Data Mining for Design and Marketing

Chapman & Hall/CRC
Data Mining and Knowledge Discovery Series

SERIES EDITOR

Vipin Kumar

University of Minnesota
Department of Computer Science and Engineering
Minneapolis, Minnesota, U.S.A

AIMS AND SCOPE

This series aims to capture new developments and applications in data mining and knowledge discovery, while summarizing the computational tools and techniques useful in data analysis. This series encourages the integration of mathematical, statistical, and computational methods and techniques through the publication of a broad range of textbooks, reference works, and handbooks. The inclusion of concrete examples and applications is highly encouraged. The scope of the series includes, but is not limited to, titles in the areas of data mining and knowledge discovery methods and applications, modeling, algorithms, theory and foundations, data and knowledge visualization, data mining systems and tools, and privacy and security issues.

PUBLISHED TITLES

UNDERSTANDING COMPLEX DATASETS: Data Mining with Matrix Decompositions
David Skillicorn

COMPUTATIONAL METHODS OF FEATURE SELECTION
Huan Liu and Hiroshi Motoda

CONSTRAINED CLUSTERING: Advances in Algorithms, Theory, and Applications
Sugato Basu, Ian Davidson, and Kiri L. Wagstaff

KNOWLEDGE DISCOVERY FOR COUNTERTERRORISM AND LAW ENFORCEMENT
David Skillicorn

MULTIMEDIA DATA MINING: A Systematic Introduction to Concepts and Theory
Zhongfei Zhang and Ruofei Zhang

NEXT GENERATION OF DATA MINING
Hillol Kargupta, Jiawei Han, Philip S. Yu, Rajeev Motwani, and Vipin Kumar

DATA MINING FOR DESIGN AND MARKETING
Yukio Ohsawa and Katsutoshi Yada

Chapman & Hall/CRC
Data Mining and Knowledge Discovery Series

Data Mining for Design and Marketing

Edited by
Yukio Ohsawa
Katsutoshi Yada

CRC Press
Taylor & Francis Group
Boca Raton London New York

CRC Press is an imprint of the
Taylor & Francis Group, an informa business

A CHAPMAN & HALL BOOK

Chapman & Hall/CRC
Taylor & Francis Group
6000 Broken Sound Parkway NW, Suite 300
Boca Raton, FL 33487-2742

First issued in paperback 2017

© 2009 by Taylor & Francis Group, LLC
Chapman & Hall/CRC is an imprint of Taylor & Francis Group, an Informa business

No claim to original U.S. Government works

ISBN-13: 978-1-4200-7019-4 (hbk)
ISBN-13: 978-1-138-11347-3 (pbk)

Library of Congress Cataloging-in-Publication Data

Data mining for design and marketing / Yukio Ohsawa, Katsutoshi Yada.
    p. cm. -- (Chapman & Hall/CRC data mining and knowledge
discovery series)
    Includes bibliographical references and index.
    ISBN 978-1-4200-7019-4 (hardcover : alk. paper)
    1. Data mining. 2. System design. 3. Design, Industrial. I. Ohsawa, Y. (Yukio),
1968- II. Yada, Katsutoshi. III. Title. IV. Series.

QA76.9.D343D3828 2008
005.74--dc22   2008044205

Visit the Taylor & Francis Web site at
http://www.taylorandfrancis.com

and the CRC Press Web site at
http://www.crcpress.com

Contents

Preface

Amidst ever-changing market conditions, the most important thing for companies today is to build a sustainable process where they can effectively grasp the needs of consumers in their market, to create products and services that answer these needs, and to appropriately convey information on such products and services to consumers. Because in recent years consumer needs have diversified and product life cycles have grown shorter, such a successful process has become increasingly difficult to realize. The ability to implement this process efficiently forms the resource of sustainable competitive advantage.

In the aspect of engineering, the concept of design has recently been extended to systems design and is affecting the wide world of business. Systems design is meant to combine subsystems, which may be basic components for making a product or a system that may be a complex product, such as a car, or a social system, such as the market. The mission of a systems designer is to create a new value that has never been realized by each one of the subsystems by combining the subsystem to form a new system.

Thus, integrating the aspects of design and marketing, we can declare it is desirable to sense and circulate information about the needs of consumers and all stakeholders as the basic resource for the creation of values. Data mining is an information technology that is particularly critical to providing this information in two senses. First, by using data mining, we can deal with vast amounts of data on consumers and thereby identify valuable patterns. These patterns aid marketers and designers in detecting the information about needs and circulating the information to coworkers in comprehensible expressions. Second, by developing visualization tools based on the computational methods of data mining, designers and marketers can uncover potential needs from the map of the market even if the needs have never been satisfied, and apply it to the creation and development of products and services with novel values. The techniques of data mining are truly growing to redesign business processes and to develop competitive products and services.

We are aware, unfortunately, that for many businesses data mining has not yet produced the significant results hoped for. The reason for this does not lie with only technical issues, such as predictive accuracy or computation speed, or with the difficulty and the advantage with data mining software used by the companies. According to our 10 years of interactions with business users of data mining, the problem is the lack of efficiency in business processes that could produce better interaction between companies and consumers or among individuals in a company. If companies can effectively design business processes, data mining can serve as a powerful engine for their growth.

In various joint research projects with more than 50 companies, we have applied data mining to marketing and designs of products and services that are among the most important corporate functions, and we have attained invaluable experience in business processes utilizing data mining. We gained important knowledge from this experience: we noticed a positive "spiraling process" in which people inside an organization learn something new from data, devise business scenarios based on this knowledge, and learn even more new things as these scenarios create valuable products if put into practice. The topics presented in this book are not only about traditional evaluation criteria of tools for data mining such as predictive accuracy or computation speed; we also offer suggestions from the perspective of creativity, and a surprise factor creates valuable products when devising new business scenarios. It is our sincere hope to be able to add something new to the research and business of this book's readers.

Yukio Ohsawa and Katsutoshi Yada
On the bridge between academia and business

Editors

Yukio Ohsawa is an associate professor in the Department of Systems Innovation, School of Engineering, The University of Tokyo. He earned his Ph.D. in communication and information engineering from The University of Tokyo. He also has worked for the School of Engineering Science at Osaka University (research associate, 1995–1999), Graduate School of Business Sciences at University of Tsukuba (associate professor, 1999–2005), and Japan Science and Technology Corporation (JST researcher, 2000–2003). He initiated the research area of chance discovery—defined as "discovery of events significant for decision making" in 1999—and a series of international meetings (conference sessions and workshops), such as the fall symposium of the American Association of Artificial Intelligence (2001). He edited the first books on *Chance Discovery* (2003) and *Chance Discoveries in Real World Decision Making* (2003, Springer–Verlag) and special issues in international and Japanese (domestic) journals. Chance discovery is growing: articles have been published in international journals—*Journal of Contingencies and Crisis Management* (2001), *New Generation Computing* (2003), *New Mathematics and Natural Computing* (2005), and *Journal on Soft Computing* in conjunction with the special issue on Web intelligence (2006). He is on the editorial board of the Japanese Society of AI and the planning board of New Generation Computing, and he is the Technical Committee chair of the IEEE-SMC technical committee of Information Systems for Design and Marketing.

Katsutoshi Yada is a professor of management information systems in the Faculty of Commerce, Kansai University, Osaka, Japan. He was previously an assistant professor in the Department of Business Administration, Osaka Industrial University, 1997–2000, and Faculty of Commerce, Kansai University, Osaka, Japan, 2000–2007. He was a visiting scholar at the marketing division of the Graduate School of Business, Columbia University, New York, 2006–2007. He received his M.A. and Ph.D. in business administration from Kobe University of Commerce, Hyogo, Japan, in 1994 and 2002, respectively. He received the Encouragement Award of Japanese Society for Artificial Intelligence (2003) and Session Best Presentation Award at SCIS and ISIS (2006). His present research interests include data mining for marketing and information strategy concerning data mining. He has been chairman and program committee member in many international data mining conferences. He is a member of IEEE, AMA, and AMS.

Contributors

Radim Belohlavek, Ph.D.
State University of New York
   at Binghamton
Binghamton, New York, and
Palacky University
Olomouc, Czech Republic

David Bergner, Ph.D.
Division of Space Biosciences
NASA Ames Research Center
Moffett Field, California

Brett Bojduj
Department of Computer Science
California Polytechnic State
   University
San Luis Obispo, California

Kuiyu Chang, Ph.D.
Mosma Research
Mosma Corporation
Singapore

Ozgur Eris, Ph.D.
Franklin W. Olin College
   of Engineering
Needham, Massachusetts

Renate Fruchter
Civil and Environmental Engineering
   Department
Stanford University
Palo Alto, California

Kenta Fukata
Graduate School of Engineering
Osaka University
Osaka, Japan

David E. Goldberg, Ph.D.
Department of Industrial and
   Enterprise Systems Engineering
University of Illinois at
   Urbana-Champaign
Champaign, Illinois

Gary Gregory, B.Sc., M.B.A., Ph.D.
School of Marketing
University of New South Wales
New South Wales, Australia

Daryl H. Hepting, Ph.D.
Department of Computer Science
University of Regina
Regina, Saskatchewan, Canada

Robert J. Hilderman, Ph.D.
Department of Computer Science
University of Regina
Regina, Saskatchewan, Canada

Kenichi Horie, M.S.
School of Engineering
The University of Tokyo, Japan

Takuma Hosoda
Department of Systems Innovation
Faculty of Engineering
The University of Tokyo
Tokyo, Japan

Wenxue Huang, Ph.D.
Generation-5 Mathematical Technologies
Toronto, Ontario, Canada

Daiji Kato
Coordination Research Center
National Institute for Fusion Science
Gifu, Japan

Milorad Krneta, Ph.D.
Generation-5 Mathematical
 Technologies
Toronto, Ontario, Canada

Limin Lin, Ph.D.
Generation-5 Mathematical
 Technologies
Toronto, Ontario, Canada

Xavier Llorà, Ph.D.
National Center for Supercomputing
 Applications
University of Illinois at Urbana-
 Champaign
Champaign, Illinois

Timothy Maciag
Department of Computer Science
University of Regina
Regina, Saskatchewan, Canada

Yoshiharu Maeno, M.S., Ph.D.
School of Business Sciences
The University of Tsukuba
Ibaraki, Japan

Naohiro Matsumura, Ph.D.
Graduate School of Economics
Osaka University
Osaka, Japan

Hiroyuki Morita, M.A., Ph.D.
School of Economics
Osaka Prefecture University
Osaka, Japan

Hiroshi Motoda, Ph.D.
Asian Office of Aerospace Research
 and Development
Air Force Office of Scientific Research
U.S. Air Force Research Laboratory
Tokyo, Japan

Izumi Murakami
Coordination Research Center
National Institute for Fusion Science
Gifu, Japan

Masaki Murata
National Institute of Information and
 Communications Technology
Kyoto, Japan

Takanobu Nakahara, M.A.
School of Economics
Osaka Prefecture University
Osaka, Japan

Asem Omari, Ph.D.
Databases and Information Systems
Institute of Computer Science
Heinrich-Heine University
Duesseldorf, Germany

Lukáš Pichl, Ph.D.
Division of Finite Systems
Max Planck Institute for the Physics
 of Complex Systems
Dresden, Germany

Akira Sasaki
Advanced Photon Research Center
Japan Atomic Energy Research
 Institute
Kyoto, Japan

Bin Shi, B.Eng., M.Eng.
School of Computer Engineering
Nanyang Technological University
Singapore

Dominik Ślęzak, Ph.D.
Infobright
Toronto, Ontario, Canada

Wataru Sunayama, Ph.D.
Hiroshima City University
Hiroshima, Japan

Manabu Suzuki
Department of Computer and
 Information Science
Graduate School of Arkansas Tech
 University
Russellville, Arkansas

Shubashri Swaminathan
Civil and Environmental Engineering
    Department
Stanford University
Palo Alto, California

Takeshi Ui, M.S.
Toppan Forms
Tokyo, Japan

Mark D. Uncles, B.Sc., Ph.D.
School of Marketing
University of New South Wales
New South Wales, Australia

Vilem Vychodil, M.Sc., Ph.D.
State University of New York
    at Binghamton
Binghamton, New York, and
Palacky University
Olomouc, Czech Republic

Takashi Washio, Ph.D.
The Institute of Scientific and
    Industrial Research
Osaka University
Osaka, Japan

Jianhong Wu, Ph.D.
Laboratory for Industrial and Applied
    Mathematics
Department of Mathematics and
    Statistics
York University
Toronto, Ontario, Canada

Noriko Imafuji Yasui, M.S., Ph.D.
Department of Industrial and
    Enterprise Systems Engineering
University of Illinois at
    Urbana-Champaign
Champaign, Illinois

Lihua Zhao, M.Sc., Ph.D.
School of Marketing
University of New South Wales
New South Wales, Australia

1 Sensing Values in Designing Products and Markets on Data Mining and Visualizations

Yukio Ohsawa

CONTENTS

1.1 INTRODUCTION: DESIGN AND MARKETING AS THE PROCESS TO VALUE SENSING

The application of data mining to business has grown explosively in the last decade. For example, the following provide benefits to real companies:

Predicting sales quantity of commercial items[1,2]
Finding the associations among commercial items, such as "if a customer buys bread, he or she tends to buy butter at the same time"[3]
Predicting stock prices[4]
Predicting network faults[5]

These analyses have been regarded as methods for showing objective conclusions because they are based on real data: facts according to a well-arranged sensing system such as error detectors in computer/telephone networks, news of stock prices,

1

points of sale, and registers in a supermarket, for example. As a result, the decision makers in business tend to rely on the "trustworthy" results obtained by tools of data mining and make decisions such as "we can recommend butter if a customer orders bread" because of patterns demonstrated in the past.

A problem with this approach occurs because humans often outperform the algorithm of data mining. For example, when a student orders a book by entering the title in the search engine of an online bookshop site, he may find a list of five books recommended. However, the student already possesses two of the books and he is already planning to purchase the other three. As a result, the system cannot give him any new information, because he has been keenly sensitive to newly published books and knows more than the search results.

Some recommendation systems have introduced devices to suggest items that are not far from but not too close to the request based on the product order history.[6] For example, if a customer orders bread, recommending wine may be more reasonable than recommending butter, because the customer is used to buying the set {butter, bread} for breakfast and considers bread as food as a different category, such as for a side food to wine. A strategy for recommending this may be to show item X, which does not co-occur with "bread" by high conditional probability (or confidence of the association rule of "bread $\rightarrow$ X") as 5%, but does by 1% or 2%. Some online book shops have already introduced heuristics to present *not-close not-far* items.

When discussing *not-close not-far* items, consider that there are a huge number of proverbial trees within 10 meters of the mountaintop in comparison to those within 1 meter. We need additional strategies for bringing customers' attention to a meaningful subset of items obtained by the *not-close not-far* items heuristics, because the "not-close" condition involves a huge number of candidate items. Otherwise, the recommendation may overwhelm customers with too much information. Marketers instead want a strategy for computing the utility of each item for the customer. There is a question we have to answer first, however: "What is the utility of an item?" To answer this question, consider how the customer is planning to use the item. For example, the high utility of "wine" with bread can be understood by considering that the customer takes bread as a starting food for dinner and the wine to serve with a steak dinner. Thus if a customer buys bread with wine, it means he or she may also buy beef to grill and vegetables for side dishes. On the other hand, to evaluate the utility of "butter" with bread, we should consider the scenario of eating bread for breakfast and having butter with the bread and assume the customer will not buy additional expensive items. Thus a marketer has to notice a scenario to connect a commercial item to a situation (such as dinner or breakfast) in evaluating the item's utility.

This principle relates also to finding the good design of a product. In a development section of our Japanese sponsor, equipment to find scratches on CCD film (Figure 1.1, left side) has been designed. A film sample is placed on the right-hand edge of the belt and conveyed on the left. On the way, lights are shone onto the surface of the film. At the first point where the film meets the light (I), cameras take an image of the light's reflection. Then, running some more distance, the film meets the second light (II), at which time the image of the light coming through the film is taken by the cameras (II). Both of the images taken by the two camera sets are sent to the computer (image processor) and the scratches on the film are diagnosed.

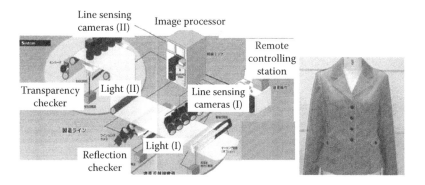

FIGURE 1.1 A problem in product design: how can we mix and combine multidisciplinary knowledge to design and redesign these products?

To redesign this system, it would be necessary to choose the most essential component or component set that would provide an effective method for such an improvement. For example, if there are new types of scratches that are hard to distinguish from each other, a new combination of existing components, or, in a complex case, new components altogether, might be required. Considering the end result is important for understanding the merit of each new design.

Similar requirements for user scenarios are important to such products as clothes (Figure 1.1, right side). Before selling a product, the marketer needs to predict the consumer's response (the extent of satisfaction) by drawing a scenario such as "the consumer will wear this clothing and go out for lunch on a cold day in autumn." This scenario is useful for designing clothing as well as marketing the clothing. If a textile is found to be suitable for making clothing to wear for going out to lunch on a cold day, and if there is consumer demand to go out for lunch in winter, the clothing would be accepted by consumers if designed well and the textile will be bought by apparel industries where the cloth is designed and sold.

These scenarios outline the relation of a person who is a customer or a decision maker in business, a group of coworking staff members of a company, or the huge number of consumers to events and situations in the environment. Value sensing, to feel associated with things in the environment, has been defined as a particular dimension of human awareness in the literature of educational psychology.[7] It is meaningful to extend this concept to an aspect of creativity in business. The "value" here can be dealt with as a new relationship to the social and natural environment, which business workers and customers create from their interaction via their products and services and through which they eventually redesign the market.

1.2 TWO CASES: MARKETING AND DESIGN WITH COMMUNICATIONS ON VISUALIZED DATA

Let us continue with the example of textile. A textile company has been strongly seeking to develop and sell new products (i.e., new kinds of textiles to be accepted by the market). The company is well aware that the three major parts of its market are

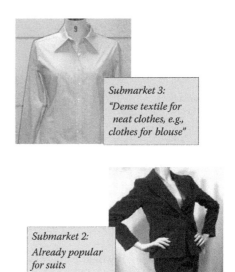

Submarket 1:

Textiles for "worn-out" style clothes, for outdoor use

Submarket 3:

"Dense textile for neat clothes, e.g., clothes for blouse"

Submarket 2:

Already popular for suits

FIGURE 1.2 How can we combine multidisciplinary knowledge for satisfying the consumers/ users?

related to textiles for business suits (*Submarket 1*), business underwear (*Submarket 2*), and casual wear (*Submarket 3*). Typical designs of these clothes are shown in Figure 1.2.

Although the company has mature markets of these kinds of products, it wanted to develop new markets starting from a niche product (i.e., a product that may not be popular for the time being but can expand the market in the future). The company started from data collected in exhibition events in which the product (textile) samples were arranged on tables, and customers representing apparel companies picked samples and left a list of preferred samples. Previously, such a list had been used only as an order card on which the textile company could send samples to the customers. However, now the company has found that the same list, if put into an electronic dataset, could be a source of ideas for designing and marketing new products. In comparison with data on past sales, the data from exhibition events include customers' preferences for new products that had not yet been sold.

The marketers of this textile company visualized the data using decision trees, correspondence analysis, etc., and looked for the best tool for achieving this goal. They decided on KeyGraph,[8–10] which shows (1) clusters of frequent items in the data (i.e., popular item sets ordered by the same customer) and (2) items bridging clusters (i.e., that appear rarely but appear in the same baskets as items in multiple clusters). (The reader is referred to Appendix A for more information about KeyGraph and Pictorial KeyGraph, a novel version of KeyGraph with an interface to attach pictorial information onto the scenario map obtained by KeyGraph.[8])

The scenario map was obtained as in Figure 1.3, where the black nodes linked by black lines show the clusters of (1) mentioned previously, and the red nodes and the

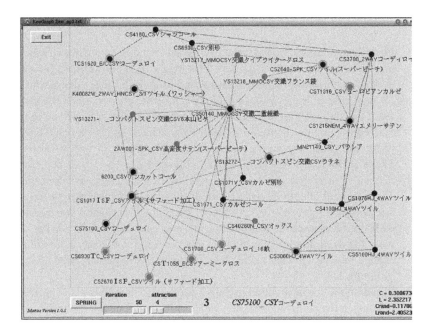

FIGURE 1.3 Scenario map from KeyGraph for the data on textile exhibition party.

red lines show items of bridges in (2) and their co-occurrence with items in the clusters, respectively. This figure, however, is difficult for the marketers to understand because of the complex names of products (i.e., complicated sequences of numbers and letters corresponding to the features of the textile materials). The marketers therefore attached the product samples, as in Figure 1.4, to sense the smoothness, thickness, and colors themselves.

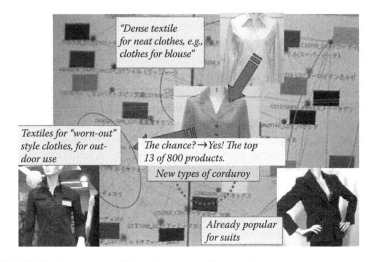

FIGURE 1.4 Marketing as a problem of value sensing on the scenario map.

The meeting by the 10 members of the marketing section ran as follows:

1. First, the marketers noticed the clusters corresponding to popular item sets mentioned in (1). Three marketers who were experts in women's blouses noticed the meaningful cluster at the top of Figure 1.4 (i.e., "dense textile for neat clothes [e.g., clothes for blouse]"); three others noticed the cluster at the right of Figure 1.4 corresponding to business suits. Two others noticed the popular item, not linked to any clusters of (1) via black lines, in the left of the diagram corresponding to materials of casual clothes. These correspond to the submarkets in Figure 1.2.

2. Second, a marketer who had been working for the company more than 15 years paid attention to the relationship of the other marketers' opinions with the three submarkets above. He pointed out that women using daily business wear (a combination of suits and blouse) do not like to wear the same kind of clothing for the weekend but, instead, desire to change into casual wear made of such a textile as in the left-hand cluster of Figure 1.4.

3. Based on the scenario found in Step 2 above, the marketers paid attention to items in the large meta-cluster, which is the combination of the clusters at the top, on the right, and the popular items on the left. These "between" nodes are red nodes (i.e., items lying between popular clusters), on which the marketers finally calculated a scenario to design a new semicasual (or semiformal) cloth that women can wear both to the workplace and to lunch or dinner with friends. As a result, the material indicating the red node, in the dotted circle in Figure 1.4, produced a historic sales hit of the 13th highest sales among their 800 products (previously, the sales of new products had been normally lower than the 100th highest).

This example (see previous work for more details on the technical aspect of this case[11]) implies three important principles. First, data collected on the users' (in this case, marketers') sense of value (i.e., the relationship of target events to their interest) leads the company to success in marketing by designing products to sell. Second, the visualization tool presents a workplace in which coworkers bring their multidisciplinary expertise to bear and create new business scenarios from the teamwork. Third, not only visualization of the raw data, but also devising a new interface for showing it to suitable users, as done with attaching real textile pieces, plays a role as a strong support of creative decision in business.

Here is another example. The company's aim is to redesign a machine (Figure 1.1, left side). As mentioned earlier, this machine is a complex system composed of cameras, light, computer, software, and a mechanical belt conveyer. The company's development section employs technicians from various engineering domains such as optical engineering, computer science, and mechanical engineering. It is difficult for the manager of this section to organize projects to redesign this complex machine, because it is essential to combine the expertise of these professionals for making the whole system run collaboratively. In other words, looking over the variety of

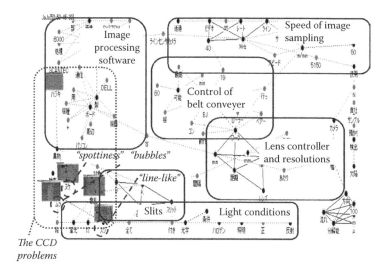

FIGURE 1.5 The visualization of business reports on the technicians' communications with users.

knowledge from a bird's-eye viewpoint is required, but is hard for a manager to do alone.

To cope with this problem, the manager collected the customer reports written by the technicians in this section. These reports have been based on the technicians' communications with the users of the machine, such as film manufacturers (because the users are also technicians who are highly trained and have technical knowledge, this company did not send the sales force team but the technicians to the customers' working place). Because the collected reports included technical terms hard to understand for the manager, who is the decision maker who decides what products to develop in which way to redesign the machine, the reports hardly reflected the decision consensus of the section.

However, after viewing the collected reports and depicting each frequent word by a black node, the co-occurrence of these frequent words in the same reports by black lines—cluster of (1) mentioned in this section—and rare words co-occurring with words in multiple clusters—items of (2)—the overall structure of reports came out clearly, as in Figure 1.5. The major parts of this diagram are as follows. (A) The upper-left part of the figure corresponds to software techniques for image processing, (B) the upper-right and center of the figure are about mechanics for moving the belt conveyer and the lens of cameras, and (C) the bottom shows the variety of light conditions. The words about scratches are located in the bottom left, between the image processing and the light conditions. The manager organized meetings with the members of his section to share and look at the figure as a scenario map. The participants were allowed to draw auxiliary lines, to explain their understanding of this figure's structure and to put annotations with letters expressing scenarios they thought of, on the printed-out scenario map.

After discussions, they understood that different types of scratches can be detected by using different types of techniques. For example, the scratch called "spottiness" should be distinguished from others by combining special light conditions and image processing software. As a result, this team registered for new patents and now is the top sales brand in the market of film scratch inspection. The reader is referred to details of this case's analysis elsewhere[12] and its extension to creating new ideas from patent documents in previous work.[13]

1.3   DATA COLLECTION AS THE ROOT OF EVERYTHING: EVIDENCE OF OBJECTIVITY AND SUBJECTIVITY

We can summarize the cases above as Figure 1.6. The process started from *collection of data*, which is based on keen attention to the emergence of new values. For example, in the case of the textile company, it started from the motivation to develop new textile products and then collect preference data from product exhibition events. In the case of the film-scratch inspecting machine, the manager had a severe problem in developing and redesigning products from his communication with technicians or from the technicians' communications with customers (the machine users). Then, they introduced the *visualization of data* using suitable tools, which happened to be KeyGraph. Looking at the visualized diagram, the map of their markets, they discussed the scenarios of developing and selling products. Through this discussion, the marketers in the textile company and the technicians in the machine company obtained novel scenarios that led them to success.

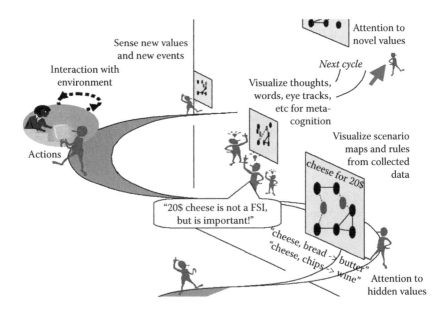

FIGURE 1.6 Spiral process with white board: Data as objective evidences are the results of subjective interests, and vice versa. Both data are visualized and always shown to user(s).

A point not mentioned previously is that the discussants were also visualizing their thoughts during the meetings. In the textile case, they were writing the discussion outlines on a whiteboard. In the machine company, words were typed into KeyGraph during communications and were visualized on their co-occurrences in the same sentences as in the center of Figure 1.6. Objective data from the real world or (*not exclusive*) subjective data from their thoughts were visualized. Thus, participants of group decisions were always aware of their own priorities and interests and understood which of their targets were linked to the teammates' main interests and how these links could produce benefits. We have called the process a "double helix" because humans and computer always run up the spiral, where humans give data to a computer and a computer gives visualized results to humans.[14] However, in this chapter, we may call this the *whiteboard* process, because successful users really referred to two or more *scenario maps* obtained throughout the collaboration process.

1.4   SCENARIO MAPS AS A BASIS OF CHANCE DISCOVERY

The common point between the two cases is that they developed new attention to a small part of their market, which had not been previously considered. In the case of the textile company, the corduroy material that finally led to a sales hit had rarely been ordered by customers. In the case of film-scratch inspection machines, technicians had not noticed that some scratches were distinguished by the combinations of light and image processing software. And, on the visualized maps, they found these items to be a significant part of a new scenario.

To understand this effect, refer to Figure 1.7, which visualizes a customer's behavior in a supermarket, as a scenario map. Suppose the customer is used to buying only liquor and the store manager finds it difficult to recommend he buy food in this store. To attract such a poorly motivated customer, the store manager placed an expensive ($20) cheese on the shelf close to the liquor. The customer became interested in

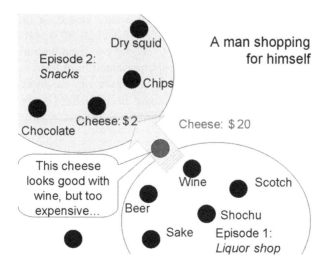

FIGURE 1.7 A scenario map, showing frequent episodes and an between-lier product.

the nice-looking cheese. However, he did not buy it because of the high price. The manager was disappointed and thought of getting rid of the cheese from the shelf. However, this customer walked up to the shelf of snacks and chose to buy several low-cost items such as chips and cheese-type snacks. This action was the result of the manager "suggesting" the taste of cheese, which then motivated the customer's interest in things to eat with beer and wine.

By thinking of such scenarios and looking at a scenario map, we can interpret the behavior of such a customer and understand the role of the $20 cheese, because the cheese affected the customer's decision to buy other items than just the liquor he was accustomed to buying. This is good thinking on the part of the supermarket manager, who needs to decide which items to arrange on the shelves. The $20 cheese seldom appears in the point of sale data, because visitors tend to just pick it out and return it to the shelf, as this customer did. Items and events that significantly influence people's decisions may be rare in the data, insomuch as we collect data on the final decision of consumers/customers/product users only.

KeyGraph, as in the examples shown previously, assisted business decisions to take advantage of rare or novel items, because the information presented by the graph was a map of the market, as simplified in Figure 1.7. Thus the diagram had to have clusters of (1) in Section 1.2, corresponding to the liquors and the snacks in Figure 1.7, and items as bridges in (2) of Section 1.2 between multiple clusters, corresponding to the $20 cheese. For details of KeyGraph algorithms, the reader is referred to previous work;[8] this tool was invented 10 years ago and is prevalent in industries mainly in Japan. We started studies on chance discovery under the definition of "chance" as an event significant for people's decisions from international sessions in 2000 (i.e., IECON2000, KES2000, and AAAI fall symposia 2001) and journal special issues (*Journal of Crisis Management Contingencies* in 2001, *New Generation Computing* in 2002 and 2003, *New Mathematics and Natural Computing* in 2006, and *Information Sciences* in 2008). For all articles and books, we stand on the simple principle that a decision means choosing one from multiple future scenarios of actions and events. Based on this principle, a chance can be regarded as an event at the cross-point of scenarios, because people are presented with a new stimulus to choose one from multiple scenarios. The bridging events or items that KeyGraph presented have been candidates of chances. This way of looking at diagrams, as in Figure 1.6, was more useful than the diagrams themselves, according to the real users of KeyGraph working on marketing and design.

1.5 META-COGNITION AS THE EFFECT OF DATA VISUALIZATION

Presented here is an experiment in which we hired a marketer who had been working on textile materials design. We had him wear an eye movement tracker made of glasses with two cameras: one detecting eye movement and the other tracing the target object, so we could acquire his eye movement on the KeyGraph diagram. First, he looked at the two major clusters of popular items, as in Figure 1.8. Then he glanced for 1 second at the item pointed to by the arrow in Figure 1.8; for 10 seconds after that, his eyes traced the dotted line. During the 10 seconds, the eyes moved

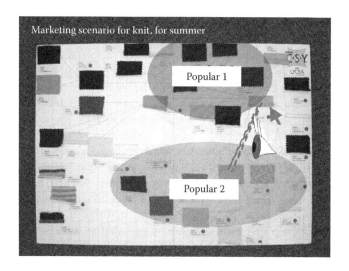

FIGURE 1.8 Eyes catch scenarios from a data-based scenario map.

quickly like a saccade and then moved slowly. After this specific movement, his eyes drifted all over the diagram for 5 minutes.

I asked him if he found any "chance," i.e., event significant for his decision, in this experiment. He said he found none. Then I showed the dotted lines in Figure 1.8 and told him these were extracted from his own cognitive process. He was deeply impressed and said, "Yes, I looked at the interesting textile pointed [to] by the arrow. This was a material for making thin clothes such as women's business-appropriate underwear. However, in this experiment, I noticed that the color and the smoothness in touching this textile material may be rather suitable for casual wear. I shall propose a new way to sell this material." As a result, this item achieved a high sales performance as a material for casual wear.

This example clarifies that the user's attention to a "chance" can be further stimulated by meta-cognition (i.e., cognition of one's own cognition).[15] This encourages users to talk about scenarios coming to their minds, through which the words may stimulate meta-cognition and accelerate the spiral process of chance discovery.

1.6 GAP BETWEEN ADVERTISERS AND DESIGNERS: RESULTS OF VISUALIZING MESSAGES

Throughout this section, we focus attention on people who make a living directly or indirectly from the design of products. They are the products' (1) designers, (2) advertisers, and (3) evaluators from the viewpoint of working outside the manufacturing company (i.e., users and professional evaluators). We expect people in (1) to work on strong inspiration and motivation to create new products, which may not be a motivation shared with people in group (3). A hypothesis is that people in (2) may be a good bridge between people in (1) and (3). If this hypothesis is correct, we can say that the concept (the reason for giving priority to a product's unique features) behind a design may not be well understood by people outside the manufacturing company.

We do not mention "users" for item (3) because our goal is to see how the designers' intentions trickle down from *in* to *out* of the community of people engaged in manufacturing. However, we cannot provide statistic validation of our hypotheses because we cannot set a hypothesis in a simple form such as "product X is designed under the concept of Y, but the user does not say they relate X and Y" because of the vocabulary gap[16] between designers and users in calling. In this sense, interviewing different categories of people about each product is not meaningful.

However, we may expect designers to say "products X1 and X2 are designed under the concept Y," whereas the user says "X1 is felt to be Y1, and X2 is also like Y1," where Y is not equal to Y1. They are talking in different vocabularies, but the two real worlds of products expressed can be regarded as similar, considering the similarity in the co-occurrence of those products. On the other hand, if the user says "X1 is felt to be Y1, but X2 is like Y2," where Y1 and Y2 are different, his or her world is different from the world in the designers' minds.

Instead of statistic validation, we chose to compare the positions of products of people in different categories. We collected the data on cellular phones that won the Good Design Award between 2003 and 2005,[17] and we analyzed the data as follows:

1. For each year between 2003 and 2005, we collected the three kinds of data for designed products (cellular phones):
   a. The documented designers' comments
   b. The documents from the Web pages where the product is advertised
   c. The referees' answers to questionnaires about each product's design
2. For the data set of each year, we visualized the positions of products in the map visualized with KeyGraph.
3. We measured to what degree each company's products are isolated in the map from those of other companies.

1.6.1 THE RESULTS AND IMPLICATIONS

The results of Pictorial KeyGraph (see Appendix A) are shown in Figure 1.9, Figure 1.10, and Figure 1.11, respectively, for the three data sets below, for the award-winning cellular phones in 2004.

Data a took the form as:

Da = Product 1: I tried to smooth and …
        Product 1: feature 1) Smooth and soft …
        Product 1: feature 2) Easy use of …
        Product 2: This design is dedicated to …
        Product 2: feature 1) The camera is good…
        Product 2: feature 2) Photos can be sent…
        …   (Equation 1.1)

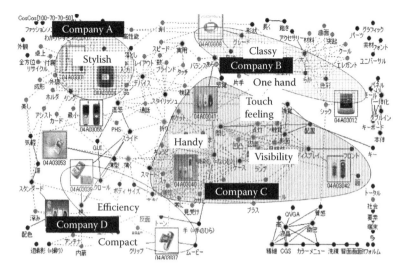

FIGURE 1.9 Pictorial KeyGraph applied to the comments of designers of the best designed cellular phones in 2004. The isolation degree is 11.0 for the four major companies.

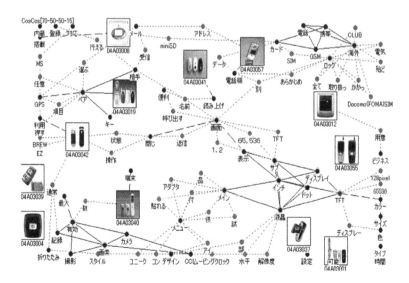

FIGURE 1.10 Pictorial KeyGraph applied to the advertisements on the Web for the best designed cellulars in Figure 1.9. No companies exist of which the products form isolated clusters. The isolation degree is 4.0 for the four major companies. Do not read Japanese characters: the isolation degrees are the point of this figure.

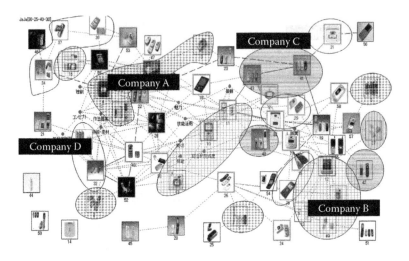

FIGURE 1.11 Pictorial Key Graph applied to the judgments of referees for the best designed cellular phones. No companies exist of which the products form isolated clusters. The isolation degree is 7.49 for the four major companies.

Then data b were taken from the Web pages of companies' cellular advertisements, and the formats were similar to Da. Data c were

Dc = Beautiful: 1, 3, 15, 17, 19…
       Novel: 2, 5, 15, 21, …
       Useful: 1, 2, 15, …   (Equation 1.2)

where the numbers show the identification numbers of products and the lines are the item evaluation criteria in the questionnaire. In Equation 1.2, product numbers 1, 2, 15, etc., were useful to the referees. Each year, we had 30–58 well-designed cellular phones, and each product was designed by between one and five designers. The referees judged mostly just by investigating the products, rather than hearing from designers.

These data can be visualized by KeyGraph to show the positions of products in the map of cellular phones. As marked by the shadows we show in Figure 1.9, the designers' comments are clearly separated in areas of products designed by different companies.

In Figure 1.9, each company's area is featured by words representing the designer's motivations, which are rare in the comments but connect the products of the company. These are ambiguous words, but can be understood by looking at the embedded pictures. For example, we find "compact" and "efficiency" for company D. This combination of words is hard to understand, but the unique look of the small products in the pictures shows rich functions such as movable and television-like displays in a small surface of a cellular. We can understand these products are compact and efficient. As well, we find "classy" as a part of the design concept in company B. This is another word difficult to understand, but the silver-colored body of the cellular phones in the area for company B in Figure 1.9 expresses the word's meaning.

This result shows that the designers in a company share some concepts, but that their low frequency may hide their existence. That is, if the concepts are expressed as frequently in words as in the figure's islands of black nodes, the company's staff and consumers would have had many opportunities to express those words. Because of the rareness, we can really expect those concepts to be discounted by people living inside and outside the company. This expectation is clearly supported by introducing a new criteria factor of how clustered the product set of each company is. We call these criteria *isolation degree*, defined by the procedure below for each map:

1. Take N companies whose numbers of products on the map are the largest. Call them *major* companies.
2. For each major company j ($1 < j < N$), surround as many products from company j as possible with one closed rim without crossing with itself or other rims. If any products of company j are not surrounded in the rim, make a new rim until all products of company j are surrounded by some rim. The set of products in a rim is called a rim-cluster.
3. Compute *Iso*, the isolation degree of the map with the following equation:

$$Iso = \text{The number of products produced by the } N \text{ majors}$$
$$/\Sigma_{j=1 \text{ to } N} \{\text{the number of clusters of } j\text{-th major company}\}$$

(Equation 1.3)

Intuitively, Iso is large, if products from each company make a cluster that is isolated from other companies' clusters.

According to Figure 1.9, we find that the designer's comments in the same company tend to form a group, sharing some concept for design (shown as the letters in Figure 1.9). On the other hand, words in the product advertisements (Figure 1.10) from one company are scattered all over the map, and we cannot separate each area by each company. Finally, we find from Figure 1.11 that referee comments restore the hidden clusters of products from companies. The value of isolation degree is not as large as in Figure 1.9, but larger than in Figure 1.10. (See Iso values in the figure captions.)

We conducted similar experiments for the data on the design competition from 2003, 2004, and 2005. That is, we have three sets of {data a, data b, data c} for the corresponding 3 years. For all 3 years, we obtained similar results, as reported above. The isolation degree was largest for Data a, the least for Data b, and the second for Data c.

Thus, we can conclude that the designers in the same company share their concepts for design, and these concepts tend to be hidden to people in the market. This occurs in a product path starting from the designers all the way to the marketers/advertisers, because of the weak impression of designers' opinions to other members in the company. Referees do communicate among themselves when deciding to award the best products, with some sort of design expertise that is common to concepts in the minds of designers.

1.7 CONCLUSIONS

In the two cases presented, we have shown the collaborations by marketers and designers of new products. These collaborations were executed based on scenario maps created by KeyGraph for the data on sales and patents. By following the well-organized communication process for sensing novel values in the market, the participants successfully developed hit products.

However, collaborations in a company do not always work, especially if participants come from different working sections. We analyzed the thoughts of designers and the people surrounding designers. Pictorial KeyGraph has been introduced for this comparison. The ideas originally shared by the designers belonging to the same company can be clearly expressed by words, even though they might be engaged daily in different projects for creating different products. However, these designers' ideas tended to be hidden in the products' path from the marketers/advertisers because of the weak impression of the designers' communication with other members of the company.

Thus we should consider the difference of inter- and intrasection communications in design and marketing and invent methods for aiding integration of these communications into creating business strategies of a company. The belief underlying this book is that tools of data mining and their well-organized coupling with human communication have the possibility to achieve this goal. The reader is referred to articles on the same project by heterogeneous members for creative design, such as Eris and Fruchter.[18,19] We are encouraged also by the literature of cognitive sciences for design, which says ambiguous information can trigger design creations.[20] All in all, information from other teams, which might be ambiguous, may motivate creative designs with rich originality, although it may not be as familiar and well understood as messages from collaborators. Data mining and visualization play an important role to provide a scenario map on which collaborators can exchange ambiguous but useful information.

REFERENCES

1. Fader, P.S. and Hardie, B.G.S. Forecasting repeat sales at CDNOW: a case study. The Marketing Department, Working Paper No. 99-023. Wharton, Philadelphia, PA, 1999.
2. Prasun, D. and Subhasis, C. (2007) Prediction of retail sales of footwear using feedforward and recurrent neural networks. *Neural Comp Appl.* 16, 491–502.
3. Agrawal, R., Imielinski, T., and Swami, A. (1993) Mining association rules between sets of items in large data. *Proc ACM SIGMOD.* 207–216.
4. Yamashita, T., Hirasawa, K., and Hu, J. (2005) Multi-branch neural networks and its application to stock price prediction, in *Proc KES Conf.* Springer, LNCS3681.
5. Weiss, G.M. and Hirsh, H. Learning to predict rare events in event sequences, in *Proc Fourth Int Conf Knowledge Discovery Data Mining (KDD-98).* AAAI Press, Menlo Park, CA, 1998, 359–363.
6. Hirooka, Y., Terano, T., and Otsuka, Y. Extending content-based recommendation by order-matching and cross-matching method, in *Proc Electron Comm Web Technol: First Int Conf.* Springer, LNCS1875, 177–190, 2000.
7. Donaldson, M. *Human Minds.* AAllen Lane, 1993.
8. Ohsawa, Y., (2003). KeyGraph: visualized structure among event clusters, in *Chance Discovery*, Ohsawa, Y. and McBurney, P., eds., Springer-Verlag, 2003, 262–275.
9. Ohsawa, Y., Nels, E.B., and Yachida, M. (1998) KeyGraph: automatic indexing by co-occurrence graph based on building construction metaphor. *Proc Adv Digital Library Conf* (IEEE ADL'98), 12–18.

10. Okazaki, N. and Ohsawa, Y. Polaris: an integrated data miner for chance discovery, in *Proc Third Int Workshop Chance Discovery Manage*. Greece, 2003.
11. Ohsawa, Y. and Usui, M. Creative marketing as application of chance discovery, in *Chance Discoveries in Real World Decision Making,* Ohsawa, Y. and Tsumoto, S., eds., Springer, Berlin, 2006.
12. Horie, K. and Ohsawa, Y. (2006) Product designed on scenario maps using pictorial KeyGraph. *WSEAS Trans Information Sci Application*. 3:1324–1331.
13. Horie, K., Yoshiharu, M., and Yukio, O. (2007) Human-interactive annealing process with pictogram for extracting new scenarios for patent technology. *Data Sci J*. 6, S132–S136.
14. Ohsawa, Y. and Nara, Y. (2003) Understanding internet users on double helical model of chance-discovery process. *J New Generation Comp.,* 21, 109–122.
15. Suwa, M. Meta-cognitive verbalization as a tool for acquiring expertise through differentiation and problem-framing. *Poster Abstracts Vol 2nd Int Conf Design Computing and Cognition (DCC'06)*. 43–44, 2006.
16. Chen, H. Approach on the vocabulary problem in collaboration. In: *Proceedings National Science Foundation Coordination Theory and Collaboration Technology Workshop*, Arlington, VA, 1993.
17. Good design finder: a library of good design award (2005). http://www.g-mark.org/search/index.jsp
18. Eris, O. *Effective Inquiry for Innovative Engineering Design*. Kluwer Academic, MA, 2004.
19. Fruchter, R., Ohsawa, Y., and Matsumura, N. (2005) Knowledge reuse through chance discovery from an enterprise design-build enterprise data store. *New Math Natural Comp*. 3, 393–406.
20. Gaver W.W., Beaver, J., and Benford, S. (2003) Ambiguity as a resource for design. *Proc Comp Human Inter.*, pp. 233–240.

2 Reframing the Data-Mining Process

David Bergner and Ozgur Eris

CONTENTS

2.1 INTRODUCTION

Imagine that two different data-mining teams of apparently comparable makeup and competence were given the same tools, access to the same data sets, and equal time to work. Later, the business managers who sponsored the projects looked back on their outcomes, and observed that one team's results were highly valued and influenced the business, whereas the other team's results were insignificant and soon forgotten. Imagine the managers now seeking to determine why two apparently identical projects could produce such different results. How would we help them? How would we study the problem? What performance variables would we measure? One way to address these questions is to consider how data mining can shape business decisions.

In this chapter, we extend prior models of the human role in data mining. We build on prior literature regarding decision-making, design, and team interaction to model relationships of data-mining processes to business decisions. Based on this model, we suggest ways to measure and manage the data-mining process to enhance business value creation. We *reframe* the data-mining process to further emphasize its social and organizational, rather than computational aspects, and to focus explicitly on how the process can improve decision quality.

The notions of *frames*, *framing*, and *reframing* are central to our discussion of how interaction processes shape decisions. A *frame* establishes context and determines what is considered part of an activity, problem, or decision; it determines what is worthy of attention and discussion and what is not. *Framing* and *reframing* refer to the processes by which individuals and teams establish and shift their frames. Although *frames* have substantial implicit aspects, here we are concerned with their explicit aspects, which are revealed in communication, and provide a basis for empirical investigation and analysis of frames (Bergner, 2004).

This chapter's title, "Reframing the Data-Mining Process," has two distinct meanings. First, it refers to shifts in the way we as theorists and practitioners conceive of data mining—what aspects of the data-mining process will receive our attention. Second, it refers to ongoing shifts in the way data-mining teams and their sponsors conceive of their projects—what aspects of the data and the business will receive their attention. In the following sections we deal with these two topics, and then consider how to measure and manage data-mining team processes to create business value.

2.2   THE DATA-MINING PROCESS REFRAMED

Fayadd, Shapiro, and Smith (1996) showed that successful *knowledge discovery* from data mining hinges not only on the data sets and data-mining tools available, but perhaps even more so on human interpretation and choices that shape the data-mining process and results. Ohsawa (2002) built on this model to provide an even richer description of the human role in observing, interpreting, selecting, and evaluating data and explaining the significance of discoveries in terms of decision making. Considering factors beyond the discovery of knowledge per se, Ohsawa was concerned with the *discovery of chance* (Ohsawa & McBurney, 2003)—a *chance* being an event or situation having significant impact on decision making or problem solving, and *discovery of chance* entailing both learning of such an event or situation and explaining its significance for decision making or problem solving. Drawing on insights from decision theory and decision analysis practice, Bergner (2004) elaborated on Ohsawa's model by focusing on the second criterion for discovery of chance—explaining how the discovery is significant for decision making. This could provide a test of the value created by a data-mining process—we would ask what decisions were influenced by the process outcomes, what was the nature of the influence, and how important were the decisions. Projects applying data mining for design and marketing, given their business context, are concerned with discovery of *chance* to the extent project sponsors will expect actionable results from the process (*actionable:* capable of being acted on [Merriam-Webster OnLine]; relating to or being information that allows a decision to be made or action to be taken [www. answers.com]).

Ohsawa (2002) also introduced the concept of *subject-data*—data generated by the team members as they interact—in contrast to *object-data*, which are the data the team intends to mine. The term *object-data* simply reflects that the data set is the object of the data-mining activity. Subject-data reflects knowledge, perspectives, and interpretations of the team members themselves, which emerge in communication and shape the course of the data-mining process. Subject data include data about the team members (such as who talks the most, who has expertise in a given field), as well as data they explicitly supply about the object-data or about the world in general. Such data would be found in records and artifacts of team interaction, such as documents, presentations, and even marker board notes, or, given a systematic knowledge capture process, perhaps in videotapes, audiotapes, transcripts of team interaction, or notes taken by trained observers. In the next section, we suggest ways to collect and interpret subject-data, but first we consider how the foregoing literature reframes the data-mining process.

Figure 2.1 shows two frames for the data-mining process, *Frame-1* and *Frame-2*. Because *Frame-2* contains *Frame-1*, *Frame-2* represents a broader perspective. $Process_1$ and $Process_2$ are subparts of the entire data mining process considered in this chapter. In general, our notion of *process* entails, for example, team interactions; tools, techniques, and procedures employed; starting and ending criteria; inputs; and results.

Frame-1 focuses on the computational aspects we typically attribute to data mining: a team with technical expertise employs particular tools and algorithms to mine some data set (the *object-data*), and somehow, the results should generate knowledge relevant to business decisions. From the perspective of *Frame-1*, the quality of the outcome hinges on qualities of the data set, the data-mining technologies and techniques employed, and the technical expertise of the team. *Frame-1* considers business decisions, but decisions are more central to *Frame-2*.

Frame-2 focuses on social aspects emphasized in the literature cited previously: team members with unique roles, expertise, and perspectives generate *subject-data* through communication as they make interpretations and interact in an organizational setting to accomplish $Process_1$. $Process_2$ captures and mines these subject-data and shapes $Process_1$. In addition, $Process_2$ elicits knowledge relevant to business

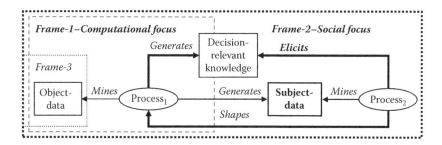

FIGURE 2.1 Data-centric decision-design.

decisions, which may be formally elicited from business decision makers or emerge dynamically based on subject data generated by $Process_1$. In this sense, to *elicit* means to draw out and structure. The structure of decision-relevant knowledge is discussed in Section 2.3.1, "The Decision Basis," and Section 2.3.2, "The Decision Frame."

The bold arrows in Figure 2.1 depict key information flows by which business decisions both inform and are informed by the data mining process. Accumulation and interpretation of subject-data are central to these information flows. From the perspective of *Frame-2*, the quality of the outcome hinges on qualities of team inter-action and interpretation, and team interaction with business decision makers is critical to inform the data-mining process and to communicate insights that shape decisions. We call this "data-centric decision-design" to emphasize the overall goal of the activity—to create decision opportunities for business decision makers based on synthesis of insights obtained from the object data and the team members.

We do not wish to imply that *Frame-1* and *Frame-2,* as we have described them, constitute the entirety of frames and framing processes relevant to data mining. For example, we could consider another frame, *Frame-3*, around the object-data itself, partially overlapping *Frame-1* and *Frame-2* but also including unknown computa-tional, organizational, and subjective factors that influenced processes by which the object-data were created and came to be the object of a data-mining project. Or we could consider *Frame-0* (not depicted in Figure 2.1), a broader frame that would subsume *Frame-2* while including additional factors, such as aspects of the organi-zational decision-making practices, setting, and cultural context in which the entire process is carried out. Regarding this broader frame, we assume data-mining projects are undertaken by teams with sponsors who have the power to commit resources and may act on decision-relevant knowledge that is generated. Further modeling of busi-ness decision-making practices is beyond our scope. Focusing on *Frame-2* allows us to carve out a manageable piece of the overall framing problem.

To varying degrees, the fundamental concerns of *Frame-2* would be reflected in all successful data-mining processes. However, *Frame-2* places novel emphasis on purposefully capturing and interpreting subject-data to shape a dynamic and con-textually richer iterative process and systematically eliciting knowledge relevant to business decisions. This emphasis motivates us to consider additional tools, tech-niques, and procedures suitable for eliciting, capturing, and mining subject-data and modeling decisions and also motivates new perspectives on team composition. Such an approach would depend on team interaction models, as well as a rich set of dis-tinctions regarding decisions and decision-making processes. We consider decision making next, and then team interaction.

2.3 DECISION QUALITY

This discussion of decision quality draws on Bergner (2006), Howard (1988), and McNamee and Celona (2001). We assume the business context is *challenging* (i.e., having aspects such as uncertainty, complexity, a changing strategic environment, new situations, long time horizons, or lack of established precedents). This appears congruent with contexts where data mining would be applied for design and market-ing. Decision making in challenging contexts requires careful thought, ingenuity, innovation, and collaboration by individuals with varied expertise and resources. Therefore we argue that data mining to better inform business decisions should also be thought of as a challenging task, and that traditional computation-focused approaches are inadequate in this regard.

Recall that *discovery of chance* (by definition) can hinge on our ability to explain how the discovery is significant for decision making. In this section, we introduce distinctions from the decision-making literature to provide a foundation for making such discoveries and explanations. These distinctions also help us model and measure team interaction. Thus the distinctions discussed in this section lay a foundation for characterizing and managing *Process₂* (depicted in Figure 2.1), which is the key to understanding how data-mining processes should influence business decision making.

The most essential distinctions pertain to the *basis* and the *frame* of a decision. The *decision basis* consists of three elements: *alternatives* the decision maker considers acting on; *information* describing how these alternative actions could influence future states of the world; and the *preferences* the decision maker has for reaching those future states by taking selected alternatives. The *decision frame* is a description, or more formally, a set of propositions that accounts for why certain alternatives, information, and values are included in the decision basis, whereas others are excluded. These concepts help clarify specifically how data mining can improve decision quality through the emergence of new basis elements and the *reframing* of decisions.

2.3.1 THE DECISION BASIS

Our primary concern here is with the decision frame, so we discuss the *decision basis* only briefly. We adopt the term *decision basis* from the decision analysis literature. The general idea is that a decision can be broken down, in a systematic way, into more fundamental structural elements. A decision basis has three elements, "the *choices or alternatives* the decision maker faces, the *information* that is relevant, and the *preferences* of the decision maker" (Howard, 1988; p. 681, emphasis added). In mathematical terms, we can represent the decision basis as a network consisting of variables, probabilistic relationships between variables, and calculations based on the variables. The variables may be control variables or random variables (uncertainties). Choices or alternatives are represented by combinations of control variables. The basis information is represented by the uncertainties, the probabilistic influence of the decision variables on the uncertainties, and the probabilistic relevance of the uncertainties to each other. These *influence* and *relevance* relationships capture information about causality—how our choices affect future states of the world. Information about preferences, which includes explicit value criteria and tradeoffs, is represented mathematically as a utility function calculated based on the states of control variables and random variables.

We use the term *basis element* to refer to any aspects of the decision basis, such as control variables, uncertainties, relevance relations (i.e., probabilistic dependence), and influence relations (the influence of the control variables on the probability distributions of the uncertainties). Value criteria, tradeoffs, and time preferences, as expressed in the utility function, are also basis elements. Please refer to Howard (1988), Howard and Matheson (1989), or McNamee and Celona (2001) for more information on decision analysis and the decision basis.

2.3.2 THE DECISION FRAME

High-quality decisions depend on appropriate frames, because frames determine what is included in decision bases. Although frames have substantial *implicit* aspects (such as cultural context and psychological factors), we limit this discussion to *explicit* aspects of frames reflected in the subject-data generated through team communication. From this perspective, the decision frame is reflected in *framing propositions* that account for the constitution of the decision basis. For example, the statement "We *have to* consider the Chinese market" entails a proposition that *requires inclusion* of numerous (as yet unnamed) basis elements logically associated with the Chinese market. If this proposition is accepted, then further discussion of these basis elements would logically follow, shaping the decision basis. The proposition entailed in the statement "There is *no way* we can have this product ready to participate in the trade fair in May" *requires exclusion* of alternatives for participation, and also tends to exclude consideration of outcomes that might occur given participation in the trade fair. If this proposition is accepted, then these alternatives and possible outcomes most likely would not be discussed, and would be excluded from any decision basis. Collectively, such framing propositions constitute frames by providing explicit criteria for inclusion as well as exclusion of basis elements, and by shaping the dialogue that follows.

Framing propositions often arise as a reaction to potential basis elements, and become part of the team's shared frame, tending to constrain the basis. If they are questioned, challenged, supported, qualified, or elaborated on, then additional propositions enter the shared frame through the dialogue process, which may cause the frame to shift (and perhaps, to expand) as a result. For example, the proposition entailed in "Why can't we do the trade fair in May? Could we at least show a prototype?" reacts to the previous framing proposition with a challenge, and simultaneously works to bring the concept "prototype" into the frame. New concepts and basis elements often enter the frame in this way, associated with a qualification or challenge to a prior framing proposition. Such framing propositions *that arise in reaction to prior framing-propositions* also become part of the shared frame and have special significance because they exhibit some level of reflection on the emerging frame, or *frame reflection* by the team. Later, we describe a way to measure frame reflection by analyzing subject-data. Frame reflection is crucial to decision quality, because it can motivate reframing that improves *comprehension of prospects*, discussed next (Bergner, 2006; Matheson, 1990).

2.3.3 HOW PROCESS AFFECTS QUALITY—COMPREHENSION OF PROSPECTS

In this section, we expand on the data-centric decision design model depicted in Figure 2.1 by explaining how the data-mining process influences decision quality. The model motivates us to mine *subject-data*, and its expansion, as depicted in Figure 2.2, further clarifies how that can be accomplished.

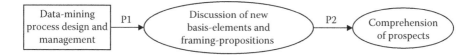

FIGURE 2.2 How the data mining process influences decision quality.

The fundamental assumption behind the model is that the data-mining process can improve decision quality by improving *comprehension of prospects*. *Comprehension of prospects* entails two senses of meaning: to effectively perceive, understand, and mentally grasp prospects that decision makers face; and to take in or include significant factors pertaining to the prospects.

A *prospect* constitutes a coherent combination of a decision alternative with its possible outcomes, faced by the decision maker when choosing. Prospects may entail scenarios or sequences of events that include many decision variables and uncertainties, interrelated through probabilistic correlations and causality. Miscomprehension of prospects, whether from failure to understand or failure to include, can involve any aspect of the basis, for example, variables, distinctions between control and uncertainty, relevance, influence, or value criteria and tradeoffs. Miscomprehension of prospects compromises decision quality, so improving comprehension of prospects can improve decision quality.

In Figure 2.2, "data-mining process design and management" is shown as a rectangle to signify that we control aspects of the process, whereas the other model parameters are shown as ovals, signifying that these parameters are uncertainties influenced by how we design and manage the process. The data-mining process referred to here is meant to include both *Process₁* and *Process₂* depicted in Figure 2.1, so it includes team dialogue processes as well as the computational processes involved in data mining. The arrows signify the influence of process design and management on the parameters, and the relevance of the parameters to each other.

Postulate P1 suggests the data-mining process can lead the team to consider new decision basis elements and new framing propositions, depending on how the process is designed and managed. This is simply a more explicit, detailed way of stating that data mining may or may not produce knowledge and insights that influence decisions. However, this postulate also implies that data mining can foster a dynamic interaction of the basis and frame that leads to *reframing* and improved comprehension (Bergner, 2006). Discussing new basis elements can lead the team to discuss new framing propositions that come as a reaction or response, and, conversely, new basis elements can enter the dialogue when framing propositions are discussed or reflected on. (Brief examples of this dynamic were provided in the previous section.)

Postulate P2 suggests that discussing new basis elements and framing issues improves comprehension of prospects. Such dialogue can help the team to discover alternatives, information, and preferences that were previously overlooked, and to clarify the subtler issues of influence and relevance, refining the basis information and *reframing* the decision. Discussing new framing propositions improves comprehension as the team explicitly reflects on frames and pools of knowledge regarding framing issues and rationales that support framing propositions. Note that Figure 2.2

depicts an abbreviated version of the *decision-dialogue model* (Bergner, 2006), which shows that *framing* and *reframing* are keys to decision quality, and suggests ways to measure and manage these aspects of the team process.

In summary, the data mining process can improve comprehension of prospects by helping a team become aware of new basis elements, such as decision variables and uncertainties, correlations and causal relationships, and value criteria and tradeoffs. To create business value, these new insights must be reflected in processes that entail the *framing* or *reframing* of decisions; otherwise, they will not affect the actions of business decision makers. By employing these distinctions to mine the subject-data reflected in dialogue, we can better understand how the data-mining process influences decision bases and frames. Next, we consider actual examples from studies of design teams, which suggest specific ways to mine subject data. We then build on those examples and further consider how mining subject-data provides a tool to measure and manage the data-mining process. We believe our previously collected dataset on design team interactions is relevant to business decision making because designers, especially during conceptual design, navigate similarly complex and challenging contexts that are rather dynamic, undefined, and uncertain.

2.4 MEASURING TEAM INTERACTION PROCESSES

In this section, we briefly cover two theories of how team interaction data—here referred to as *subject-data*—can be mined for insights regarding the influence of team interaction processes on the quality of team performance. According to Eris's theory, team performance can be predicted by analyzing the types of questions posed by team members, whereas, according to Bergner's theory, team performance can be predicted by the team's degree of frame reflection (Eris et al., 2006).

To develop practical methods based on these theories, first we precisely define observable types of events that occur in team communication (e.g., a type of question was asked; a type of framing proposition was uttered), as motivated by the theoretical models. Then, we apply the definitions to *code* team interaction data (such as videotapes and transcripts of team dialogue), which means to label observed events according to the defined event types. The observed event frequencies provide a basis for quantitative analysis, and tests of underlying theoretical models. This approach is a form of *content analysis* (Krippendorff, 1980). A related approach known as *protocol analysis* (Ericsson & Simon, 1993) is employed in cognitive science to analyze verbal data for insights into cognitive processes.

2.4.1 A MEASURE OF FRAMING

Our measure of *framing* is based on a *conceptual exploration* model developed by Bergner (2006) to explain the role of team communication in framing and generation of alternatives in decision making and design. This model is based on a small set of *dialogue acts*. Dialogue acts are types of utterances that play specified roles in dialogue, sharing certain kinds of information among the participants, reflecting intentions of the speakers and relationships between utterances (Traum, 2000). (For example, *greeting*, *threat*, and *promise* are types of dialogue acts.) The full conceptual exploration model is beyond our scope here, so we provide definitions of only two types of dialogue acts, which Bergner calls *framing acts*.

Type 1. *Limit*: To exclude or "rule out" a concept or a set of concepts; generally, with reference to certain attributes or characteristics of the concepts. *Limit* has two forms: first, the *negation*, or direct exclusion, which contains or implies words such as "no" or "not," and second, the *anchor*, or indirect exclusion, which contains or implies words such as "must" or "have to" or "only." A *limit* generally entails a limiting assertion regarding possibility, relevance, control, influence, preferences, or process that tends to reduce the span of basis elements considered worthy of further discussion in a given design or decision-making context.

Type 2. *Limit handling*: To implicitly or explicitly question, challenge, qualify, or support a *limit* or prior *limit-handling* act.

Examples of these dialogue acts were provided above in Section 2.3.2, "The Decision Frame." The reader may wish to review that section now and apply the definitions given here to identify the types of framing acts in those examples.

Note that here a *limit* is defined as a dialogue act—an observable event and not a cognitive state, psychological perspective, or physical or social condition. Because dialogue acts are observable events, their frequencies and sequences provide an empirical basis for computational models and quantitative measures of team interaction (and support qualitative analysis as well). The observed frequency of *limit*s provides a measure of basic framing activity, because *limits* entail framing propositions (as described previously) that pertain to basis elements.

The observed frequency of *limit handling* provides a measure of higher-order framing activity or *frame reflection*, because *limit-handling* acts pertain to prior *framing acts* on which they conceptually depend for their meaning and interpretation. If a *limit-handling* act (e.g., question, challenge) results in retraction or revision of a *limit*, then a wider span of basis elements may be considered worthy of further discussion. Bergner's theory predicts that given a challenging task, higher performing teams will exhibit a higher level of *frame reflection*, as measured by the frequency of *limit-handling* events observed in their dialogue, because *frame reflection* improves comprehension of prospects, as described previously.

2.4.2 A Measure of Inquiry

Our measure of inquiry is motivated by the following postulates (Eris et al., 2006):

1. Behind every decision there is a constellation of questions—which are motivated by unmet needs, an intention to influence future states of the world, uncertainty, and ambiguity—that populates the decision space; hence, questions can be tracked to understand and model decision-making processes.

2. The corollary is that behind every question there is a constellation of decisions that populates the question space; hence, decisions can be tracked to understand and model question-making processes.

In other words, questions asked should be motivated by decisions (to ensure the relevance of their answers), and decisions should motivate question asking (to improve comprehension).

Eris observes that inquiry takes place in two fundamental modalities: divergent and convergent (2004). These two thinking modes manifest in two classes of questions observed in team dialogue: deep reasoning questions (DRQs) as defined by Graesser in a learning context (Graesser, Lang, & Horgan, 1988), and generative design questions (GDQs), a new class of questions proposed by Eris that are characteristic of design thinking. The key distinction between the two classes of questions pertains to the truth value of propositions that could be offered as answers: answers to DRQs are expected to hold truth value because their answers fundamentally depend on causal relationships established by prior knowledge, whereas the answers to GDQs do not hold truth value because their answers fundamentally depend on future possibilities and prospective knowledge. For example, "Why *did* the product fail?" is a DRQ, whereas "How *could* the product fail?" is a GDQ. Graesser's DRQ definitions and Eris's GDQ definitions both are based on a taxonomy developed by Lehnert (1978)— five of Lehnert's original 12-question categories were termed DRQs by Graesser, and Eris proposed five GDQ types as extensions. See Eris (2004) for definitions of question categories. Eris's theory predicts that more effective teams will exhibit a higher degree of inquiry as well as a *balance* of convergent and divergent thinking, as exhibited by frequencies of DRQs and GDQs observed in their dialogue.

2.4.3 PRIOR RESULTS

Previously, we applied these two distinct theoretical approaches to analyze the interactions of design teams (via audiovisual records), and through this analysis sought to unify our theoretical models of team performance in design and decision making. See Eris et al. (2006) for a detailed description of the experiment, the design task, and the results. To accomplish this prior work, we developed a metric based on each theory.

The *frame-reflection metric* is simply a count of *limit handling* acts that occur over a given time period, whereas the *inquiry metric* is calculated according to the equation *inquiry metric* = $(DRQ)^{1/2} \times (GDQ)^{1/2}$, where DRQ is the count of deep-reasoning questions and GDQ is the count of generative design questions occurring over a given period. This mathematical form, known as a Cobb-Douglas function, is often employed in economic analysis and utility models. This function mathematically represents Eris's theory that divergent and convergent thinking should be balanced, because it has a maximum where DRQ = GDQ (for a fixed number of questions), and it approaches zero as the count of either question type approaches zero. As one question type (or thinking mode) becomes more frequent, or "overused," this function gives increasing utility for the underused type and decreasing utility for the overused type. The simple sum (*inquiry metric$_1$* = DRQ + GDQ) also yielded a significant predictor of team performance, but the Cobb-Douglas function better captures Eris' theory in mathematical form, and also yields a result with a stronger correlation ($R2 = 0.872$, versus 0.817) and higher statistical significance (P value = $.0064$, versus $.0133$). See Eris et al. (2006) for a fuller

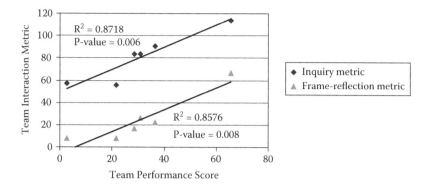

FIGURE 2.3 Design-team performance scores correlated with interaction process metrics.

description of the experiment and additional results. (Note the metrics were scaled linearly to improve readability of the graph in Figure 2.3.)

As shown in Figure 2.3, each model successfully characterized a significant relationship between our quantitative dialogue processes metrics and team performance scores. The approach also underpinned qualitative analysis and modeling to complement the sort of statistical analysis we showed here. The successful application of these two theoretical models to "mine" design team interaction data to correlate process measures with outcome measures suggests that the *subject-data* of data-mining teams could be mined in a similar fashion, as an integral part of the data-mining process, to provide process insights that could improve team performance.

2.5 DISCUSSION

The basic distinction employed in the data-centric decision design model presented in this chapter—computational focus versus social focus—can be further articulated by considering how decision-relevant knowledge would be generated in the absence of *Process₂* and how it would be elicited in the absence of *Process₁*.

In the absence of *Process₂*, the focus would be on the computational frame only, which means the criteria used in mining object data to generate knowledge to support business decision making would be built, or *hard-coded*, into the computational model that is used to process information. This would require the data-mining team that is creating the computational model to predetermine the criteria for the most part. That approach is clearly not particularly opportunistic because it would not allow for interaction among the team, the data, and the criteria. The team would not be able to respond to the potentially relevant connections that might emerge during data mining in real time, and would have to try to work, or *guess*, its way back to those opportunities from the output of the computation. Also, this approach could result in the decision flaw Russo and Schoemaker (1989) call *frame blindness,* in which the decision maker is unaware of key factors that shape the decision basis and frame.

On the other hand, in the absence of *Process₁*, there is no object- or subject-data to be mined, and the approach would be reduced to the team's eliciting business decision information from its preexisting knowledge that is relevant to the decision under consideration; the team's existing knowledge base would become subject-data. That could clearly constitute a rather limited, and perhaps even misleading, decision basis.

Interestingly, the two scenarios outlined previously are not that unlikely, and they may occur often in poorly managed decision-making approaches in the real world. As we have argued throughout the chapter, a more effective approach would entail the symbiotic combination of $Process_1$ and $Process_2$.

Finally, we recognize that the identity of the decision maker in our data-centric decision design model is open to discussion. Although we have set up our framework so that the data-mining team is charged with the task of generating and eliciting decision-relevant knowledge for a sponsor, who would ultimately act on the knowledge to make business decisions, we have not explicitly discussed the identity of the sponsor and his or her relationship with the team. One critical variable in that consideration would be to understand the implications of modeling the decision maker as an individual versus a group. However, that consideration is beyond the scope of this chapter.

2.6   IMPLICATIONS

We now return to the questions that originally motivated our discussion. Why could two data-mining projects, apparently equivalent from a technical perspective, have substantially different impacts on business decisions? How would we study the problem? What would we measure? In general, we would measure the degree to which teams attend to framing and basis development, and communicate with decision makers. We also consider the question, "What would we do to manage the data-mining process given what the measures reveal?" Based on the foregoing discussion, we offer possible answers to these questions, based on three aspects of a data-mining project: team composition, team interaction, and decision focus.

2.6.1   TEAM COMPOSITION

The participants could be the *most important* component in a data-mining process for design and marketing, because they provide the *subject-data*. Recall that *subject-data* reflects the knowledge, perspectives, and interpretations of team members. From the *Frame-1* perspective (see previous discussion), we would, of course, include team members with data-mining expertise and deep understanding of the object-data.

The *Frame-2* perspective broadens our concerns regarding team composition. We would include team members with expertise across the business domains (i.e., domain experts) to provide knowledge, perspectives, and interpretation during the project to shape its course and contribute to its outcomes. For example, we might wish to include team members with expertise in design, production, and marketing to ensure diverse perspectives on emerging decision bases and frames. Because we would measure success in terms of the decisions that emerge, we would include experts in decision-making processes to elicit knowledge from business decision makers and domain experts regarding the business's strategic situation and priorities, to obtain feedback throughout the process from stakeholders with the authority and resources to implement proposed alternatives, and to help frame potential decisions as they emerge. Because we are concerned with interaction processes, we would include experts in observing and facilitating team interaction, and those who could mine and interpret subject-data.

2.6.2 TEAM INTERACTION

Even if the right people are on the team, the way they interact, and each member's degree of participation, could be critical. Teams may exhibit very different interaction dynamics, for example, with respect to inquiry and framing (as discussed previously). Even if team members interact effectively among themselves, they could still fail by lacking effective interaction with project sponsors and business decision makers to frame and reframe their efforts appropriately. Based on analysis of subject-data, we would seek to facilitate and enhance the interaction process to address these issues.

Research in specific business contexts may be necessary to learn how to optimize team processes, for example, by collecting and analyzing subject-data and outcomes for several data-mining projects. For example, consider different types of data-mining projects for design and marketing that could be undertaken in a given company: develop a new market for an existing product; develop a new product for an existing market; or develop a new product for a new market. Clearly, unique characteristics of these business situations could entail unique process concerns and measures for research in the business context.

However, general models and concepts, such as those presented in this chapter, would guide such research, and may provide insights that apply to a wide range of project types. Based on our models, we would look for a balance of generative questions and deep-reasoning questions and a high level of frame-reflective dialogue. This would indicate the team is getting to the heart of issues and pooling knowledge to build a shared frame and develop ideas. We would look for the emergence of insights to shape significant business decisions and expect to observe deep inquiry motivated by these emergent decisions to improve comprehension. Deficiencies in these areas, revealed through analysis of subject-data, may suggest the need for process facilitation or changes in team composition.

2.6.3 DECISION FOCUS

The distinctions defined above in Section 2.3, "Decision Quality," help us break down the relatively abstract notion of a *decision* into more basic elements, providing a foundation for understanding how decisions shape a project, and how a project shapes decisions. In fact, in decision analysis practice (Howard & Matheson, 1989), these distinctions underlie a *prescriptive* methodology for *eliciting* knowledge from decision makers and modeling their decisions. We would expect to see elicitation of such decision-related information from organizational decision makers and project sponsors, to ensure the project is properly formulated and kept on track. For example, in formulation meetings and reviews we would expect to see *framing acts* as well as discussion of value criteria and tradeoffs.

In a *descriptive* sense, these distinctions—control, uncertainty, influence, relevance, value criteria, tradeoffs, frames—provide a way to observe and more clearly describe what happens in team communication, with respect to team decision making. As the successful team interacts with each other and with the object-data, we would expect to see them collaboratively explore interrelated issues of control, influence, relevance, and preferences, and develop new insights regarding these issues. For example, we would expect the discussion of control variables to motivate inquiry regarding uncertainties, as well as value criteria and tradeoffs. We would expect discussion of value criteria and tradeoffs to motivate discussion of influence and control. As insights and potential decision bases emerge, we would expect to see them framed effectively as *limits* are introduced, questioned, challenged, qualified, and supported in a frame-reflective process. We would expect to see emergent decisions communicated to project sponsors and organizational decision makers for their evaluation and possible reframing.

2.7 LIMITATIONS

Although there is a broad literature on analyzing and measuring team interaction, we discussed only two approaches that focus on team communication and information sharing. This information-processing perspective may offer a natural extension to data mining, but it leaves out substantial social and psychological factors. Our emphasis on information-processing issues reflects an implicit assumption that the teams function well from a social-psychological and organizational perspective. Yet our models emphasize *frames* and *reframing*, as well as deep and generative inquiry, which may involve inherent psychological and organizational complexity. For example, Brocklesby and Mingers (1999) explore various *cognitive limits* on our ability to reframe and question optimism that reframing will generally lead to more effective action. Palmer and Dunford (1996) observe that it may be difficult to sustain a "within-dialogue" frame shift when we return to the organizational context (outside the dialogue context), in which our ingrained patterns of interaction and dominant frames bias action toward established conventions. Power and values of those both within and external to the dialogue may operate in opposition to reframing.

Our approach to analyzing frames—based on sets of propositions—is designed to be relatively simple, incisive, and empirically useful. However, focusing on empirical aspects of *frames* carries the risk of oversimplification. Sets of propositions may be only crude indications of frames when cultural, organizational, and psychological issues come into play. However, even the deep implicit aspects of frames may reveal themselves in explicit framing acts, which present an entry point for elicitation. Deeper levels of frame analysis are possible, but present additional operational challenges (Bateson, 1955; Goffman, 1974).

2.8 CONCLUSIONS

Our main goal here was to describe and explore a new, more inclusive frame for the data-mining process. Our treatment of how we would actually use this frame to manage the process has been limited to brief illustrations. The general model is motivated by prior literature and stands on theoretical grounds, but further empirical work would be necessary to test the ideas and put them into practice. Essentially, the model we present constitutes an agenda for applied research in organizational settings on aspects of the data-mining process that can make the difference between success and failure of data-mining projects.

REFERENCES

Bateson, G. A theory of play and fantasy, in *Steps to an Ecology of Mind*, Bateson, G., Ed., Chandler Publishing Company, San Francisco, 1955.

Bergner, D. From decision frames to discovery frames. Paper presented at European Conference on Artificial Intelligence (ECAI 2004), 4th International Workshop on Chance Discovery, at Valencia, Spain, 2004.

Bergner, D. Dialogue processes for generating decision alternatives. Doctoral Dissertation, Department of Management Science and Engineering, Stanford, Palo Alto, 2006.

Brocklesby, J. and Mingers, J. The cognitive limits on organisational reframing: a systems perspective based on the theory of autopoeisis. Paper presented at The 17th International Conference of The System Dynamics Society, at Wellington, New Zealand, 1999.

Ericsson, K.A. and Simon, H.A. *Protocol Analysis: Verbal Reports as Data*, MIT Press, Cambridge, MA, 1993.

Eris, O. *Effective Inquiry for Innovative Engineering Design*, Kluwer Academic Publishers, Boston, 2004.

Eris, O., Bergner, D., Jung, M., and Leifer, L.J. ConExSIR: a dialogue-based framework of design team thinking and discovery, in *Chance Discoveries in Real World Decision Making*, Ohsawa, Y. and Tsumoto, S, Eds., Springer, New York, 2006.

Fayyad, U., Shapiro, G.P., and P. Smyth. From data mining to knowledge discovery in databases. *AI Mag.,* 17, 37–54, 1996.

Goffman, E. *Frame Analysis*, Harper and Row, New York, 1974.

Graesser, A., Lang, K., and Horgan, D. A taxonomy for question generation. *Quest. Exch.,* 2, 3–15, 1988.

Howard, R.A. Decision analysis: practice and promise. *Manage. Sci.,* 34, 679–695, 1988.

Howard, R.A. and Matheson, J.E., Eds., *The Principles and Applications of Decision Analysis*, Strategic Decisions Group, Menlo Park, CA, 1989.

Krippendorff, K. *Content Analysis: An Introduction to Its Methods*, Sage, London, 1980.

Lehnert, G.W. *The Process of Question Answering*, Lawrence Erlbaum Associates, Hillsdale, NJ, 1978.

Matheson, D.E. When should you reexamine your frame? Doctoral Dissertation, Engineering Economic Systems, Stanford University, Palo Alto, 1990.

McNamee, P. and Celona, J. *Decision Analysis for the Professional*, SmartOrg, Menlo Park, CA, 2001.

Ohsawa, Y. Chance discoveries for making decisions in complex real world. *New Generation Comp.,* 20, 143–163, 2002.

Ohsawa, Y. and McBurney, P.J. Chance discovery, in Jain, L.C., Ed., *Advanced Information Processing*, Springer-Verlag, New York, 2003.

Palmer, I. and Dunford, R. Reframing and organizational action: the unexplored link. *J. Organiz. Change Manage.,* 9, 12–25, 1996.

Russo, E. J., and Schoemaker, P.J. *Decision Traps*. Fireside, New York, 1989.

Traum, D.R. 20 Questions on dialogue act taxonomies. *J. Semant.* 17, 7–30, 2000.

3 The Use of Online Market Analysis Systems to Achieve Competitive Advantage

Lihua Zhao, Mark D. Uncles, and Gary Gregory

CONTENTS

3.1   INTRODUCTION

The focus of this chapter is the development and application of online market analysis systems (OMASs) to provide automobile manufacturers and dealerships with easy-to-use and effective managerial decision support tools. OMASs make use of information and software from geographical information systems (GIS) and Internet technologies to generate online (Web-based) environments for data management, analysis, and visualization in map format. These platforms are integrated and synchronized with market analysis techniques and customer relationship management (CRM) systems to produce effective approaches for identifying market opportunities and estimating automobile sales performance. In this way, a bridge is established between marketing science, GIS and Internet technologies, and practical problem-solving, with a view to developing competitive advantages for manufacturers and dealers who are able to harness the potential of these systems.

3.2   THE NEED FOR ONLINE MARKET ANALYSIS SYSTEMS

Managers seek to gain competitive advantage by conducting market analyses and by refining their forecasts of market potential. An effective and practical approach for doing this is to combine GIS information with CRM databases and to visualize analytical results using maps and graphs (Duke, 2001). This approach can be extended to integrate very different sources of data held by diverse players in a market, doing so in a dynamic and timely way. WebGIS is one such example, and applications of this have been developed and tested for purposes of urban planning and resource management (Kingston et al., 2000). But applications in marketing are nascent and raise distinct challenges that are not faced by urban planners (e.g., the competitive nature of business is a crucial issue to confront); therefore, the challenge is to develop a dynamic OMAS with the specific needs of business in mind.

Some progress has been made. Within marketing, there is clear support for the analysis and mapping of geo-referenced customer/consumer data to enhance CRM and marketing activities, typically making use of GIS technologies (Harris et al., 2005; Hernandez, 2005; Longley et al., 2005; Sleight, 2002). However, an issue is the timeliness of these analyses. All too often a very static description of the marketing landscape is presented.

At the same time, marketers have come to recognize that the Web provides ready access to a vast array of global information resources and facilitates the gathering of valuable competitive intelligence and information. As the network of Internet users expands, marketers are increasingly turning to the Web to conduct market surveys, focus groups, virtual shopping experiments, new product concept tests, and customer satisfaction measurement—all of which can be used to assist in decision making (Burke 1996, 2005; Prasad et al., 2001; Quelch & Klein, 1996; Rust et al., 2004; Urban, 2005a, 2005b).

In addition, the development of information and communication technologies has led to more and more techniques from other disciplines being integrated and applied in marketing research. For example, data-mining techniques have been used in online environments to provide timely trend analyses and customer profiling information that is valuable in making effective marketing-mix decisions (Kalakota & Whinston, 1997; Prasad et al., 2001; Ravi et al., 2005).

In light of these developments, it is only natural to look to OMASs, and specifically WebGIS, for a solution to the problem of how to conduct more timely and dynamic analyses. The practical development of an online marketing decision support system (DSS) consists of building an online system by integrating CRM and spatial databases; implementing a model-based system by integrating online analytical techniques, spatial analysis, and data-mining techniques for market potential analysis and for generating spatial visualization (maps, graphs, and tables); and developing an easy-to-use online interface for decision makers to make use of the proposed online system.

In the next section, we review the infrastructures and technologies used in this field of research and introduce a framework for WebGIS-based OMASs that integrates all systems and technologies. We then examine the benefits with respect to efficacious analysis and decision making in the automobile industry. Finally, we comment on how the capabilities of the system can affect both theory and practice in marketing and outline some issues for the future.

3.3   INFRASTRUCTURE FOR OMASs

Information technology infrastructure is used in all e-business initiatives to connect different parts of an organization and to link suppliers, customers, and allies (Weill & Vitale, 2000). For an OMAS, the infrastructure comprises four elements (Figure 3.1): (1) very general public/external infrastructures such as the Internet and telecommunications networks (associated with technologists' views of infrastructure); (2) enterprise-wide infrastructures in the form of CRM/data servers, firewalls, and shared information technology services (associated with users' views of infrastructure); (3) business unit infrastructures, such as the intelligence used to translate

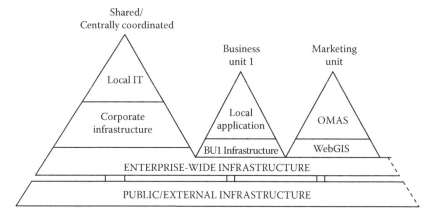

FIGURE 3.1 Infrastructure for online market analysis systems (adapted from Weill and Vitale, 2000).

information technology components into services that users in human resources and marketing can draw on; and (4) local applications for specific tasks within the business unit, such as market analysis.

OMAS fits into the four-part infrastructure as a fast-changing local application. WebGIS is the business unit infrastructure that provides spatial data management, spatial data analysis, and map display functions. In turn, this OMAS is linked to broader enterprise-wide and public/external industry-based infrastructures (such as credit and bank payments systems and automotive industry supply chain networks).

Within the context of these infrastructures, key components for the development and realization of OMASs are outlined next.

3.3.1 THE INTERNET

This integrated system of networks and connections provides a dynamic environment for accessing data, presenting information, and analyzing results. The Internet has become a global common platform where organizations and businesses communicate with each other to carry out e-commerce activities and to provide value-added services (Feeny, 2001; Fensel & Bussler, 2002). Today, e-commerce provides ready access to a vast array of information resources and facilitates the gathering of valuable competitive intelligence. As noted earlier, marketers are increasingly turning to the Web for market research information to help make decisions. Furthermore, more and more techniques from other disciplines are being integrated for e-commerce activities (such as the use now made of data mining). Applying GIS technology in e-commerce is another example of the provision of market intelligence, in this case by focusing on the spatial context.

3.3.2 A WEBGIS PLATFORM

A conventional GIS is a computer system capable of capturing, storing, analyzing, and displaying geographically referenced information (i.e., data identified by location) (Longley et al., 2005). GIS also can be seen as including the procedures, operating personnel, and spatial data that go into the system. Decision science researchers have shown that use of maps results in faster problem solving than tables and that, as task difficulty increases, maps are more effective for problem solving (Smelcer & Carmel, 1997). Also, a GIS can convert existing digital information, which may not yet be in map form, into formats it can recognize and use. For example, tabular customer address data can be converted to maplike form and serve as layers of thematic information in a GIS. Increasingly, this versatility is recognized by marketers who see GIS as a way to analyze internal and external marketing intelligence data in a helpful format and to integrate such internal and external data to greatly improve the effectiveness of marketing decisions (Hess et al., 2004).

A WebGIS platform combines GIS systems with Internet technologies to provide powerful online data processing and display systems. The power of a WebGIS for business decision support, as compared with conventional GIS, is its ability to manage spatial and aspatial data from a number of sources, display the data online dynamically, and provide spatial analysis modeling and decision-support services via online maps, graphs, and tables. However, to date, applications outside urban planning and resource management have been limited (e.g., exploring ways to acquire and query geo-referenced data or images, as in the case of online maps for tourists). The development of OMASs here goes further: it enables the use of continually updated data from existing and potential customers/consumers, grouped into different time frames or grouped into classes by age, sex, occupation, brand buying behavior, or shopping patronage, combined with the thematic mapping capabilities of GIS, for visualization (Zhao et al., 2005).

3.3.3 CRM

CRM describes software solutions that help organizations manage relationships with their customers (e.g., a database containing detailed customer information that management and salespeople can access to match customer needs with products, and inform customers of service requirements). CRM is not only an information system; it is also a business strategy that gives rise to conceptual, organizational, and operational changes within organizations (Payne & Frow, 2005). Underlying CRM is the belief that an organization's most valuable asset is the customer and the organization must manage its customer relationships wisely. Having various departments (e.g., marketing, sales and service) gather qualified information creates a database that is of real value to the organization. Establishing defined processes for data retrieval allows for effective use of the data and provides a uniform platform for managing relations with customers. When successfully implemented, CRM maximizes business potential within the existing customer base, optimizes ongoing service levels, capitalizes on sales opportunities throughout the service process, and broadens relationships with customers/consumers.

In OMASs, CRM is combined with GIS. The attractions of doing this are threefold. First is the ability to overcome any weaknesses embedded within each system by integrating GIS capabilities with the power of CRM. Second is the ability to make effective use of data from different sources (e.g., census data combined with sales records). Third is the advantage for users of being able to visualize spatial data in different forms (e.g., to visualize the spatial distribution of data on maps before further market analysis). In these ways, a platform is created for more refined market analysis and decision support, such as for solving practical marketing problems related to retail chain network planning based on demographic analysis, market positioning, and consumer targeting.

3.3.4 DATA MINING

Data-mining techniques consist of a wide range of tools to facilitate goal definition, data selection, data preparation and transformation, data exploration, and pattern discovery and pattern usage (Han & Kamber, 2006). These methods provide a new generation of analysis techniques and procedures for market analysis, prediction and the identification of practically useful patterns of information (Berry & Linoff, 2004). A driving force behind data mining has been the extraordinary growth in the quality, quantity, and complexity of geospatial data. The ready availability of such data, on a scale unthinkable a couple of decades ago, poses new challenges for the geospatial and marketing research community. Although conventional market analysis and spatial statistics methods retain their power and popularity in numerous studies, innovative data-mining techniques and approaches are appearing in response to the newly available geospatial data (such as cellular automata, agent-based modeling, and qualitative and fuzzy reasoning). These techniques are efficient and effective in discovering hidden structures, patterns, and associations within geospatial data (Arentze & Timmermans, 2006). At the same time, emerging visualization and interaction technologies provide powerful tools for obtaining additional insights from geospatial data. There is increasing convergence of analytical reasoning and visualization toward the creation and discovery of geospatial knowledge for real-world marketing applications (Florkowski & Sarmiento, 2005; Hanaoka & Clarke, 2007; Jank & Kannan, 2005, 2006).

Although the technologies and methodologies are developing rapidly, what is already available has the capacity to assist in the process of business planning and market research. Forward-looking businesses are already applying approaches similar to those described. Unfortunately, however, current approaches tend to be very disjointed, often requiring the manual movement of data between various software applications. This limits the use of these technologies to those who have advanced skills in database management and programming, data analysis, and predictive modeling. There is a need, therefore, for tools that will integrate the necessary technologies, enabling marketers/mangers to focus on the business opportunities instead of the technical barriers to implementation. OMASs meet this need. Here we do not focus on the technological developments per se; rather, we address the issue of integrating the GIS and data-mining tools for market analysis and decision support.

3.4   ARCHITECTURE AND DESIGN OF OMASs

The growth of the Internet and the delivery of content on the Web are changing methodologies for displaying, reading, and using spatial information. A primary goal is to capitalize on these changes to produce and deliver spatial analysis results and maps for marketing business customers, doing so in as efficient a way as possible. The online market analysis system provides decision makers with a flexible, problem-solving online environment with a geographic foundation. This is achieved using scripts and programs to link open-source and commercial products. The online mapping component has the capacity to gather and display existing customer information; generate buyer profiles based on customer information and demographic variables; create dynamic maps from data stored in a GIS; allow users to display (scale and pan) map information for different areas of interest; and produce map layouts with cartographic components (e.g., titles, legends, scales).

3.4.1 SYSTEM ARCHITECTURE

Systems integration is becoming a critical component in most custom software development projects and commercial off-the-shelf software package installations. With the widespread use of the Internet, industry is experiencing a significant growth in three-tier

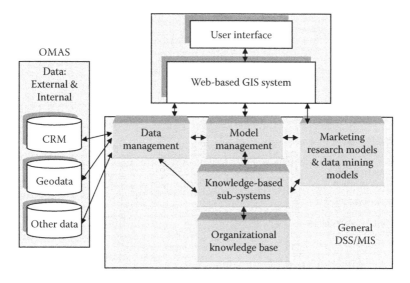

FIGURE 3.2 Architecture of WebGIS-based online market analysis systems.

Web-based applications. This three-tier approach allows the system to be separated into three layers: presentation (the graphical user interface), business logic (the rules that define business processing and provide decision-making support), and the data layer (the underlying spatial database that integrates the spatial information and customer data from CRM). This separation of layers provides for efficient development, reduced maintenance, and increased data consistency. By extending the development of marketing applications to a three-tier model, Web-based GIS systems can be integrated seamlessly and provide better analysis, presentation, and data sharing.

The architecture framework (Figure 3.2) consists of six key components: a database management system, model-based market management, marketing research models, knowledge-based subsystems, graphic display generator, and a user interface. The graphic generator is a GIS-specific component for the spatial analysis and display of information in map format. The module for marketing research models is a specific component embedded in the framework for market analysis. The other four components are identical to the concept of a general DSS (Turban & Aronson, 2001; Turban et al., 2005). With this WebGIS-based OMAS, Internet technologies and e-business concepts have been incorporated into the system to provide accessible and cost-efficient online decision support.

3.4.2 FUNCTIONAL COMPONENTS

The WebGIS-based OMAS is designed to use systems tools (infrastructure) and system components as key building blocks across the three interrelated layers (user layer, application layer, and service layer), having regard to the efficiency of information flow, data protection, and integrity of the whole system (Figure 3.3). In this OMAS,

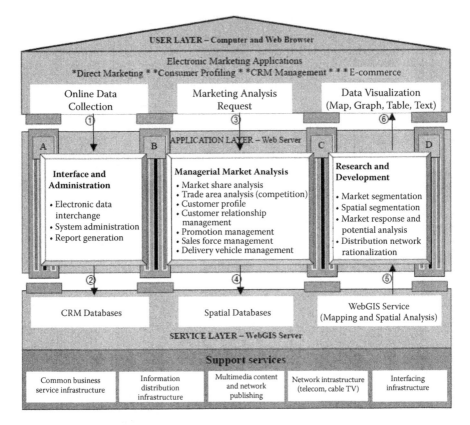

FIGURE 3.3 Functional components of WebGIS-based online market analysis systems.

the user layer is described as a client, whereas the application and service layers are described as servers. The Internet and TCP/IP, a special language, are used to link layers with one another. To meet the requirements of different users in understanding current market performance, and working out a solution for marketing planning based on daily business practice, this WebGIS-based OMAS consists of four major functional components (shown as supporting pillars in Figure 3.3).

3.4.2.1   Communication and Administration (Pillar A)

In this module, administration refers to the periodic collection and management of market information from the retail outlets. Some examples of this function are system administration, information user group management, information collection and assortment, and internal management. With these functions designed, data from different sources can be incorporated and integrated into the system using GIS and database management. This also enables users from different groups to access information at different content levels.

Geographical mapping is used to improve communication efficiency and effectiveness by putting comprehensive marketing information into an easy-to-understand map format. With maps, the enormous and complicated marketing analysis and spatial modeling results can be vividly presented. The presentation also can help system users and decision makers easily link or integrate results with their own experiences and their own knowledge.

3.4.2.2 Current Market Analysis (Pillar B)

As the comprehensive marketing information is organized in GIS-based relational databases, the system is implemented with a combination of marketing analysis functions (e.g., total sales—by brand, by product origin, by type, by subcategory, by functional specification) and spatial distributions (e.g., for sales, market shares, projected demand). These functions are designed to offer market analysis and development modules in a standardized form, making it easier and cheaper to update the entire analytical system without big changes on the user side. This reduces the overall cost of market analysis for all users or the industry in general. In addition, the system is designed to offer scope for mass customization to meet the needs of different users under different conditions by compacting and integrating the various market analysis and knowledge discovery modules (such as extension modules for spatial segmentation, for "if-then" multicriteria scenario analysis, and optimization/operations research).

3.4.2.3 CRM and Sales/Customer Analysis (Pillar C)

A GIS-based CRM system can go beyond the functionalities provided by general CRM systems. The system links CRM customers with geography; thus, users gain information about sales performance over space and about the spatial distribution and spatial location of high-value areas/clients. Example analyses include sales performance by zip or postal code/census collection district (CCD) and customer value evaluation by suburbs.

3.4.2.4 Operational/Decision Support Issues (Pillar D)

Different from conventional DSSs, GIS-based OMASs provide additional special facilities for spatial analysis, such as logistics management, area-based optimization, and retail outlet rationalization. Thus the system can provide decision makers with practical tools to coordinate members of a distribution channel and to conduct operational planning.

3.4.3 Processing Data and Information

The structure shown in Figure 3.3 provides efficient information flow and generates useful market analysis knowledge and intelligence for various users and decision makers. The system provides both users and decision makers with a flexible, problem-solving online environment with a geographic foundation. A key requirement here is the provision of accurate and up-to-date information to track market trends online. Six steps are involved in this process.

Step 1: Data collection, data entry, and data coding. On a regular (e.g., daily) basis, users of the system update sales data for their own area from their own computer. This updated information is passed through the Internet to a server. The electronic data interface structures the updated information from users for a broad geographical area in an identical format. This standardized and automated operation for data entry and coding improves the efficiency of data collection, entry, and coding within the whole industry/system.

Step 2: Sales data updating. The structured sales information is automatically passed to the central sales database via TCP/IP.

Step 3: Marketing analysis requests. Requests for analysis are sent out from users to the server. General marketing analysis tools are requested by users, and more sophisticated and specific research can be conducted via interactive communications between system users and the marketing analysis system. This research and strategy development module includes market and spatial segmentation, market response, retail network rationalization, and budget optimization. Within this application layer, CRM and delivery vehicle management modules are incorporated. For instance, the link with CRM enables promotional letters/advertisements to be sent directly to the target market. Delivery vehicle management automatically coordinates the distribution schedule based on the principle of minimizing the total distribution cost by considering the travel path distance, traffic flows, and labor costs. Thus, in this layer, all the functions of e-commerce are to be found (i.e., e-operations, e-marketing, and e-services).

Step 4: Data communication and results generation request. Sales and relevant spatial databases are requested and incorporated during these analysis and exploration processes, and the results generation request is sent out to the WebGIS server for analytical output.

Step 5: GIS mapping and output exporting. Through the WebGIS server, the sales database is routinely updated and geocoded. The sales database is then incorporated into a basic spatial database for spatial analysis and mapping (not only for market share analysis and spatial segmentation, but also for distribution network rationalization). At the end of these analyses, maps are created within the WebGIS server.

Step 6: Result browsing. Maps (output images) are exported from the WebGIS server and packaged into a customized format in the application layer according to requests from the user. Eventually, this formulated output will be displayed by the user's Internet browser.

3.4.4 INTEROPERABILITY BETWEEN USERS

In terms of functionality, the focus is on practical development of a managerial DSS, but also of importance is the need for system design based on open standards that encourage interoperability between users. There are both technical and data considerations.

From a technical viewpoint, the approach adopted is similar in spirit to open GIS: an end user does not have to understand the technicalities of GIS to perform analyses and mapping using GIS. Thus users do not have to become involved with the relatively complicated GIS concepts and techniques, but they are still able to perform GIS analyses and other forms of spatial modeling. With the advent of WebGIS, sophisticated analyses can be processed dynamically via the Internet without having to rely too much on the assistance of technological specialists. For example, MapXtreme, the WebGIS server developed by MapInfo, provides a dynamic online mapping tool to help marketing professionals identify sales patterns and make sound decisions at different spatial scales. As for using data-mining techniques, users can choose the type of results they would like to have. All technique selection and analysis processes are automated.

Regarding data, consideration is based on the manipulation of very large amounts of primary data, which includes data transfer from CRM databases to geo-referenced data records and the warehousing of data from different sources. In particular, transferring customer records into geo-referenced data, and integrating this with census variables, takes considerably longer than traditional marketing survey data collection. This is similar to the experience of those working with data mining; for example, Pyle (1999) showed that those using data mining to generate decision support scenarios spent 75% of their time on data preparation, 20% on data analysis, and 5% on data modeling. In addition, the online market analysis system involves substantial time for the integration of different systems and the development of online displays.

A further issue concerns the sharing of data. First, there is sharing of the spatial database located on the online server. Data from each CRM provided by different companies are aggregated into small spatial units based on customer location. The data manipulation is to maintain customer privacy and also to match demographic data for market analysis. The aggregated data from up-to-date CRMs provide a precise overview of the current market and a basis for forecasting. Second, an equally important component of a CRM is the sharing of data about prospective (potential) customers. To maximize future value, exploration based on existing customer data is not sufficient, because the market is changing, lifestyles of the whole community are changing, and the culture is changing—markets are dynamic, not static. The impacts of these changes need to be captured, and online data collection is an important way to facilitate this. From the viewpoint of planning future marketing activities, the enhanced datasets described here hold the promise of being more useful than existing customer databases.

With such online systems, although the spatial databases and market analysis techniques will be shared by different users from different organizations, CRM information is covered by confidentiality agreements between all participating parties and no specific customer information is divulged to third parties. Company performance analysis is based on only their own CRM data. However, aggregated data generated from the CRM data are used for competitor analyses and market trend analysis.

3.4.5 Testing and Assessment of the Resulting System

Testing and evaluation of OMASs stems from three interfaces: (1) the user interface (do users find the OMAS easy to use?); (2) the interface between the user and the decision-making organization (does the OMAS enhance decision-making processes?);

and (3) the interface between the organization and the environment (does the use of OMAS lead to better performance?). Empirical tests and comparative assessments (e.g., compared with non–Web-based GIS systems) also can be used to show gains in marketing effectiveness and efficiency. We consider technical validity (e.g., accuracy, reliability), user assessments (e.g., perceived usefulness, decision confidence), and organizational gains (e.g., cost-savings, time savings). This is in keeping with the framework for evaluation of DSSs put forward by Adelman and Donnell (1986) and adopted widely (Laudon & Laudon, 2007; Turban et al., 2005) and is in line with marketing research practice (Wierenga et al., 1999).

Based on these factors, three observations about OMASs are made. First, a WebGIS provides an easy-to-use interface, which is integrated with the Internet browser. The user interface design has been considered both from a design perspective (Figure 3.2) and a user evaluation perspective (functional components in Figure 3.3).

Second, most strategy researchers agree that effective management and use of information is a valuable asset that can help gain a competitive advantage (Hoffman, 2000). In some situations, making better, faster, and more effective decisions can create "decision superiority." The implementation of the proposed system serves this purpose in the marketing field.

Third, the state of the art concerning the measurement of the contribution to an improvement of DSS performance is poor. In theory and in practice there is a high degree of agreement with regard to the contributions of DSS usage for the marketer: time benefits in accessing information; uniformity of information or presentation of information; and an improved understanding of the organization and market position. But at present not enough research has been carried out into the evaluation of the performance of DSSs. There is an apparent need for innovative methods and techniques, as we discuss later in this chapter.

3.5 APPLICATIONS OF ONLINE MARKET ANALYSIS SYSTEMS

Applications are discussed in the context of the development and implementation of an innovative business-to-business e-marketing solution in the Australian automobile industry. The OMAS developed for the automobile industry serves as a case study, showing some of the benefits of integrating WebGIS, CRM, data mining, and market analysis.

An initial investigation into online market reporting systems available to Australian automotive manufacturers and dealers shows that current systems are mainly based on tabular reporting of market share and other key performance indicators at quite aggregated levels (e.g., national or state levels). However, the automobile industry is looking for methods to aggregate various types of data into easy-to-understand systems at far more detailed spatial levels (e.g., at the level of suburbs, postcodes, or CCDs comprising roughly 250 households) (Department of Industry Science and Resources, 2001). Analysis at these levels enables manufacturers and dealers to examine demographic opportunities, customer opportunities, and potential marketing opportunities in ways that were previously unthinkable.

The challenge for the automobile industry is to develop affordable solutions that build on existing systems and are tailored to meet the needs of individual automobile businesses (e.g., dealerships). Such solutions need to provide timely access to information for decision support in a dynamic environment. Working with an industry partner, Mapdata Interface, VSTATS (http://vstats.test-drive.com.au) is developed as a prototype OMAS for the automobile industry. The broader application illustrates a range of issues, from improvements to information flows, to efficient business processing, and to reduced costs compared to some of the alternatives. Here, only a couple of examples are elaborated on increasing competitiveness and improving sales performance.

3.5.1 Increasing Competitiveness

Sharing information and obtaining market analysis outcomes through the Web will provide business decision makers with up-to-date information and knowledge. This solution will not only reduce costs for established businesses, but will also help to avoid the cost of wrong decisions for new entrants. This may give rise to competitive advantages.

Using the system designed, the information flow delivered to automobile business decision makers could be improved through the advanced analysis technologies, analysis dimensions, and time frames. Figure 3.4 illustrates these information flows for the automobile market.

In Figure 3.4, four different types of information flow are gathered and integrated into the system engine. One is the company's own sales data (CRM) within its

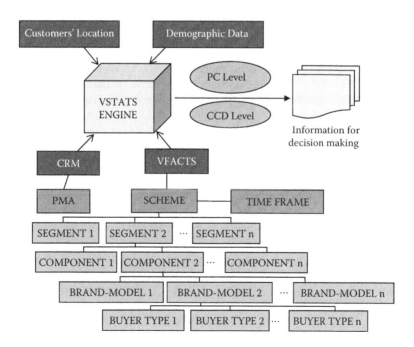

FIGURE 3.4 Information flows for automobile decision makers.

primary marketing area (PMA). The second type of data is VFACTS—automobile sales data in different regions and time periods published monthly by the Federal Chamber of Automotive Industries. The third type is various demographic information including census data on population and housing. The fourth type is customer location data, including other spatial background data, which are used to build spatial links among different types of data. With the support of these datasets, information can be delivered to decision makers for supporting their management and marketing activities.

Examples of major integrated analyses include overall analysis of the automobile industry; sales by brand, time, and postcode; advertising expenditure by test drive campaigns; top sellers by postcode; difference analysis (by brand/time); pump in/pump out analysis; customer locations in postcode/CCD; and demographic distributions in postcode/CCD.

Such analyses can be undertaken along different dimensions, such as by time (monthly, yearly); by geographical boundaries (PMAs, postcodes, CCDs); by demographics (e.g., sex, age, income, occupations, number of vehicles per household); and by point data (customer locations).

The OMAS for automobile sales comprises schemes, segmentations, and components. The VFACTS scheme is a user-defined analysis scheme (e.g., competitors for an automobile model, selling patterns of one or many models, user-defined segments and time frames). VFACTS-defined segments are user-defined segments (e.g., 4×4, ATM, LIG, LUX). VFACTS components include brand (e.g., AUD, BMW, CHR), model (e.g., 156 2.0L, M5, MAGNA), and buyer type (e.g., private, fleet).

The improved interpretation and value of business information through GIS and CRM not only supports improved decision making from the wealth of information already being retained, but it also facilitates the distribution of business information throughout a corporation and its business relationship network (e.g., customers, dealers, retailers, manufacturers).

OMAS can be used to provide comprehensive information about the entire automobile industry and competitors' business performance to help different companies better focus on a specific customer segment and hence gain an advantage in meeting that segment's needs.

As an example, Figure 3.5 shows a map generated by the system to display sales opportunities. On the map, monthly automobile segments analysis by postcode is displayed in different shades. The best segment by location in that month (December) should easily attract the decision maker's attention. Together with the map, the table on the left lists the sales by brand/segment for each postcode.

Sales trends are displayed over space, competitors, sales are updated in a timely way, and allowance is made for new model launches and promotion campaigns, all of which enable manufacturers/dealers to better plan their own promotions.

This is undertaken in different ways at different levels. At the head office level, the priorities are to identify opportunities for each of its planned and future automobile models; analyze each dealer's PMA by postcode/CCD to identify potential marketing opportunities; use demographic/customer buyer profile information to better target direct mail campaigns; conduct real-time analysis using current monthly VFACTS data comparing its sales and that of its competitors' performance; and identify "hot spot" geographical areas to target. The priorities at dealer PMA level are better

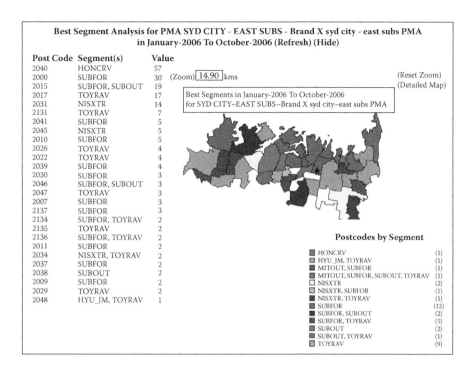

FIGURE 3.5 Best segment analysis: an example.

targeting of direct mail, together with a clearer follow-up analysis capability to show what has or has not worked; better understanding of who the customers are and how to find them; and improved sales performance. At the level of service garages, the focus is on competitor market analysis and the determination of automobile servicing requirements for brands and auto products using updated sales and car registration information for segments at the postcode level or for customized spatial units.

3.5.2 IMPROVING SALES PERFORMANCE

Use of the designed OMAS could help firms to generate revenue (through a better understanding of actual and potential market demand) or reduce costs (through efficiency gains). OMAS uses maps and graphics to help communicate dynamic demand forecasts and accurate prediction results, enabling a distributor/dealership to see at a glance its current and target market shares. These results can be used either by an existing auto dealer or manufacturer or by someone thinking of opening an auto dealership and trying to select the right geography and target market. All these courses of action would be expected to lead to improved sales performance.

Traditionally, automobile distributors determine orders based on the previous yearly or half-yearly sales statistics and market forecasts. This static procedure tends to generate a large stock of inventory; consumers normally receive the huge benefit of discounts via stock sales at the end of the financial year or end of the model year.

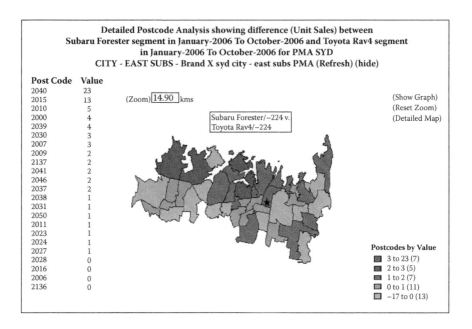

FIGURE 3.6 Sales performance analysis: an example.

The offering of cheaper price could reduce the profit margin up to 10% of a car sales price or even more. With a dynamic OMAS, the sales data and market demand analysis can be updated daily or weekly and more accurate amount ordering can be achieved, thereby reducing inventory and improving sales performance.

Figure 3.6 displays an example of sales performance analysis: monthly sales for Brand X in the 4WD segment is displayed by postcode. On the map, the postcode areas in the north region shows better sales performance. The results of sales performance analysis in different geographical regions also provide relevant information to service garages, who can maintain an improved supply mix for possible demands of different brands and amounts of sales in their business regions.

Examples of similar analyses and visualizations include current and potential customer distribution in each PMA; current marketing distribution in each PMA; historic changes of marketing distribution in each PMA; marketing distribution comparison with competitors; market volume forecasts in each postcode area; and key performance indicators in each region.

Automating the collection and analysis of such marketing information would result in timely marketing and sales decisions, and their quality would be greatly improved. This would lead to improved efficiency of the marketing and sales staff.

3.5.3 IMPLICATIONS FOR MANAGERS

The focus on OMASs shows how improvements to marketing analysis are achievable through the use of cutting-edge technologies developed across several disciplines.

This has the potential to deliver broad benefits in the automotive industry (e.g., improved information flows, efficient business planning, even cost reductions). Some of the most noticeable benefits for managers are as follows.

Timeliness. Automating the collection and analysis of marketing information results in timely marketing and sales decisions. Electronic data interface and online data collection and processing facilitate the automation of sales and customer support, all of which have the potential to improve the effectiveness of marketing and sales personnel in both business-to-consumer and business-to-business activities.

Advanced spatial analysis. The information flow delivered to business decision makers is improved through advanced analysis technologies. Some examples using spatial and analysis technologies are overall analysis of automobile industry statistics; sales by brand, time, and postcode; advertising expenditure by test drive campaigns; top sellers by postcode; difference analysis (by brand/time); pump in/pump out analysis for dealership PMAs; customer locations by postcode/CCD; demographic distributions by postcode/CCD; market potential within 20-minute zones around service stations; competitors' market penetration by model of automobile; market volume forecasts in each postcode area; and key performance indicators in each geographical area/region.

Visualization. The way information is presented to marketers and sales personnel has an influence on the quality of the decision made. Maps, when used appropriately, serve as a form of decision support and have a positive influence on the quality of decisions. OMASs use maps and graphics to help communicate results of analyses, enabling an automobile distributor/dealership to see at a glance its current and target market shares. These results can be used either by an existing auto manufacturer or dealership or by someone thinking of opening an auto dealership and trying to select the right geography and target market. The results of sales performance analyses in different geographical regions also provide relevant information to service garages, which can maintain an improved supply mix for possible demands of different brands/components in their trading areas.

Scenario building. Users welcome the ability to test different assumptions and different scenarios in an interactive setting, thereby paving the way to more informed marketing decision making.

Market responsiveness. WebGIS-based OMASs help decision makers undertake automobile market segmentation to create a new vision of how particular markets are structured and operate and uncover the needs and wants of the targeted segments therein. This has the potential to create better understanding of consumer needs in each segment of the market, resulting in the identification of new marketing opportunities; help develop new products and marketing communications campaigns to attract custom market areas or among particular target markets; enable marketing expenses to be budgeted more effectively, according to the needs and likely returns from each

segment; assist in precision marketing to adjust product and service offer-
ings and fine-tune marketing appeals used for each segment; and help local
dealerships to plan their product assortments and the mix of vehicle types
in light of customer needs.

Decision superiority. Data-driven OMASs enable better, faster, and more
effective decisions to be made, giving users a competitive edge (Hoffman,
2000). Using data can create advantages in many ways, including improving customer relationships, identifying cost-cutting ideas, uncovering new
business opportunities, improving reactions to changes in retail demand,
and optimizing selling prices.

Cost reductions. Online systems help firms to generate revenue (through a better understanding of actual and potential market demand) or reduce costs
(through efficiency gains). In particular, use of cutting-edge technologies
may reduce costs compared with previous methods for gaining equivalent
information (compared, say, to the cost of employing or contracting a spe-
cialist researcher). The Web facilitates the sharing of nonconfidential information and, through intranets, even sensitive information can be shared.

3.6   EXTENSIONS AND ISSUES FOR THE FUTURE

OMASs can improve the effectiveness of marketing decision making. The system
features described previously show this is technically feasible—the automobile case
illustrates this in practice. However, there remain some challenges, three of which
are discussed here.

3.6.1   EXTENSION TO OTHER INDUSTRIAL CONTEXTS

The context here has been the Australian automobile industry. Many automobile manufacturers, as well as their dealers and suppliers, are continuously trying to improve
their market position by reevaluating their product and service provision, while
investing in new dealer outlets and service centers. The improved interpretation and
value of business information through GIS and data mining not only supports better
decision making, it also facilitates the distribution of business information throughout a corporation and its business relationship network (e.g., customers/consumers,
dealers, retailers, manufactures, suppliers). This informs, educates, and empowers
at all levels of the industry. By extension, it is expected that principles and practices
learned from the automobile industry can be meaningfully carried across to other
industries (e.g., grocery retailing and wholesaling, retail banking, franchised service
networks). OMASs are an ideal business tool for organizations that need to undertake precise market analysis based on powerful geodemographic information. Such
systems enable marketing professionals in these varied industries to use reliable and
up-to-date information to identify new market opportunities. Valuable customer/
consumer and market analysis information can be put into the hands of decision
makers throughout the organization. Precursors of these technologies had just this
effect in retail management in previous decades (Wrigley, 1988).

3.6.2 Meeting the Needs of Small and Medium Enterprises

One challenge is to develop affordable systems that offer practical and meaningful applications for a wide range of decision makers in different-sized enterprises. Large organizations have been able to invest heavily in market analysis, and they will continue to do so with online systems. By contrast, small- and medium-sized enterprises traditionally have been at a disadvantage because of the high costs involved. However, OMASs offer the prospect of giving cost-effective solutions to small- and medium-sized organizations. Such systems are affordable and easy to implement by small businesses, which commonly operate on tight budgets, with few resources, little time, and only basic information technology skills. Also significant for small- and medium-sized enterprises is the way OMASs integrate seamlessly with other office systems. Specifically, system requirements are very basic for end users—they only need to have the general systems that are normally installed with every computer (e.g., Microsoft Windows 9x, Me, NT/2kx operating systems; Microsoft Internet Explorer 6.0 or higher; Internet connection). This solution, moreover, is compliant with privacy principles. Thus, access to customer records that are stored on a central server is limited to those with access authorized by the CRM manager, ensuring that dealerships/service providers maintain control over who has access to their records. Despite these attractions, the high costs of spatial data collection and GIS technical support are hard for small and medium enterprises to afford. This remains a challenge, although in other realms of marketing research the problem is resolved through syndication/subscription services (e.g., in the way the costs of establishing and maintaining scanner panels are shared among subscribers), and this solution might be equally appropriate here.

3.6.3 Assessing the Performance of OMASs

OMASs are a form of marketing DSS and, as such, they share similar attractions and challenges. DSS usage by marketers implies that information is captured, that various alternatives are taken into account and evaluated, and that this results in better decisions and better performance. Unfortunately, performance gains are not always easy to demonstrate. Studies into DSS performance have been criticized for their lack of an adequate theoretical basis (Benbasat & Nault, 1990; Waalewijn & de Arons, 1997). This sentiment is echoed by marketers: Wierenga and Van Bruggen (1997) acknowledge that implementation of information systems does not automatically lead to better decision making, and Kayande et al. (2006) conclude that a lot more work still has to be done to assess DSS performance. Effective marketing decision making is dependent on a combination of factors (e.g., the marketing decision maker and the characteristics of the individual, the DSS, the type of marketing problem, the environment, organizational characteristics). There is an absence of well-structured evaluation methods, and too little research has been carried out into the effect of action strategies, organizational characteristics, and environmental factors on the performance of DSSs. Case studies, in which performance outcomes are compared for alternative decisions, are beginning to provide some answers.

3.7 CONCLUSIONS

The OMASs described in this chapter are designed to facilitate information and knowledge exchange between marketing analysts and decision makers in the automobile industry (e.g., marketers, dealers, sales personnel, suppliers). The integration of CRM and WebGIS provides a dynamic database management and market analysis platform, which is expected to give rise to better understanding of the potential of particular market areas or target markets and to help identify the strengths and weaknesses of competitors in particular market areas or among particular target market segments. Such market analysis strategies are likely to provide competitive advantages for those organizations and individuals who are able to harness these systems.

Furthermore, decisions are likely to be more informed and timely, not only resulting in better decisions in themselves, but also avoiding the costs associated with poor decisions. OMASs achieve this by going some way to resolve the problem of data overload that besets decision makers today. On the one hand, the availability of comprehensive and timely data extends the knowledge base of decision makers, but, on the other hand, the overload and under-utilization of data confuse and frustrate decision-makers. OMASs cut across these difficulties by providing customized market analysis systems, enabling "if-then" scenario spatial analysis and vivid computer mapping.

"Organizations that fail to invest in proper analytic technologies," writes Davenport (2005), "will be unable to compete in a fact-based business environment." Online market analysis systems lie at the heart of these new analytic technologies and are central to contemporary marketing and management.

ACKNOWLEDGMENTS

We are indebted to Alan Mann, M.D., Mapdata Interface Pty Ltd., for his help, advice, and collaboration (http://vstats.test-drive.com.au). The project was funded with a grant from the Australian Research Council (ARC Grant LP0348935).

REFERENCES

Adelman, L. and Donnell, M.L. Evaluating decision support systems: a general framework, in *Microcomputer Decision Support Systems: Design, Implementation and Evaluation*, Andriole, S.J., Ed., QED Information Sciences, Wellesley, MA, 1986, pp. 285–309.

Arentze, T. and Timmermans, H. Multi-agent models of spatial cognition, learning and complex choice behavior in urban environments, in *Complex Artificial Environments: Simulation, Cognition and VR in the Study and Planning of Cities*, Portugali, J., Ed., Springer, Heidelberg, 2006.

Benbasat, I. and Nault, B.R. An evaluation of empirical research in managerial support systems, *Decision Supp. Syst.* 6, 203–226, 1990.

Berry, M.J.A. and Linoff, G.S. *Data Mining Techniques: For Marketing, Sales, and Customer Relationship Management,* 2nd ed., Wiley, New York, 2004.

Burke, R.R. Virtual shopping: breakthrough in marketing research. *Harvard Bus. Rev.* 74, 1230–1129, 1996.

Burke, R.R. The third wave of marketing intelligence, in *Retailing in the 21st Century*, Krafft, M., and Mantrala, M.K., Eds., Springer, Heidelberg, 2005.

Davenport, T. Analytic technologies can provide organizations a competitive edge, 2005. Available online at: http://www.DMReview.com. Accessed April 29, 2005.

Department of Industry Science and Resources. *Positioning for Growth—Spatial Information Industry Action Agenda*. Department of Industry Science and Resources, Canberra, Australia, 2001.

Duke, P. Geospatial data mining for market intelligence. *PC AI.*, 15(2) March/April, 48–49, 2001.

Feeny, D. Making business sense of the E-opportunity. *MIT Sloan Manage. Rev.* 42, 41–51, 2001.

Fensel, D. and Bussler, C. The Web service modeling framework WSMF. *Electron. Comm. Res. Appl.* 1, 113–137, 2002.

Florkowski, W.J. and Sarmiento, C. The examination of pecan price differences using spatial correlation estimation. *Appl. Econ.* 37, 271–278, 2005.

Han, J. and Kamber, M. *Data Mining: Concepts and Techniques*, 2nd ed., Morgan Kaufmann, San Francisco, 2006.

Hanaoka, K. and Clarke, G.P. Spatial microsimulation modelling for retail market analysis at the small-area level. *Comp. Environ. Urban Sys.* 31, 162–187, 2007.

Harris, R., Sleight, P., and Webber, R. *Geodemographics, GIS and Neighbourhood Targeting*, John Wiley & Sons, Inc., Chichester, UK, 2005.

Hernandez, T. Visual decisions: geovisualisation techniques within retail decision support, *J. Target. Measure. Anal. Marketing* 13, 209–219, 2005.

Hess, R.L., Rubin, R.S, and West, L.A. 2004. Geographic information systems as a marketing information system technology, *Decis. Supp. Sys.* 38, 197–212, 2004.

Hoffman, N.P. 2000. An examination of the 'Sustainable Competitive Advantage' concept: past, present, and future, *Acad. Marketing Sci. Rev.* 4, 1–16, 2000.

Jank, W. and Kannan, P.K. Understanding geographical markets of online firms using spatial models of customer choice, *Marketing Sci.* 24, 623–634, 2005.

Jank, W. and and Kannan, P.K. Dynamic e-targeting using learning spatial choice models, *J. Interactive Marketing* 20, 30–42, 2006.

Kalakota, R. and Whinston, A.B. *Electronic Commerce: A Manager's Guide*, Addison Wesley, Reading, MA, 1997.

Kayande, U., de Bruyn, A., Lilien, G., Rangaswamy, A., and Van Bruggen, G. *How Feedback Can Improve Managerial Evaluations of Model-based Marketing Decision Support Systems*, Erasmus Research Institute of Management, RSM Erasmus University, Rotterdam, 2006.

Kingston, R.S.C., Evans, A., and Tutton, I. Web-based public participation geographical information systems: an aid to local environmental decision-making, *Comp. Environment Urban Sys.* 24, 109–125, 2000.

Laudon, J.P. and Laudon, K.C. *Essentials of Business Information Systems, 7th ed.,* Prentice Hall, Upper Saddle River, NJ, 2007.

Longley, P.A., Goodchild, M.F., Maguire, D.J., and Rhind, D.W. *Geographical Information Systems and Science*, 2nd ed., Wiley, Chichester, UK, 2005.

Payne, A. and Frow, P. A strategic framework for customer relationship management, *J. Marketing* 69, 167–176, 2005.

Prasad, V.K., Ramamurthy, K., and Naidu, G.M. The influence of internet-marketing integration on marketing competencies and export performance, *J. Int. Marketing* 9, 82–110, 2001.

Pyle, D. *Data Preparation for Data Mining*. Morgan Kaufman, San Francisco, 1999.

Quelch, J.A. and Klein, L.R. The Internet and international marketing. *Sloan Manage. Rev.* 37, 60–75, 1996.

Ravi, V., Raman, K., and Mantrala, MK. Applications of intelligent technologies in retail marketing, In *Retailing in the 21st Century*, Krafft, M. and Mantrala, M.K., Eds., Springer, Heidelberg, 2005.

Rust, R.T., Ambler, T., Carpenter, G.S., Kumar, V., and Srivastava, R.K. Measuring marketing productivity: current knowledge and future directions, *J. Marketing* 68, 76–89, 2004.

Sleight, P. Optimising retail networks: a case study of locating Camelot's lottery terminal, *J. Targeting Measure. Anal. Marketing* 10, 353–365, 2002.

Smelcer, J. B. and Carmel, E. The effectiveness of different representations for managerial problem solving: comparing tables and maps, *Decision Sci.* 28, 391–420, 1997.

Turban, E. and Aronson, J.E. *Decision Support Systems and Intelligent Systems*, Prentice Hall, Upper Saddle River, NJ, 2001.

Turban, E., King, D., Lee, J., and Vieland, D. *Electronic Commerce 2006: A Managerial Perspective*, Prentice Hall, Upper Saddle River, NJ, 2005.

Urban, G.L. *Don't Just Relate—Advocate! A Blueprint for Profit in the Era of Customer Power*, Wharton School Publications, Upper Saddle River, NJ, 2005a.

Urban, G.L. Customer advocacy: a new era in marketing? *J. Public Pol. Marketing* 24, 155–159, 2005b.

Waalewijn, P. and de Arons, S.H. Are decision support systems helping marketers? (A framework for analysis and a literature review). Technical report. Erasmus University, Rotterdam, 1997.

Weill, P. and Vitale, M. What IT infrastructure capabilities are needed to implement e-business models, *MIS Q. Exec.* 1, 17–34, 2000.

Wierenga, B. and van Bruggen, G.H. The integration of marketing problem-solving modes and marketing management support systems, *J. Marketing* 61, 21–37, 1997.

Wierenga, B., Van Bruggen, G.H., and Staelin R. The success of marketing management support systems, *Marketing Sci.* 18, 196–207, 1999.

Wrigley, N, Ed. *Store Choice, Store Location and Market Analysis*, Routledge, London, 1988.

Zhao, L., Lu, H., and Yu, Y. Designing and implementing an online WebGIS-based decision support system, in *Proceedings of ICEB2005*, Fifth International Conference on Electronic Business, Hong Kong, 2005.

4 Finding Hierarchical Patterns in Large POS Data Using Historical Trees

Takanobu Nakahara and Hiroyuki Morita

CONTENTS

4.1 INTRODUCTION

Advancements in information technologies have resulted in the inexpensive and easy accumulation of a large amount of data in various fields. In retail stores, managers have employed customer relationship management tools to forge better relationships with their customers, who have the potential to bring in considerable future revenue. One of these tools is the frequent shopper program. Here, customers earn points in direct proportion to the total amount paid by them. These points promote future purchases and are designed to help build good relationships with customers. Additionally, by using frequent shopper programs, retail stores can accumulate a large amount of historical purchasing data on the basis of identification information because customers use their member cards to earn their points. This enables the retail stores to understand their customers better and provide more efficient services by using data mining.

Recently, graph-mining methods have been proposed by some researchers, applicable mainly to the fields of organic chemistry and Web analysis. In addition to the features of traditional methods, these methods incorporate the relationship between variables as explanatory variables. During the last decade, these methods have yielded successful field applications. These methods are powerful, and it is possible to apply them to other fields, such as various businesses. However, business data have very wide diversities and the amount of data is huge. Therefore it is difficult to apply existing algorithms from the viewpoint of computational costs.

In this chapter, we propose a pattern-mining method using historical purchasing data. Our method comprises two steps. The first step is to transform the time series transaction data into a tree-structured data, which is a type of graph-structured data. We refer to it as a "historical tree" (HT). The second step is to find effective patterns from the HT by using a multiobjective evolutionary algorithm (MOEA). Finally, a decision tree model is constructed using the patterns and other given attributes. By using our method, computational experiments were performed on two types of practical data. One involves historical purchasing data by credit cards; the other is the point-of-sale (POS) data in a supermarket. In the former case, we show that some meaningful patterns can be extracted to increase the number of customers who use revolving credit. For the latter case, to determine the purchasing features of loyal customers, some interesting patterns can be extracted. In the experiments, we have shown that our method outperforms traditional methods and provides some practical interpretations for both of the above-mentioned cases.

4.2   RELATED WORK

Graph mining is a promising new approach in research on data mining. It was developed focusing mainly on sophisticated fields of organic chemistry and Web analysis; further, some efficient algorithms were proposed in the last decade.[1,3–6] The study of algorithms in this field is categorized into two groups: research to find effective subgraphs from a collection of general graphs and research to count patterns appearing frequently in a tree graph. The typical algorithms in the former group are Apriori-Based Graph Mining (AGM),[3] Frequent Subgraph Mining (FSG),[4] and gSpan,[5] and those in the latter group are Frequent Tree Miner (FREQT)[1] and TreeMiner.[6] AGM and FSG represent graphs using adjacency matrices and extract frequent subgraphs by using an apriori-based approach. These differences are types of extractive subgraphs. AGM can extract every type of subgraph. However, FSG cannot extract induced subgraph from isolated graph in order to reduce calculation costs. FREQT and TreeMiner use depth-first search (DFS) trees—not an a priori–based approach—to extract frequent subtrees. These algorithms are very similar to each other, except in the manner in which they update their patterns. Further, gSpan extracts frequent subgraphs from graph-structured data using DFS trees.

The performance of these methods with regard to existing applications is efficient. The substructures extracted using graph mining, which incorporate the relationships between several variables, yield useful knowledge about the business field. However, it is not a trivial task to apply graph mining techniques to business data. There are several reasons for this. First, business data are large, and these data are stored according to their identification; these data include many items and many customer identifications. The second reason is data structure. The existing applications of graph mining originally have some graph structures such as those involving chemical compounds and XML as the raw data. However, we have to construct similar graph structures using raw data for business applications because these data are not structured. Although this is possible, such graphs have extremely complicated relationships. The last reason is to identify a set of target customers. In business applications, target customers change according to the objective of the analysis. When we apply graph mining to business data, we have to identify the target customers and clarify a gap between the target customers and other customers. Therefore, although existing graph mining methods consider only one objective variable to extract the frequent substructure, we need to extract patterns from the bi-objective viewpoint.

There exist studies that have employed the graph mining method in business data.[7,8] In Kuroda et al.,[8] a market basket analysis between alcoholic beverages and some foods was performed, and some practical suggestions have been proposed. Further, in Yada et al.,[7] the gap between general customers and customers who pay attention to their health in terms of some items, such as eggs, milk, and salad oils, was analyzed. Further, this clarifies that health-concerned customers prefer purchasing higher-priced products for their health.

As compared with previous studies, the following points are different. Yada et al.[7] and Kuroda[8] reveal good results from the viewpoint of item analysis. Our study is similar to these results; however, the viewpoint focusing on historical purchasing patterns using multilevel layered structures based on time relationships differs. Further, they defined a single objective problem and used AGM to extract the patterns, whereas our study defined biobjective optimization problems and the MOEA approach[9] was used for pattern extraction.

In this study, we have investigated a method to express historical purchasing data with multicategories as tree-structured data (HT). By expressing data using a multilevel-layered structure, our method can maintain the time relationship between the data. Using HT, we obtain some promising subgraphs among HTs to clarify the features of target customers. After identifying the target customers and other customers, we define two biobjective combinatorial optimization problems to find subgraphs of HT, which have large differences with regard to their support value. To optimize these problems, we use the MOEA approach and extract some promising purchasing patterns. By using these patterns and other attributes, a decision tree model is constructed and some practical knowledge is illustrated.

4.3   OVERVIEW OF OUR METHOD

It is possible to express various types of graph structures for business applications. Among these, we focus on the total sales of all or specific categories (or items) for each customer, along with incorporating the dimension of time. To implement this idea, we express the values as tree-structured graphs. It is important and meaningful to consider a total paid-with-time relationship. Assume there are two types of customers: in a particular week, customer A pays only on Monday and customer B pays only on Saturday in the same week, and their payments are the same. Then, we formulate a pattern according to which customer A is supposed to be meaningful and a pattern according to which customer B is supposed to be trivial. It is not easy to extract such patterns from the historical purchasing data, because the independent aggregation of the total paid with time interval cannot express such patterns. In our study, we propose a method for extracting such patterns with time relationship and we show our method is effective for some practical data in a later chapter.

The flowchart of our proposed method is shown in Figure 4.1.

First, raw data are cleaned and some basic analyses are performed to determine the target customers, similar to that in other traditional methods. Subsequently, the amount paid by each customer is totaled at each time level given in the previous transaction and each total is mapped to some type of code representing the extent of purchasing for each time level. By expressing each code as a multilevel layered tree structure, the HT for each customer is completed. To apply our MOEA, each HT is converted into gene tracing by the order of the DFS from the root node. The MOEA can determine some approximate Pareto solutions for each biobjective optimization problem, and the solutions are decoded into HT subgraphs as purchasing patterns. By using these patterns and other given attributes, we formulate a decision tree model to discriminate target customers, and its model and rules are interpreted.

4.3.1   Historical Purchasing Data and HT

Although there are many time levels, such as 1 day, 1 week, and 1 year, to aggregate the purchasing data of a customer, it is not easy to determine the most effective time

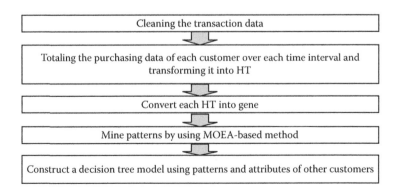

FIGURE 4.1 Flowchart of the proposed method.

level for performing an analysis. Although it is possible to use all the total amounts paid for all the time levels, it is inefficient from the viewpoint of computational cost. However, the interrelationships among these time levels probably add more valuable knowledge. Although such interrelationships between variables are not incorporated in traditional data mining methods, our method can simultaneously handle all the necessary time levels and extract such patterns.

The procedure for converting raw POS data into HT is as follows. First, the required time levels are provided. We can provide arbitrary time levels depending on the time interval of the given data. Then, the aggregation extent is determined. In one case, we consider the total purchasing amount, and in the other case, we independently consider the purchasing amounts of some specific categories or items. Next, for all the given time levels, each purchasing amount is aggregated for each customer. Each value is mapped into two codes—a personal code and the entire code; each code has four types of values (none, low, middle, and high). These codes indicate the following details for each time level.

Personal code: the degree of purchasing amount as compared to the distribution of the customer.

Entire code: the degree of purchasing amount as compared to the distribution of all the customers.

These codes are required when a considerable gap exists between the distribution of the personal purchasing amount and the distribution of the entire purchasing amount. When this gap is small, only the entire code is used. Finally, HT is completed by constructing each code and maintaining the time relationship.

More precisely, given the time levels, the number of items that belongs to t is calculated regularly, namely, t_j, $j = 1,\ldots, r(t)$. Further, the number of categories to aggregate is given, namely, $m = 1,\ldots, M$. If only the total purchasing amount is used, $M = 1$. Then, $C_m^{t_j}$ denotes the jth total purchasing amount of category (or item) m at time level t. $P^t(C_m^{t_j})$ and $E^t(C_m^{t_j})$ represent the functions that map $C_m^{t_j}$ to the personal code and to the entire code at time level t, respectively. Here, we suggest $P^t(C_m^{t_j})$ for each standardized $C_m^{t_j}$ as follows:

$$
P^t\left(C_m^{t_j}\right) = \begin{cases} \text{if } C_m^{t_j} \text{ is } (-\infty, v - s) \text{ then } 1, \\ \text{else if } [v - s, v + s] \text{ then } 2, \\ \text{else if } (v + s, \infty) \quad \text{ then } 3, \\ \text{and} \quad \text{otherwise} \quad 0 \end{cases}
$$

(4.1)

Further, for $E^t(C_m^{t_j})$, after sorting $C_m^{t_j}$ of all the customers in an increasing order at each value of t, they are divided into three equal parts. Then, each group is mapped by 1, 2, and 3 from small ones. When $C_m^{t_j} = 0$, the code is 0.

Figure 4.2 shows an example of HT with five time levels, $T = 5$. In the figure, each node has M categories and each category has both personal and entire codes, as shown in Figure 4.3. In this case, the year is 1, season is 2, and so on. The number of

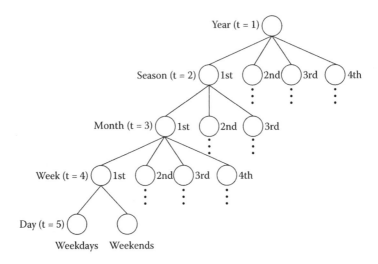

FIGURE 4.2 An image of HT.

nodes for each value of t (season, month, and week) is 4, 12, and 52, respectively. In this case, each week has two nodes—weekdays and weekends. Consequently, there are 104 nodes at the day level. As a result, this HT has a total of 173 nodes. The following section explains the extraction of patterns from the HT while maintaining their time relationships.

4.3.2 PATTERN MINING USING MOEA FROM HT

To apply the MOEA to the HT, we initially transform it into a gene-tracing node from a root node by the order of the DFS. Figure 4.4 shows an example of this transformation.

In this case, $T = 4$ and $M = 1$ are provided, and the numbers in the upper and lower squares denote the personal and entire codes, respectively. Further, the number located at the bottom right or below the lower square denotes the DFS order from the root node. According to this order, both the codes are transformed into a gene, as shown in Figure 4.4. Moreover, the time code that denotes the time level is added to both these codes. After extracting a pattern with length 1 from the genes, we can

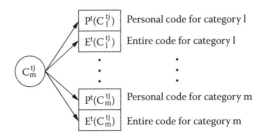

FIGURE 4.3 Purchasing amount and both the codes.

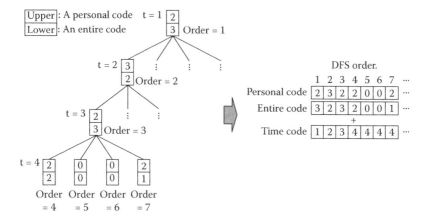

FIGURE 4.4 HT and gene.

decode it into a subgraph in HT by maintaining this time code, as shown later in the experimental results.

In this pattern mining procedure, we use two types of customer sets—target customers (TC) and other customers (OC). Suppose that P_1 comprises a set of patterns with length 1. Here, we define each support as follows:

$$SUP(TC, p) = \frac{|TC_p|}{|TC|} \quad \text{and}$$

$$SUP(OC, p) = \frac{|OC_p|}{|OC|},$$

(4.2)

where $|\cdot|$ denotes the number of items in the set and TC_p and OC_p represent the sets that include $p \in P_1$ for each TC and OC set, respectively. Here, p is a good pattern when there is a considerable gap between $SUP(TC, p)$ and $SUP(OC, p)$, whereas it is meaningless if $SUP(TC, p)$ is similar to $SUP(OC, p)$. Then, the desired patterns are extracted to achieve the following two biobjective combinatorial optimization problems:

$$(P1) \begin{cases} \text{maximize } SUP(TC, p) \\ \text{minimize } SUP(OC, p) \end{cases}$$

(4.3)

$$(P2) \begin{cases} \text{maximize } SUP(OC, p) \\ \text{minimize } SUP(TC, p) \end{cases}$$

(4.4)

Therefore, given a pattern of length 1, two biobjective pattern mining problems can be solved by using the MOEA. To be applicable to pattern mining, our MOEA approach is a modified version of that proposed previously;[2] however, the basic idea remains the same.

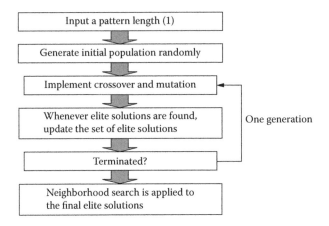

FIGURE 4.5 Flowchart of our MOEA.

Figure 4.5 shows the flowchart of our MOEA. Given a pattern length from l = 1,..., L (L: the maximum length of the genes), the number of extracted patterns decreases with an increase in L. The maximum pattern length is obtained from preliminary experiments in each case. First, the pattern length l is input and an initial population is randomly generated. The crossover and mutation operations are performed at every generation. Whenever an elite solution is found during these processes, the set of elite solutions is updated. Here, elite solutions denote the approximate Pareto solutions. If the elite solutions are dominated by a new solution, the new solution becomes the new elite solution, and the older elite solutions that are dominated by the new one are removed from the set of elite solutions. After all the operations are performed in one generation, it is verified whether the evolutionary algorithm process should be terminated or not. Here, we stop the process if no elite solution is found during the predetermined consecutive generations (i.e., stp). Otherwise, the process is continued in order to find new elite solutions. After the evolutionary algorithm process is terminated, a neighborhood search is performed on the final elite solutions. With the exception of the crossover operation, existing methods can be applied during these processes. In the crossover operation, it is difficult to apply conventional methods to multiple genes. Here, we split multiple genes into a number of single genes—personal code and entire code for each category—and the time code. For each personal code and entire code, the existing crossover method (e.g., one-point crossover, uniform crossover method) is independently performed. For the time code, the two types of genes extracted from the parent are duplicated to maintain feasibility. Each code has two types of candidate single genes; thus, 2^{2M+1} new offsprings are generated by combining them.

Figure 4.6 shows a simple case in which M = 1. In these patterns, the use of wildcards that are equal to any of the codes within the personal and entire codes is permitted.

Figure 4.7 shows an example of using wildcards. Patterns A and B are not strictly identical. If we can use four wildcards like that in pattern C, we can consider patterns

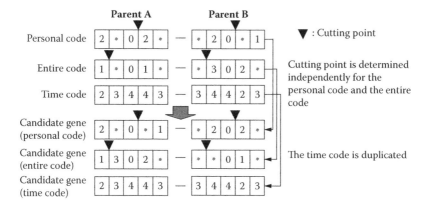

FIGURE 4.6 Crossover method used in our experiments.

A and B to be the same. In business applications, a partial difference between the codes is interpretable and useful. However, too many wildcards generate meaningless patterns. In our experiments, the number of wildcards is restricted for each experiment, and they need to be efficiently used.

Throughout these processes, the number of meaningful candidate patterns is extracted. Among these patterns, some of them are similar and some of them are not, and the classification of these patterns is not so easy. Here, we use the existing decision tree method to select more meaningful patterns and to systematically elaborate on the explanatory variables from the viewpoint of practical usage.

In the following two sections, we employ our method in two different practical data sets, and we reveal good performance and practical interpretation from the computational experiments.

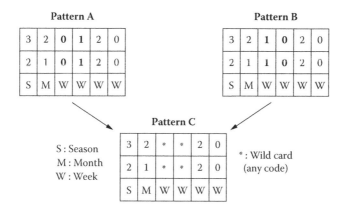

FIGURE 4.7 Example using wild cards.

4.4 APPLICATION TO CREDIT CARD DATA

4.4.1 HISTORICAL PURCHASING DATA BY CREDIT CARDS

In this section, by using historical purchasing data by credit cards over a 2-year period, we show some computational results obtained using our method and discuss the results. The data source is a Japanese credit card company. (The data were obtained from 2005 Data Analysis Competition, which was sponsored by the Joint Association Study Group of Management Science). In these data, customer attributes such as gender, date of birth, and occupation are provided. Although the payment amount and the means of payment are provided, the items purchased by the customers are unclear. In general, the customer attributes and the amount paid for some items are used as explanatory variables to construct the models.

4.4.2 BASIC ANALYSIS AND OBJECTIVE OF THIS ANALYSIS

A credit card payment can be done in two ways: lump-sum payments and revolving credits. Further, credit cards can be used for obtaining cash and for store purchases. From our preliminary basic analysis, we confirmed that the main part of credit card use is buying something in a shop, and the data revealed that the most common payment style was lump-sum payment. There is nothing special about the lump-sum style of payment, but it is popular in Japan. As a result, Japanese credit corporations are encouraging customers to use revolving credit in order to increase the corporations' profits in the future; this is the purpose of this experiment.

To achieve this, we define two sets of customers—TC and OC. Although both make only lump-sum payments during the first year, in the second year, the mode of payment for the OC group does not change, but the TC group adopts the revolving credit method. In other words, the TC and OC groups indulge in a similar mode of payment during the first year; however, both exhibit a gap in the payment style during the second year. The differences observed between the sets of customers in the data for the first year are interesting for business applications. Our objective is to find effective patterns that identify TC from these two groups using only the transaction data obtained during the first year.

In this experiment, we consider five types of time levels: year, season, month, week, and day. Among them, all the time levels use a normal time interval, except the day level. For the day level, we use two time intervals—weekdays and weekends—to avoid redundancy in the mining patterns. The daily purchase for a majority of customers was zero; the reason for this is that credit cards are not commonly used on a daily basis in Japan. We employ only one category in aggregation, because the names of the categories and items are unclear. According to the time levels, the total amount paid by each customer is recorded.

4.4.3 ANALYSIS TO IDENTIFY PROMISING CUSTOMERS USING REVOLVING CREDIT

Each parameter that is used to construct the HT and to perform MOEA is listed in Table 4.1. Here, a node of the HT is expressed by a pair of personal and entire codes using each customer's total purchasing amount. Further, in the MOEA, the pattern

TABLE 4.1
Parameters Used by Historical Tree and Multiobjective Evolutionary Algorithms

Numbers of Categories	$M = 1$
Time levels	$T = 5$ (year, season, month, week, and day [weekdays and weekends])
Length of patterns	$l = 2, \ldots, 12$
Upper limit of wild cards	1
Size of initial population	200
Number of crossovers	100/generation
Number of mutations	150/generation
Stopping rule	$stp = 100$ generations

length ranges from 2 to 12, and the upper limit of wild cards is restricted to 1. All the computational experiments in this chapter are performed on a Pentium M 1.5 MHz with 512 MB RAM; the MOEA programs are coded in C.

Figure 4.8 shows an example of the final elite solutions obtained by our MOEA when $l = 7$. The upper left side shows the elite solutions for P2 and the lower right side shows the elite solutions for P1. A solution in this figure represents a promising pattern to discriminate TC.

To validate the performance of our MOEA, we compare our solutions with the Pareto solutions. We can find all the Pareto solutions up to $l = 4$ by enumerating.

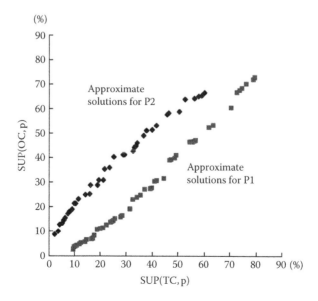

FIGURE 4.8 Example of elite solutions by MOEA.

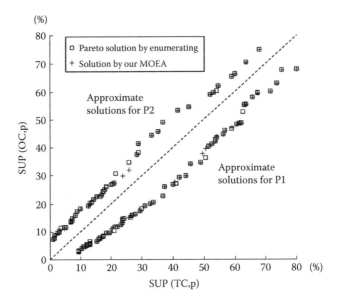

FIGURE 4.9 Comparing our solutions with Pareto solutions.

Figure 4.9 shows the plots of the Pareto solutions and our approximate solutions. For P1 and P2, 49 and 70 Pareto solutions exist, and the detection ratios of our approximations are 73.47% and 81.43%, respectively. Although some approximate solutions found are not exact, we observe that alternative solutions are found near them. On the whole, our solutions yield a good approximation.

The average computational time for each value of l is shown in Figure 4.10. In the experiments, data from 12,160 customers were input. From the figure, it can be seen that the computational time greatly depends on l. Although a large computational

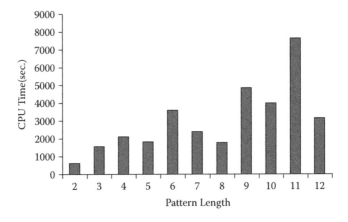

FIGURE 4.10 Average CPU time to find approximate solutions.

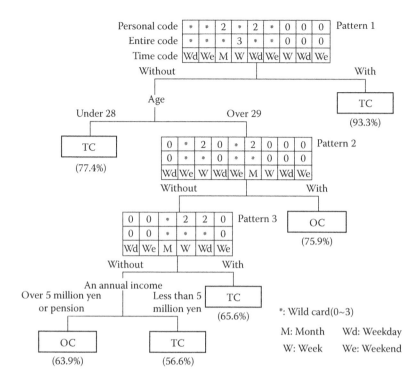

FIGURE 4.11 Decision tree using our patterns.

cost is needed for l = 11, it is completely acceptable because we can implement them as offline in practical usage.

From the computational experiments, 492 promising patterns are observed to identify TC. To construct a decision tree model, we input the identification of TC or OC as the objective variable, and the patterns extracted and the given attributes of the customer are used as explanatory variables. After sampling, if the |TC| and |OC| are identical, a decision tree (shown in Figure 4.11) is constructed.

In this figure, TC and OC denote leaves that are identified as the expected group. A numerical value in the parentheses under a leaf denotes the discrimination accuracy. The total accuracy of this model is 66% starting from 50%. As compared to commonly used decision tree models that do not use patterns as explanatory variables, we can improve the discrimination accuracy by approximately 10%.

In this figure, three patterns are used as strong explanatory variables. In the patterns, "*" denotes a wildcard present in the personal and entire codes. Further, the characters in the time code denote each time level, as shown in the figure. Pattern 1 has a characteristic pattern showing that the monthly purchasing amount was normal, but the purchasing occurred during the first week of the month and not during the second week. The customers with this pattern are identified as TC. Pattern 2 shows that the monthly purchasing is similar to pattern 1; however, there is normal purchasing during the last week of the previous month and not during the first week of the month. The customers with this pattern are identified as OC. Pattern 3 is similar to pattern 1, and customers exhibiting this pattern are identified as TC. As a result, these patterns show that purchasing during the first week of a month introduces customers to using revolving credit, and purchasing during the last week of a month introduces them to using only lump-sum payments. This is because of a gap between the account day and the payment day of the credit cards. The account day is the last day of month and the date of payment is the day in the following month. Based on this, if the customers approve of pattern 1 or pattern 3, they can delay their payments. When such customers strongly desire to buy an item, they are expected to shift from being only under the lump-sum payment system to the revolving credit system.

4.5   APPLICATION TO POS DATA

In this section, as another type of application data, we use the POS data collected during 2 years (these data are obtained from Customer Communications, Ltd.). The volume of the data includes approximately 2,500,000 records and approximately 12,000 identifications provided from a certain supermarket in Japan. The item category comprises 2 types of large categories, 12 types of middle categories, and 95 types of small categories. We cannot specify the item name; hence, only the item code is provided. The gender and age are provided as the only customer attributes.

Table 4.2 lists the ratio of each sale to the total sales and a ratio of the number of purchasers to the total number of customers in the middle category. We can see that processed food composes a major part of the sales in this supermarket. Sales of only three categories, namely, processed foods, beverages, and confectioneries, occupy a major portion of the total sales. Similarly, most of the customers purchase items belonging to these three categories; however, for the other categories, the ratio of the purchasers decreases quickly.

TABLE 4.2
Ratio of Purchases for Middle Category

Middle Category	Ratio of Sales	Ratio of Purchasers
Processed foods	62.4%	97.3%
Beverages	17.1%	92.0%
Confections	13.2%	90.1%
Everyday goods	2.6%	54.5%
Household utensils	1.5%	53.2%
Other foods	1.3%	16.5%
Cosmetics	0.6%	23.2%
Perishable foods	0.6%	43.6%
Pet goods	0.4%	7.8%
Medical goods	0.1%	2.0%
Do-it-yourself goods	0.1%	7.5%
Other everyday goods	0.1%	2.9%

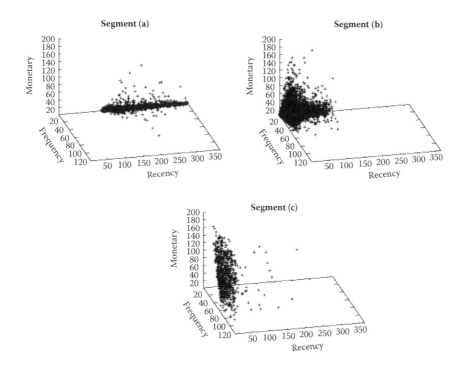

FIGURE 4.12 Segmentation by using K-means method.

To specify a set of target customers, the available data are divided into two parts—first year (data between April 2002 and March 2003) and second year (data between April 2003 and March 2004). Using these data, the standardized Recency, Frequency, Monetary (RFM) value (as recency, the number of days is counted from the final day of each year) of each part is separately calculated for each customer. Figure 4.12 shows three segments of customers classified with these RFM values by using the K-means method. Further, Table 4.3 lists the characteristics of these segments using the data obtained during the first year.

Segment A exhibits poor R, F, and M values. In segment B, although the R value is not bad, the F and M values are not so good. Segment C has all good values, and

TABLE 4.3
Segment Characteristics

	Segment A	Segment B	Segment C
Total purchasing amount	13,305,901	153,241,071	246,828,349
Number of customers	2040	6257	1506
Amount of average purchases	6522.5	24491.1	16,3896.6
Number of average visits	4.5	16.3	105.3
Recency	229.5	31.5	4.6

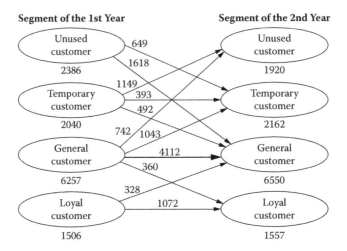

FIGURE 4.13 Movement between the segments from the first year to the second year.

it represents the desirable customers. Therefore, we term segments A, B, and C to be temporary customers, general customers, and loyal customers, respectively.

Figure 4.13 shows the variation in the customers among the segments from the first year to the second year as a bipartite graph. The values under the nodes denote the number of customers who belong to it. The unused customer attribute denotes the customers who do not purchase items within that period. More than 3% of all the customers are denoted by arcs.

The movement from the general customer segment in the first year to the general customer segment in the second year is the largest of all the arcs, having approximately 4000 customers. Further, 360 customers move from the general customer segment to the loyal customer segment. However, except for self-movement, considerable movement from the other segment to the loyal customer segment is not confirmed. On the contrary, we can see that 328 customers move from the loyal customer segment to the general customer segment and that the number of loyal customers does not change. Namely, we can see that the change from unused customers and temporary customers to loyal ones is rare; therefore, many loyal customers do not become poor customers. To increase the number of loyal customers, it is important to decrease the movement from the loyal customer segment to the general customers and to guide the general customers to the loyal customer segment.

Based on these observations, by using the proposed method, we analyze the characteristics of the customers who move from the general customer segment to the loyal customer segment and those who drop from the loyal customer segment.

4.5.1 ANALYSIS OF CUSTOMERS FOR BECOMING LOYAL CUSTOMERS

Here, we focus on the customers who move from the general customer segment to the loyal customer segment and who remain in that segment for 2 years. The former is the target customer, |TC| = 360 customers, and the latter is the other customer,

TABLE 4.4

Parameters Used by Historical Tree and Multiobjective Evolutionary Algorithms

Numbers of Categories	$M = 1$
Time levels	$T = 5$ (year, season, month, week, and day [weekdays and weekends])
Length of patterns	$l = 2,..., 9$
Upper limit of wild cards	L
Size of initial population	300
Number of crossovers	150/generation
Number of mutations	200/generation
Stopping rule	stp = 100 generations

$|OC| = 4112$ customers. Note that in the following analysis, we only use the data for the first year, in which both types of customers belong to the same segment.

Each parameter used to construct the HT and to perform the MOEA for the experiment is listed in Table 4.4. Here, HT is expressed as a pair of personal and entire codes using each customer's total purchasing amount. The minimum time level is weekdays and weekends. Further, in the MOEA, the pattern length ranges from 2 to 9, and the upper limit of wildcards is restricted to l.

Figure 4.14 shows an example of the final elite solutions obtained by using our MOEA approach when $l = 3$, as shown in the previous section. In total, 236 patterns

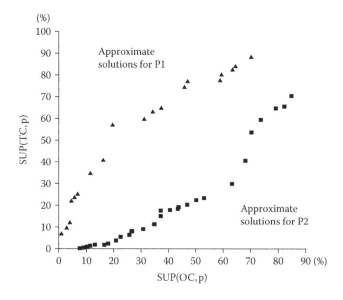

FIGURE 4.14 Approximation using MOEA.

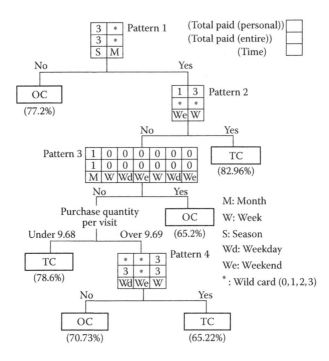

FIGURE 4.15 Decision tree model for promising customers using extracted patterns.

were extracted and used as the candidate explanatory variables to construct a decision tree model similar to the previous one. The other explanatory variables calculated from the preliminary analysis include the number of visits, total amount paid, quantity purchased per visit, and so on.

Figure 4.15 shows the model obtained by decision tree analysis: this figure is identical to the results obtained in the previous section. The accuracy of the model is 72% in 10-fold cross-validation; however, if these patterns are not used, the accuracy is 69%. A slight improvement is confirmed.

Table 4.5 shows the interpretation of each pattern. The most promising customers to be TC are those who exhibit both patterns 1 and 2. Here, patterns 1 and 2 are

---

TABLE 4.5
Patterns Used in Decision Tree Model in Figure 4.15

	Interpretation
Pattern 1	Large amount paid on both personal and entire codes during a season
Pattern 2	Large amount paid during a week and small amount paid during the previous weekends
Pattern 3	Small amount paid during the latter half of a month
Pattern 4	Large amount paid during a week and previous weekdays

---

independent from the viewpoint of time level. Hence the TC group indulges in large purchasing amounts at least during one season and at least for 1 week. As a practical interpretation, both these patterns probably indicate that continuous purchasing is needed during one season to be considered as TC. Moreover, customers who exhibit pattern 1 and do not exhibit patterns 2 and 3 and whose purchasing quantity per visit is fewer than 9.68 items are promising, too. Based on the assumption that they do not exhibit pattern 3 and the number of items purchased during one visit is small, they indicate the necessity of continuous purchasing.

Among these, we suggest that it is possible to mine pattern 1 using a traditional method; however, the other patterns are characterized using our method. By using these characteristic patterns, our method can outperform the traditional decision model.

However, from the observations of these patterns, the personal and entire codes seem redundant for these data because the same code emerges at almost all the positions. In the following section, we eliminate the personal code and use only the entire code for the two types of categories and make a decision tree model to retain the loyal customers.

4.5.2 Analysis to Retain Loyal Customers Using Data from Two Categories

Here, TC comprises 1072 customers who are retained in the loyal customer segment for 2 years, and OC comprises 328 customers who change from the loyal customer segment to the general customer segment during the second year. Note that in this analysis, the data during only the first year are used, similar to that in the previous analysis.

Table 4.6 lists the purchasing scenario for each category of TC and OC. The important categories are processed foods, beverages, and confectioneries, similar to

TABLE 4.6
Situation of Purchasing Each Category

	Rate of the Number of Purchases		Average Number of Times of Purchase		Share of the Amount of Money	
	Loyal	General	Loyal	General	Loyal	General
Processed foods	100%	100%	106.12	68.13	62.71%	63.23%
Beverages	99.91%	100%	65.62	41.45	16.03%	16.43%
Confectioneries	99.53%	100%	60.28	38.95	13.67%	12.69%
Household utensils	93.38%	88.41%	13.31	8.41	1.79%	1.70%
Everyday goods	87.50%	83.54%	12.8	8.23	2.81%	2.59%
Perishable foods	72.76%	65.24%	7.36	4.97	0.56%	0.60%
Cosmetics	48.60%	37.80%	3.44	2.93	0.80%	0.59%
Other foods	35.35%	26.52%	4.27	3.05	1.03%	1.47%
Do-it-yourself goods	19.22%	14.02%	1.83	1.22	0.05%	0.07%
Pet goods	14.65%	14.94%	9.83	5.61	0.37%	0.42%
Other everyday goods	8.68%	7.01%	1.62	1.13	0.10%	0.08%
Medical goods	6.06%	3.05%	4.02	2.2	0.07%	0.14%

TABLE 4.7

Parameters Used by Historical Tree and Multiobjective Evolutionary Algorithms

Numbers of Categories	M = 2
Time levels	T = 5 (year, season, month, week, and day [weekdays and weekends])
Length of patterns	l = 2,..., 8
Upper limit of wild cards	1
Size of initial population	100
Number of crossovers	150/generation
Number of mutations	200/generation
Stopping rule	stp = 100 generations

the results in Table 4.2. Of the three candidate categories, we use our preliminary analysis data to confirm that the beverage category exhibits poor results. Then, we use the remaining two categories—processed foods and confectioneries—in the following analysis.

Each parameter used by the HT and MOEA is listed in Table 4.7. The personal code is not used in this analysis. Although each category only has the entire code, two types of categories are expressed. Then, the gene is tripled, similar to that in the previous analysis (as shown in Figure 4.16).

In this case, 212 patterns with pattern lengths of l = 2,..., 8 are discovered by our method. Similar to the previous analysis, all the patterns and other attributes, such as gender, age, and number of visits, are used to construct a decision tree model. Figure 4.17 shows the decision tree model, and the accuracy of the model is 70% in 10-fold cross-validation. As compared with the model that does not employ patterns, the accuracy is improved by approximately 6%.

Table 4.8 lists the interpretations of the patterns used in the decision tree model. From the observations of the model, a customer was categorized as a loyal customer if there was no gap in purchasing under both the categories for more than 2 weeks. On the contrary, a customer was categorized as a general customer if such a purchasing gap existed. They are common features, and it reveals the importance of blank periods during purchasing. Although a pattern including only the 0 code seems trivial, it is very interesting. In the general analysis, the act of not purchasing at a certain time is not interesting because many single 0s exist. However, in our method, a series

(Processed food (entire))	3	3	2	2	0	3	3	3	...
(Confectioneries (entire))	3	3	2	2	0	3	2	2	...
(Time)	1	2	3	4	4	3	4	4	...

FIGURE 4.16 Gene with multicategories.

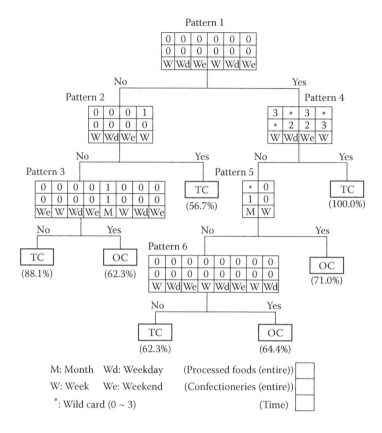

FIGURE 4.17 Decision tree model in order to retain loyal customers.

TABLE 4.8
Patterns and Their Interpretations

Interpretation

Pattern 1	Processed foods and confectioneries are not purchased for 2 weeks
Pattern 2	Low purchasing of processed foods during 1 week and no purchasing of both categories during the previous week
Pattern 3	Low purchasing of both categories during a month. However, no purchasing during both the last week of the previous month and the first week
Pattern 4	Large amount of processed foods purchased during a week and the weekend, normal amount of purchasing confectioneries during weekdays and weekends, and large amount of purchasing during the following week and the amount of purchase is not low
Pattern 5	Low purchasing amounts of confectioneries during a month; however, no purchasing during the first week
Pattern 6	No purchasing of both the categories for 3 weeks

of 0s indicates that there is no purchasing during a particular period; this was ascertained by using the time code.

In this model, only some patterns emerged as explanatory variables and no variable of the other attributes emerge. It implies that the extracted patterns are effective in this analysis, similar to that in the previous section.

4.6 CONCLUSION

In this chapter, we proposed a method to transform historical purchasing data into tree-structured data using HTs; we also proposed the MOEA approach to extract powerful patterns to discriminate target customers. Using the actual historical purchasing data and general POS data, two types of applications that use our method were introduced. In both these cases, we can extract many candidate patterns by using our MOEA and construct practical decision tree models. As compared with ordinary decision tree models, we improve the accuracy of the models by several percentage points. Moreover, we showed that the patterns used in the decision tree models are interpretable from the viewpoint of business applications.

It is possible to apply our method to other historical purchasing data with IDs. Here, the maximum number of categories under consideration was two ($M = 2$). Owing to the data characteristics, although it is difficult to use a value of $M > 3$, we can use greater values for the other data sets.

By extending the applications of our method to various practical data, we would like to show the performance of our method in advanced works.

ACKNOWLEDGMENT

This work was supported by grant-in-aid for JSPS Fellows (0196928).

REFERENCES

1. Asai, T., Abe, K., Kawasoe, S., Arimura, H., Sakamoto, H., and Arikawa, S. Efficient substructure discovery from large semi-structured data, *Proceed. SDM2002*, 158–174, 2002.
2. Gandibleux, X., Morita, H., and Katoh, N. The supported solutions used as a genetic information in a population heuristic, First International Conference on EMCO, Springer-Verlag, *Lect. Notes Comp. Sci.*, 1993, 429–442, 2001.
3. Inokuchi, A., Washio, T., and Motoda, H. An a priori-based algorithm for mining frequent substructures from graph data. Proceedings of the 4th European Conference on principles of data mining and knowledge discovery, Springer-Verlag, *Lect. Notes Comp. Sci.*, 13–23, 2000.
4. Kuramochi, M. and Karypis, G. Frequent subgraph discovery, *Proc. IEEE ICDM'01*, 313–320, 2001.
5. Yan, X., and Han, J. gSpan: graph-based substructure pattern mining, *Proc. IEEE ICDM'02*, 721–724, 2002.
6. Zaki, M. J. Efficiently mining frequent trees in a forest, *Proc. SIGKDD'02*, ACM, 71–80, 2002.

7. Yada, K., Motoda, H., Washio, T., and Miyawaki, A. Consumer behavior analysis by graph mining technique, *Proc. KES 2004*, LNAI3214, Springer-Verlag, 800–806, 2004.
8. Kuroda, M., Yada, K., Motoda, H., and Washio, T. Knowledge discovery from consumer behavior in an alcohol market by using graph mining technique, *Proc. Jt. Workshop Vietnamese Soc. AI*, SIGKBS-JSAI, ICS-IPSJ and IEICE-SIGAI, 111–116, 2004.
9. Morita, H., and Nakahara, T. Pattern mining for historical data analysis by using MOEA, *Proc. 7th Int. Conf. Multi-Objective Program. Goal Program.*, 2006.

5 A Method to Search ARX Model Orders and Its Application to Sales Dynamics Analysis

Kenta Fukata, Takashi Washio,
Katsutoshi Yada, and Hiroshi Motoda

CONTENTS

5.1 INTRODUCTION

In market research, the dynamic effects exerted on purchase behaviors have been analyzed by two approaches. The first is a structural and deterministic approach that introduces the domain knowledge-based structure into the model of the objective and dynamic system while taking into account the relevant dynamic factors, and then examines the validity of this model in terms of the consistency with some static data associated with the objective system. Neslin et al. (1985) modeled the effect exerted on the results of sales promotions by some factors, including the purchase interval, the home inventory, and the purchase volume of customers. Gupta (1988) built a model of the dynamic factors on sales intervals in concert with the brand selection probability. Both of these studies investigated the impact of the factors to the sales promotion. Taylor and Neslin (2005) extended their static database approach to analyze the relationship of the factors and the effects over two periods. Moreover, Bass et al. (2007), Lachaab et al. (2006), and the others estimated the parameters of given structural models by applying more advanced statistical techniques under the consideration of the effect of complex factors on sales results over a long period. However, the structural models representing extremely complicated market processes tends to be large and complex, and it easily induces overlooking or misunderstanding of important factors. This possibility becomes particularly high under the acquisition of diversified data in the recent business environment.

The second approach is an empirical and statistical framework based on the time series analysis that uses some advanced statistical principles to derive dynamic models characterizing the objective systems underlying the data. Leone (1983, 1987) evaluated important factors such as stockpiling, which affect substantial sales increases, by applying an autoregressive integrated moving average (ARIMA) model to a given empirical data set. Dekimpe and Hanssens (1995) evaluated the long-term effects of advertisements in printed matter and television via the analysis based on an autoregressive (AR) model and an autoregressive moving average (ARMA) model, and they suggested the appropriate selection of the media to be adopted in the required marketing strategies based on the evaluation. The reader is advised to consult Dekimpe and Hanssens (2000) for a detailed survey of the statistical time series analysis in past marketing research.

However, these conventional approaches have the following two drawbacks in capturing the dynamics of the objective systems in the analysis of the given time series data. The first drawback is that only the short time dependence among the factors and the effects over the periods up to three sampling intervals has been considered in the models. The second is that the number of exogenous factors considered in the model is limited to one at maximum. For example, the model of Leone (1983, 1987) is limited to the third order (i.e., the consideration of the dynamic dependence over the past three sampling intervals), and that of Dekimpe and Hanssens (1995) is limited to the second order. Neither has exogenous factors. Contrarily, in real-world problems, the periods of the dynamic dependence in the objective systems are far longer than the sampling interval, and many exogenous factors often exist in the systems. Consequently, the conventional approaches are not widely applicable because of these limitations.

The approaches of these previous studies are considered to have been developed to conduct long-term market predictions under stationary environments. However, as the business environments and the associated market structures dynamically changed in recent years, their analysis under given model structures such as the conventional approaches becomes difficult. Hence the importance of the time series analysis extended to capture the highly dynamic behaviors of the customers based on the daily sales data has become significant. This study proposes a new time series analysis method by using higher-order auto-regressive eXogenous (ARX) models, including multiple exogenous factors based on the historical data of the daily sales and advertisements while addressing some technical issues for its application to the practical marketing data analysis. The proposed approach has been applied to time series data consisting of an objective item sales amount, two exogenous variables of the television advertisement amount, and the in-store promotion strength. If we can appropriately grasp the dynamic contributions of each exogenous factor to the objective item sales amount through the analysis, some useful business implications will be provided because the efficiencies of the advertisement and the promotion can be precisely evaluated.

5.2   RELATED WORK

5.2.1   TECHNICAL ISSUES

One of the representative and quantitative dynamics modeling approaches that have often been used in the time series analysis is ARX input modeling (Ljung, 1987). Similar to the many other empirical modeling approaches based on given time series data, a main issue in this modeling is to determine an appropriate model complexity well, capturing the dynamic structure of the objective system. In terms of the ARX modeling, its complexity is defined by the model orders that are the finite numbers of past consecutive quantitative states to take into account under a constant time interval sampling. This issue has been explored in many aspects, including the indices of the Akaike information criterion (AIC) (Akaike, 1969), Bayesian information criterion (BIC), (Kuha, 2004), and minimal description length (MDL) (Graunwald et al., 2004). However, these works assume that the time series data are observed from the system without any uncertainty and distortions such as sensing accuracy limit, discretization errors from analog to digital information, and unexpected biases not following any statistical expectations and distributions. This assumption strongly limits the applicability of these criteria to determine the model complexity in many practical modeling problems. This issue on the use of the information criteria in practical situations has been partially discussed, and some ideas to use the difference of the indices between two candidate models such as DAIC (Akaike, 1973) have been proposed. However, any generic and systematic approach to select the appropriate model order based on the indices has not yet been established.

Another important issue that has not been explored in the selection of the appropriate ARX model orders is the efficient and complete search algorithm of the orders having the optimal index value. In conventional approaches, a simple line search is used in which the index of each model order is exhaustively computed up to a limit order. However, if an ARX model has multiple exogenous inputs, the number of the parameters to define the model orders is also more than one. Because the number of the parameter combinations of the ARX model to be explored within some order limit is exponential to the number of the parameters, the search of the optimal model orders becomes easily intractable under the increase of the exogenous inputs.

In this chapter we address these issues by providing a novel information criterion named DAIC*, which is an extension of the DAIC and an efficient and complete search algorithm of the parameter combination of the optimal model orders under the criterion.

5.2.2 STATE OF THE ART

5.2.2.1 Auto-Regressive eXogenous Input Model

An auto-regressive eXogenous input (ARX) model is a linear recurrence equation to relate the current value of an objective variable $x(s)$ with its past finite time series and the past finite time series of the other exogenous input variables y_g ($g = 1,..., h$), as follows.

$$x(s) = \sum_{i=1}^{p} a_i x(s-i) + \sum_{j_1=1}^{q_1} b_{j_1} y_1(s - j_1 - k_1) + \cdots + \sum_{j_h=1}^{q_h} b_{j_h} y_1(s - j_h - k_h) + e(s) \quad (5.1)$$

where s is a current time step, a_i the contribution coefficient of an i-step past value of the objective variable to its current value, b_{jg} the contribution coefficient of the j-step past value of an exogenous input variable y_g, k_g the time lag of the propagation delay of the exogenous input variable, and p, q_g ($g = 1,..., h$) the model order parameters which define the finite and maximum time steps of the contributions from the objective and the exogenous variables. In addition, let $\hat{x}(s)$ be a prediction of $x(s)$ and $e(s) = x(s) - \hat{x}(s)$ their prediction error. The model coefficients a_i ($i = 1,..., p$) and b_{jg} ($j_g = 1,..., q_g$, $g = 1,..., h$) are determined by the least squares principle on the variance of the prediction error $e(s)$ over a given time series data. The combination of the time lags k_g ($g = 1,..., h$) which are integers is determined by a greedy method to search the combination which provides less least squares prediction error on the combination lattice. The model orders, i.e., the parameter values of p, q_g ($g = 1,..., h$), are conventionally determined by the AIC index as explained in the next subsection.

5.2.2.2 Conventional Order Determination

The selection of the appropriate orders of the ARX model is crucial, and it has been performed by using AIC (Akaike information criterion) in the conventional and standard approach. AIC is an information measure to evaluate the difference between the actual probability distribution of the value $x(s)$ and that of the predicted value $\hat{x}(s)$. AIC can be defined by the following Eq. (5.2) as the measure of the difference between these two probability distributions based on the Kullback-Leibler quantity of information.

$$\text{AIC} = N \log\left(\hat{\sigma}_M^2\right) + 2 \, |M|, \quad (5.2)$$

where N stands for the total number of data and $\hat{\sigma}_M^2$ the variance of the model prediction error $e(s)$. Moreover, $|M|$ stands for the total number of coefficients in the ARX model $M = [p, q_g \ (g = 1,..., h)]$. The smaller value indicates that the estimated distribution function is closer to the true distribution function.

An important issue on this AIC is the limitation in its practical use due to its strong assumption on the linearity of the objective system and the absence of observation error. If the objective time series data are observed from a linear system without any observation error, AIC should have a clear bottom on a model complexity. Thus, the optimal model complexity is uniquely determined by the bottom of AIC. However, the AIC curve does not follow the ideal case when some nonlinearity of the system and some observation error exist and does not show any clear bottom in many cases. This happens since the errors induced by the nonlinearity and the observation are incorporated in the evaluation of AIC as if they are some meaningful errors. Accordingly, more practical measures to determine an appropriate model order must be established.

5.3   PROPOSAL OF DAIC*

DAIC (Akaike, 1973), which takes the difference of the AIC between consecutive model orders, provides a criterion to determine some appropriate order of the autoregressive (AR) model, which has only a unique order parameter. In the principle of the difference of the AIC (DAIC), a model order that shows a significant decrease of the AIC value is selected as an appropriate order instead of the minimum value of the AIC. This is because the significant decrease of the AIC value may not occur when the model incorporates the errors but may occur when it incorporates major characteristics of the objective system. This principle can be similarly applied to the models having multiple model order parameters such as the ARX model. However, to our best knowledge, no approach had addressed the application of this principle to the case of the multiple model order parameters.

Given a parameter vector $M = [p, q_1, q_2, ..., q_h]$ and the AIC under M as AIC_M, DAIC* is defined as the minimum difference of AIC_M from AIC_{Mp} and AIC_{Mqg} ($g = 1, ..., h$), where $M_p = [p - 1, q_1, q_2, ..., q_h]$ and $M_{qg} = [p - 1, q_1, ..., q_g - 1, ..., q_h]$. More formally, DAIC* is described as follows.

$$DAIC^* = \max(DAIC_p, \max_{g=1,...,h} (DAIC_{q_g})), \tag{5.3}$$

where

$$DAIC_p = AIC_M - AIC_{Mp},$$

$$DAIC_{qg} = AIC_M - AIC_{Mqg}. \tag{5.4}$$

Note that the minimum difference between two AICs corresponds to the maximum value of the difference because their values are always negative. By definition, DAIC* stands for the least improvement of the AIC under a unit extension of the model complexity. On the other hand, the best model order is considered to be the order that provides the maximum improvement of the AIC similarly to the principle of the DAIC. Accordingly, the order providing the maximum improvement of the AIC should be selected as the appropriate model order by using the DAIC*. This is done by seeking the model order parameter vector M providing the minimum value of the DAIC* because of its negativeness. This approach enables selection of the model order to achieve the maximum value of the least improvement of the AIC among the order parameter changes. The purpose of this strategy is to discover the model where any simplification certainly and significantly reduces the accuracy of the model beyond the errors. When an order parameter is zero, DAIC* including the parameter cannot be computed because the further simple model for the parameter does not exist. In this case, DAIC* is evaluated by Equation 5.3 while excluding the zero-order parameters because the variables corresponding to the zero-order parameters are not included in the model.

From Equation 5.4, the AIC for the model simpler by one order parameter is as follows.

$$\text{AIC}_{M'} = N \log \left(\hat{\sigma}^2_{M'} \right) + 2(|M|-1),\tag{5.5}$$

where $\hat{\sigma}^2_{M'}$ is the variance of the prediction error $e(s)$ by the simpler model. Accordingly, the concrete formula of DAIC* in Equation 5.3, which is the difference between Equation 5.4 and Equation 5.5, is represented as

$$\text{DAIC*} = N \log \frac{\hat{\sigma}^2_{M}}{\min\limits_{g=1,\dots,h} \left(\hat{\sigma}^2_{M_p}, \hat{\sigma}^2_{M_{q_g}} \right)} + 2.\tag{5.6}$$

Instead of the original definition of DAIC* in Equation 5.3, this formula is used for the computation of DAIC* and the search for the optimal ARX model.

5.4   SEARCH FOR OPTIMAL MODEL ORDER

The simplest and most complete way to search the optimal model order vector M by DAIC* under a given time series data is the thorough search by using loops for all order parameters. However, the computational complexity of this algorithm is $O(L^{h+1})$, where L is the upper limit of the order to search, and hence the computation becomes intractable when the number of the exogenous variables or the upper limit of the order is large.

For an efficient search of the optimal M based on DAIC*, we introduce A^* search (Hart et al., 1968; Nilsson, 1980). A^* search uses a lower bound f of an objective function f to minimize instead of the objective function itself. This f is DAIC* in our context. Starting from an initial model order vector $M_{\min} = [1,\dots,1]$ where all parameters are one, the algorithm evaluates $f_1 = \text{DAIC*}(M_{\min})$ for the vector, further increases one of the elements of $M_{\min}$ as $M_{\min}^+$, and evaluates the lower bound $f_2 = \text{DAIC*}(M_{\min}^+)$. If $f_2 > f_1$, this fact implies that no M deduced by the further increments of $M_{\min}^+$ does not have the smaller value than f_1, and hence the depth first search beyond the $M_{\min}^+$ is pruned. This pruning principle is recursively applied at every step to evaluate the model order vector and its corresponding model. As easily understood by this explanation, A^* search is complete (i.e., not to miss the optimal solution). The main issue of the A^* search is to design an efficient lower bound f that

Main

(1) Given $M = M_{min}$ and M_{max}.

(2) Compute DAIC*(M) and $\underline{D}$AIC*(M).

(3) Let $M_{opt} = M$ and DAIC*(M_{opt}) = DAIC*(M).

(4) If DAIC*(M) $\geq$ $\underline{D}$AIC*(M) then

$$[M_{opt}, DAIC^*(M_{opt})] = A^*(M, M_{max}, M_{opt}, DAIC^*(M_{opt}), 1)$$

(5) end

Function $[M_{opt}, DAIC^*(M_{opt})] = A^*(M, M_{max}, M_{opt}, DAIC^*(M_{opt}), gs)$

(1) for g=gs to h

(2)   Let $q_g = q_g + 1$.

(3)   Compute DAIC*(M) and $\underline{D}$AIC*(M).

(4)   If DAIC*(M) $\leq$ DAIC*(M_{opt}) then $M_{opt} = M$ and DAIC*(M_{opt}) = DAIC*(M).

(5)   If ($r_g < L$) and (DAIC*(M) $\geq$ $\underline{D}$AIC*(M))

then $[M_{opt}, DAIC^*(M_{opt})] = A^*(M, M_{max}, M_{opt}, DAIC^*(M_{opt}), g)$

(6) end

FIGURE 5.1 A^* search for optimal model order.

is close to the actual value of f. From Equation 5.6, DAIC* is the minimum when the ratio of the variances of the model prediction error is the minimum. Because the variance monotonically decreases when any element in M increases, the ratio of the variance under $M_{max} = [L, ..., L]$ over the variance under the current M is the lower bound of the ratio, where L is the upper limit of the order to search. This derives the following lower bound of the DAIC*(M).

$$\underline{D}AIC^* = N \log \frac{\hat{\sigma}^2_{M_{max}}}{\hat{\sigma}^2_M} + 2. \tag{5.7}$$

Figure 5.1 shows the algorithm of this A^* search where M_{opt} is the optimal model order vector and DAIC*(M_{opt}) is the DAIC* under M_{opt}. The final outputs of this algorithm are M_{opt} and DAIC*(M_{opt}).

The lower boundary of DAIC* given by Equation 5.7 is sometimes too small to efficiently prune the search space, because it is based on the error variance $\sigma^2_{M_{max}}$, which is minimum within the search space. To obtain more efficient search performance, which is not complete but sufficiently practical, we introduce a heuristic measure for the pruning as follows.

$$\underline{\text{DAIC}}*^{1/n} = N \log \left(\frac{\hat{\sigma}^2_{M_{max}}}{\hat{\sigma}^2_{M}} \right)^{1/n} + 2.$$

Because the ratio of the variances always lies in [0, 1], its n-root is closer to 1, and hence Equation 5.8 gives a larger value than Equation 5.7. Though this change does not ensure the lower boundary property of the measure, the larger value of the measure enables tighter pruning, which increases the search efficiency.

5.5   PERFORMANCE EVALUATION

The performnce of the proposed approach to determine the ARX model order is evaluated by using some artificial data sets. The data sets are generated by the following semi-ARX system containing quadratic nonlinear terms:

$$x(s) = \sum_{i=1}^{p} a_i x(s-i) + \sum_{i_2=1}^{p} a_{i_2} x^2(s-i_2) + \sum_{j_1=1}^{q_1} b_{j_1} y_1(s-j_1) + \sum_{j_2=1}^{q_2} b_{j_2} y_2(s-j_2) + e(s)$$

Two order vectors $M = [p = 3, q_1 = 3, q_2 = 4]$ and $M = [p = 6, q_1 = 7, q_2 = 6]$ are used. The coefficients of a_i, b_{j_1}, b_{j_2} have been determined by a design method of infinite-duration impulse response filter while ensuring the stability of the system (Krauss et al., 1994; Lennart, 1996). The coefficients of the nonlinear terms a_{i_2} are set to be very small values compared against a_i for the stability, and they are $a_{i_2} = a_i/20$ for $M = [p = 3, q_1 = 3, q_2 = 4]$ and $a_{i_2} = a_i/500$ for $M = [p = 6, q_1 = 7, q_2 = 6]$. When the data sets containing only linear dynamics are generated, all coefficients a_{i_2} are set to 0. The total time steps for the data generation is $N = 10,000$, and the time series of the input variables $y_1(s)$ and $y_2(s)$ are chosen to be a unit stepwise form or Gaussian noise having unit variance depending on the required conditions of the evaluation. Furthermore, the objective variable $x(s)$ generated by this system is distorted by adding Gaussian noises having various relative amplitudes in terms of the standard deviation of $x(s)$.

The performance to identify ARX model orders under various conditions of the data is compared between the standard AIC and our DAIC*. The upper limit of each order parameter for the search is set to be $L = 9$. The identified orders for the system having the order parameters $M = [p = 3, q_1 = 3, q_2 = 4]$ under step/Gaussian inputs of both $y_1(s)$ and $y_2(s)$, linear/nonlinear dynamics, and various noise distortion levels are shown in Table 5.1 and Table 5.2 for the AIC and the DAIC*, respectively. The results for the case of $M = [p = 6, q_1 = 7, q_2 = 6]$ are shown in Table 5.3 and

TABLE 5.1
Orders by Akaike Information Criterion for M = [3,3,4]

Inputs	a_{i2}	Noise 0%	Noise 5%	Noise 20%	Noise 50%
Step	0	[3,3,4]	[9,3,4]	[9,3,3]	[9,3,2]
Gaussian	0	[3,4,5]	[9,8,9]	[9,9,9]	[9,9,9]
Gaussian	$a_i/20$	[6,8,8]	[3,5,1]	[9,9,9]	[9,9,9]

TABLE 5.2
Orders by DAIC* for M = [3,3,4]

Inputs	a_{i2}	Noise 0%	Noise 5%	Noise 20%	Noise 50%
Step	0	[1,1,1]	[1,1,1]	[1,1,1]	[1,1,1]
Gaussian	0	[1,2,3]	[1,2,3]	[1,2,3]	[2,2,3]
Gaussian	$a_i/20$	[1,2,3]	[1,2,3]	[1,2,3]	[3,2,3]

TABLE 5.3
Orders by AIC for M = [6,7,6]

Inputs	a_{i2}	Noise 0%	Noise 5%	Noise 20%	Noise 50%
Step	0	[6,5,7]	[9,2,4]	[9,2,2]	[9,1,0]
Gaussian	0	[7,8,8]	[9,9,9]	[9,8,9]	[9,9,9]
Gaussian	$a_i/500$	[8,9,9]	[9,9,9]	[8,8,9]	[9,9,9]

TABLE 5.4
Orders by DAIC* for M = [6,7,6]

Inputs	a_{i2}	Noise 0%	Noise 5%	Noise 20%	Noise 50%
Step	0	[4,1,1]	[3,1,1]	[2,1,1]	[2,1,1]
Gaussian	0	[5,7,7]	[5,3,8]	[3,4,4]	[5,5,5]
Gaussian	$a_i/500$	[6,3,8]	[2,3,9]	[3,4,4]	[5,5,5]

Table 5.4. Table 5.1 and Table 5.3 indicate that the orders determined by the AIC tend to be significantly larger than the true order parameters when the noise or the nonlinearity is large. In contrast, Table 5.2 and Table 5.4 indicate that our approach using DAIC* provides almost the same or slightly lower orders compared with the true order parameters in the case of Gaussian inputs. The reason for the lower-order estimations in the case of the step inputs is that the step inputs contain mainly low-frequency signal components that tend not to affect the higher-order terms of the system. In summary, DAIC* derives better results than AIC for the data containing many errors.

5.6   ANALYSIS OF REAL MARKETING DATA

5.6.1   Objective Data

The data were acquired through a marketing investigation. Between March 1 and June 30 of a certain year, the daily sales amount of a confectionery item in a store belonging to a supermarket chain was recorded. During this period, television advertisements of the item were broadcast from April 13 to May 3. In addition, the store actively promoted the item sales by placing the items on a main rack significantly exposed to the customers in some weeks, including the television advertisement period. Let the objective variable $x(s)$ be the daily sales amount of the item and the exogenous input variables $y_1(s)$ and $y_2(s)$ be the daily amount of the television advertisement and the in-store sales promotion, respectively. $y_1(s)$ is measured by an index called the *gross rating point* (GRP), representing the number of television advertisements exposed to audiences (Damani et al., 2006). This is evaluated by the sum of the audience ratings at the times when the television advertisements are broadcast. The GRP was constantly about 100 from April 15 to 26 when the television advertisements were the most actively broadcast. $y_2(s)$ is 1 during the in-store sales promotion and 0 otherwise.

5.6.2   Performance on Efficiency and Accuracy

Because the DAIC* value changes in complex manners for practical data and the search process depends heavily on the value, the computation efficiency of the search is expected to sensitively change according to the characteristios of objective data. Table 5.5 shows the efficiency in terms of the number of search steps and the search time of the thorough searches, the A^* search using Equation 5.7 and the heuristic searches using Equation 5.8 with $n = 2,\ldots, 5$ under the upper-order limit $L = 9$. Because the loop-based thorough search uses simple pointer management, it is faster than the A^* search under this upper-order limit. However, they become almost identical 630 sec under $L = 15$, because the loop-based thorough search has high computational complexity $O(L^{h+1})$. Accordingly, the A^* search is advantageous for the large-scale problems in terms of the number of input variables and the upper-order limits. The heuristic searches based on Equation 5.8 search the solution far faster than the A^* search. Even when we apply the fourth-rooted ratio, the optimal solution

TABLE 5.5
Search Steps and Times for Sales Data

Algorithm	Steps	Time (sec)	$p, q_1, q_2, k_1,$ and k_2
Thorough by loops	1000	20	1,4,1,7,0
Thorough by recursions	729	99	1,4,1,7,0
A^* search	458	61	1,4,1,7,0
Search by 2nd root	231	39	1,4,1,7,0
Search by 3rd root	107	19	1,4,1,7,0
Search by 4th root	54	10	1,4,1,7,0
Search by 5th root	42	8	2,6,1,9,0

can be found. Though the fifth-rooted ratio cannot derive the optimum, the resultant solution is not very far from the optimum. In this regard, the A^* search and its associated heuristic searches are very advantageous for practical use.

5.6.3 Discussion of Analysis Result

The impulse responses of the optimal ARX model obtained in the previous subsection have been investigated to understand the dynamic relation of the sales amount of the item with the television advertisement and the in-store sales promotion. The impulse responses are a response of the sales amount under the virtual television advertisement of a unit GRP for a day and a response of the sales amount under the virtual in-store sales promotion for a day. They can be estimated by introducing an impulse time series to each input variable into the ARX model. For example, the impulse response of the sales amount to the television advertisement is derived by adding the time series of $y_1(1) = 0,\dots, y_1(s-1) = 0, y_1(s) = 1, y_1(s+1) = 0,\dots, y_1(n) = 0$ to the input of the ARX model.

Figure 5.2 represents the impulse responses for both the in-store sales promotion and the television advertisement. In both cases in the figure, the unit impulse is introduced on the 60th day from the beginning. Based on the upper response, the effect of a 1-day in-store promotion on the sales amount is about $+1000$ yen. The lower response indicates that the effect of a unit GRP advertisement on the sales amount is $\pm 10 \cdots \pm 15$ yen, and its delay is almost 9 days. This time delay indicates the time interval required to impress the item upon the customers by the television advertisement. Because the standard input amplitude of the GRP is 100, the actual response of the sales amount is about $\pm 1000 \cdots \pm 1500$ yen, which is comparable to the effect of the in-store sales promotion, whereas the response to the in-store sales promotion does not include any time delay. This is because the in-store sales promotion promptly makes an impact on the item onsite. The negative response of the sales to the GRP is not consistent with our background knowledge. This occurred by the characteristics of the ARX modeling in which the effects of the input variables

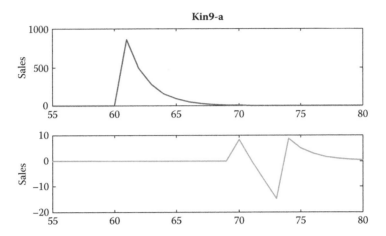

FIGURE 5.2 Sales response by DAIC*-based auto-regressive eXogenous input model. Top panel: Impulse response to in-store sales. Bottom panel: Impulse response to TV advertisement.

cannot be decomposed perfectly within the finite number of the data samples. This effect is called *cross-talk* among inputs. Even under this cross-talk problem, however, the quantitative amplitudes and time delays of the responses to the input variables can be approximately known through the analysis, and the information can be used for the detailed marketing analysis and its associated marketing strategy planning. Figure 5.3 shows the impulse response to the television advertisement of the ARX model derived by using the standard AIC. Because of the excessively high model orders, the responses do not reflect the practical behaviors of the item sales amount and are not interpreted by the marketing domain knowledge. This demonstrates the advantage of our DAIC* approach for the ARX modeling under noisy and erroneous modeling situations.

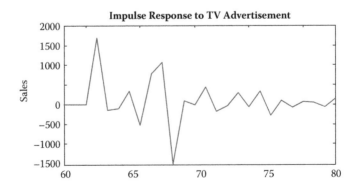

FIGURE 5.3 By AIC-based auto-regressive eXogenous input model.

5.7   CONCLUSION

In this chapter, we proposed a novel measure named DAIC* to overcome current limitations to determine the model complexity of the ARX model. In addition, we proposed some efficient complete/heuristic search algorithms to determine the optimal combinations of the model order parameters. Through the empirical evaluations, DAIC* is confirmed to suggest appropriate model complexity under practical conditions, and the algorithms are confirmed to derive the optimal or the semioptimal model complexity in high efficiency. The proposed approaches are expected to provide a novel measure for the analysis of the dynamic behaviors of customer sales in marketing.

ACKNOWLEDGMENT

This research was partially supported by Japan MEXT grant-in-aid for Scientific Research on Priority Areas, Cyber Infrastructure for the Information-Explosion Era, 18049052-A01-0008, 2006.

REFERENCES

Akaike, H. Fitting autoregressive models for prediction, *Ann. Inst. Statist. Math.,* 21, 243–247, 1969.

Akaike, H. Information theory and an extension of the maximum likelihood principle, in *Proceedings 2nd International Symposium on Information Theory,* Petrov, B. N. and Csaki, F., Eds., Akademiai Kiado, Budapest, 267–281, 1973.

Bass, F.M., Bruce, Majumdar, N.S., and Murthi, B. P. S. Wearout effects of different advertising themes: a dynamic Bayesian model of the advertising-sales relationship, *Marketing Sci.,* 26, 179–195, 2007.

Damani, R., Damani, C., Farbo, D., and Linton, J. *Online Marketing,* Imano plc, London, 2006.

Dekimpe, M.G. and Hanssens, D.M. The persistence of marketing effects on sales, *Marketing Sci.,* 14, 1–21, 1995.

Dekimpe, M.G. and Hanssens, D.M. Time-series models in marketing: past, present and future, *Int. J. Res. Marketing,* 17, 183–193, 2000.

Graunwald, P. D., Myung, I. J., and Pitt, M.A. Pitt, Eds., *Advances in Minimum Description Length: Theory and Applications,* MIT Press, Cambridge, MA, 2004.

Gupta, S. Impact of sales promotions on when, what, and how much to buy, *J. Marketing Res.,* 25, 342–355, 1988.

Hart, P.E., Nilsson, N.J., and Raphael, B. A formal basis for the heuristic determination of minimum cost paths, *IEEE Trans. Sys. Sci. Cybernetics* SSC4, 100–107, 1968.

Krauss, T.P., Shure, L., and Little, J.N. Signal processing toolbox for use with MATLAB, Cybernet Systems, Inc., 1994.

Kuha, J. AIC and BIC: comparisons of assumptions and performance, *Sociol. Methods Res.,* 33, 188–229, 2004.

Lachaab, M. Ansari, A. Jedidi, K. and Trabelsi, A. Modeling preference evolution in discrete choice models: a Bayesian state-space approach, *Quant. Marketing Econ.* 4, 57–81, 2006.

Leone, R.P. Modeling sales-advertising relationships: an integrated time series—econometric approach, *J. Marketing Res.,* 20, 291–295, 1983.

Leone, R.P. Forecasting the effect of an environmental change on market performance—an intervention time-series approach, *Int. J. Forecasting,* 3, 463–478, 1987.

Ljung, L. System identification theory for the user, 1987, Prentice Hall, Upper Saddle River, NJ, pp. 71–73.

Ljung, L. System identification toolbox for use with MATLAB, Cybernet Systems, Inc., 1996.

Neslin, S.A., Henderson, C., and Quelch, J. Consumer promotion and the acceleration of product purchases, *Marketing Sci.,* 4, 147–165, 1985.

Nilsson, N.J. *Principles of Artificial Intelligence,* Morgan Kaufmann, San Francisco, CA, 1980.

Taylor, G.A. and Neslin, S.A. The current and future sales impact of a retail frequency reward program, *J. Retailing,* 81, 293–305, 2005.

6 Data Mining for Improved Web Site Design and Enhanced Marketing

Asem Omari

CONTENTS

6.1 DATA MINING FOR WEB SITE DESIGN IMPROVEMENT

The success of a commercial company depends greatly on the success of its Web site. A successful Web site is a well-structured Web site. The Web site is well structured from the user's point of view if it contains services that satisfy users' needs, if user navigation is simplified, and if the user can reach the target page in a short time without the need to make any search or to guess where the target page is. On the other hand, from the point of view of the Web site owner, a Web site is well structured if it participates in increasing the company's overall profit, if it increases the user's trust in the company and its products, and if it participates in supporting the company's marketing strategies. A great deal of research has been done to cover different Web site

95

design techniques and strategies. The work in Gerhke[1] provides a survey of experts' recommendations of how to create an effective Web site from an e-commerce point of view. It investigates the determinants of an effective Web site. The survey indicates that the major categories of determinants are page loading speed, business content, navigation efficiency, security, and marketing/customer focus. Troyer et al.[2] present a method for designing kiosk Web sites, which are Web sites that provide information and allow users to navigate through that information. The method is based on the principle that the Web site should be designed for and adapted to its users. It starts by identifying different classes of users and describing manually their characteristics, their information requirements, and how can they navigate the Web site. The work in Lohse and Spiller[3] gives some recommendations and remarks on how to design retail Web sites. For example, stores that offer an FAQs section have more visits than those without such a section, and every Web page must have consistent navigation links to move around on the site. The author in Chou[4] presents a technique for redesigning a large and complex Web site and provide usability practices and techniques. He provides some tips and practical issues and solutions for developing a solid information architecture and for implementing Web standards. Data mining is one of the effective methods used to extract patterns of interest from the company's data warehouses and Web log files to build well-structured Web sites or to improve that structure if the Web sites are already built. In this chapter, we will see how data mining techniques can participate in building well-structured Web sites in both the design phase and in the maintenance phase, which is known as Web mining.

6.1.1 DATA MINING IN THE MAINTENANCE PHASE OF WEB SITES (WEB MINING)

Web mining is the use of data mining techniques to extract useful patterns from the Web. Those extracted patterns are used to improve the structure of Web sites, improve the availability of the information in the Web sites and the way those pieces of information are introduced to the Web site user, and improve data retrieval and the quality of automatic search of information resources available on the Web. Web mining can be divided into three major categories: Web usage mining, Web content mining, and Web structure mining.

6.1.1.1 Web Usage Mining

Web usage mining, or Web log mining, is the process of applying data mining techniques to Web log data to extract useful information from user access patterns. The Web usage data include data from Web server access logs, proxy server logs, browser logs, user profiles, registration data, cookies, and user queries. The Web usage mining process consists of three phases: data preprocessing, pattern discovery, and pattern analysis. Web usage mining has a great effect on e-commerce. It can be used to study customer behavior on the Web; it uses the extracted knowledge to facilitate navigation and services introduced to the customer and suggests particular products to the customer based on the customer's interests. In Berendt and Spiliopoulou,[5] comparisons of navigation patterns between customers and non-customers led to rules that specify how the Web site should be improved. Web personalization is the process of customizing Web sites to the needs of specific users, taking advantage of the patterns discovered from mining Web usage data and other information such as Web structure, Web content, and user profile data.

6.1.1.2   Web Content Mining

Web content mining is mining the data that a Web page contains. A lot of research has been done to cover different Web content mining issues for the purpose of improving the contents of the Web pages, improving the way they are introduced to the Web site user, improving the quality of search results, and extracting interesting Web page content. Several methods to help the user find various types of unexpected information from his or her competitors' Web sites are proposed in Liu et al.[6] Changing the content of a Web site can make the Web site better serve the requirements of a specific user. Content may be added, removed, or rearranged.[7] Those changes may include additional explanations or details that may be added or removed depending on the user's background and interests in some topic, or changing the Web site presentation language based on user language preference.

6.1.1.3   Web Structure Mining

Web structure mining describes the organization of the content of the Web. Gedov et al.[8] describe an approach that allows the comparison of Web page contents with the information implicitly defined by the structure of the Web site. In this way, it can be indicated whether a page fits in the content of its link structure and topics that span over several connected Web Pages can be identified, thus supporting Web designers by comparing their intentions with the actual structure and content of the Web page. Other studies deal with the Web page as a collection of blocks or segments. Making changes to the links of the Web site can facilitate the user's navigation of the site and minimize the time required to reach the target page. There are several techniques for adaptive links such as direct guidance, link sorting, link hiding, disabling, or highlighting.[9] Perkowitz and Etzioni[10] investigated the creation of index pages, which are pages that contain a direct link to pages that cover a particular topic, to facilitate the user's navigation of the Web site. The PageGather cluster mining algorithm takes Web server logs as input and finds collections (clusters) of pages that tend to co-occur in visits, and outputs the contents of candidate index pages for each cluster found. As a result, it is clear that making changes and adaptations to Web sites with the help of extracted patterns using different data mining techniques is very effective, but doing so in the maintenance phase can be costly and time consuming. Another approach for improving the structure of Web sites, the investment of the patterns extracted from different data mining techniques to build well-structured Web sites in the design phase, is presented in the next section.

6.1.2   DATA MINING IN THE DESIGN PHASE OF WEB SITES

As mentioned above, making adaptations and improvements to Web sites in the maintenance phase can be costly and time consuming. An alternative approach for designing retail Web sites is improving the structure of the Web site in the design phase before it is published.[11,12] In this approach, the problem of building an ill-structured Web site for some company or institution can be solved by applying data-mining techniques such as clustering, classification, sequential pattern mining, and association rule mining on the contents of the information system of the company or institution. Then, from the extracted patterns, the information to be considered in the Web site building process is gained and invested in the process of Web site design, which yields a better-designed Web site. The main advantage of this method is that it reduces maintenance time and budgetary costs for Web sites if they are built without taking into account the extracted interesting patterns from the transactions database of the company. This approach also permits the sales manager to focus on the core business and gives him or her a better view of his or her products and customers, which is very helpful in designing retail Web sites.

6.1.2.1   Example

Suppose there is a company that sells different products in its physical stores. The company has a database that contains information about customers' profiles, transactions, purchases, employees, and branches, and it has a dataset that records all customer transactions in its stores. It is decided to build a Web site for that company to give a good view about its available products and activities, to support and facilitate services introduced to customers, and to encourage customers to buy more of its products. The Web site design process starts by identifying the company's goal for building this Web site. The Web site designer looks at the database and tries to understand its structure and see what type of information is available in the database and whether that information should be presented in the Web site.[4] The Web site designer also considers some standards and recommendations adopted by Web site designers on how to build well-structured Web sites, such as the ideas that every page should be connected directly to the home page and every parent page should have a direct link to its descendants.[3] The Web site designer uses his or her knowledge and the available design tools to build the initial Web site prototype. Figure 6.1 shows the resulting prototype of the Web

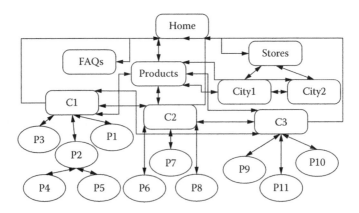

FIGURE 6.1 Initial Web site design prototype.

site structure, in which arrows represent links between pages and boxes and circles represent Web pages. The prototype is well designed with respect to Web site designer standards. Every page has a consistent navigation link to move around on the Web site. Every page is connected directly to the home page, and every page has a direct connection to its descendants—for example, from the products Web page are direct links to all product categories C1, C2, and C3. All product categories are connected to each other—for example, the C1 product category page is connected directly to C2 and C3 product category pages. The company has two stores, City1 and City2. An FAQs section is presented to facilitate the usage of the Web site. Before considering the prototype resulting from the design process, the following questions can be asked.

- Can we improve the design of this prototype?
- Is there any important information in the database that cannot be seen that, when considered, may have a good effect in improving the Web site structure, such as the relationships between customers and products?
- Will this structure really participate in increasing the company's overall profit, for example, by encouraging customers to buy more from the available products?

To improve the design of the Web site prototype in Figure 6.1, several data mining techniques can be applied on the database of the company. Then, from the extracted patterns, the Web site designer gets a better view about the customers, products, and the relationship between customers and products.

- Who are the frequent customers?
- What kinds of products are they usually interested in?
- What kinds of products are sold together?
- Which customers are interested in which sets of products?

The following patterns can be a result of one of the data mining techniques applied to the database of the company.

6.1.2.2   Association Rule Mining

Association rule mining is the discovery of association rules showing attribute values that occur frequently together in a given set of data. The following rules can be a result of applying association rule mining techniques.

1. If a transaction T contains product P8, there is a 75% chance that it contains product P11 as well, and 10% of all transactions contain both.
2. A total of 80% of the customers who buy product P9 also buy product P2, and 8% of all customers buy both P9 and P2 products.

6.1.2.3   Sequential Pattern Mining

Sequential pattern mining is mining for frequently occurring patterns with respect to time; for example, customers who buy product P7 seem to buy product P4 within 3 months.

6.1.2.4   Classification

Classification is the process of finding a set of models or functions that describe and distinguish data classes or concepts in which the models derived are based on a set of training data. The following pattern can be a result of using classification data-mining techniques.

Classify customers with respect to their age into three classes. The first class contains customers who are younger than 20 years old. The second class contains customers who are between 20 and 40 years old. The third class contains customers who are older than age 40. After analyzing the characteristics of each class, an interesting result could be that the customers who are between 20 and 40 years old are usually interested in P3, P7, and P11 products.

6.1.2.5   Clustering

In clustering, data objects have no class label. The objects are clustered or grouped based on the principle that objects in one class have high similarity to one another but are very dissimilar to objects in other clusters. For example, to extract customers' buying habits in both City1 and City2 with respect to purchasing patterns of some products, and their addresses, the result could be that customers who are living in City1 are mostly interested in set A of products, which contains P1 and P9 products. On the other hand, customers who are living in City2 are mostly interested in set B of products, which contains P5 and P6 products.

The extracted patterns from applying data mining techniques on the company's database give the Web site designer an overview about the behavior of the customers, their interestingness, the relation between customers and products, what kinds of products are usually sold together, and product buying habits with respect to different attributes such as customer age or address. Thus, the Web site designer can make some decisions that will improve the Web site design structure, such as creating direct links between products that seem to be sold together, creating links to products that are expected to be of interest for some customers or highlighting links if they already exist, and creating index pages, which are pages that suggest some products to the customers with respect to their age or address. For example. Figure 6.2 shows the effect of data mining techniques on the Web site prototype design. After studying and analyzing the previous patterns carefully, the following decisions are introduced to improve the Web site prototype.

1. From rules extracted using association rule mining and sequential pattern mining, a direct link between P2 and P9, P8 and P11, and P4 and P7 are to be created.
2. From the patterns extracted using classification techniques, an index page is to be created. This page is a collection of recommended links for customers who are between 20 and 40 years old with links to the product pages that are of interest of customers in this age interval that are P3, P7, and P11 products.
3. From patterns extracted using clustering techniques, two index pages are to be added. The first page contains a set of links to product pages that

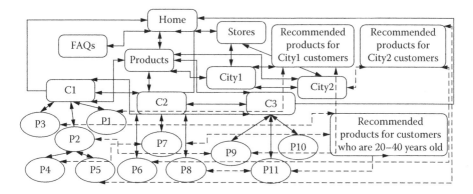

FIGURE 6.2 Improved Web site prototype with the help of data mining techniques.

are of interest of customers who are living in City1 and which contain P1 and P9 products. The second page contains a set of recommended links to product pages that are of interest of customers who are living in City2 and which contain P5 and P6 products.

As a result, it is clear that the previous improvements to the Web site prototype design will contribute to a better-designed Web site. These improvements will facilitate and improve customer navigation in the Web site, thereby encouraging the customer to buy more of the available products. The improvements also provide more opportunity to look at some products that may be of interest, and facilitate and support services introduced for customers, which will consequently increase the company's overall profit.

6.2 ASSOCIATION RULE MINING FOR ENHANCED MARKETING

One major application domain of data mining is the use of association rule mining to analyze market basket data. A transactions database contains information about customers' transactions, and each transaction is a collection of items. Association rule mining captures the relationships between different items. An association rule finds the notion that two different items occur together in the transactions database. An association rule has the form $X => Y$, where X and Y are sets of items and have no items in common. Given a database of transactions D, where each transaction $T \in D$ is a set of items, $X => Y$ denotes that whenever a transaction T contains X, then there is a probability that it contains Y, too. The rule $X => Y$ holds in the transactions set T with confidence c if c% of transactions in T that contain X also contain Y. The rule has support s in T if s% of all transactions in T contain both X and Y. Association rule mining is finding all association rules that have support and confidence values greater than or equal to a user-specified minimum support (minsup) and minimum confidence (minconf), respectively. Those rules are called interesting association rules. In this approach,[13] besides the usage of interesting association rules, the association rules that do not satisfy minimum requirements (i.e., have support and confidence values less than the user-specified minsup and minconf, respectively) are considered in the decision-making process. Suppose that we have a database of customer transactions for some store, that the store sells its products online through its own Web site, and that we have a log file that records user sessions and navigations through the Web site pages; the method is summarized as follows:

1. Periodical mining for association rules. The period length is user specified. It depends on different factors, such as the type of products available in the store, the expected time of the change of user behavior, and how often we add new products to the products set or remove some products from that set. For example, a store that has frequent addition/removal of products should have a shorter period than that of stable products.
2. From the first step we get three types of association rules:
   - *Interesting association rules,* which are rules that have support and confidence values greater than or equal to minsup and minconf, respectively.
   - *Semi-interesting association rules,* which have support and confidence values less than the user-specified minsup and minconf, respectively. However, their values are close to minsup and minconf values. For example, if the minsup is 10% and we have an association rule that has a 7% support value, then this rule is considered a semi-interesting association rule.
   - *Non-interesting association rules,* which are rules that have support and confidence values much lower than the user-specified minsup and minconf values, respectively. These rules belong to products that sell weakly.
3. We use these last three types of association rules to make decisions. Interesting association rules give an idea about the relationships between different products; for example, how often two products are sold together.

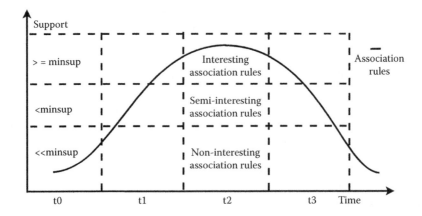

FIGURE 6.3 The interestingness of association rules in a set of products with respect to different time periods.

From that, we can, for example, make offers/discounts to encourage customers to buy those products. Figure 6.3 represents the behavior of association rules of a set of products through different periods. The x-axis represents the time in which association rules through that set of products, during t0, ..., t3 time periods, are extracted. The y-axis represents the interestingness of association rules represented by different support values. The first sector represents non-interesting association rules, represented by << minsup. The second sector represents semi-interesting association rules, represented by < minsup. The upper sector represents interesting association rules, represented by >= minsup. t0 is the first period in which we start to sell that product. We see no interesting association rules in that period. Then, in the t1 period, we get three types of association rules: non-interesting, semi-interesting, and interesting. Non-interesting association rules represent the products that still have weak sales. Usually, the sales of some products are weak because either they were recently added to the products set, the customers are not familiar with such products, or the products are too old to be interesting for the customers. In all cases, more promotions need to be made in order to increase the sales of those products. If the products have interesting association rules between them, then they are considered well-sold products. Semi-interesting association rules represent the products that start to have good sales, but they are not good enough to be considered well-sold products. This also gives an indication that those products could be a part of the set of well-sold products in the next period. To make them well-sold products, we can make promotions or offers for those products to encourage customers to buy more, which may bring those products to the set of well-sold products. The curve in the third period t2 represents interesting association rules. The goal is to keep the products in the set of well-sold products as long as possible. In the fourth period t3, the products start to have decreased sales for several reasons, for example, the availability of competitive products in other companies. To solve this problem, we can improve the sales of those products by making offers for those products in a way that attracts, the customers to our products and keeps them away from competitive products, which will bring our products back to the well-sold products set and keep them in that set longer. In that way, we give the sales manager a better view about the products and their behavior and help him or her to make the right decisions and better marketing strategies. We can also predict and control the next best sales, which will consequently increase the company's overall profit.

This method can be applied to both the transactions database of a physical store and to the log file of an online store in the case that the store has its own Web site and sells its products online. In the case of mining the log file of the online store, we can use the extracted association rules to improve/maintain the structure of the Web site, improve the way that some products are presented to the customer, and make offers and promotions on the store's Web site.

6.3   TEMPORAL FREQUENT ITEM SET MINING

A fundamental problem for mining association rules is to mine frequent item sets. In our approach,[14] we study the behavior of frequent item sets with respect to time. A method for finding interesting frequent item sets is introduced. In a Web log file, the frequent item sets represent URLs that are frequently visited by the users. To include the temporal information in our analysis, for each frequent item set $f \in FI$, the set of covering transactions cover(f) are found:

$$f \in FI, \text{cover}(f) = \{t: t \in T, f \subset t\}$$

where f is a frequent item set, FI is the set of all frequent item sets, and t is a transaction belonging to the set of all transactions T. A time series for each frequent set $f \in FI$ is constructed as follows.

First, all covering transactions cover(f) are determined for f. Second, the set of time stamps of the session corresponding to all $t \in$ cover(f) is found. Third, the found set of time stamps is ordered and forms the time series $S(f)$ corresponding to the frequent item set f. The length of $S(f)$ equals the support of f:

$$f \in FI, \text{length}(S(f)) = \text{support}(f) \geq \text{minsup}$$

6.3.1   Definition

A frequent item set A is interesting if tc-median($S(A)$) $\leq \delta$, where tc is the current time, δ is some period of time, $S(A)$ is the time series of the frequent item set A, and median($S(A)$) is the median of the ordered time series of the frequent item set A. A necessary condition for frequent item sets to be interesting is that all frequent item sets from the transactions should be within the time interval $[tc - \delta, tc]$ with respect to minimum support minsup/2. This gives a superset of all interesting frequent item sets. The necessary condition can be used either as a preprocessing step to search for frequent item sets within the determined interval or as an extension to the a priori algorithm to prune non-interesting frequent item sets. Figure 6.4 shows an example of interesting and non-interesting frequent item sets. The frequent item sets $\{b,d\}$ and $\{a,b,c\}$ are not interesting because the median is outside the time interval

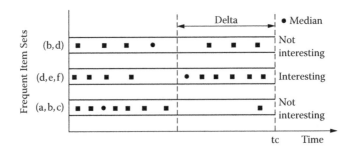

FIGURE 6.4 Interesting and non-interesting frequent item sets.

$[tc - \delta, tc]$. It is also clear that the frequent item set $\{a,b,c\}$ is too old to be interesting. On the other hand, $\{d,e,f\}$ is interesting because the median of its time series is within the determined interval. This method can be applied to different fields, for example, finding the most sold sets of products in the last 6 months. Another application area is in search engine log files to find out the most searched keywords in the last period.

6.4   SUMMARY

In this chapter, we investigated two main approaches to use data mining to improve Web site design. The first approach is using data mining to improve and maintain Web sites, getting benefit from information available from Web sites such as information about Web site usage, content, and structure. The second approach is different from the first one in that it uses data mining as a tool to help build well-structured Web sites in the design phase before those Web sites are published. In that way, much maintenance time and cost can be saved and we can ensure that the designed Web site can fit our requirements and marketing strategies. Then we saw how we can get benefit from interesting and non-interesting association rules to study, control, and predict product trends and behaviors with respect to different periods. A further method to include the temporal aspect in the process of searching for interesting frequent item sets was introduced, and a new measure to define interesting frequent item sets was also introduced.

REFERENCES

1. Gehrke, D. Determinants of successful website design: relative importance and recommendations for effectiveness, *HICSS 1999: Proceedings of the Thirty-second Annual Hawaii International Conference on System Sciences*, 50, 5042, 1999.
2. Troyer O., Goedefroy, W., and Meersman, R. UR-WSDM: adding user requirements granularity to model web based information systems, In *Proceedings of the First Workshop on Hypermedia Development Hypertext*, Pittsburgh, 1998.
3. Lohse, G.L. and Spiller, P. Electronic shopping. *Communications of the ACM*, 41, 81–88, 1998.
4. Chou, E. Redesigning a large and complex website: how to begin, and a method for success, *SIGUCCS 2002: Proceedings of the 30th Annual ACM SIGUCCS Conference on User Services*, ACM Press, New York, 2002, pp. 22–28.
5. Berendt, B. and Spiliopoulou, M. Analysis of navigational behavior in web sites integrating multiple information system, *VLDB Journal*, 9, 56–75, 2000.
6. Liu, B., Ma, Y., and Yu, P.S. Discovering unexpected information from your competitors' web sites, *Proceedings of the 7th ACM SIGKDD International Conference on Knowledge Discovery and Data Mining,* ACM Press, New York, 2001, pp. 144–153.
7. Kilfoil, M., Ghorbani, A., Xing, W., Lei, Z., Lu, J., Zhang, J., and Xu, X. Toward an adaptive web: the state of the art and science, In *Proceedings of CNSR 2003,* Moncton, Canada, 119–130, 2003.
8. Gedov, V., Stolz, C., Neuneier, R., Skubacz, M., and Seipel, D. Matching web site structure and content, *Proceedings of the WWW Conference*, 2004, ACM Press, New York, 2004, 286–287.

9. Brusilovsky, P. Efficient techniques for adaptive hypermedia, *Intelligent Hypertext,* 12–30, 1997.

10. Perkowitz, M. and Etzioni, O. Adaptive web sites: automatically synthesizing web pages, In *Proceedings 15th National Conference on Artificial Intelligence and 10th Innovative Applications of Artificial Intelligence Conference (AAAI 98/IAAI 98),* 727–73, 1998.

11. Omari, A., Conrad, S., and Alcic, S. Designing a well-structured e-shop using association rule mining, *Proceedings of 4th International Conference on Innovations in Information Technology,* Dubai, United Arab Emirates. 18–20 November 2007, IEEE Communication Society.

12. Omari, A. and Conrad, S. On the usage of data mining to support website designers to have better designed websites; *Proceedings of the Advanced International Conference on Telecommunications and International Conference on Internet and Web Applications and Services (AICT/ICIW 2006),* Guadeloupe, French Caribbean, 19–25 February 2006, IEEE Computer Society.

13. Omari, A. and Conrad, S. On controlling and prediction of next best sellings through periodical mining for {semi/non}-interesting association rules, *1st International Conference on Digital Communications and Computer Applications (DCCA2007),* Jordan University of Science and Technology, Irbid, Jordan, 19–22 March 2007.

14. Omari, A. Hinneburg, A., and Conrad, S. Temporal frequent item set mining. knowledge discovery, *Data Mining Machine Learning (KDML 2007),* 24–26 September 2007, Halle, Germany.

7 Discourse Analysis and Creativity Support for Concept Product Design

Noriko Imafuji Yasui, Xavier Llorà, and David E. Goldberg

CONTENTS

7.1 KEY ELEMENTS EXTRACTION FROM ONLINE, TEXT-BASED DISCUSSIONS

One of the biggest advantages of using network-based communication is that numerous ideas, opinions, and interests by diverse people can be easily collected. Because reading through all the communication logs is impractical, extracting key elements of the communication is an essential and important component of discourse analysis. This chapter reviews an algorithm for finding key discussants and key terms simultaneously, called the key elements extraction (KEE) algorithm.[1]

KEE is an algorithm for finding key persons and key terms of a discussion by scoring participants and terms in the context of their significance in discussions.

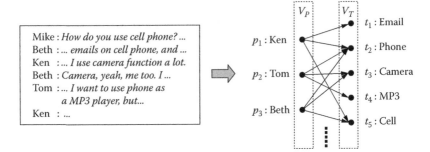

FIGURE 7.1 Building bipartite graph from discussion. V_P and V_T consist of a set of participants and a set of terms in the participants' messages, respectively.

Higher-scored participants are key persons having innovative and creative ideas or potential for producing them. Higher scored terms are key terms indicating or leading to innovative and creative ideas. KEE is based on the idea of a mutually reinforcing relationship between participants and terms: significant participants are the participants using many significant terms, and, conversely, significant terms are the terms used by many significant participants. KEE uses a HITS (hyperlink-induced topic search) algorithm[2] in an unintended way. HITS is an algorithm for ranking Web pages in terms of hubs and authorities. KEE is an algorithm applying the HITS framework to text mining and obtains scores for ranking participants and terms by an iterative calculation.

A discussion is represented by a weighted directed bipartite graph $G(V,E)$, where V and E are sets of nodes and weighted edges, respectively. Let V_P be a set of participants of the discussion and V_T be a set of terms used by the participants, $V = V_P \cup V_T$, $V_P \cap V_T = \phi$. Let denote an edge between $p_i \in V_p$ and $t_j \in V_T$ and its weight by (p_i, t_j) and $w(p_i, t_j)$, respectively. $w(p_i, t_j) = m$, if the participant p_i used the term t_j m times. Figure 7.1 depicts an example of building the bipartite graph (partially depicted).

Participants and terms are ranked by key scores of participants (or participant scores) and key scores of terms (or term scores). Let $s(p_i)$ and $s(t_j)$ denote the key score of participant p_i and the key score of term t_j, respectively. Similar to the HITS algorithm,[2] the mutually reinforcing relationship in the KEE algorithm is as follows. If the participant p_i had used many terms with high key scores, then he or she should receive a high participant score; and if the term t_j had been used by many participants with a high key score, then the term should receive a high term score.

The KEE algorithm obtains participant and term scores simultaneously by an iterative calculation. Given participant scores $s(p_i)$ and term scores $s(t_j)$, $s(p_i)$ and $s(t_j)$ are updated by the following calculations. $\alpha(t_j)$ is a weighting factor for the term t_j, which will not be argued here because of lack of space (please refer to Equation [7.1]).

$$s(p_i) \rightarrow \sum_{(p_i,t_j)\in E} s(t_j) \times w(p_i,t_j) \times \alpha(t_j) \tag{7.1}$$

$$s(t_j) \rightarrow \sum_{(p_i,t_j)\in E} s(p_i) \times w(p_i,t_j) \times \alpha(t_j) \tag{7.2}$$

7.1.1 KEE Algorithm

The KEE algorithm is as follows. A vector of participant scores and a vector of term scores are represented by S_P and S_T, respectively. k represents a natural number.

> Step 1: Initialize vectors $S_p^0 = (1,1,\ldots, 1)$, and $S_T^0 = (1,1,\ldots, 1)$
> Step 2: For $i = 1,2,\ldots, k,$
> [2-1] Obtain S_P^i by updating each entry using Equation 7.1 with S_T^{i-1}
> [2-2] Normalize S_P^i so the square sum in S_P^i to 1
> [2-3] Obtain S_T^i by updating each entry using Equation 7.2 with S_P^i
> [2-4] Normalize S_T^i so the square sum in S_T^i to 1
> Step 3: Return S_P^k and S_T^k.

Kleinberg proved theorems that S_P and S_T converge and the limits of S_P^k and S_T^k are obtained by the principal eigenvectors of $A^T A$ and AA^T.[2] A is an adjacency matrix; (i, j) entry is 1 if $(p_i, t_j) \in E$ and is 0 otherwise. Empirically, S_P and S_T converge very rapidly ($k = 6$ on the average in our experiments).

7.2 DISCOURSE ANALYSIS USING THE KEE ALGORITHM

The KEE algorithm is simple, is easy to implement, and works quite effectively. For given discussion logs, a highest-ranked participants list gives us an intuitive understanding of who was the center of the discussions. Likewise, a highest-ranked terms list tells us what topics were discussed. One of the biggest advantages of the KEE algorithm is its high applicability. Using the KEE algorithm, various aspects of discussions can be analyzed. Some essential analyses of discussions for supporting human creativity are presented in this section.

7.2.1 Summarization

The KEE algorithm can be used not only for finding important participants and terms but also for finding any types of important term sets and terms. The term sets can be sentences, paragraphs, messages, and so on. Furthermore, any type of documents (news articles, blog entries, e-mails, BBS messages, chat logs, and so on) can be analyzed by the KEE algorithm. In all cases, lists of important term sets and terms indicate the essence of the analyzed documents.

For example, suppose that we want to summarize a news article. To do so, we must find important sentences and terms in the article. The KEE algorithm is based on the mutual reinforcement relationship between sentences and terms: Important sentences are the sentences containing many important terms, and, conversely, important terms are the terms contained in many important sentences.

7.2.2 Delineating Topic and Discussant Transitions

Observing transitions of key terms and key persons enables us to understand how topics were changing and who was leading the topics. This is carried out by using

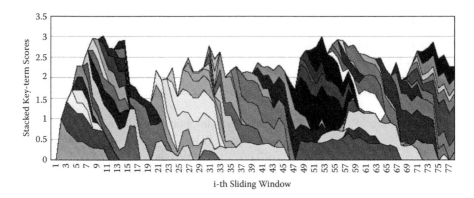

FIGURE 7.2 Key terms transition: *x* axis and *y* axis indicate sliding windows and stacked key term scores, respectively. Each area represents a term.

sliding windows over the discussion. Suppose that discussion messages are arranged in order by time stamp. A sliding window is a sequence of a certain number of messages. For each window, that is, a sequence of messages, we obtain key persons and key terms ranking lists by using the KEE algorithm. The ranking lists for each window are stored and prepared for visualizations.

Stack charts with sliding windows on the *x* axis and stacked key term scores on the *y* axis represent one of the most suitable visualizations for observing how key terms are changing and when topics are segmented. Figure 7.2 depicts an example of a key-term transition. Used sample discussion data consist of 78 messages by six participants. The main topic of the discussion is "future scenarios of cell phone usage." A sliding window consists of 10 messages, which means the *i*th window consists of the message *i* − 9 to the message *i*. The *x* axis and *y* axis indicate sliding windows and stacked key term scores, respectively. Each area represents a term.

Some term areas grow parallel, and blocks with the term areas can be observed. Each block indicates a topic. For example, the blocks can be found in the windows between 9–17, 25–33, 48–58, and 74–78, and the extracted key terms are 9–17:{talk, call, vibration, make answer}, 25–33:{function, instant, Bluetooth, Internet, phonebook}, 48–58:{computer, keyboard, screen, small, simply}, and 74–78:{battery, player, music, MP3, problem}.

The line chart in Figure 7.3 shows key participants transitions for the same data. The *x* axis and *y* axis indicate sliding windows (starting from the 11th window) and key persons scores, respectively. Each plotted line indicates each participant. From this chart, one can observe that Auth2 was leading the discussion in the early stage of the discussion, and conversely, Auth3 became the lead as the discussion was approaching its end.

Comparing two charts gives us much information in another important and interesting aspect: *Who is interested in which topic?* For example, look at the end of the discussion. Auth3 was dominating the discussion with the key terms *battery, player, music, MP3,* and *problem,* which enables us to have an assumption that Auth3 has

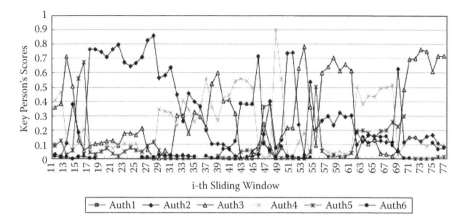

FIGURE 7.3 Key persons transition x axis and y axis indicate sliding windows and key persons scores, respectively. Each line represents each participant.

an interest in using a cell phone as a music player such as an MP3 but has concerns about batteries.

7.2.3 Social Network Analysis

Online discussion using BBS is preceded by participants' message positing and replying. A social network can be easily obtained by using the post-and-reply relationships between participants and the key term and key participant scores by the KEE algorithm. The social network is represented by a weighted directed graph and tells us which pair of participants was sharing the important topics in the discussion. The social network is represented by a weighted directed graph $G(V, E)$, where V and E are a set of participants and a set of weighted edges, respectively. Let $w(u, v)$ be a weighted edge from a participant u replying to another participant v. The edge weight $w(u, v)$ is measured by the sum of the scores of common terms in the messages from u to v, which is given by $w(u,v) = \sum_{k=1}^{n} r_k(u,v)$, where $r_k(u, v)$ is a post-reply relationship from a message m_u by participants u replying to a message m_v by other participants v, and $r_k(u,v) = \sum_{t \in T} c(t) \times s$, where T is a set of common terms in the messages m_u and m_v, and $c(t)$ is a key term score given by the KEE algorithm. S is a tuning parameter used for presenting $w(u, v)$ with a larger value. Because $c(t)$ is less than 1, $w(u, v)$ tends to be quite small. Figure 7.4 depicts a simple example of building the social network. If Jane is replying to Mike, the directed edge from Jane to Mike with the weight w(Jane, Mike) is equal to a sum of the key term scores of the common terms *phone*, *camera*, and *function*.

7.3 INTEGRATED DISCOURSE ANALYSIS: MESSAGE FEATURE MAP

The method and the discourse analyses presented in the previous section help us to understand the mainstream idea or interests of discussion participants. However, for enterprises, rare, not mainstream, opinions and ideas are also quite important.

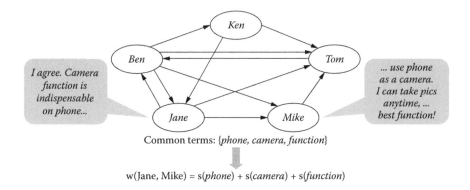

FIGURE 7.4 Sample of the message feature map. Each message is plotted at the point with its centrality and novelty.

Truly original new products or services come out of something people have never imagined before. We need a method for detecting not only the mainstream, but also the periphery. This section introduces a message feature map and visualization of message plots on a plane with two axes: centrality and novelty. A classification of message characteristics into four types is also discussed.

7.3.1 MEASURING MESSAGE FEATURE: CENTRALITY AND NOVELTY

Each message can be characterized in various aspects. To have creative ideas for new products, the most important aspects are the centrality—something many people support—and the novelty—something new. In the following, we introduce two metrics for measuring *centrality* and *novelty*.

7.3.1.1 Centrality

The centrality metric measures how much messages are center, and conversely peripheral, in the discussion. Remember that the KEE algorithm can be used for detecting not only key persons and key terms but also key messages and key terms: *important messages contain a lot of important terms, and conversely, important terms are contained in a lot of important messages.* The centrality metric uses the message score obtained by the KEE algorithm. If the centrality of the message (or the message centrality) is high, the message would be center of the discussion. Conversely, if the centrality is low, the message would discuss the peripheral topic.

Suppose a discussion can be represented by a sequence of messages $(m_1, m_2,..., m_n)$. By using the KEE algorithm, we calculate the score for each message k times with different sets of messages. The message centrality is obtained as the highest score in the k message scores. Let M be a message score vector obtained by the KEE algorithm and $M(m_i)$ be the score for the message m_i. Denote the centrality of the message m_i by $c(m_i)$, defined as $c(m_i) = \max_{i \le j < i+k} M_j(m_i)$, $0 \le c(m_i) < 1$, where $M_j(m_i)$ is a score of the message m_i by the calculation of a set of k messages $\{m_{j-k+1},...,m_{j-1},m_j\}$.

The centrality is transformed so that the values are in the range of -1 to 1. Let C be a vector which stores message centralities. Denote the transformed centrality by $c'(m_i)$, which is defined as follows. For simplification, instead of using a continuous mapping function on $[-1, 1]$ with three control points $0 \rightarrow 1$, $e \rightarrow 0$, and $1 \rightarrow 1$, the discontinuous mapping is used.

$$c'(m_i) = \begin{cases} c(m_i)/e - 1 & \text{if } c(m_i) < e \\ \{c(m_i) - e\}/(1-e) & \text{if } c(m_i) \geq e \end{cases}$$

e is a *virtual median* of centralities. The message score vector is normalized so that the square sum of the scores equals 1 (see line four in the KEE algorithm). Let e_i be the message score. In the case of the calculation of a set of k messages, $\sum_{i=1}^{k} x^2 = 1$. Suppose $x_1 = x_2 = \ldots x_k$; then $x_i = 1/\sqrt{k}$. We use $1/\sqrt{k}$ as e.

7.3.1.2   Novelty

The novelty metric measures how much messages include something new: ideas, topics, opinions. We assume that the message is novel if the messages contain many terms that are not previously used. Thus, the novelty is based on the number of new terms in each message. We define a new term in a message as a term that has not appeared in previous messages. If the novelty of the message (or the message novelty) is high, the message would contain something new and initiate a new topic. Conversely, the low novelty indicates the message would be following the existing topic, or the message would be of no importance (in the case of short messages).

Suppose a discussion can be represented by a sequence of messages $(m_1, m_2, \ldots, m_n)$. Denote the novelty of the message m_i by $n(m_i)$, which is defined by $n(m_i) = N^1(m_i)$, where $N^1(m_i)$ is a number of terms that do not exist in a set of the messages $\{m_{i-1}, \ldots m_{i-1}\}$.

The novelty is also transformed so that the values are in the range of -1 to 1. Let N be a vector that stores message novelties. Denote the transformed novelty by $N'(m_i)$. $N'(m_i)$ is defined as follows. Note that max indicates a threshold; if $n(m_i) >$ max, then $n(m_i) = 1$. min N indicates the lowest value in N.

$$n'(m_i) = \frac{2 \times n(m_i)}{\text{max} - \text{min } N} - 1$$

7.3.2   Message Feature Map

The message feature map plots each message on a centrality–novelty plane. Figure 7.5 depicts a sample of a message feature map. The horizontal axis indicates the centrality. The "more right" messages plotted are the more central of the discussions, and conversely, the more left, the more peripheral. The vertical axis indicates the novelty. The upper messages plotted are the higher novelty, and conversely, the lower, the more conventional. In this sample, messages are plotted with different shapes for each discussant.

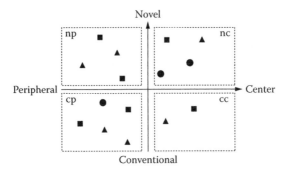

FIGURE 7.5 An example of a social network. Edge directions are based on the post/reply relationships. Each edge has weight obtained from key term scores.

7.3.2.1   Message Feature Classification

As seen in Figure 7.5, the message feature map has four areas; np (upper left), nc (upper right), cc (lower right), and cp (lower left). The message characteristics are different in the four plotted areas. The following are the plotted areas and the corresponding message characteristics.

> *np: Potential chances.* The messages plotted in this area have high novelties and low centralities. The messages of this type have new but rare ideas, opinions, and topics to which no other discussant is paying attention or of which no discussion is talking about further. These messages may turn out to be the sources of ideas for a new product or service.
>
> *nc: Topic triggers.* The messages plotted in this area have high novelties and high centralities. The messages of this type bring new ideas or topics to the discussions. Originating from these messages, the current discussion topics are shifted to the topics of these messages. This leads to a discussion mainstream, which can be detected by observing these messages.
>
> *cc: Topic followers.* The messages plotted in this area have low novelties and high centralities. The messages of this type give more ideas or deeper insights on the current topics. The discussion topics are somehow converged by these messages. The discussion mainstream can be detected by observing these messages.
>
> *cp: Trifles.* The messages plotted in this area have low novelties and low centralities. The messages of this type do not influence the ongoing discussion. The message content does not have any specific topic. Questions by discussion facilitators, yes-and-no answers, and simply short messages are plotted in this area. The discussion is inactive if many messages are plotted in this area.

Figure 7.6 depicts the message feature map for the same sample discussion (discussion topic: "future scenarios of cell phone usage") as used in the previous section. The horizontal axis represents the centrality and the vertical axis represents the novelty.

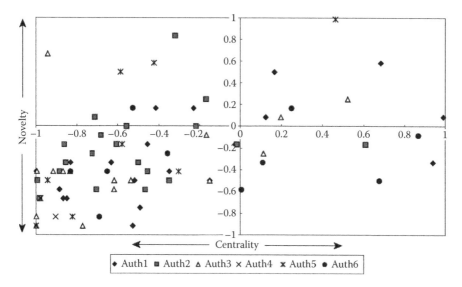

FIGURE 7.6 Message feature map. Each message is plotted with different color (or shape) for each participant.

Each message is plotted with a different color or shape for each participant. In the example, we used $k = 10$ for the centrality and $l = 10$ for the novelty. Because approximately 90% of messages contained fewer than 30 new terms, we used max = 30.

We can find some interesting facts in the messages by observing the map. By examining the messages plotted on the right, we could understand the mainstream discussion topics. For example, one of the messages plotted in the right-most in the nc area was about camera function on a cell phone, which had not been popular in the United States at the time of the discussion but became popular some time after the discussion. The messages plotted in the np area contained many variable minority opinions and ideas. For example, an idea of using a cell phone for money withdrawal was found in these messages. Typically, this type of message, which has no salient features based on term frequency, is difficult to detect without reading through all the messages. We can also observe participants' behaviors from the message feature map, for example, that participant Auth3 posted some messages with high novelties and that participant Auth5 tended to post messages having high centralities.

7.3.2.2   Message Feature Transition

The message feature transition can be represented as a weighted directed graph (see Figure 7.7), which we call a *message transition graph*. Denote the message transition graph by $G(V, E)$, where V is a set of vertices, that is, np, nc, cc, and cp. E is a set of edges between the

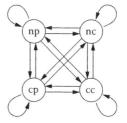

FIGURE 7.7 Sample of message feature transition graph.

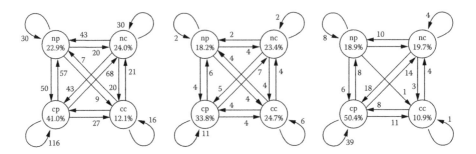

FIGURE 7.8 Message transition graphs for eight discussions (left), discussion1 (middle) and discussion2 (right). Each number beside the arrow indicates the edge weight. The rate in each area indicates the percentage of the messages plotted in the area.

vertices. Suppose a message transit from m_i to m_j means that the message m_i replies to the message m_j, and m_i and m_j are plotted in the area np and nc, respectively; then E contains an edge from np and nc. Observing the message feature transition graph gives us an insight into discussion dynamics.

Figure 7.8 depicts the message transition graphs for sample discussions. The sample consists of eight discussions with different groups of participants. The left graph was obtained by using all the discussions, and the middle and the right graphs were obtained by using two of the sample discussions, which we call discussion1 (the middle) and discussion2 (the right). Each discussion consists of 60 to 100 messages with 6 to 10 participants. Each number beside the arrow indicates how many times the messages transit from one area to the other. The rate in each circled area indicates the percentage of the messages plotted in the area.

On average, there is a tendency for many messages to be plotted in the area cp, and conversely, there are fewer messages plotted in the area cc. Compared with the average, in discussion1, many messages are plotted in the cc area. This indicates that the discussants in discussion1 tend to discuss certain topics deeply. In fact, the thread tree structure of discussion1 had many deep message chains. Conversely, compared with the average, in discussion2, many messages are plotted in the cp area. This indicates that the discussants in discussion2 tend to briefly give their opinions or ideas but not discuss certain topics deeply. In fact, the thread tree structure of discussion2 was very wide but had few deep message chains (the longest was four).

7.4   CREATIVITY SUPPORT FOR CONCEPT PRODUCT DESIGN

Generally, in the case of face-to-face discussions, one or more facilitators carefully observe the discussions, for example, participants' facial expressions, discussion activeness, and topics of interest. How skillfully they can control the discussions is the key element of maximizing profit from discussions such as focused group discussions and brainstorming discussions. Unlike face-to-face discussions, online discussion is done by communication with text only. How clearly and easily facilitators can catch hidden information behind the text is the key to success in online discussions.

Analyses in various aspects are much more significant than a deep analysis in one aspect. The message feature map discussed in the previous section is one of the most effective approaches for detecting various information and observation in a single visualization. Here are some examples of how to use the message feature map and the message transition graph to make discussions more profitable:

- Get the novel and unconventional ideas from the messages plotted in the area np. Conversely, catch the trends and get the ideas many people support from the messages plotted in the area cc.
- Let the discussion facilitators ask questions or talk to the discussants, whose messages are plotted in the area nc or np, when a lot of messages are plotted in the cp area, because it indicates the discussion is contracting.
- Make a group with the discussants whose messages are plotted in the area nc to have survey-type discussions, which, for example, begin with the question *Where do you want to go on summer vacation?* Conversely, make a group with the discussants whose messages are plotted in the area cc to have brainstorming-type discussions, which, for example, begin with the message *Please make the best plan for summer vacation.*

7.5   CONCLUSIONS

This chapter argues online discussion analysis for creativity support and consumer-based market strategy. Analysis from various aspects is essential for enhancing discussion creativities and understanding consumer needs. The KEE algorithm can be a core methodology of the analysis that enables us to have a clear understanding of discussions and understand participants' behavior. The message feature map gives us an intuitive understanding of the message feature and helps to identify the messages that should be focused on from the marketing viewpoint. The message feature graph can be polished using probabilistic models. Simulating discussions flow for a given set of participants can be very interesting as a next challenge. The simulation will be a very useful tool for discussion planning—determining the discussion goal, grouping people, and building discussion facilitation strategies.

REFERENCES

1. Imafuji, N.Y., Llorà, X., Goldberg, D.E., Washida, Y., and Tamura, H. Delineating topic and discussant transitions in online collaborative environments, *Proceedings of the 9th International Conference on Enterprise Information Systems (ICEIS 2007)*, 2007.
2. Kleinberg, J.M. Authoritative sources in a hyperlinked environment, *J. ACM*, 46, 604–632, 1999.

8 Data Crystallization with Human Interactions Applied for Designing New Products

Kenichi Horie, Yoshiharu Maeno,
and Yukio Ohsawa

CONTENTS

8.1 THE CHALLENGE IN THE BASIS: DETECTING ZERO-FREQUENCY KEY EVENTS

This chapter is dedicated to experts working in real domains where discoveries of unobservable events are desired. For example, consider an intelligence analysis in which analysts of criminal group behaviors are exploring missing links among members. The head (see the unobservable person at the top of Figure 8.1) of the criminal organization may phone subleaders managing local sections (Mr. A and Mr. B in

FIGURE 8.1 Intelligence analysis seeking hidden leader.

Figure 8.1) a few times. By responding to these top-level commands, each local section keeps its own internal communication via different media from that the boss used for contacting the subleaders. Then, the subleaders may meet to achieve consensus before responding to the boss. The boss may not attend these meetings. In this way, a person who is hidden from meetings' data may be the real boss.

We have been challenged to reveal events potentially important but never observed. Because unobservable events cannot be included in given data, existing data-mining methods have not worked well in identifying such events.

Data crystallization is the answer to this problem as an extension of our challenge of "chance discovery" in 2000.[1–3] Chance discovery is to discover a chance, defined as an event significant for decision. This has been a challenge beyond data mining, in that the goal was understanding of the meaning of rare events for people's decisions rather than learning rules for predicting rare events as done elsewhere.[4,5] For example, developers of cellular phones are seeking the opinions of users. Users' comments to the manufacturer significantly affect the decision of developers to redesign cellular phones; therefore, they can be regarded as "chances." Given these comments, data/text-mining tools can present relations among words and also predict the occurrence probabilities of words. On the other hand, methods of chance discovery show the relation of concepts behind the words and aid human–computer interactions for finding influential events, ideas, and people in the market,[6–8] recognizing the uncertainty of the future. For aiding this creation in the future rather than the prediction, tools of data visualization have been developed.[9–11]

However, the complexity of the real world is sometimes even beyond the reach of chance discovery: a few users of cellular phones, who never contact the manufacturer, may be likely to create a new way of using a phone to influence other users. The developers' question is "Where can we find users' real requirements when we do not hear from them?" Here arises the problem of data crystallization—finding important ideas and events that never appear in existing data.

8.2 DATA CRYSTALLIZATION AND ITS LIMITS

The objective of data crystallization is to understand the role of (not only rare, but also) unobservable significant events in the user's decision. In this chapter, we show how to integrate two new methods for the breakthrough from the current state in chance discovery.

The first is a method for visualizing data by inserting artificial dummy items. These dummy items mean unobservable events, of which the entity is totally unknown and is not included in the given data. By this, the user can see the overview of the real world, with the potential existence of significant but hidden (unobservable/unknown) events. The second is the person's cognitive process for understanding the role of hidden events in the real world. For example, if the boss of a criminal group is unobservable, the intelligence analyst should become interested in someone contacting leaders in local meetings (Mr. A and Mr. B in Figure 8.1). Then the analyst can go to the dangerous areas to observe the environments of Mr. A and Mr. B and collect the data on relevant events. As a result, the analyst can look at the visualization of the data by a computer and identify the most important part of the output figure. Basically, the process of chance discovery so far has been following the double helix process presented elsewhere.[2,12] The effect of this process, in which the granularity of information about chances is tuned, enables applications such as selling new products in marketing,[6,7] detecting earthquake indicators,[13] treatment opportunities of hepatitis,[14] and designing products.[19] To create finer strategic scenarios in real business, data crystallization is expected to work for introducing unobservable events to the creation, in which the previous methods of chance discovery introduced rare events included in the data. We present a new process of data crystallization with human–machine interaction in this chapter for enabling application of data crystallization to the problem of designing new products.

8.2.1 KEYGRAPH: THE BASIC TOOL FOR VISUALIZING EVENT MAPS

KeyGraph is a tool we developed for visualizing relationships among events. If the environment here means the existing activities are a criminal group, KeyGraph shows the relation of members on their coexisting frequencies (see previous work for details[9,15]). In Equation 8.1, let data D1 express a set of meetings, putting a period (".") at each end of meeting.

"Member1" in Equation 8.1 can be regarded as "member1_attend" (i.e., an event at which member appeared in a meeting place). Regarding each item in the data as an event rather than an object is meaningful in interpreting KeyGraph as a scenario map, where the sequence of events should be grasped from the connections among nodes.

$$D1 = member1\ member2\ member3.$$
$$member1\ member2\ member3\ member4.$$
$$member4\ member5\ member7\ member8.$$
$$member5\ member2\ member3\ member7\ member8.$$
$$member1\ member2\ member7\ member8\ member9.$$
$$member5\ member7\ member8\ member9. \tag{8.1}$$

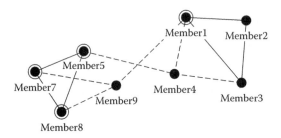

FIGURE 8.2 An output of KeyGraph.

The KeyGraph[9,16] of the following steps is then applied to D1. Figure 8.2 is obtained as a result.

>   *KeyGraph-Step 1:* The M1 most frequent events in the data (e.g., "member1" in Equation 8.1) are depicted with black nodes. The M2 most strongly co-occurring events–pairs get linked with black lines. Here, the co-occurrence is computed on the Jaccard equation in Equation 8.2, where Freq(X) means the number of baskets (lines in Equation 8.1), including elements of X. member1, member2, and member3 are connected with solid lines in Figure 8.2. Each connected graph forms one island, implying a basic context shared by its members.
>
>   *KeyGraph-Step 2:* M3 events co-occurring with multiple islands the most strongly (e.g., member9) are obtained as hubs. A path of links connecting islands via hubs is called a bridge. If a hub is rarer than black nodes, it is colored in a different color (e.g., red or white) than black. We regard such a hub as a candidate of chance, because it can be meaningful for a decision to jump from an island, corresponding to a context represented by the cluster of events, to another island.

Islands are obtained from D1, including sets {member1, member2, member3} and {member5, member6, member7}, respectively. The nodes in the islands show frequent events, and member4 and member9 show rare hubs bridging islands.

$$\mathrm{Ja}(e_i, e_j) = \frac{\mathrm{Freq}(e_i \cap e_j)}{\mathrm{Freq}(e_i \cup e_j)} \tag{8.2}$$

Figure 8.2 helps in making a scenario of criminal behaviors, such as "member1, member2, and member3 are working together, and member5, member6, member7 form another group. When they meet member9, member9 gives commands to both groups from a higher level of organization," via recollecting information about the members from the memory of intelligence analysts. The appearance of a bridging member can be a central topic to the analysts. Discussion of analysts by looking at the output diagram of KeyGraph may resolve the uncertainty about whether member4 or member9 is the real leader, because people can reflect the knowledge acquired from the real interaction with the external environment.

8.2.2 DATA CRYSTALLIZATION: EXTENDING KEYGRAPH FOR ANALYSIS OF HIDDEN EVENTS

Data crystallizing aims at presenting the hidden structure among events, including unobservable ones. This is realized with inserting dummy items, which may correspond to unobservable events, into the given data on past events. The existence of unobservable events and their relations with other events are then visualized by applying KeyGraph. The core of data crystallization is represented in the following algorithm:

Hidden_0 := {}; line_0 :={}; {M1 , M2}: given values
For all i, j in {0, 1, ..., N} such that j G.E. i do
    if line_i and line_j are same then Insert (D, i, j);
H: = KeyGraph (D, M1, M2, M3, = M1/2);
For j = 1 to N do
    If j is in H then Delete (D, j);

Here, D is the data set given. N is the number of lines (co-occurrence units) in the data. A dummy item gets inserted into each line of D. If two or more lines have the same set of items, the same dummy item is inserted into all those lines, supplied with the line number of the first of those lines. KeyGraph is applied to this data set with inserted dummy nodes. Formally, D is to be analyzed by the function KeyGraph (D, M1, M2, M3). The value of M1 represents the number of nodes to be visualized by KeyGraph. M2 is the number of links in each island and is set larger (smaller) if the user likes to see a small (large) number of large (small) islands. Then dummy items that did not appear on the bridges of KeyGraph get deleted from D.

Insert (D, i, j) means to insert dummy_j, the dummy node for the j-th line, in to the i-th line of data D and from data D. The second and the third lines of the procedure mean to insert dummy_i into the dummy_j-th line, and, if there is a line (the i-th line) of the same set of items as the j-th line, dummy_j is inserted into all those lines. Delete (D, j) means to delete dummy_j, the dummy item for the j-th line, from all its appearances in data D. H represents the set of line numbers where the dummy items, which appeared on the bridges of KeyGraph, are positioned in the data.

Data crystallization works similarly to snow crystallization. A dummy item plays the role of a particle of dust connecting molecules of water in the air. The increase in M2 corresponds to the decrease in temperature. In the case of snow, a well-structured crystal is made because the temperature is decreased gradually and water molecules are collected via dust participles.

To show a simple example, let us take a series of meetings in a team of 21 members as the target data to analyze. In Da, in Equation 8.3, part of the data on the participants is listed (obtained in Step 2) because of the concern with the real leader. In Equation 8.3, each line corresponds to a meeting.

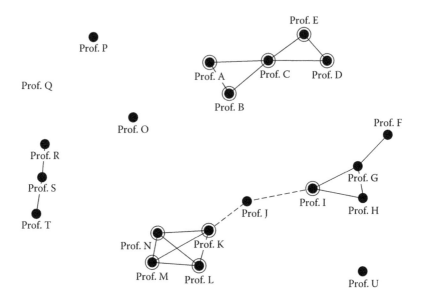

FIGURE 8.3 The original KeyGraph for members of a group.

Da = Prof.U Prof.K Prof.O Prof.J
       Prof.Q Prof.M Prof.A Prof.N Prof.I
       Prof.U Prof.K Prof.J Prof.I
       Prof.I Prof.J Prof.G
       Prof.O Prof.A Prof.U Prof.I Prof.N
       Prof.N Prof.L Prof.U Prof.M
       Prof.F Prof.G   (8.3)

Figure 8.3 is the result of KeyGraph, for M1 = 20, M2 = 20, and M3 = 20, from Da. Even though KeyGraph searches 20 hubs bridging among islands, we find that all islands without hubs connect. That is, the team looks like a set of groups irrelevant to each other. Thus, we should investigate hidden levels. The dummy nodes are inserted as 1_x for the x-th line, to obtain Db below.

Db = Prof.U Prof.K Prof.O Prof.J dummy1_1
       Prof.Q Prof.M Prof.A Prof.N Prof.I dummy1_2
       Prof.U Prof.K Prof.J Prof.I dummy1_3
       Prof.I Prof.J Prof.G dummy1_4
       Prof.O Prof.A Prof.U Prof.I Prof.N dummy1_5
       Prof.N Prof.L Prof.U Prof.M dummy1_6
       Prof.F Prof.G dummy1_7   (8.4)

Figure 8.4 is the output of KeyGraph for Db in Equation 8.4. Some dummy nodes appear in the graph, bridging among islands. For example, dummy1_5 between

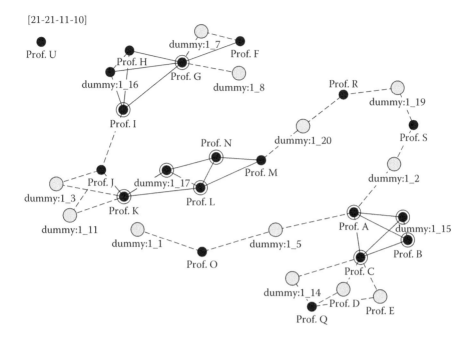

[21-21-11-10]

Prof. U

dummy:1_7

Prof. F

Prof. H

Prof. G

dummy:1_16

dummy:1_8

Prof. R

dummy:1_19

Prof. I

Prof. N

dummy:1_20

Prof. S

Prof. M

dummy:1_2

Prof. J

dummy:1_17

dummy:1_3

Prof. L

dummy:1_11

Prof. K

Prof. A

dummy:1_15

dummy:1_1

dummy:1_5

Prof. B

Prof. O

Prof. C

dummy:1_14

Prof. D

Prof. E

Prof. Q

FIGURE 8.4 The output for data with first-order dummies (1_x).

Prof.A and Prof.O means some hidden thing relevant to the fifth meeting (the fifth line in Equation 8.4) made a significant bridge.

From the new figure obtained by data crystallization, we can obtain newer findings. For example, dummy1_1 means there might have been some powerful leader who just sent a command such as "call a meeting for this problem!" to the members of the first meeting. He or she may not have appeared in the meetings, but the command can be regarded as the first voice of the meeting (i.e., he or she is the hidden leader).

Obtaining the diagram in Figure 8.4, we obtain the new data set as in Equation 8.5 by leaving dummy items appearing in Figure 8.4. The two dummies as dummy1_4 and dummy1_6 are discarded, because they do not appear in Figure 8.4.

$$
\begin{aligned}
Dc = \ &\text{Prof.U Prof.K Prof.O Prof.J dummy1\_1} \\
&\text{Prof.Q Prof.M Prof.A Prof.N Prof.I dummy1\_2} \\
&\text{Prof.U Prof.K Prof.J Prof.I dummy1\_3} \\
&\text{Prof.I Prof.J Prof.G} \\
&\text{Prof.O Prof.A Prof.U Prof.I Prof.N dummy 1\_5} \\
&\text{Prof.N Prof.L Prof.U Prof.M} \\
&\text{Prof.F Prof.G dummy 1\_7} \qquad\qquad\qquad\qquad (8.5)
\end{aligned}
$$

Ohsawa presented a method to automatically decrease M2, corresponding to the temperature in winter.[16] The expected result is that changing granularity of a crystallized structure can be obtained. For example, in the application of Ohsawa's data crystallization to the data on people's meetings, relations were shown between a lower-level leader, such as the leader of a small subgroup, and the top leader, such as the dean of a school faculty. However, according to the experiments, his method worked only for a small number of items in the data.[16] For a larger number of items, meaningless dummy nodes appear in the output of a graph of data crystallization. Although Ohsawa proposed combining the talent of humans to the data crystallization algorithm, it was a sheer extension of the existing double helix process of chance discovery. For real application of data crystallization, because dummy nodes do not have names corresponding to real entities in the real world, people demand to see more simplified structures.

8.3   REFINEMENT BY HUMAN-INTERACTIVE ANNEALING

Human-interactive annealing is a new technique; the basic procedure has been presented by Maeno and Ohsawa.[17,18] The process is similar to the annealing in materials science and simulated annealing. A graph (i.e., scenario map, as mentioned previously) is used to represent crystallized unobservable events. The annealing process is a combination of two complementary elements: interpretation by humans and crystallization by a computer. The two elements are combined as in Figure 8.5.

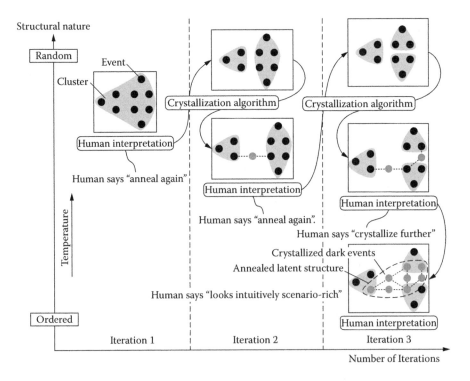

FIGURE 8.5 Human-interactive annealing: iteration of human's interpretation and data crystallization.

Here, temperature is the single control parameter representing the depth of people's understanding of the real world's structure. When the understanding should be more complete, the temperature should be set higher, resulting in more complex hidden structures among many islands (co-occurrence clusters of observable events). This leads to the discovery of novel and unexpected scenarios. On the other hand, when the understanding should be simplified, the temperature should be set lower. Then the user tries to understand the basic structures from the graph. This iteration in the annealing process is continued until users are satisfied with their understanding of the material.

As the temperature increases, the following three structural changes occur on the graph. These are embedded in the annealing process and independent of the stable deterministic crystallization algorithm.

1. Weaker intercluster links (i.e., connecting dummy events and clusters) are destroyed.
2. Weaker intracluster links (i.e., connecting events within a cluster) are destroyed.
3. The events are divided into a larger number of clusters.

In this annealing-based crystallization, the computer basically analyzes the occurrence frequencies and the co-occurrence of events. As in Figure 8.5, in the heating step up to the specified peak temperature, the number of edges between visible events decreases (i.e., weak associations are destroyed and crystallized unobservable events disappear). Then a cooling step comes after the heating step, where event relations are solidified as the temperature goes down. The number of unobservable events between clusters of visible events, corresponding to islands in KeyGraph, increases in the graph. As a result, the clusters are connected to each other to form a single large structure. The crystallization is followed by a user's interpretation, where it is checked whether the termination condition is fulfilled (i.e., if the user is satisfied with his or her understanding).

It has been shown that human-interactive annealing successfully obtains hidden leaders even if they do not appear in the given dataset.[18] The method has been applied to a large data set of people's meetings produced from an artificial human network produced by a community simulator. The results showed that people who meet many people can be restored by this method, even though they had been deleted from the original dataset. The scalability of the method has been thus evaluated, because the network included 100 nodes, which was much larger than the 20 nodes they had been testing. However, this was a problem: the application to real-world problems is still open to data crystallization and human-interactive annealing.

8.4 APPLICATION TO DESIGNING NEW PRODUCTS FROM PATENT DOCUMENTS

8.4.1 REDESIGN OF SURFACE INSPECTION SYSTEM

Here, the human-interactive annealing method has been applied to improve a surface inspection system (SIS), a machine for detecting defects on works by charge-coupled devices (CCD). As shown in Figure 8.6, an SIS carries a roll of film on its belt conveyer,

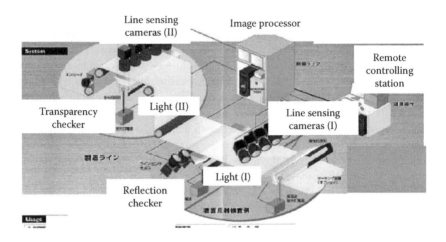

FIGURE 8.6 Outline of liner CCD surface inspection system (SIS).

and lights are shone from over and under the film. Then CCD cameras take the pictures of the reflected and transpired lights and send the images to the computer. This computer runs the image analysis software and detects and classifies the detected defects into classes useful for understanding the cause of the defects on the film. The function of the SIS has been realized and refined by the combination of the staff members' multidisciplinary expertise.

A problem in developing and improving this system was that the development staff members were from different domains (i.e., experts of camera, lights, computer programming, and the controlling system of the belt conveyer). This caused difficulty in communicating about each other's technology, and, as a result, each person had to be confined in his or her fixed area of thoughts and proposals. Thus, the company desired an efficient redesign method.

The original method of chance discovery was applied using KeyGraph to show the structure of words in the combined text of business reports showing the claims of customers.[19] The text was dealt with as the data in the form of Equation 8.1, by regarding each word as a meeting member and regarding each sentence as a basket (i.e., as a line corresponding to a meeting in Equation 8.1). Because each development staff member reported on a restricted focus on his or her domain, the islands in the obtained KeyGraph (as in Figure 8.7) corresponded to established knowledge specific to those domains. Also, the bridging nodes showing the rare words showed some bridges between these specific domains. A useful point was that the nodes at these bridges were the words meaning some type of defects on the CCD film. As a result, they understood that the detection of each kind of defect required a specific combination of technologies (e.g., a defect called "spottiness" can be detected by a combination of technologies of light and of image analysis software). In the end, the company registered five patents and developed a new machine that was the highest ranked in SIS by inventing a design scenario to detect some kinds of scratches by combining new software and lighting conditions.

Their next challenge was to remain the leading company in the SIS market, not only responding to the claims of customers but also finding new combinations of

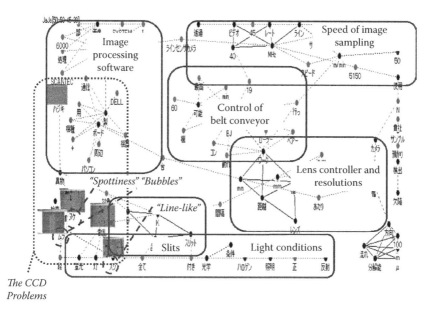

FIGURE 8.7 The simple KeyGraph applied to designing a CCD scratch inspection system.

technologies, which customers rarely notice. For this purpose, the company now focused attention on the rich public document text on patents. This new data set, however, was not easy to deal with by the KeyGraph in Appendix A, because each patent was described by words narrowly restricted to specific technical terms than the business reported. As a result, the collection of patent documents seldom had bridging words i.e., item, such as the "spottiness" in the example of their previous work.

Thus, in this chapter, we present our application of data crystallization with human-interactive annealing to patent documents for discovering hidden ideas that underlie the dummy nodes bridging the islands.

8.4.2 Preliminary Study and Tasks

We executed a preliminary test based on text data made from combining the documents of six Japanese patents of marking systems for defects on CCD detected by SIS. All claims in these patents were used for text data and processed by data crystallization with human-interactive annealing (DCHA). After the iterations in the human-interactive annealing, an event map was shown on KeyGraph.

We executed the test for 2 hours, with four examinees (one sales manager, two sales engineers, and one engineer). They were instructed to communicate while looking at the output graph of KeyGraph (a result of data crystallization), in which each opinion was to be a scenario for developing products.

However, only one engineer understood the meaning of all clusters in the diagram and created scenarios of each cluster. Neither new words corresponding to the hidden events nor new scenarios were communicated or created. We interviewed all examinees after the preliminary test and found the major problems as listed below:

1. There were too many hidden events to predict and it was difficult to think of suitable words to express the hidden events connecting other words in clusters.
2. The word structure was complex, reflecting the complexity of patent documents, composed of multiple contents such as purposes, implementations, and technologies.

8.4.3 IMPROVEMENT OF TASKS

The improvements listed below were obtained, heuristically, for solving the problems above in the preliminary tests.

Improvement 1: Choose topics from patent claims for text data to focus on limited topics.

Improvement 2: Add each patent number to the end of the corresponding claim, as if they were words to be dealt with by KeyGraph.

Improvement 3: Mark each island (cluster) with a keyword summarizing the cluster.

Improvement 4: Make Pictograms (Figure 8.8) for all patents. A Pictogram is a visual summary of each patent, composed of the patent number, the flow

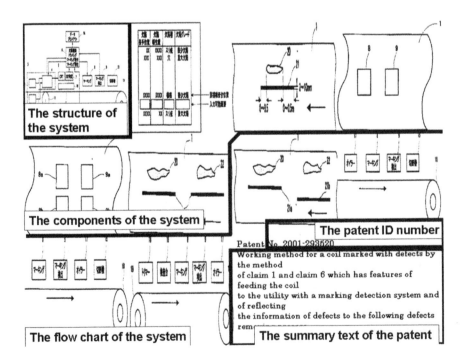

FIGURE 8.8 A sample Pictogram.

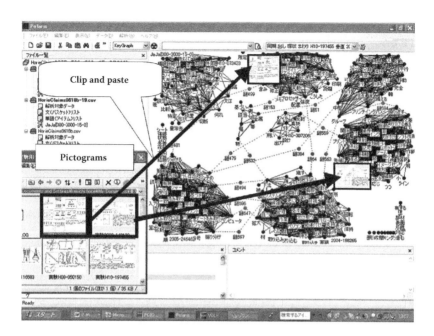

FIGURE 8.9 Pasting *Pictogram* on the event map.

chart of the patented system, and drawings of components corresponding to the claims in the patent. When a user is interested in a part of the output graph KeyGraph, Pictograms including the words in that part are extracted and shown to the user. Then the user chooses the suitable Pictogram and pastes it onto the KeyGraph (Figure 8.9).

Improvement 5: Set the presentation timing of Pictograms to examinees to first show the Pictogram of patent numbers for the reinterpretation of clusters that have been interpreted. Then show Pictograms corresponding to the hidden events, when scenarios are about to be considered. Here, examinees are instructed to consider as many hidden events as possible to connect islands in creating new scenarios. This order of presentation is based on the results of Horie et al.,[19] in which users who successfully created useful scenarios first paid attention to clusters and then to the bridges in applying KeyGraph to product designs.

8.5 THE APPLICATION OF DCHS TO PATENT DOCUMENTS

8.5.1 EXPERIMENT CONDITION AND THE PROCESS

We adopted the new proposals for the application of the DCHA process to 106 Japanese patents. These included both "marking systems" and "inspection," and the real test was executed by the six steps below for 2 hours with five examinees: one sales manager, two sales engineers, and two engineers working in a company (called Company A hereafter) to develop and sell SIS machines. Following the steps below

TABLE 8.1
Cluster Title and Scenarios

Cluster	Item	Scenarios
1	Title	Technology for the marking system
	Scenario	System to remove specific defects from unmasked planate area by irradiating laser beam
2	Title	Controller of marking system
	Scenario	Control system that transmits a position of defects on the film by measuring the distance between defects
	Correction of scenarios	Control system to transmit the positional information to the back-end equipment, which identifies the position of defects
3	Title	Driving mechanism of marking system
	Scenario	Marking equipment that moves in parallel with the travel direction of film on roll and is able to mark multiple defects
4	Title	Inkjet marking system
	Scenario	Robotic arms, by which inkjet heads are automatically moved to a position of defects on the product and mark the defects by ink
5	Title	Back-end inspection system
	Scenario	Computational system to detect the position of defects and separate controversial defects for aiding visual inspections at the back ends
6	Title	Post process of CCD inspection
	Scenario	System to allocate the number to each defect on the film
	Correction of scenarios	Computer system for assigning products in allocated gates by reading number issued by image sensor beforehand

and reflecting the improvements (Improvement 1 through Improvement 6), the examinees undertook a design communication by looking at the result of KeyGraph with data crystallization.

[Phase of presenting the scenario map]
Step 1: See the event map visualized by KeyGraph with data crystallization on the text data obtained by combining the documents of 106 patents.
[Phase of discussing islands]
Step 2: Interpret events underlying each cluster in the graph and write the title corresponding to the meaning of each cluster on the presented graph (Table 8.1).
Step 3: Talk about scenarios using words in each cluster and write them on the whiteboard during the discussion (Table 8.1).
Step 4: Find suitable Pictograms (Figure 8.10) to be pasted to patent numbers in clusters depicted as circles in Figure 8.10 and reinterpret the clusters referring to them.
[Phase of discussing bridges]
Step 5: Paste Pictograms corresponding to dummy nodes in the graph, considering hidden events (e.g., "Hidden events1," "Hidden events2," and so on) to connect the clusters in the graph (Figure 8.11). Then write newly created

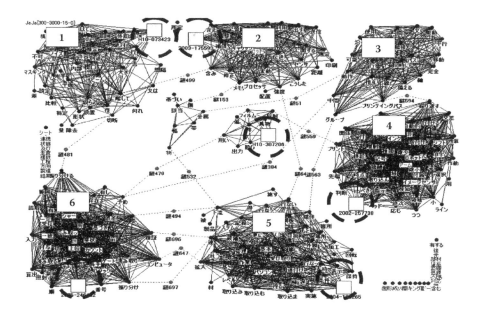

FIGURE 8.10 Pasting Pictogram on each cluster (Step1 to Step4).

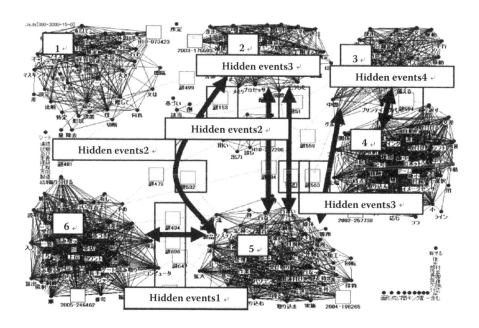

FIGURE 8.11 Pasting Pictogram on hidden events (Step5 to Step6).

scenarios on the whiteboard. For example, subjects may create a scenario "change the speed of conveyer with the progress of the film on the belt; then the back-end checking may be realized" by combining cluster No. 5 of "technology for back-end inspection system" and cluster No. 6 of "technology for control of CCD inspection" via the four hidden events (a double-headed arrow) at "Hidden events1."

Step 6: Select new scenarios that can be agreed on by all participants and evaluate them from the point of view of feasibility in development and marketing and of the product's novelty.

8.5.2 EXPERIMENTAL RESULTS

We evaluated the results of the procedure using the following criteria. It should be noted that the purpose of this evaluation was to see if the proposed procedure in Section 8.5.1 supplied users with the ability to obtain novel and acceptable ideas in their forthcoming teamwork. Thus, we do not include a comparison of KeyGraph with other methods but compare the scenarios obtained for the various bridging hidden events with scenarios and check if the difficulties stated in Section 8.4.2 were solved. Doing this, we can investigate if the hidden events, which play a significant role in the structure of the graph, really contributed to creating scenarios.

1. Creativity in reinterpreting clusters and correcting scenarios: Each scenario was finely reinterpreted with Pictograms on patents in each cluster at Step 4. Here, the two scenarios of clusters No. 2 and No. 6 were corrected (Table 8.1). The drawings and the charts on each Pictogram aided examinees in their different expertise to reinterpret the meaning of each cluster precisely. In comparison to the previous test in Section 8.4.2, we found an apparent improvement here.

2. Creating new scenarios via bridging dummy nodes: New scenarios emerged from the six clusters referring to Pictograms of hidden event numbers on the event map at Step 5 of Section 8.5.1. All the five examinees initially paid attention to "Hidden events1," which connected the No. 5 cluster titled "back-end inspection system" and the No. 6 cluster titled "post-process of CCD inspection." Then they paid attention to "Hidden events2" and "Hidden events3" following the procedures described in Step5. As a result, new scenarios continuously emerged, and those scenarios corresponded to the combination of scenarios underlying multiple clusters being bridged by the "hidden events." The meanings of hidden events were understood by the Pictograms, and these understandings were reflected to the created scenarios here.

After the experiment, the new scenarios were evaluated from the viewpoints of novelty of ideas and feasibility of development. Scenarios 4 and 6 after correction in Table 8.1 were selected and introduced into Company A's new products.

8.5.3 Discussion

In the DCHA process, 106 patents were separated into six clusters as a hidden structure and named with conceptual titles (Figure 8.11, Table 8.1). It is difficult, however, to find scenarios suitable for redesigning their products because only the top 300 nodal words appeared over excessive links in clusters. Our new method, showing a Pictogram of each patent number in creating scenarios, aided the examinees not only in interpreting each cluster deeply, but also in making the cross-disciplinary communication creative, as expected in the literature on creative groups of people.[20,21] All six clusters were reinterpreted and the initial two scenarios were corrected as in Table 8.1.

Furthermore, in the new scenario creation step after the reinterpretation of each cluster, the Pictograms on hidden events stimulated the creativity of the user, which had been born from the ambiguity in the information of dummy nodes[22] or possibly from asking questions such as "What is the meaning of these dummies?" as in Eris.[23] As a result, examinees perceived new and useful scenarios by bridging the basic clusters via their interpretation of dummy nodes on the additional information in the pasted Pictograms.

8.6 CONCLUSIONS

We applied DCHA to product redesigning in a real company. The results show the effect of inventing new industrial products design.

In this chapter, the DCHA process was performed well by creating new scenarios for new products and aiding in making a significant decision to develop them. No. 3 "Driving mechanism of marking system" in Table 8.1 was chosen and was started to develop a prototype model. It has been evaluated on basic functions by the company and is expected to be a new commercial product at its final stage in the near future. The tasks below, however, should be solved for efficiency in creating scenarios:

- Improve the visualization of words on each cluster to show the relation of them easily.
- Prepare multilateral data of nodes on clusters that are connected to hidden events to narrow the degree of ambiguity of hidden events.
- By modifying and improving these tasks of the DCHA process, the other application for real business can be expanded to patent analysis, analysis of consumer behaviors in marketing, and the analysis of disciplinary boundaries in science.

REFERENCES

1. Chance Discovery Consortium. Available online at: http://www.chancediscovery. com/english/index.php. Accessed June 30, 2008.
2. Ohsawa, Y. and McBurney, P. Eds. *Chance Discovery, Advanced Information Processing,* Springer-Verlag, Heidelberg 2003, pp. 2–15.

3. Ohsawa, Y. and Tsumoto, S. *Chance Discovery in Real World Decision Making, Series on Computational Intelligence,* Springer-Verlag, 2006.
4. Joshi, M., Kumar, V., and Agarwal, R. Evaluating boosting algorithms to classify rare classes: comparison and improvements, in *Proceedings of the First IEEE International Conference on Data Mining,* 2001.
5. Weiss, G.M. and Hirsh, H. Learning to predict rare events in event sequences, in *Proceedings of the Fourth International Conference on Knowledge Discovery and Data Mining (KDD-98),* AAAI Press, Menlo Park, CA, 1998, pp. 59–363.
6. Ohsawa, Y. and Usui, M. Creative marketing as application of chance discovery, in *Chance Discovery in Real World Decision Making, Computational Intelligence,* Ohsawa, Y. and Tsumoto, S., Eds., Springer-Verlag, 2006, pp. 253–272.
7. Ohsawa, Y. and Fukuda, H. Chance discovery by stimulated group of people—an application to understanding rare consumption of food, *J Contingencies Crisis Manage.,* 10, 129–138, 2002.
8. Yada, K., Motoda, H., Washio, T., and Miyawaki, A. (2005). Consumer behavior analysis by graph mining technique, *New Math. Natural Comput.,* 2, 59–68, 2005.
9. Ohsawa, Y. KeyGraph: visualized structure among event clusters, in Ohsawa, Y. and McBurney, P., Eds., *Chance Discovery,* Springer Verlag, 2003, pp. 262–275.
10. Okazaki, N. and Ohsawa, Y. Polaris: an integrated data miner for chance discovery, In *Proceedings of the 3rd International Workshop on Chance Discovery and Its Management,* Greece, 2003.
11. Matsumura, N., Matsuo, Y., Ohsawa, Y., and Ishizuka, M. (2002). Discovering emerging topics from WWW, *J. Contingencies Crisis Manage.,* 10, 73–81, 2002.
12. Ohsawa, Y. and Nara, Y. Understanding Internet users on double helical model of chance-discovery process, *New Generation Comp.,* 21, 109–122, 2003.
13. Ohsawa, Y. KeyGraph as risk explorer from earthquake sequence, *J. Contingencies Crisis Manage.,* 10, 119–128, 2002.
14. Ohsawa, Y., Fujie, H., Saiura, A., Okazaki, N., and Matsumura, N. Process to discovering iron decrease as chance to use interferon to hepatitis B, in *Multidisciplinary Approaches Theory in Medicine,* Paton, R., Ed., Elsevier, The Netherlands pp. 209–229, 2004.
15. Ohsawa, Y. Scenario maps on situational switch model, applied to blood-test data from hepatitis C patients, in *Chance Discoveries in Real World Decision Making,* Ohsawa, Y. and Tsumoto, S., Eds., Springer-Verlag, 2006, pp. 69–80.
16. Ohsawa, Y. Data crystallization: chance discovery extended for dealing with unobservable events, *New Math. Nat. Sci.,* 1, 373–392, 2005.
17. Maeno, Y. and Ohsawa, Y. Understanding of dark events for harnessing risk, in *Chance Discoveries in Real World Decision Making,* Ohsawa, Y. and Tsumoto, S., Eds., Springer-Verlag, 2006, pp. 373–392.
18. Maeno, Y. and Ohsawa, Y. Human-computer interactive annealing for crystallization of invisible dark events, *IEEE Trans. Industrial Electron.,* 54(2), 1184–1192, 2006.
19. Horie, K., Ohsawa, Y., and Okazaki, N. Products designed on scenario maps using Pictorial KeyGraph, *WSEAS Transitions Info. Sci. Appl.,* 3, 1324–1331, 2006.
20. Goldberg, D.E. *The Design of Innovation: Lessons from and for Competent Genetic Algorithms,* Kluwer Academic Publishers, Boston, 2002.
21. Fruchter, R., Ohsawa, Y., and Matsumura, N. Knowledge reuse through chance discovery from an enterprise design-build enterprise data store, *New Math. Nat. Comput.,* 3, 393–406, 2005.
22. Gaver, W.W., Beaver, J., and Benford, S. Ambiguity as a resource for design, in *Proceedings of Computer Human Interactions,* pp. 233–240, 2003.
23. Eris, O. *Effective Inquiry for Innovative Engineering Design,* Kluwer Academic, 2004.

9 Improving and Applying Chance Discovery for Design Analysis

Brett Bojduj

CONTENTS

9.1 INTRODUCTION

The activity of design is the activity of creating an artifact through the selection and composition (that is, the order in which the designer makes the selection) of available materials. Bertel, Freksa, and Vrachliotis[1] describe the process of architectural design, in particular, as follows.

> There are lots of variables designers can "play around" with: They include spatial dimensions like lengths, widths, or heights; shapes, materials, colors, to name but a few. Abstractly speaking, we can view design as consisting of a large feature space spun up by such variables.

If one takes Bertel et al.'s[1] way of looking at the design process as a "play" with features on a "large feature space," then it becomes apparent that choosing the correct feature to apply (i.e., choosing an action to perform) at each step in the design process becomes a complex problem in the sense that one action must be chosen out of many valid potentialities. The complexity of design is further increased by the subjective nature of determining the utility of a particular action to perform on a design. The application of an action to a design can be met both with favor and with opposition, based on the subjective judgment of individual aesthetics. Thus each action performed in the process of design should be carefully determined, as it will influence the outcome of the design artifact.

Because the process of design is a composition of sequential actions performed on a design, the need for an aid in design decision making becomes apparent. At each step in the design process, the designer must choose from a potentially large set of possible actions that can be applied to transform a design artifact. These actions do not merely have local effects, but rather have a direct effect on the final outcome of the design artifact. Thus if a methodology could be introduced to improve the designer's knowledge of the current state of a design artifact, the designer may be able to apply this better understanding to make better design decisions (i.e., choosing better actions to apply). In this chapter, a methodology is introduced that uses chance discovery to help guide the actions that are chosen in the design process, based on a chance discovery analysis of a design artifact as it currently is. First, we will spend some time explaining what is involved in the design process. Then we will discuss chance discovery and one of its visualization methods, KeyGraph. We will talk about an extension of KeyGraph, a hierarchical visualization method, which lends itself particularly well to design analysis. Finally, we will present an example of using chance discovery for the design of a software product.

9.2   DESIGN

We present a methodology that uses chance discovery for analysis of the current state of a design artifact, which can then be used to influence future design decisions and thus the final outcome of the design process (i.e., the artifact). To discuss how chance discovery can be used to guide a design process, we must first define more formally what we mean by "design." In our work here, it is useful to take Bojduj et al.'s definition of design.[4]

> Given a set of actions that can be applied to a concept, design is the process of selecting and applying one of the actions to the concept.

Though this definition of design may not be applicable in all cases, it is particularly useful for our work here because of its emphasis on both iteration of the design process and on selection out of an applicable set of actions. This definition of design conceptualizes design as an activity that begins with a concept. An example of such a concept could be the concept that a software program is needed to perform a certain task. Given the concept, there are certain actions one can take. For the concept of a needed software program, one can perform actions such as interviewing customers to determine requirements or writing software code to implement requirements that he or she already has. When one applies the action to the concept (i.e., implementing a requirement in software code), then it transforms the state of the design artifact. The concept may also change as the design artifact changes. This is an iterative process that is repeated until the designer has completed the design task. Thus the process of design can be defined as the selection and application of actions in accordance with a concept.

Based on the observation from Herbert Simon that humans are bounded in their rationality,[26] we argue that selecting actions in a design process is not likely to achieve optimal results, but rather only "good enough" results. This is because it can be argued that humans are unable to properly judge the utility of all the possible actions that can be applied to a design because they do not necessarily know the outcomes of those actions. Furthermore, as a consequence of being bounded in rationality, even if humans could know the outcome of all their actions, they would not have the cognitive knowledge processing capabilities to determine the best course of action.[25] Also, because many design decisions can be subjective in nature, it can be possible that there is no "right" way to do design. Bertel, Vrachliotis, and Freksa[2] state that in architectural design, "many design tasks or subtasks do not seem to have any solution at all." We believe that this same problem also exists in other design tasks because of the subjective nature inherent in many design decisions. In many design tasks, different humans will judge the outcomes differently; thus there really can be no way for designers, bounded in their rationality as they are, to know what design decisions will be universally accepted. This is an essential difficulty of design, which must be accepted and dealt with properly. To deal with the inherent complexity of design tasks, chance discovery can be used to analyze and thus achieve a greater understanding of the current state of a design artifact. This understanding can then be used to guide future design decisions.

9.3   CHANCE DISCOVERY

Chance discovery is "the realization of an opportunity or a risk in a decision-making environment."[3] In the context of chance discovery, a "chance" can be defined as "an event significant for decision making."[20] The premise behind chance discovery is that realizing a chance in a decision-making environment will present the decision maker with greater understanding of the dynamics of the problem domain. This allows chance discovery to provide "a means to invent the future rather than to predict the future."[15] Chance discovery accomplishes this by providing a collaborative methodology between a computer with data mining faculties and a human decision maker to expand the human decision maker's knowledge and understanding of the domain in which he or she is working.

Chance discovery has been successfully used to aid decision making in many disparate fields. Ohsawa[21] explored the use of chance discovery in the prediction of earthquakes by discovering relations between faultlines. Chance discovery has also been used to explore eating patterns and to provide a means for finding ways to alter eating patterns.[9,23] Additionally, chance discovery has been used to provide analysis of credit risks,[10,11] create a methodology for designing new patents,[12,13] and aid in the understanding of Internet users,[24] to name but a few of its successes.

Within the framework of chance discovery, Ohsawa and Fukuda[23] laid out three criteria for the evaluation of the efficacy of a chance.

1. Proposability—the ease with which a chance can be proposed
2. Unnoticeability—the difficulty of getting others to accept the chance
3. Growability—the rate at which people accept the chance

Within the context of using chance discovery for the analysis of the current state of a design artifact, these criteria can be used to determine the efficacy of a chance, because a chance that can easily be proposed and accepted by others is likely to be useful in a design environment, since typically other people will have to agree with a designer's design decisions if a product is to be successful. Because there exist no universally accepted quantitative value that satisfies each of these criteria, these criteria can be considered to be primarily qualitative in nature. However, this is a strength of these criteria and not a weakness, because, as Minsky puts it, "We turn to using quantities when we can't compare the qualities of things."[17] Also, as Freksa and Röhrig state, "Qualitative knowledge can be viewed as that aspect of knowledge which critically influences decisions."[8] Therefore, qualitative criteria such as these should be embraced.

Chance discovery is unequivocally a collaborative process between a computer, which analyzes and presents data to a human user, and a human user who assigns an interpretation to the presented data. In many situations, humans can work more efficiently with spatial representations compared with sentential representations.[7,14,27] This is an intuitive conclusion from the theory that humans are bounded in their rationality,[26] because spatial representations allow humans to relieve some of the burdens on their memory, thus freeing up cognititive capacities for other reasoning. Because humans are seemingly bounded in their rationality, presenting data visually assists the chance discovery process by allowing human collaborators in the process to offload a large burden from their memory. For visualizing relations among data in chance discovery, several methods have been developed.[16,22] In particular, we will focus on one of these methods: KeyGraph.

9.4   KEYGRAPH

KeyGraph is both a program and an algorithm for displaying information to aid the process of chance discovery.[22] KeyGraph displays relations among events in such a way that groups of related events can be grouped together visually. An example output from KeyGraph is shown in Figure 9.1. The output of KeyGraph can be categorized as events, event clusters, visible events, and chances. Events are data

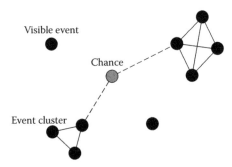

FIGURE 9.1 KeyGraph visualization of data. (Adapted from [15].)

items describing something significant in the problem domain. Many times these events are in the form of textual data describing the problem domain, where words or groups of words can be considered single events. Events that are closely related are grouped together into event clusters. The events within these clusters typically have a frequent co-occurrence together in the problem domain. To mark their high co-occurrence, events in event clusters are linked together by solid black lines. Visible events are events that occur frequently in the problem domain but do not have any strong relation (i.e., high co-occurrence) with other events. Thus visible events are not connected to any lines. Chances are events that occur infrequently but which have a high co-occurrence with events or event clusters. Because chances are infrequent, but related strongly to other events, they can have a potentially large impact on the system, particularly if they are related to multiple event clusters. If a chance is related to multiple event clusters, then it is possible that it may be a way to get from one group of events to another. KeyGraph marks chances by drawing connections to them with dashed lines. The circular marker for chances is also gray, instead of black. Figure 9.1 shows all these visualization components.

9.4.1 KeyGraph for Visualizing Events in Design

Our definition of design implies an iterative process, because only one action is applied at each design iteration. Unless there is a way to explicitly view which actions were performed on a design in the past, and in what order, these data are lost and future designers will not have access to this knowledge of the design. Understanding the actions that were performed on a design in the past provides context to the design, thus helping to understand the design's current state. Because the KeyGraph visualization graphs all data together on one graph without temporal constraints being considered, KeyGraph is not able to show explicitly when certain events occurred. Because this temporal information could be considered vital to understanding the design and for making design decisions, an extension of KeyGraph is needed that allows constraints, such as temporal groupings, to be embedded in the visualization. Thus we turn to a hierarchically organized variant of KeyGraph.

9.5 HIERARCHICAL VISUALIZATION

The hierarchical visualization method for chance discovery presented by Bojduj and Turner[3] allows modeling of hierarchical constraints. This is an extension of the KeyGraph visualization method and is inspired from work done in the field of sociology on target sociograms.[18,19] A target sociogram is composed of rings of concentric circles. In sociology, sociometric data are plotted on the concentric rings to show a hierarchical structure, represented by relating the data to the distance from the center. For example, Northway[18,19] used the target sociogram to model hierarchical social relations among a group of people. The hierarchy in this case of Northway's work was used to rank the popularity among the group of individuals.

The hierarchical concepts in the target sociogram were extended by Bojduj and Turner[3] to be applicable to chance discovery by defining the concentric rings of the target sociogram to be representative of any arbitrarily defined hierarchical constraints, rather than sociometric relations. This allows a visualization method based on the target sociogram to support the modeling of constraints directly in the visualization. The advantages of this, as Bojduj and Turner point out, are that:

1. Constraints specific to the problem domain can be explicitly modeled.
2. Explicitly modeling the constraints provides context, which can aid the chance discovery process.[3]

Explicitly modeling the constraints that are part of the problem domain allows the hierarchical visualization method to make the relationships among the presented data clear, such that misinterpretations of the data are less likely to occur. This is because the addition of explicit constraints increases the context of the data, which can help human collaborators to carry out the process of chance discovery, because greater context allows the computer to better collaborate with a human user.[6]

In the hierarchical visualization method for chance discovery, the same conventions for displaying events, event clusters, visible events, and chances are followed. These conventions are extended, as shown in Figure 9.2, by creating rings of concentric circles and placing the data in the graph in the correct region bounded between the concentric rings. Each region bounded between the concentric rings can be assigned a constraint, such as holding events from a set of design iterations (i.e., from one or more actions applied in the process of design). In this manner, constraints can be imposed on the data and, because the rings allow the assignment of a hierarchical

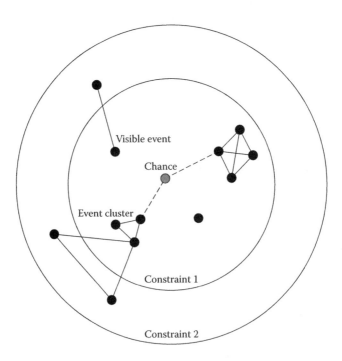

FIGURE 9.2 Extension of the KeyGraph visualization to add constraints.

structure, with respect to distance from the center ring, hierarchical constraints can be defined. For a complete explanation of the hierarchical visualization method for chance discovery, see Bojduj and Turner.[3] Together, these modifications of KeyGraph allow the visualization of events to be used for the analysis of a design.

9.5.1 HIERARCHICAL VISUALIZATION FOR VISUALIZING EVENTS IN DESIGN

Specific to using chance discovery for design analysis, the hierarchical visualization method allows data from multiple design iterations to be modeled. The events graphed on the hierarchical visualization graph in a region bounded by two concentric circles are a grouping of actions applied to a design, such that the grouping makes conceptual sense given the problem domain. For example, if the designer is designing requirements for a software program, then events—in this case textual data—from multiple requirements would be visualized in one of the regions bounded between two concentric rings on the hierarchical graph. Then future iterations of the design process would build on the previous iterations (e.g., building on the previous software requirements) by graphing the events in a different circular region, farther away from the center than the region before it.

Because we define the design process to be primarily an activity of selecting among applicable potential actions, the usefulness of grouping iterations of the design process in an explicit manner becomes apparent. Chance discovery is useful for design because it provides a methodology for discovering knowledge about a design, which can then be used to select an appropriate action to drive future design iterations. Through preserving the context of previous design iterations, the hierarchical visualization method for chance discovery can help the designer to make better design decisions (i.e., to choose a more appropriate action to apply to a design). To illustrate the efficacy of using the hierarchical visualization method for chance discovery for design analysis, the next section will explore the role of chance discovery in the design of a software product.

9.6   CASE STUDY: STAFF SCHEDULING PROGRAM

To demonstrate the usefulness of chance discovery for design, we used chance discovery in the software design process for a staff scheduling software product. For our purposes here, we define software design to be the process of developing requirements for a software product. Software design makes a great test area for chance discovery, because software itself can be viewed as essentially complex.[5] If the complexity of software is part of its essential nature, as Brooks Jr. argues, then there can be no hope of completely eliminating it. Furthermore, as Brooks Jr. states:

> The hardest single part of building a software system is deciding precisely what to build. No other part of the conceptual work is as difficult as establishing the detailed technical requirements… No other part of the work so cripples the resulting system if done wrong. No other part is more difficult to rectify later. Therefore, the most important function that the software builder performs for the client is the iterative extraction and refinement of the product requirements.[5]

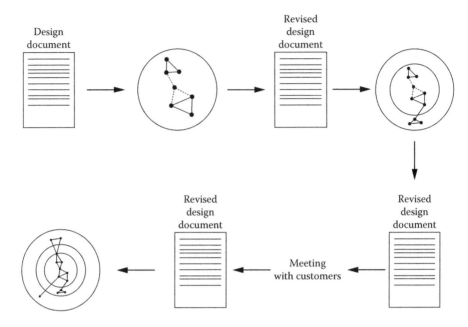

FIGURE 9.3 Overview of using chance discovery for the design of a software product.

Thus designing software, rather than building it, can be considered not only the hardest part of the software creation process but also the most important. It is for this reason that the design of a software product was chosen as an example. An outline of the methodology that was followed is shown in Figure 9.3.

As shown in Figure 9.3, first a preliminary design document was created, outlining the software requirements in textual form. Then the text of the document was processed by KeyGraph. The abstracted output of this processing is shown as the center circular region in Figure 9.4. Through analysis of the resultant graph, it was seen that employers were underrepresented in the design document, so we went back and added more requirements concerning the role of employers in the scheduling software. The additions to the design document yielded more events, which are shown diagrammatically in the second circular region in Figure 9.4. We then met with a group of customers, going over the description of the software product in the design document. From the meeting with the customers, we discovered that the details of how customers are scheduled needed to be better explained in detail. For example, it might be extremely helpful to have the personalities of employees considered for certain tasks. These requirements were added to the software design document and this new document was processed by KeyGraph; the results were merged as another iteration into the hierarchical visualization. This is shown as the third circular region in Figure 9.4. After reviewing the new graph, it was found that requirements specifying the scheduling of employees to multiple projects were underspecified. The design document was then revised to provide better specification of how employees should be scheduled to multiple projects. The KeyGraph output of this is shown as the outer circular region in Figure 9.4.

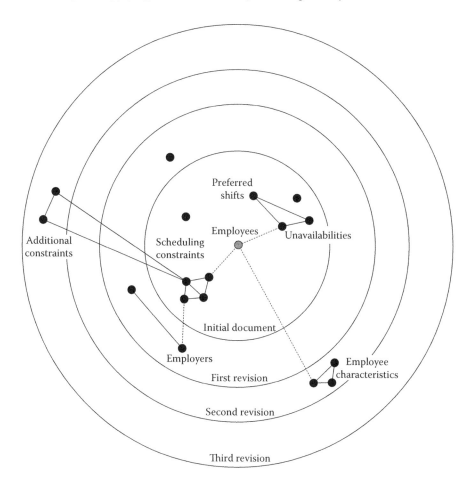

FIGURE 9.4 Abstracted output of hierarchical visualization graph for the design of a software program.

Through this iterative process, it can be seen that chance discovery can provide decision support for a designer who is attempting to choose an action to perform on a design. The example of using chance discovery to make modifications to a software design document is just one of the ways that this technique can be used. Further exploration of domains for using chance discovery to handle design tasks is left to future work, though the concept of using chance discovery to choose appropriate design decisions should be applicable across many domains.

9.7 CONCLUSIONS

Chance discovery is a technique used to identify rare but important events in a decision-making environment. It is especially useful for trying to understand complex tasks, such as the design of an artifact. Chance discovery can assist a human designer in understanding the current state of a design artifact by presenting information about previous actions applied to the artifact. Because a design task is made up of a set of sequential actions performed on a design, at each iteration, the designer must choose an action to perform. These actions heavily influence the final outcome of the design task. To improve the designer's ability to choose good actions and thus improve the quality of the resultant artifact, we introduce chance discovery as a method to aid decision making. Chance discovery helps the designer of an artifact understand the current state of the artifact so that further changes can be made. Through the illustrative design of a software product, it is shown that chance discovery can be a viable aid in the design process. In future work, further study is planned to analyze how chance discovery can aid the process of design across many domains.

REFERENCES

1. Bertel, S., Freksa, C., and Vrachliotis, G. Aspectualize and conquer in architectural design, in *Visual and Spatial Reasoning in Design III*, Gero, J.S., Tversky, B., Knight, T., Eds., Key Centre of Design Computing and Cognition, University of Sydney, 2004, pp. 255–279.
2. Bertel, S., Vrachliotis, G., and Freksa, C. Aspect-oriented building design: toward computer-aided approaches to solving spatial constraints in architecture, in *Applied Spatial Cognition: From Research to Cognitive Technology*, Allen, G.L., Ed., Lawrence Erlbaum Associates, Mahwah, NJ, 2007, pp. 75–102.
3. Bojduj, B. and Turner, C. Hierarchical visualization for chance discovery, in *IEA/AIE 2007, LNAI 4570*, Springer, Berlin, 2007, pp. 786–795.
4. Bojduj, B., Weber, B., Richter, K.F., and Bertel, S. Computer aided architectural design: wayfinding complexity analysis. *The 12th International Conference on Computer Supported Cooperative Work in Design (CSCWD)*, Xi'an, China: IEEE Computer Society, 919–924, 2008.
5. Brooks Jr., F.P. No silver bullet: essence and accidents of software engineering, *Computer* (IEEE Computer Society Press) 20, 10–19, 1987.
6. Dey, A.K. and Abowd, G.D. Towards a better understanding of context and context-awareness, *CHI 2000 Workshop on the What, Who, Where, When, and How of Context-Awareness*, The Hague, Netherlands 2000.
7. Freksa, C. Spatial aspects of task-specific wayfinding maps. A representation-theoretic perspective, in *Visual and Spatial Reasoning in Design*, Gero, J.S., Tversky, B., Knight, T., Eds., Key Centre of Design Computing and Cognition, University of Sydney, 1999, pp. 15–32.
8. Freksa, C. and Röhrig, R. Dimensions of qualitative spatial reasoning, in *Qualitative Reasoning in Decision Technologies, Proc. QUARDET '93,* Carreté, N.P. and Singh, M.G., Eds., Barcelona, 1993, pp. 483–492.
9. Fukuda, H. Application to understanding consumers' latent desires, in *Chance Discovery*, Ohsawa, Y. and McBurney, P., Eds., Springer, Berlin, 2003, pp. 383–396.
10. Goda, S. Chance discovery in credit risk management—estimation of chain reaction bankruptcy structure by chance discovery method, in *Chance Discoveries in Real World Decision Making*, Ohsawa, Y. and Tsumoto, S., Eds., Springer, Berlin, 2006, pp. 347–355.
11. Goda, S. and Ohsawa, Y. Chance discovery in credit risk management—estimation of chain reaction bankruptcy structure by chance discovery method, *ICSMC '06, IEEE International Conference on Systems, Man and Cybernetics,* Taipei, Taiwan: IEEE Computer Society, 2006, pp. 2127–2132.

12. Horie, K., Maeno, Y., and Ohsawa, Y. Designing new product scenarios for patent by human-interactive annealing with pictogram, *ICDM Workshops 2006, Sixth IEEE International Conference on Data Mining Workshops,* IEEE Computer Society, 2006, pp. 559–564.

13. Horie, K., Maeno, Y., and Ohsawa, Y. Human-interactive annealing process with pictogram for extracting new scenarios for patent technology, *Data Sci. J.* 6, 132–136, 2007.

14. Larkin, J.H. and Simon, H.A. Why a diagram is (sometimes) worth ten thousand words, *Cognit. Sci.* 11, 1987, 65–99.

15. Maeno, Y. and Ohsawa, Y. Human–computer interactive annealing for discovering invisible dark events, *IEEE Trans. Industrial Electr.* 54, 1184–1192, 2007.

16. Matsumura, N. Topic diffusion in a community, in *Chance Discovery*, Ohsawa, Y. and McBurney, P., Eds., Springer, Berlin, 2003, pp. 84–97.

17. Minsky, M. *Society of Mind,* Simon & Schuster, New York 1986.

18. Northway, M.L. A method for depicting social relationships obtained by sociometric testing, *Sociometry* 3, 144–150, 1940.

19. Northway, M.L. *A Primer of Sociometry,* University of Toronto Press, Toronto, 1967.

20. Ohsawa, Y. Data crystallization: chance discovery extended for dealing with unobservable events, *New Math. Nat. Sci.* 1, 373–392, 2005.

21. Ohsawa, Y. Detection of earthquake risks with keygraph, in *Chance Discovery*, Ohsawa, Y. and McBurney, P., Eds., Springer, 2003, pp. 339–350.

22. Ohsawa, Y. Keygraph: visualized structure among event clusters, in *Chance Discovery*, Ohsawa, Y. and McBurney, P., Eds., Springer, 2003, pp. 262–275.

23. Ohsawa, Y. and Fukuda, H. Chance discovery by stimulated groups of people. Application to understanding consumption of rare food, *J. Contingencies Crisis Manage.* 10, 129–138, 2002.

24. Ohsawa, Y. and Nara, Y. Understanding Internet users on double helical model of chance-discovery process, *Proceedings of the 2002 IEEE International Symposium on Intelligent Control*, 2002, pp. 844–849.

25. Pohl, J. Some thoughts on human nature: a discussion of human strengths and weaknesses, *InterSymp-2002, Focus Symposium on Collaborative Decision-Support Systems,* Baden-Baden, Germany, 2002.

26. Simon, H. *The Sciences of the Artificial,* MIT Press, Cambridge, MA 1996.

27. Tversky, B. and Lee, P.U. How space structures language, in *Spatial Cognition, An Interdisciplinary Approach to Representing and Processing Spatial Knowledge*, Freksa, C., Habel, C., and Wender, K.F., Eds., Springer, Berlin, 1998, pp. 157–175.

10 Mining for Influence Leaders in Global Teamwork Projects

Renate Fruchter, Shubashri Swaminathan,
Naohiro Matsumura, and Yukio Ohsawa

CONTENTS

10.1 INTRODUCTION

The process of designing and constructing modern buildings depends for its success on the effective communication of ideas among individuals with different backgrounds who are likely to be geographically distributed as well. Historically, the most effective communications occur during face-to-face meetings where multiple members of the team are able to interact and participate in project-wide problem solving.

The entire architecture, engineering, and construction (AEC) industry has adopted Internet-based technologies such as e-mail and incorporated them into the daily routine. These technologies offer a combination of advantages such as direct one-to-one communication similar to phones, asynchronous modes such as written communications, along with the ability to store and retrieve the communications in electronic form. However, the effectiveness of ordinary e-mail for team collaboration is limited by the distributed storage and the lack of organization that would facilitate tracking, sorting, searching, and retrieval. Commercial Web-based portals offer a formal mechanism for storing and tracking official project communications. However, these tend to be structured along traditional contractual lines to provide a legal "chain of custody" and tracking data relative to information flow. Consequently, project portals are not designed to foster and support the fluid process of concept generation and development, problem solving, and discussion that take place among project stakeholders. What is needed to support the creative design process is an electronic environment that facilitates the asynchronous discourse among project stakeholders situated between the spectrum defined by the unstructured chaos of proliferating e-mail and the overstructured commercial portals. The ThinkTank discussion forum developed at the Project Based Learning Laboratory (PBL) at Stanford University is an asynchronous collaboration technology that aims to address these needs. Discussion forums are an online communication genre that is offered today by many Web-based services and collaboration technologies (e.g., Yahoo, MS SharePoint, Buzzsaw). ThinkTank is a discussion forum that was customized for project teamwork activities. Text-based information extraction is a growing area of research and development that is one of our points of departure. Many computer-supported collaborative work studies, natural language processing, and data mining focus on leveraging the growing online information as well as corporate resources. For instance, Tacit (www.tacit.com) integrates and mines corporate communications to connect distributed participants by identifying "who-," "when-," and "why-" based on real-time organizational activities. Other studies focus on social networks aiming to maximize the spread of influence in social networks (Kempe et al., 2003). An interesting latent opportunity for corporate competitive advantage is leverage of such data stores as ThinkTank to discover chances for business or project improvement and new business opportunities. An area related to our study is *chance discovery*, which has been gaining in interest since 2000 (Fruchter, 2006; Ohsawa, 2003; Ohsawa & McBurney, 2003). Chance discovery does not mean discovery by chance, but discovery of a chance from a pool of interlinked events. The word *chance* means an event or a situation significant for the decision of a person. In a dynamic environment, a person must continue to make decisions and stay sensitive to chances. That is, one's *concern* with chances should be deepened through involvement in the dynamic environment of discourse to be ready to capture information about an event or global perspective of team performance as a chance. In other words, a *chance favors a prepared mind*. As one deepens the concern regarding a chance, one becomes *aware* of a chance and begins to understand its meaning for future decisions or team process. Finally, one can decide to take action. Chance discovery is such a process, rather than a momentary happening, in which the occurrence, the awareness, and the understanding of chances interleave and lead to actions.

Global project teamwork is communication intensive and relies heavily on synchronous and asynchronous information and collaboration technologies (ICT) (O'Hara-Devereaux & Johansen, 1994). The use of ICT is shaping and reshaping work processes and social interactions among team members. Team members also reshape ICT and the way it is used. We explore here how ThinkTank (a Web-based asynchronous collaboration and discussion forum [Fruchter et al., 2003]) reshaped the work process of AEC global teams and how the interaction with this ThinkTank by 53 teams over 8 years (1999–2007) reshaped the purpose and benefits of its use. In addition to improved communication and collaboration, ICT such as ThinkTank contains tacit and implicit information about the people on the team and the critical topics raised at different times during the project. For instance, team members might influence leaders without being the assigned project leader. Mining enterprise archives such as the one produced by ThinkTank and discovering who the influence leaders in project teams are can be beneficial and important from a corporate management perspective, because they can guide or motivate the team toward successful actions and outcomes.

Influence is generically defined as the ability to indirectly affect the beliefs or actions of other people. An interesting framework to describe influence (Centrerion Canadian politics, 2006) that can be related to teamwork scenarios offers five ways to be influential: "(1) express an original idea or a common one in an insightful new way, (2) meet and speak to more people, (3) raise issues and opinions ignored by others, (4) volunteer with a group, (5) gain expertise by researching a subject." Other studies focus on leadership and influence and trust in teams (Macy, 1991; Song, 2006). Leaders influence people. In his book *On Leadership,* Gardner stresses the interdependence between leaders and the followers. "Leadership is the process of persuasion or example by which an individual or team induces a group to pursue objectives held by the leader or shared by the leader and his or her followers" (Gardner, 1990).

Leadership is a complicated notion that includes the art and science of creating a vision; clearly, concisely, compellingly, and consistently communicating that vision; and enabling others to "own" the vision and contribute to achieving it. As such, leadership is an attribute, not a position. It has been said that management is "doing what it takes to get there" and leadership is "determining where we should be going." Although management and leadership are related, they are not the same thing. John P. Kotter, professor of organizational behavior at the Harvard Business School, calls leadership and management "two distinctive and complementary systems of actions." Management is "about coping with complexity, leadership is about coping with change" (Kotter, 1997). How can individuals and organizations anticipate and lead change? One answer is provided by Maxwell (1998). In his influential book *The 21 Irrefutable Laws of Leadership*, he states "Leadership is influence— nothing more, nothing less."

10.2   THINKTANK

One of the ongoing efforts in the PBL Laboratory at Stanford University studies issues related to interdisciplinary collaboration across disciplines and geographically distributed teams for the past decade. Design teams of architects, engineers, and construction managers from a variety of partner universities and industry companies worldwide from Europe, Asia, and the United States are engaged in the PBL testbed. They have accepted the challenge to collaborate and produce building designs on a tight schedule as part of the annual AEC Global Teamwork Design Course (Fruchter, 1999, 2004). Early on it became apparent that an efficient means of asynchronous communication across distance and time zones was required. The limitations of e-mail quickly became apparent, and the PBL Lab team set out to develop a custom tool that would address the project communication requirements. The objectives in developing the tool included the following.

- Providing an efficient means of asynchronous communication (i.e., European, Asian, and U.S. teammates needed to be able to carry on a meaningful dialogue even though they would not be collocated). Ordinary e-mail supports this need rather well. The objective was not to develop a collaboration tool that would replace or compete with e-mail applications, but to leverage the existing e-mail work habits and processes practitioners are used to and integrate them into the new collaboration tool, consequently keeping a clear distinction between the benefits and use situation of the two applications—e-mail and asynchronous collaboration tool.
- Providing a means to capture the individual conversations that occur among team members and keep the individual threads organized in a way that would facilitate re-creating the thought process underlying the team decisions, consequently capturing not only the product (i.e., design decision, concept, or detailed drawing) but also the process it was created through.
- Provide a means to share and make visible the entire transcript of each discussion accessible to everyone on the team without duplicating the underlying data and without creating enormous amounts of clerical overhead.
- Provide a means to capture reference material such as sketches, CAD drawings, and pictures needed to aid in communication linked to the specific discussion to keep it in context. Implicit in this requirement is the capture of versions of sketches as the design evolves.
- Provide a means to foster collaboration, exploration, and communication among team members from different cultural backgrounds.

What emerged from these requirements was a Web-based discussion forums tool called ThinkTank, with a user interface that created an asynchronous meeting cyberspace, providing structure to the communications, and performing the clerical operations transparently in the background. The underlying concept of ThinkTank is that rather than typing e-mail that will end up in multiple in-boxes across the globe, team members type their correspondence into ThinkTank, where it is archived in a database for future tracking, sharing, sorting, searching, reuse, or repurposing. ThinkTank is based on the Web-based discussion forum principles. Many commercial and free Web discussion forum tools are available (e.g., Google, Yahoo!, Microsoft).

ThinkTank was tailored for project communication needs. The underlying Microsoft Access or Oracle database is organized by groups, with each group having a private, password-protected, virtual asynchronous meeting room. Within the group meeting rooms the content is organized based on the "book" metaphor with three levels of organization: *Forums* representing key topics or project phases similar to book chapters, *Subjects* representing issues brought up within a Forum, similar to

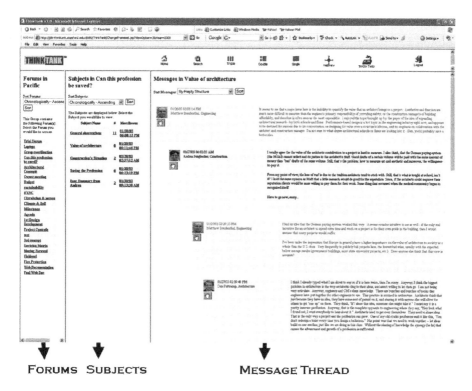

FORUMS SUBJECTS   MESSAGE THREAD

FIGURE 10.1 ThinkTank interface structure.

section within a chapter of a book, and threaded *Messages* representing the actual ideas captured and shared among team members, similar to the paragraphs within a section of a book (Figure 10.1). Messages are created as needed over the course of the project by the team members. Each group can create any number of forums, and within each forum there can be any number of subjects, within subjects any number of threads, and within threads any number of messages. Within the context of ordinary project communications, there are no practical limits to the numbers of each. Each message may have document attachments. This allows documents to be kept in the context of the dialogue.

10.2.1 CREATE-CAPTURE-SHARE

ThinkTank enables project members to create forums, subjects, and messages, capturing and sharing their ideas with the team. After these are submitted, ThinkTank archives them automatically in the database. ThinkTank enables the creator of a message to specify who in the team should be notified. The notification mechanism links the corporate e-mail system to ThinkTank, enabling a smooth transition among the applications. The receiver of the notification will receive an e-mail message with a direct "quick-login" to the specific forum, subject, and message sent that requires his or her attention. This eliminates time-consuming browsing through large archives

10.2.2 ALERT

When the user logs in to review messages, ThinkTank indicates the new/unread messages through "alert" red bullet markers. This addresses the information overload.

10.2.3 REPLY

The user has two options to reply to a reviewed message: (1) reply through the ThinkTank functionality or (2) reply through e-mail ThinkTank functionality, which switches to the corporate e-mail system in case a user chooses a private communication channel for feedback.

10.2.4 WHO, WHEN, WHAT

Each message contains information regarding the originator, his or her picture, profession and role in the team, the time stamp when the message was submitted, and its content that can be text and attachments. The picture of the originator attached to the message provides a persistence presence that sustains relationships among geographically distributed team members.

10.2.5 SEARCH AND SORT

One of the advantages of linking the ThinkTank discussion forum to a database is to enable searching and sorting. The search functionalities allow for simple keyword searches and advanced searches based on author, discipline, level of granularity in the database, and text data mining, respectively. The search is valuable for knowledge reuse and quick access to specific items produced in the past. Sorting allows users to view the content chronologically in ascending and descending order. In addition, users can sort by author, for instance, when the user needs to review all the messages posted by a specific person (e.g., the structural engineer or the architect) in a threaded discussion, or by reply structure, when the user wants to review the discussion as an ongoing asynchronous conversation among team members.

10.3 INFLUENCE DIFFUSION MODEL

Our observations of communication and collaboration in teams or larger communities of interest show that people who were inspired or affected by another person's thought would consider the same perspective or respond to that perspective, often using the same words as the originator. In the context of global project teams, the same phenomenon can be observed. A team member's thoughts or behaviors often affect others' thoughts or behaviors. Such a team member who has a strong influence on others can be considered as an *influence leader* in the team. However, the influence leader is not always the assigned project leader. Discovering who the influence leaders in project teams are can be beneficial and important from a corporate management perspective, because they can guide or motivate the team toward successful actions and outcomes. Influence diffusion in a team is one way to measure influence. We consider a simple influence diffusion model (IDM) that formalizes the process of identifying the influence of people, messages, and terms mathematically (Matsumura, 2003). IDM defines the influence based on the propagation of terms throughout discussion threads (i.e., in the context of ThinkTank that will correspond to the message thread within one subject in a specific forum). For example, if message C_y replies to C_x, the influence of C_x onto C_y, $i_{x,y}$, is defined as

$$i_{x,y} = \frac{|w_x \cap w_y|}{|w_y|}$$

where $|w_y|$ denotes the count of terms in C_y and $|w_x \cap w_y|$ denotes the count of propagated terms from C_x and C_y. In addition, if C_z replies to C_y, the influence of C_x onto C_z via C_y, $i_{x,z}$, is defined as

$$i_{x,z} = \frac{|w_x \cap w_y \cap w_z|}{|w_z|} \cdot i_{x,y}$$

where $|w_z|$ denotes the count of terms in C_z, and $|w_x \cap w_y \cap w_z|$ denotes the count of propagated terms from C_x and C_z.

It is generally considered that the more a message affects other messages, the more the influence increases. Therefore, the influence of C_x is measured by the sum of the influence diffused from C_x (i.e., $i_{x,y}+i_{x,z}$ if there are only three messages C_x, C_y, and C_z).

To understand the procedure of measuring the influence of messages in more detail, let us measure the influence of messages in the illustrated discussion thread in Figure 10.2, where C_1 is replied to by C_2 and C_4, and C_2 is replied to by C_3. In this

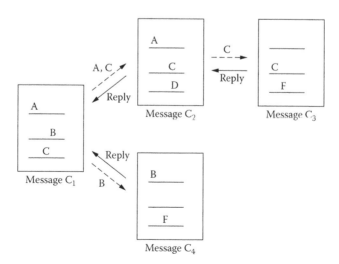

FIGURE 10.2 A discussion thread of three messages.

case, terms A, C are propagating from C_1 to C_2, term B is propagating from C_1 to C_4, and term C is propagating from C_2 to C_3. Here, the influence of C_1 is calculated as follows:

–The influence of C_1 on C_2:
  The number of propagated terms from C_1 to C_2 is two (A, C), and the number of
    terms in C_2 is three (A, C, D). Thus, the influence of C_1 on C_2 is 2/3.
–The influence of C_1 on C_4:
  The number of propagated terms from C_1 to C_4 is one (B), and the number of
    terms in C_2 is two (B, F). Thus, the influence of C_1 on C_4 is 1/2 .
–The influence of C_1 on C_3 through C_2:
  The number of propagated terms from C_1 to C_3 via C_2 is one (C), and the num-
    ber of terms in C_2 is two (C, F). Considering that the influence of C_1 on C_2
    is 2/3, the influence of C_1 on C_3 via C_2 becomes 2/3 × 1/2 = 1/3.

The influence of C_1 in Figure 10.2 is calculated as (the influence from C_1 to C_2) + (the influence from C_1 to C_4) + (the influence from C_1 to C_3) = 2/3 + 1/2 + 1/3 = 3/2. Similarly, the influence of C_2, C_3, and C_4 are calculated as 1/2, 0, and 0, respectively. Therefore, C_1 is selected as the most influential comment in Figure 10.2.

The influence of people is measurable by applying the same principle. By assuming that C_1, C_2, C_3, and C_4 in Figure 10.2 are posted by person P_1, P_2, P_3, and P_3, respectively, the relationship between people, called the *human-network*, is illustrated in Figure 10.3. Here, the influence of P_1 on P_2 is equal to the influence of C_1 on C_2, whereas the influence of P_1 on P_3 is the sum of C_1's influence on C_3 via C_2, and of C_1 on C_4. Referring to the above results, the influence of P_1 on P_2 becomes 2/3, and the influence from P_1 to P_3 becomes 2/3 × 1/2 + 1/2 = 5/6. Therefore, the influence of P_1 is

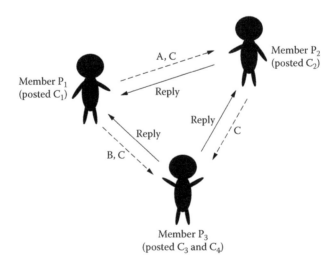

FIGURE 10.3 Human network in the discussion thread in Figure 10.2.

calculated as (the influence from P_1 to P_2) + (the influence from P_1 to P_3) = 2/3 + 5/6 = 3/2. Likewise, the influence of P_2 and P_3 is calculated as 1/2 and 0, respectively. From these calculations, it is clear that P_1 is the influence leader in the discussion thread.

10.4   INTEGRATION OF THINKTANK AND IDM

The objective of integrating ThinkTank and IDM is to assist global team members to find valuable information about influential comments and opinion leaders (i.e., knowledgeable people who affect the decision-making process in a team). Such information is embedded implicitly in discussions. We define a comment chain as the relation of comments in each message that indicates the influence of a specific message. The integration of ThinkTank-IDM builds on the assumption that a person's idea is expressed and propagated through words or terms in the context of ThinkTank's asynchronous discussions. Consequently, influence diffuses along the comment chain through the medium of words. Following is an example of the representation and calculation of IDM influence propagation in a ThinkTank discussion thread. It illustrates a group of people discussing which programming language to use for their software development (Figure 10.4). For instance, IDM determines Shuba's total influence in the discussion as the sum of her influence on Matt and on Nao. To calculate Shuba's total influence, the following terms are defined:

- *Term1* as Shuba's influence on Matt,
- *Term2* as Shuba's influence on Nao, and
- *Term3* as Shuba's influence on the final decision.

Shuba's influence on Matt, *Term1*, is ½, because Matt used one of Shuba's words, "XMP," in his discussion. Shuba's influence on Nao, *Term2*, is 0, because Nao did not use any of Shuba's words. Shuba's influence on the final decision, *Term3*, is determined by two parts: *direct influence* and *indirect influence* on the final decision. The direct influence of Shuba on the final decision is 1/3, because she used one of the three keywords present in the final decision. Shuba's indirect influence on the final decision is: $1/2 \times 2/3 = 1/3$, because she influenced Matt, who was also involved in making the final decision. Therefore, Matt's influence on the final decision was 2/3 and Shuba's influence on Matt was 1/2. Consequently:

Term3 = direct influence + indirect influence = 1/3 + 1/3 = 2/3.
Total influence of Shuba = *Term1* + *Term2* + *Term3* = 1/2 + 0 + 2/3 = 5/6.
IDM calculates the *Total Influence of* Matt = 4/3
   and *Total Influence of* Nao = 2/3.

Because Matt's influence is the highest, Matt could be considered as a potential opinion leader in this discussion.

The following describes the ThinkTank-IDM integration. The first step entails extracting the content from the project team ThinkTank database archive and creates a text file, *team_name.txt*. This text file contains the following data: text from

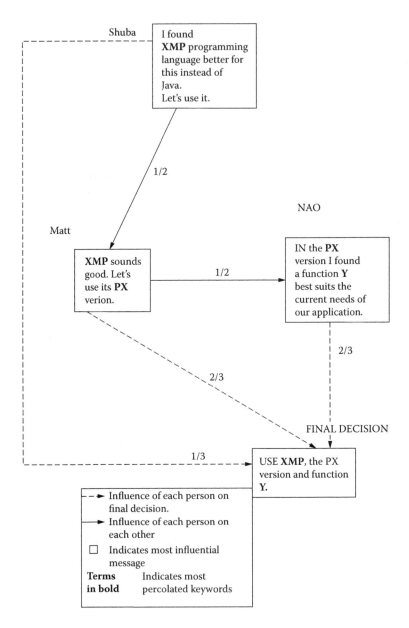

FIGURE 10.4 Representation of influence diffusion model propagation in a ThinkTank discussion thread.

messages written by team members, names of the authors, content and structure (*reply structure*) of messages from ThinkTank, and subject of discussion. To create the text file, the entire threaded conversation (i.e., *Forum*) is downloaded from ThinkTank as a Word document and saved as a *team_name.txt* file. This text file is converted to IDM format *team_name.xml*. The following shows a sample of the XML markups created through this conversion:

- *<id>#0000008</id>* → indicates the message number
- *<name>Shuba</name>* → indicates name of the team member
- *<replyid></replyid>* → indicates whether the message is a reply to a message or a new message
- *<body>* send response post Shuba *</body>* → indicates the content of the message

The *team_name.xml* file is the input to the IDM.pl module that calculates the influence of team members, messages, and terms.

10.5 TESTBED ENVIRONMENT

To validate the ThinkTank-IDM integration and its potential value from a team and corporate management perspective, we used the AEC Global Teamwork program offered since 1993 at Stanford University in cooperation with partner universities in Europe, Asia, and the United States (Fruchter, 1999). The AEC Global Teamwork program is based on the PBL methodology of teaching and learning that focuses on *problem*-based, *project*-organized activities that produce a *product* for a client. PBL is based on reengineered *processes* that bring *people* from multiple disciplines together. It engages faculty, industry practitioners, and students from architecture, engineering, and construction management disciplines who are geographically distributed. The core atom in this learning environment is the AEC student team, which consists of an architect, two structural engineers, and two construction managers from the M.Sc. level. One of the innovative features of this course is the mentoring model that engages professors and industry experts who play the role of master builder mentors to the AEC student teams in the program (Fruchter & Lewis, 2003).

The AEC Global Teamwork program is a two-quarter class that engages architecture, structural engineering, and construction management students from partner universities (i.e., Stanford University, UC Berkeley, Cal Poly San Luis Obispo, Georgia Tech, Kansas University, and University Wisconsin Madison in the United States; Puerto Rico University; Stanford Japan Center in Kyoto, Japan, and Aoyama Gakuin University in Tokyo, Japan; University of Ljubljana in Slovenia; Bauhaus University in Weimar, Germany; ETH Zurich and FHA in Switzerland; Strathclyde University in Glasgow, Scotland; Manchester University in the United Kingdom; KTH in Stockholm, Chalmers University, and IT University Goteborg in Sweden; and TU Delft in the Netherlands). Every year there are 3 to 12 AEC student teams. Each team is geographically distributed and has an owner/client with a building program, a location, a budget, and a timeline. The core activity of each team is a building project with a program, a budget, a site, a time for delivery, and a demanding owner. The project is based on a real-world building project that has been scaled down to address the academic time frame of two academic quarters. AEC teams model, refine, and document the design product, the process, and its implementation. Because all participants are geographically distributed, each student has four challenges: cross-disciplinary teamwork, use of advanced collaboration technologies, time management and team coordination, and multicultural collaboration.

One of the asynchronous collaboration technologies used by each team is ThinkTank. We used the ThinkTank archive (created 1999–2007) as the testbed for the ThinkTank-IDM validation. The testbed consisted of 53 AEC project teams that engaged 228 participants. The team size varied from three to seven member teams. The size of the overall archive considered for the testbed was approximately 5 GB, 14,000 messages, and 3000 subjects. Of the 53 teams, we have performed ThinkTank-IDM retrospective analysis on 39 and used ThinkTank-IDM for real-time analysis on 14 teams since starting this study in 2004. As we performed the ThinkTank-IDM analysis of influence leaders in all 53 teams, we validated the results by triangulating the data about each team's dynamics known by Dr. Fruchter, the instructor of the AEC Global Teamwork program, and the results obtained from Ms. Swaminathan, the analyst. Dr. Fruchter observed all team members and teamwork as she participated in 75% of the team activities and coached all teams. Her observations related to influence leaders on each team focused on communication, collaboration, and coordination tasks. The analyst did not know the team data from the program or the team members. The result of the ThinkTank-IDM analysis identified correctly the influence leader of 50 teams of the 53 analyzed teams. The remaining three teams had a homogeneous teamwork with shared leadership behavior and similar influence of all team members. These ThinkTank-IDM results aligned with the qualitative observations made by Dr. Fruchter.

10.6   THINKTANK-IDM SCENARIOS AND OBSERVATIONS

We describe in this section a number of relevant scenarios of use resulting from the ThinkTank-IDM analysis.

10.6.1   TEMPORAL ANALYSIS OF INFLUENCE LEADERS IN AEC PROJECT TEAMS

A first perspective of our research focused on the influence of the members of the team during the AEC project. To illustrate the results, we chose one of the teams from the year 2002–2003. The team's name was *Pacific*, and its participants are shown in Table 10.1. The Pacific team used ThinkTank to discuss key issues of their

TABLE 10.1
Pacific Team Roles and Location

Name	Discipline	Location
DP	Architect	Kansas University
MB	Engineer	Stanford University
BM	Engineer	KTH, Sweden
AJ	Construction manager	Bauhaus, Germany
CP	Construction manager	Stanford University
TH	Owner/client	Japan

TABLE 10.2
Sample Term Ranking

Sample Output: Term Ranking			
Rank	Term	Influence	Term Frequency
1	Steel	14.708	52
2	Concrete	13.706	40
3	Architects	7.319	36
4	Elevation	7.002	18
5	Atrium	5.705	11

building project. Because all the messages in ThinkTank are stored with timestamps, it afforded us the ability to study the influence of messages over time as the project progressed. The ThinkTank-IDM team analysis allowed us to identify the overall influence leader and the range of influence topics discussed in the project. Table 10.2 illustrates ThinkTank-IDM results, ranking the top five terms used in the concept development phase of the project. They represent terms that initiated many influential topics of discussions. Table 10.3 presents sample output data regarding the ranking of the top five comments mentioned in ThinkTank messages. Table 10.4 shows a sample output of participant ranking that indicates one of the construction managers, Mr. CP, as the top influence leader. Mr. TH was the owner/client of the Pacific team who posted three messages at milestone project deadlines. Figure 10.5 provides an illustration of the Pacific Team ThinkTank-IDM participant ranking and the comment chain. Renate was the instructor who was coaching the team.

We used ThinkTank-IDM to study the dynamic change in influence leadership over time as different disciplines raised critical challenges in the project and the respective team members moved to the center of the activity becoming an influence leader for a period of time. We plotted time history graphs and set them side by side to observe the relationship among team members and influence. The x axis

TABLE 10.3
Sample Comment Ranking

Sample Output: Comment Ranking		
Rank	Comment	Influence
1	#0000108	22.34
2	#0000039	22.11
3	#0000164	14.73
4	#0000165	14.18
5	#0000040	14.15

TABLE 10.4
Ranking of Participants

	Sample Output: Participant Ranking		
Rank	Participant	Influence	Number of Posts
1	CP	84.91	44
2	MB	67.52	55
3	DP	67.11	31
4	AJ	21.38	43
5	BM	19.08	14
6	TH	2.42	3

indicates when the messages were posted and the y axis shows the message's influence. Figure 10.6 shows examples of such graphs obtained for the architect, Mr. DP, and one of the engineers, Mr. MB. Note that these AEC team projects start the third week of January and end the first week of May every year. All team members travel

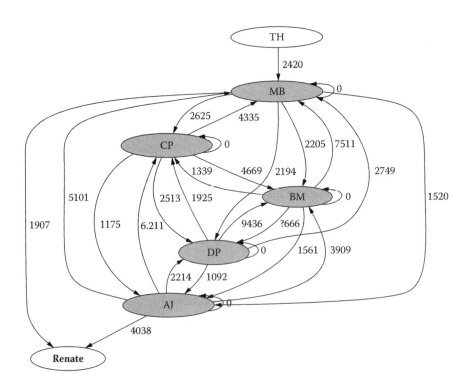

FIGURE 10.5 ThinkTank–influence diffusion model participant ranking and comment chain.

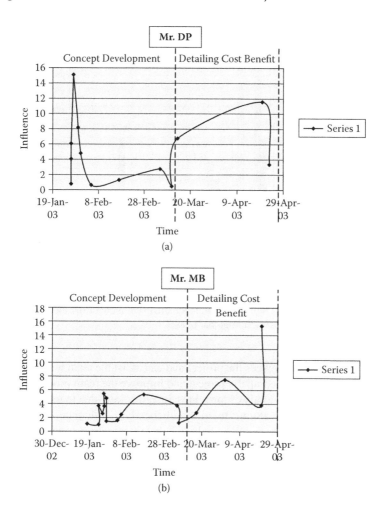

FIGURE 10.6 Temporal analysis influence–example of time history of influence messages posted by different team members: (a) Mr. DP, architect, and (b) Mr. MB, one of the engineers of the Pacific team.

to Stanford and are collocated the first week and last week of the project. In addition, there is spring break in the middle of March. These events are reflected by dips in communication shown in the graphs (i.e., when team members are collocated, they tend to capture fewer of their discussions, issues, and decisions).

By comparing, for instance, the two time histories of the architect and one engineer, we observe that Mr. DP, the architect, was the influence leader for the first 2 weeks as he was tasked to develop a vision and an architectural concept for the project and start the cross-disciplinary collaboration with the engineers and construction managers. As the project progressed, the engineers started to raise critical issues and their messages became influential. Such information can be valuable for the

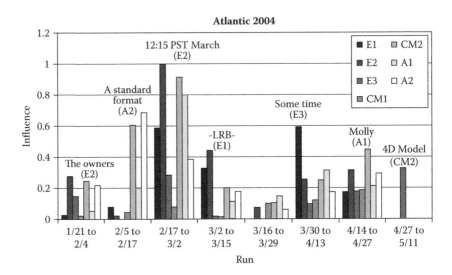

FIGURE 10.7 Overview of ThinkTank–influence diffusion model time history of an architecture, engineering, and construction global team.

general contractor who oversees the project and can assist the team with timely input and resources that can speed up the project and improve the team process.

The ThinkTank-IDM analysis provides insights into the team dynamics in terms of the interactions among team members, their influence, and the influence topics created by them. We analyzed the intersection between influence leader and influence topic over time and illustrate a number of interesting types of situations observed through this analysis. Note that in this analysis the x axis indicates a Run representing a time frame of 1 to 2 weeks and the y axis indicates the influence. We abstract the names of the team members to the following symbols: A1: architect 1; A2: architect 2 (during 1 year, there was an experiment with two architects per team); E1: engineer 1; E2: engineer 2; E3: engineer 3; CM1: construction manager 1; and CM2: construction manager 2. The labels over the bars indicate the influence topic and its originator (e.g., steel truss [E3] means the influence topic was "steel truss" originated by engineer E3). The bars indicate the influence leaders and the degree of their influence. Figure 10.7 provides an overall example of the ThinkTank-IDM time history of the Atlantic 2004 AEC project team from the second week of their project through completion. Further detailed analysis of the intersection between influence leader and influence topic over time revealed interesting types of social interactions that include the following.

> *Strong leadership: influence leader and influence topic coincide*, as illustrated by the examples in Figure 10.8 (i.e., influence leader E2 triggered the influence topic "seismic spreadsheet" in the Atlantic 2003 team, and influence leader E1 triggered the influence topic "trusses" in the Ridge 2005 team).

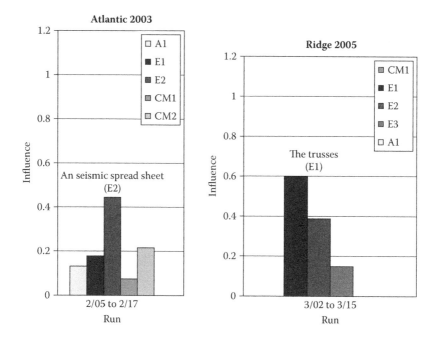

FIGURE 10.8 Strong leadership–influence leader coincides with the influence topic.

Cross-disciplinary engagement: influence leader builds on influence topic from another discipline that highlights cross-disciplinary attention and engagement, as illustrated by the example in Figure 10.9 (i.e., the influence leader is architect A1, who discusses the influence topic "structural engineer" triggered by engineer E1).

Discipline centric teaming: influence leader builds on influence topic raised by a team member from the same discipline (i.e., influence leader and influence topic are not the same). This is illustrated by the example in Figure 10.10 (i.e., the influence leader E2 builds on the influence topic "structural solution" originated by E1 from the same discipline).

Interdisciplinary leadership interweaving: influence leader of previous phase of project triggers the response and influence leader from a different discipline in the next project phase, as illustrated by the example in Figure 10.11 (i.e., in the second and third runs, the influence leaders build in the influence topic originated by a different discipline). This leads to an interweaving of influence topics and influence leaders that indicates high engagement and responsiveness among team members. In the first run, the influence leader and influence topic coincide (i.e., engineer E1). In the second run, the influence leader is the construction manager CM1, who builds on the influence topic of the previous run initiated by E1. In the third run, the influence leader is the architect A1, who builds on the influence topic proposed by construction manager CM1.

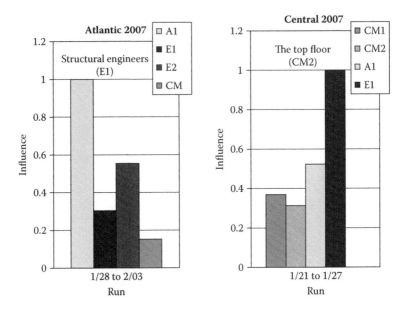

FIGURE 10.9 Cross-disciplinary engagement–influence leader builds on influence topic from another discipline.

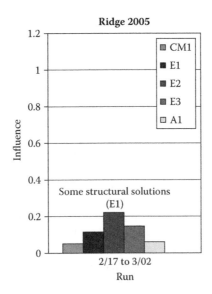

FIGURE 10.10 Discipline-centric teaming–influence leader builds on influence topic brought up by a team member from the same discipline.

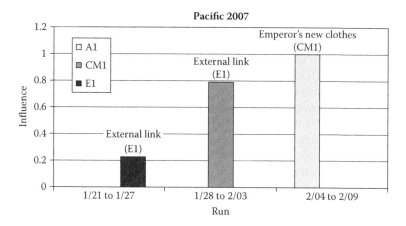

FIGURE 10.11 Interdisciplinary leadership interweaving–influence topic in previous phase of project triggers the response and influence leader from a different discipline in the next project phase.

Balanced team engagement: team dynamics revealed by time history analysis of ThinkTank-IDM shows a balanced communication and contribution to the dialogue by all team members, as illustrated in Figure 10.12. It also reveals that the architect is responsive to the engineer's and construction managers' information requests and suggestions. However, the architect generates few topics of influence in the early phase of the project.

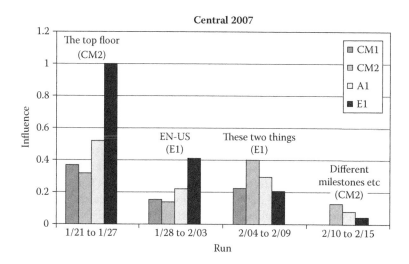

FIGURE 10.12 Balanced team engagement–team dynamics time history reveals balanced contribution of all team members on each influence topic.

10.7 CONCLUDING REMARKS

This chapter presents a new perspective on data mining and information extraction focused on small- to medium-sized teams (3–10 members) that is modeled using an integrated ThinkTank-IDM system. ThinkTank-IDM provides an effective communication environment that allows users to observe, understand, leverage, and augment the social interactions and intelligence that evolve in the team mediated by ICT, on one hand. On the other hand, ThinkTank-IDM processes the project team dialogues. This facilitates the design of a new social intelligence perspective for the people about the people on the team, their interactions, and topics of interest.

The use of ThinkTank is shaping and reshaping work processes and social interactions among team members, on one hand. On the other hand, team members reshape ICT and the way it is used as ThinkTank-IDM analysis information becomes visible to the team members and corporate management. We validated ThinkTank-IDM in a testbed composed of a database archive of 53 AEC global teams collected over 8 years. We demonstrated how the use of ThinkTank-IDM applied in the context of global teamwork discussion forums can assist in identifying influence leaders, influence topics, and social interaction dynamics over time in global teams. We used ThinkTank-IDM to study the dynamic change in influence leadership over time. In addition, we analyzed the intersection between influence leader and influence topic over time. This analysis revealed a number of interesting types of situations that characterize specific social team interactions:

- *Strong leadership:* influence leader and influence topic coincide.
- *Cross-disciplinary engagement:* influence leader builds on influence topic from another discipline.
- *Discipline centric teaming:* influence leader builds on influence topic raised by a team member from the same discipline.
- *Interdisciplinary leadership interweaving*: influence leader of a previous phase of a project triggers the response and influence leader from a different discipline in the next project phase.
- *Balanced team engagement:* there is balanced communication and contribution to the dialogue by all team members.

From a project teamwork perspective, ThinkTank leads to effective communications, reduced reply cycle from days to hours, and increased productivity. Because ThinkTank is a collaboration technology, it requires participants to engage in the discourse, contribute by sharing their ideas, and provide feedback to other's ideas. We identified two key factors in effective adoption and use of ThinkTank: responsiveness and timeliness (Fruchter et al., 2003). *Responsiveness* is revealed by the feedback replies participants provide online to other participants' messages. It is an indicator of engagement, reciprocity, care, and interest in others' ideas, goals, constraints, and problems they face. If team members continuously submit their ideas but no one else participates in the discourse, they will typically abandon the effort of sharing their ideas. *Timeliness* is the second key factor in the effective use of ThinkTank to increase productivity and improve communication among stakeholders. Timeliness is a key behavior of a participant in a communicative event, where the information provider will not only be responsive but also provide the information in a timely manner to the information seeker, because information received after the deadline is in many cases useless. In addition, we observed emergent work processes that engaged team members in more frequent, short, and focused communicative events; sharing of ideas; making their local activities visible; behavioral changes that entailed awareness of the importance of responsiveness; and timeliness.

The integration of the messages with relevant material in the form of attachments—for example, documents such as sketches, CAD drawings, or spreadsheets—keeps the content in context. This enables users to understand and evaluate the content they review. It eliminates the time project members typically spend to search and retrieve the referenced material from diverse locations and people.

The adoption of a collaboration technology such as ThinkTank is motivated and justified by space and time constraints, such as situations in which participants are in different geographic locations or in different divisions (e.g., engineering and detailing) or when participants have different schedules that preclude them to interact face to face.

Finally, our observations showed that the deployment and adoption of a technology such as ThinkTank-IDM require the development of new work behaviors, team dynamics, and corporate processes that indicate clear economic/business justifications, work process and individual benefits, as well as a corporate culture that provides incentives, fosters, and encourages knowledge and experience capture and sharing. As this technology is used in new and diverse use scenarios, it is improved to serve specific data, information and knowledge creation, capture, sharing, and reuse in learning and corporate environments.

REFERENCES

Centrerion Canadian politics. Available online at: http://centrerion.blogspot.com/2006/01/5-ways-for-you-to-be-influential.html. Accessed June 30, 2008.

Fruchter, R. Global Teamwork: Cross-disciplinary, collaborative, geographically distributed e-learning environment, in *Collaborative Design and Learning: Competence Building for Innovation,* J. Bento, J. Duarte, M. Heitor, W. Mitchell, Eds., Praeger, Westport, Connecticut, 2004, pp. 265–298.

Fruchter, R. Is there a needle in the haystack? in *Chance Discoveries in Real World Decision Making,* Ohsawa, Y. and Tsumoto, S. Eds., Springer-Verlag, Berlin 2006, pp. 287–314.

Fruchter, R., Demian, P., Yin, Z., and Luth, G. Turning A/E/C knowledge into working knowledge, *Proceedings ASCE Computing in Civil Engineering,* Flood, I., Ed., 2003 (CD).

Fruchter, R. and Lewis, S., Mentoring models in support of P⁵BL in architecture/engineering/construction global teamwork, *IJEE,* 19:5, 663–671, 2003.

Gardner, J.W. *On Leadership*, Free Press, New York, 1990.

Kempe, D., Kleinberg, J., and Tardos, E., Maximizing the spread of influence through a social network, in *KDD '03 Proceedings of the Ninth ACM SIGKDD International Conference on Knowledge Discovery and Data Mining,* Washington, DC, SIGKDD, ACM, 2003, pp. 137–147.

Kotter, J. What leaders really do? in *Leadership: Understanding the Dynamics and Power and Influence in Organizations,* Vecchio, R.P., Ed., University of Notre Dame Press, Notre Dame, IN, 1997, 24–34.

Macy, M.W. Chains of cooperation: threshold effects in collective action, *Am. Sociol. Rev.*, 56, 730–747, 1991.

Matsumura, N. Topic diffusion in community, in *Chance Discovery,* Ohsawa, Y. and McBurney, P., Eds., Springer-Verlag, Berlin, 2003, pp. 84–97.

Maxwell, J.C. *The 21 Irrefutable Laws of Leadership,* Thomas Nelson Publishers, Nashville, TN, 1998.

O'Hara-Devereaux, M. and Johansen, R. *GlobalWork, Bridging Distance, Culture, and Time,* Jossey-Bass Publishers, San Francisco, 1994.

Ohsawa, Y. Modeling the process of chance discovery, in *Chance Discovery,* Ohsawa, Y. and McBurney, P., Eds., Springer-Verlag, Berlin 2003, pp. 2–15.

Ohsawa, Y. and McBurney, *Chance Discovery,* Springer-Verlag, Berlin, 2003.

Rogers, E.M. *Diffusion of Innovation,* The Free Press, New York, 1962.

Song, F. Trust and reciprocity in inter-individual versus inter-group interactions: the effects of social influence, group dynamics, and perspective biases, *J. Exp. Econ.,* 9, 179–180, 2006.

Tacit. Available online at: http://www.tacit.com. Accessed June 30, 2008.

11 Analysis Framework for Knowledge Discovery Related to Persuasion Process Conversation Logs

Wataru Sunayama and Katsutoshi Yada

CONTENTS

11.1   INTRODUCTION

As the economy recovers and business activities expand in Japan, the growing disparity in income levels has become a problem. In recent years, the structure of the economy has undergone vast changes, and the proportion of direct business transactions with end-use consumers, or business-to-customer business, has been rapidly expanding because of factors causing serious conditions to arise. For example, depending on the company involved, difficulties concerning customer payments have been increasing. In business-to-customer business, the numbers of customers involved are so large that in many cases it has become necessary for companies affected to rationalize and improve the efficiency of such operations.

In Yada and Matsumura (2006), the problem of collecting overdue payments related to Japan's telecommunications companies is discussed. For these companies, operators contact negligent customers and negotiate these overdue payments. The success of such negotiations depends to a large extent on the persuasion skills of individual operators. In 2007, because of an organizational problem, more than half of the experienced employees left the company. Thus it became necessary for company managers to act quickly to transfer these special, but tacit, unrecorded skills of successful operators to other employees. The authors divided the current employees into those with good collection skills and those with bad collection skills and analyzed the actual verbal content and structure to determine the factors that might account for differences in their levels of success and to discover ways to transfer this newly discovered knowledge.

The persuasion patterns, which were created from the data from Erwin (2001), contained such major basic elements as getting customers to acknowledge the problem and changing their attitudes and behavior. One critical factor affecting the success or failure of persuasion procedures is the actual communication content, in other words, the actual information communicated during conversations. Yada and Matsumura (2006) combined text mining and statistical methods and discovered groups of special vocabulary items, including words and phrases. After measuring the frequency of these key terms, they were able to identify and extract knowledge that underlies superior negotiating skills. In the case of these skills, the quantitative frequencies of the use of these words and phrases in negotiation conversations and underlying structures were clarified. However, although the static characteristics of these conversations and interplay became known, understanding of the dynamic aspects of these processes remains clearly insufficient: the knowledge gained is not yet readily usable.

Most studies in persuasion and negotiation process have focused on structural causes (Fishbein & Ajzen, 1981). For example, frameworks were proposed that figure out influence on persuasion success by message acceptance or impact (Kunda, 1990; Lutz, 1975). However, there is no study that treats the dynamic persuasion process, that is, a real conversation among people who persuade. As far as we know, there is no study that quantifies the conversation process and reveals a cause-and-effect relationship between its success and failure. Such an understanding of the persuasion process brings us theoretical contributions and has practical significance for marketing experts (Ahluwalia, 2000).

Thus, in this study, labels were created that identify the various words and phrases contained in these conversations and the roles that they play in the flow of these conversations. These terms are presented and used as a framework for analyzing the persuasion processes involved. In addition, analyzing the conversation logs of the actual late payment collection problems of the company demonstrated that by converting to knowledge clearly indicated concerning negotiating skills, a useful, effective analysis framework was established. The main objective of this study is to develop such a framework to make it possible to create a model of the persuasion process and to verify its usefulness using actual company data.

11.2   FRAMEWORK FOR THE PERSUASION COMMUNICATION PROCESS

In this section, we describe a persuasion communication framework that can be used to explain our intention and extract explicit knowledge related to persuasion skills. Figure 11.1 shows the analysis framework for the persuasion process.

This framework mainly includes "Modeling of a Persuasion Process," as in the upper left of Figure 11.1, which divides persuasion communication into stepwise aspects, and "Persuasion Process Analysis," as arrows connect processes in Figure 11.1, which analyzes each modeled process.

11.2.1   MODELING OF A PERSUASION PROCESS

Persuasion communication never ends in a short message but progresses gradually. Such communication includes the following processes.

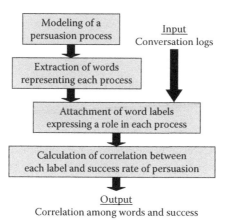

FIGURE 11.1 Analysis framework for persuasion process.

[Persuasion Process]

A. Necessity explanation for action
B. Creation of a climate to act
C. Negotiating on an action method
D. Final confirmation of action

That is, a man who wants to persuade initially informs a target person of the necessity of action (A) and convinces him or her to accept the intention to act (B). If the target agrees with the action, concrete methods to act are negotiated (C) and final confirmation is given to him or her (D). In practice, this process model depends on the content of the persuasion and is modified by eliminating or dividing processes for its application. The model for a debt-collecting process is described in the next section.

11.2.2 FLOW OF PERSUASION PROCESS ANALYSIS

Each modeled process is used to analyze which process leads to the success or failure for acquiring skills to use words and knowing which process should be concentrated on. In this framework, words representing each process's subject, called theme keywords, are prepared. By analyzing which word is used with theme keywords, we can know how each word is related to the subject. Then each word is labeled as the name of the relationship toward the subject. Finally, correlations between labels and success/failure are calculated as knowledge clues that lead to persuasion success.

11.3 MODELING OF A DEBT-COLLECTING PROCESS

In this section, we describe a process model for a debt-collecting problem by applying the framework described in the last section. That is, a debt-collecting process corresponds to the persuasion process as follows.

[Debt-Collecting Process]

A. Necessity explanation for payment
B. Creation of a climate to pay
C. Negotiating on a payment method
D. Final payment confirmation

The subject of persuasion is "debt collecting," and the desired action is replaced with customer "payment." However, process zero is not concerned because the customer has used the services under recognition of the obligation to pay, although he or she may pretend not to know. In the rest of this section, the details of each process are described.

11.3.1 CREATION OF A CLIMATE TO PAY

When persuading late payers, the emotions and feelings of the party being persuaded are likely to affect the success (McGuire, 1985). The late payer, regarding requests for payment, will not necessarily take a positive attitude and may look for opportunities to offer excuses why he or she will not pay and attempt to avoid paying. For the operator to convince the late payer to change his or her attitude toward the debt, it is necessary to supply the late payer with detailed information concerning the situation and to warn him or her of possible consequences while remaining calm. First, the late payer, who has already been officially notified several times that this bill is overdue, has chosen to ignore such notifications. The late payer is likely to negatively react to persuasion for the required payment (Boyd, 1995). Therefore it is necessary to change his attitude using warnings and communicating the facts.

11.3.2   NEGOTIATING ON A PAYMENT METHOD

When these persons are themselves contributing to this process and when they sufficiently understand the content of the persuasion, based on this information, they tend to change their attitudes (Petty & Cacioppo, 1986). To get them to follow through with payment, in the case of such negotiations, the operator must usually indicate specific and concrete methods of payment several times. Such conversation may involve the late payer more positively and also help the late payer accurately understand the problems involved when paying late. This process significantly improves the recovery success ratio.

11.3.3   FINAL PAYMENT CONFIRMATION

When recovering late payments, because the late payer will use such excuses as misunderstanding and forgetting to deflect requests for payment, to keep the late payer from avoiding payment, the operator must often reconfirm the payment method to which the late payer has agreed. Repetition strengthens the understanding of the content and promotes changes in the attitude of the late payer (Hasher, 1977). By repeating the content of the negotiation, the operator has the opportunity to restress the content and get the late payer to take action.

11.3.4   KEY POINTS CONCERNING RECOVERY OF LATE PAYMENTS

A basic factor is to surround the late payer with a climate to pay using the payment persuasion process described above. The sequence probably begins with negotiation on the payment method and then moves to reconfirmation, for the last time, of the payment method. The operator must carry this process out quickly and effectively to encourage the late payer to pay. When the operator is responsible for a relatively large number of late payers, it is necessary to handle this matter as simply as possible without spending too much time on a given late payer. It is better not to spend a whole hour on one late payer even if successful but, rather, to divide 1 hour among six late payers and collect from two of them. This approach leads to the recovery of greater sums. Using these factors, it was possible to clarify the structure of the persuasion content of late payment collection procedures. However, using a new framework was necessary for expressing the time flow–related changes in the persuasion content of the conversations. To acquire knowledge making it possible to conduct the persuasion procedures more quickly, a method of analyzing persuasion content had to be created.

11.4 DISCOVERING NEW KNOWLEDGE CONCERNING THE PERSUASION PROCESS USING BUSINESS

In this section, we describe an analysis method to find a significant process and how to use words for effective persuasion communication. The procedures for analysis are as follows.

1. Decide topics and vocabulary items contained in communication concerning the major important themes (theme vocabulary).
2. Assign term labels to all vocabulary items in communication based on distances between each item and a theme vocabulary.
3. Calculate relationship between frequency of use of various themes (and theme-related) vocabulary and information concerning success/failure of the persuasion process.

11.4.1 THEMES AND THEME VOCABULARY ITEMS

For the above analyzing procedure of the persuasion process, the first step is to create theme vocabulary items to identify each persuasion communication process. Concerning themes directly related to collection of overdue payments, three different category titles were established: "Creation of a climate to pay," "Negotiating on a payment method," and "Final payment confirmation."

For this chapter, the vocabulary items used in conversation logs concerning overdue payment collection, by analyzing the various factors involved, and using the results obtained elsewhere (Yada & Matsumura, 2006), these factors were divided into groups that consisted of appropriate key element words. The words included in each group are called "factor keywords." However, the data that we used were actual company data that contained many background noises. Because the data contained many vocabulary items with low relevance to the factor keyword categories, the vocabulary items in each category with the highest relevance to the critical themes were selected and called "theme keywords." Table 11.1 shows a list of factor keywords.

TABLE 11.1
Theme Vocabulary Items by Factor Analysis and Selected Theme Keywords

Process Title	Factor Keywords	Theme Keywords
Creation of a climate to pay	letter, money, arrears, interest, shop, defense, can use, promise, document, request for payment, lawyer	request for payment, letter, document, arrears, interest
Negotiating on a payment method	confirmation, request, remit, partial payments, remittance, full payment, letter, full amount, arrival, defense, promise	sum, remittance, full payment, partial payment, full amount
Final confirmation of payment	request, partial payment, can pay, receive, court, courthouse	pay, can pay, receive, submit, make payment

Words appearing in multiple processes are underlined.

TABLE 11.2

Six Function Labels and Their Roles as a Word

Label	Meaning
TOPIC	Conversation theme vocabulary item (theme word corresponding to theme/factor keyword)
FLOW	Theme-related word (also, previously used word)
NEW	Newly introduced word (first use)
INC	Word incorporated into theme-related vocabulary items, not related at first use
BYWAY	Previously used, non-related theme vocabulary item
FLOOD	First used vocabulary item not related to a theme

---

and theme keywords. (These words were extracted by a Japanese morpheme analysis system [ChaSen] and translated to English [Matsumoto et al., 2000].)

11.4.2 ASSIGNMENT OF LABELS

In conversations between the overdue customers and collectors, a number of vocabulary items were used (including nouns and verbs). To carry out the analysis, explanatory function labels were used. In other words, for the vocabulary items used in the conversations, the six function labels in Table 11.2 were used based on the accompanying definitions.

Theme vocabulary items given in the last subsection are labeled as TOPIC and the others can be divided into two major categories that include the various label types with a clear relationship to themes (FLOW, NEW, INC) and less closely related/nonrelated to theme items (BYWAY, FLOOD). Classification by relevance to a given theme is based on whether a given item appears within the 10 preceding given theme words or within the 10 words following a given theme word. A given item that satisfies this rule at least once is classified as a "theme-related vocabulary item." In Figure 11.2, based on this degree of given theme-relatedness, the item that first appears is labeled as (NEW) or (FLOOD), if suitable. When a term that is labeled as NEW at first is encountered again, the term is labeled as (FLOW). When a term that is labeled as FLOOD at first is encountered again, the term is labeled as (BYWAY) if the term is not encountered within a 10-word location from any theme keywords. If a term that is labeled as FLOOD or BYWAY is encountered again within a 10-word location, it is labeled as (INC) only this time and labeled as (FLOW) if the term is encountered more often.

For example, suppose the theme of this subsection is "label"; because the word "function" is used with "label" at any time, "function" is labeled as (NEW) at first and as (FLOW) after that. On the other hand, because "item" is far from "label" at first and near in the second use, "item" is labeled as (FLOOD) at first, as (INC) at the second use, and as (FLOW) after that.

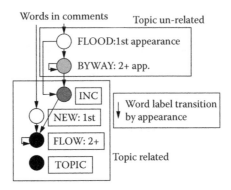

FIGURE 11.2 Six function labels and their transition patterns, along with a word appearance repetition.

11.4.3 ANALYSIS METHOD FOR CONVERSATION LOGS

To analyze which conversation is effective, the information contained in successful conversations is important. Therefore correlation coefficients between success/failure and the number of labeled words are calculated using such transactions where success or failure is expressed as one or zero, respectively.

Because the conversation logs handled by this chapter did not have information about persuasion success, we used an operator overdue payment collection ratio, defined as the number of customers the operator successfully persuaded divided by the customers the operator tried to persuade in advance.

Equation 11.1 calculates the correlation coefficients for conversation i, label j, occurrence $rate_i(j)$ using the number of label j appearances in i, $num_i(j)$ given as Equation 11.2 and p_i, conversation i for operator overdue payment collection. The terms in Equation 11.1, overlined values mean each averaged values given as Equation 11.3 and Equation 11.4.

$$cor(j) = \frac{\sum_{i=1}^{n}((rate_i(j) - \overline{rate(j)})(p_i - \overline{p}))}{\sqrt{\sum_{i=1}^{n}(rate_i(j) - \overline{rate(j)})^2 \sum_{i=1}^{n}(p_i - \overline{p})^2}} \tag{11.1}$$

$$rate_i(j) = \frac{num_i(j)}{\sum_j num_i(j)} \tag{11.2}$$

$$\overline{rate(j)} = \frac{1}{n}\sum_{i=1}^{n} rate_i(j) \tag{11.3}$$

$$\overline{p} = \frac{1}{n}\sum_{i=1}^{n} p_i \tag{11.4}$$

In each process, if labels have positive/negative correlations with collection ratios, the recovery ratio will be improved by not using negative labeled words but by using positive ones.

11.5   EXPERIMENTS

In this section, experimental results are described to verify the effect of the analysis framework and acquired knowledge for debt-collecting persuasion.

11.5.1   CONDITIONS FOR EXPERIMENTS

The data for this experiment, which were provided by a telecommunications company, included billing for amount (whether overdue reminders were sent out was not a condition) and records of conversations with late payers aimed at collecting late payments. The experiment involved 15 operators who carried out a total of 108 conversations with late payers to collect overdue payments. Table 11.3 shows collection ratios calculated by operators, who were supplied with the vocabulary items that included the factor and theme keywords of Table 11.1.

First, term (label) usage ratios for each conversation by each operator were calculated. Then the collection ratio correlations with each theme label were calculated, from which the most effective given theme-related terms (labels) were identified.

TABLE 11.3
**Number of Conversations by Operators
and Their Collection Ratios**

Operator No.	Number of Conversations	Collection Ratios
1	7	0.231
2	8	0.174
3	9	0.171
4	3	0.156
5	5	0.152
6	5	0.152
7	11	0.147
8	7	0.133
9	8	0.132
10	9	0.122
11	9	0.122
12	9	0.116
13	7	0.112
14	8	0.110
15	3	0.105
	Total 108	**Average 0.142**

TABLE 11.4
Correlations by Label for Successful Collection

Process Title		TOPIC	FLOW	NEW	INC	BYWAY	FLOOD
Creation of a climate	Factor	0.07	0.09	0.14	0.26	−0.17	0.03
to pay	Theme	0.06	−0.35	−0.30	0.28	−0.01	0.13
Negotiating on a	Factor	0.23	−0.06	0.11	0.16	−0.11	0.01
payment method	Theme	0.48	0.55	0.48	0.19	−0.32	−0.20
Final payment	Factor	0.31	0.44	0.14	0.35	−0.27	0.03
confirmation	Theme	0.20	−0.17	−0.06	0.19	−0.08	0.10
Total process	Factor	0.42	−0.04	0.18	0.58	−0.32	−0.09
	Theme	0.53	0.12	0.26	0.51	−0.44	−0.11

It was possible to interpret the flow of a given conversation and suggest effective collection strategies.

11.5.2 RESULTS OF EXPERIMENTS

Table 11.4 shows the correlation results for each respective theme label, where the table results are based on the calculations for all vocabulary items for all theme categories by Equation 11.1. For the various labels, correlations indicate the relative levels of successful collection when the given term is used. In addition, negative correlations (when indicated) mean that collection rates are higher than when these negative correlation label vocabulary items are not used.

Figure 11.3 summarizes Table 11.3 by two sets of words, theme-related labels and non–theme-related labels. The theme-related words include TOPIC, FLOW, DIV, and INC. The non–theme-related words include BYWAY and FLOOD.

11.5.2.1 Results of Factor Keywords

In Table 11.4, when the related correlations for respective labels are examined, the values for factor keywords have relatively weak correlation. One possible interpretation indicates that, for each respective process, vocabulary items with different meanings such as "shop," "defense," and "court" have been included. In addition, common words in multiple processes such as "letter," "defense," "promise," "request," and "partial payment" are included. Therefore the division for each process was insufficient to analyze the persuasion process.

The correlation of the last process, "final payment confirmation," was high because of the words "request," "partial payment," and "court" that do not appear in theme keywords. However, because "request" and "partial payment" also appeared in the other processes mentioned above, these words are not definitely related only to final confirmation. In addition, "court" does not mean final confirmation but instead a threat to a customer such as "If you don't pay, we'll go to court."

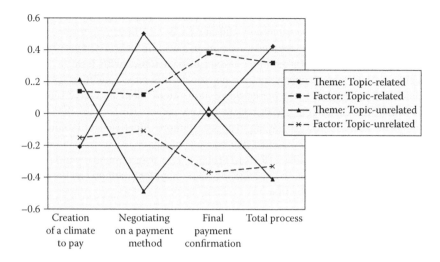

FIGURE 11.3 Correlations by topic relation for successful collection.

11.5.2.2 Results of Theme Keywords

In Figure 11.3, the "negotiating on a payment method" process was the most relevant to successful results, and other processes were low. This result suggests that good operators who have high performance ratios spend their time "negotiating on a payment method" process and do not waste time on other processes. If concrete methods are discussed in the process, the last process, the "final payment confirmation," is not so relevant.

The correlation of label FLOW was highest in the "negotiating on a payment method" process in Table 11.4, which suggests words related to payment method should be frequently and positively used during persuasion.

The correlation of label INC, which refers to words incorporated from unrelated ones to related, was high in the total process. Therefore, words should be clearly connected to the subject—even words that the customer might know tacitly.

The correlation of label BYWAY was negative in the total process, which suggests that topics unrelated to the subject lead to failure. Therefore, if an operator feels the conversation drifting off the subject, he or she should return to the topic and should not continue the current topic.

As a result, theme keywords were effective for acquiring considerable results and interpretation in the persuasion process analysis compared to factor keywords output by factor analysis.

11.5.2.3 Implications Related to Payment Persuasion Process

The frequent use of the vocabulary items related to the three late payment collection themes "creation of a climate to pay," "negotiating on payment method," and "final payment confirmation" appears to help raise levels of successful collection

However, based on the new knowledge of the process that we gained, the "creation of a climate to pay" theme seemingly did not have very high importance, and the time spent negotiating on "method of payment" was, in contrast, more important for successful collection. In addition, conversational topics with little or no direct relevance to the major themes tended to negatively influence collection levels. Such diversions seemingly made the persuasion content ambivalent, and there seems to be a possibility that such irrelevant factors negatively affect efforts to get the late payer to change his attitudes toward paying. It appeared more effective to communicate the assumption that the late payer must pay because of his or her responsibility and to eliminate, as much as possible, efforts to produce a positive climate toward payment. The most emphasis was put on "negotiating about payment method" as the best way to increase the level of collection.

11.5.3 ADDITIONAL EXPERIMENTS BY RECONSTRUCTED THEME KEYWORDS

The above experiment found that the most important process for the debt-collecting persuasion process was "negotiating on a payment method." To reconfirm this result and to analyze more precisely, additional experiments were executed using new theme vocabulary items.

First, we extracted all words from all conversation logs and calculated correlation coefficients between each word and each operator's collection ratio. Equation 11.1 was applied where $rate_i(j)$ had one or zero whether each log i included each word j. Then new processes "payment method" and "situation confirmation" were created using words that had high or low correlation. Table 11.5 shows correlations by new theme vocabulary items for successful collections.

High-correlation words express conversations about payment methods and how much a customer remits this month and next month, including arrears interests. Low-correlation words express conversations about such situation confirmations as "you should have a request letter that confirmed your use, and you promised to pay." These new processes make concrete the former processes of "negotiating on a payment method" and the "creation of a climate to pay" and express other words.

TABLE 11.5
Correlations by New Theme Vocabulary Items for Successful Collection

Payment Method	Correlation	Situation Confirmation	Correlation
This month	0.169	Request for payment	−0.116
Next month	0.310	Letter	−0.157
Remittance	0.346	Document	−0.172
Sum	0.244	Arrival	−0.171
Receive	0.172	Use	−0.120
Submit	0.162	State	−0.156
Arrears	0.128	Payment	−0.059
Interest	0.161	Promise	−0.113

TABLE 11.6

Correlations by Labels Successful Collection

New Process Title	TOPIC	FLOW	NEW	INC	BYWAY	FLOOD
Payment method	0.79	0.66	0.65	0.80	−0.62	−0.44
Situation confirmation	−0.57	−0.11	−0.41	−0.47	0.16	0.36

Table 11.6 and Table 11.7 show correlations by label for successful collection by giving new theme vocabulary items.

In Table 11.6, the "payment method" process had a positive 0.8 correlation in TOPIC. By contrast, the "situation confirmation" process had a medium −0.5 correlation in TOPIC.

In Table 11.7, because the "payment method" process has high correlation not only in TOPIC but also in FLOW, NEW, and INC and has negative correlation in BYWAY and FLOOD, the conversation should be preceded by a limit in the concrete payment method that avoids other non-relational topics.

In the "situation confirmation" process, correlations are negative in TOPIC, NEW, and INC and weakly negative in FLOW. This result suggests that when an operator confirmed a customer's situation, topics sometimes varied so that the operator wasted time without collection.

11.5.4   DISCUSSION OF WORD USAGE IN DEBT-COLLECTING PROBLEMS

This subsection discusses word usage that leads to debt collection. Table 11.8 shows high-frequency words in all conversation logs with correlations to collection ratios. The top seven words, from "call" to "contact," indicate almost zero or negative values in correlation, which implies that the debt will not be collected, even if the operator repeats the same words. Table 11.8 includes both positive and negative words that will be classified into two sets: realized collection or not. Based on the results of previous experiments, these words are classified into "payment method" and "situation confirmation." Thus operators should steer their conversations toward "payment method."

This result is related through an operator having initiative in his or her conversation. Figure 11.4 shows the cumulating appearance ratio, the number of unrelated words over the number of used words in each 10-folded conversation, and topic-related words along with a conversation stream in which high operators denote

TABLE 11.7

Correlations by Theme-Related Labels for Successful Collection

New Process Title	Theme-Related Labels Total	Theme-Unrelated Labels Total
Payment method	0.81	−0.82
Situation confirmation	−0.46	0.47

TABLE 11.8
Correlations by High-Frequency Words

Word	Frequency	Correlation
Call	362	−0.028
Say	257	−0.186
Payment	242	−0.059
Think	214	−0.070
Invoice	185	0.005
Pay	179	−0.013
Contact	154	−0.012
This month	138	0.169
Today	131	−0.066
Division	127	0.041
Number	124	0.106
Cellular phone	119	0.043
Remit	118	0.175
Contract	112	−0.046
Submit	106	0.162
Remittance	104	0.346
Go	102	−0.160
Letter	101	−0.157

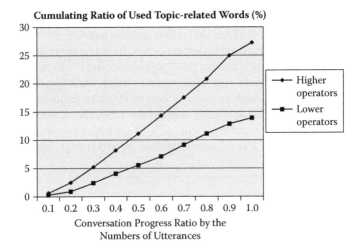

FIGURE 11.4 Cumulating appearance ratio of topic-related words along with conversation stream.

averaged value by the seven whose collection ratios are above average and low operators mean the other eight. Comparing both lines, they differ from 0.2 or 0.3, and there are twice as many high operators as low. This depends on who takes the initiative first; topic-related words cannot be appeared if a customer takes. In other words, if an operator has an initiative, the topic will be "payment method," but if the customer controls the conversation, the topic will be excuses for the debt.

Even if an operator takes the initiative, debt collection may fail without considering a customer's intention. This is confirmed by Table 11.7, which shows 0.8 correlation in INC. This label is given to words initially unrelated to the topic but related as the conversation proceeds. Table 11.9 shows words labeled as INC once with the collection ratio where it includes cases in which the words are not labeled as INC. Because the label INC is given to each word only once in each log, the number corresponds to the number of logs.

Because the top eight words in Table 11.9 are common words in Table 11.8, they are necessary for debt-collection persuasion. However, collection ratios are not so high compared with the ratio of new theme vocabulary items in Table 11.5. Therefore these words have high collection ratios when labeled as INC because these necessary words were used without verbal omission of theme words and utilized clear explanations and understandings.

In addition, 120 kinds of words were labeled INC. Low-frequency words included customer situation terms such as "job," "salary," "company," "student," and "income."

Persuasion will not succeed as part of a one-sided conversation. Conversations using the words of the late payer are summarized as follows.

1. Expressing sympathy
2. Showing understanding of the situation
3. Considering the level of understanding

Because a person who pays is not an operator but a debtor, grasping his or her intention by using his or her words is the most effective way to collection.

TABLE 11.9
Words Labeled as INC

Word	Frequency	Correlation
Call	15	−0.028
Payment	13	−0.059
Think	9	−0.070
Say	8	−0.186
Division	7	0.041
Pay	7	−0.013
Remit	7	0.175
Invoice	7	0.005
Charge	6	−0.030
Wait	6	−0.027
Make payment	6	0.061

11.6 CONCLUSION

In this chapter, to analyze the payment persuasion process, various parts of negotiation conversations were given labels indicating their role in the process. Then these content items were quantified and a framework for their analysis was presented. Using actual company data for experimentation, we demonstrated that the analysis framework was effective. Results showed that to increase the collection of overdue payments, more emphasis must be placed on "negotiating on a payment method" and eliminating other processes as much as possible. In addition, operators must take the initiative and express sympathy to customers and negotiate using the words of customers themselves that lead to debt collection.

REFERENCES

Ahluwalia, R. Examination of psychological processes underlying resistance to persuasion, *J. Consumer Res.*, 27, 217–232, 2000.

Boyd, H.C. Effects of fear appeal format and consumer personality on ad processing and persuasion: a preliminary analysis, *Marketing Lett.*, 6, 211–220, 1995.

Erwin, P. *Attitudes and Persuasion,* Psychology Press, Philadelphia, PA, 2001.

Fishbein, M. and Ajzen, I. Acceptance, yielding, and impact: cognitive processes, in *Persuasion, Cognitive Responses in Persuasion,* Petty, R.E., Ostrom, T.M., and Brock, T.C., Eds., Erlbaum, Hillsdale, 1981, pp. 339–359.

Hasher, L., Goldstein, D., and Toppino, T. Frequency and the conference of referential validity, *J. Verbal Learning Verbal Behav.*, 16, 107–112, 1977.

Kunda, Z. The case for motivated reasoning, *Psych. Bull.,* 108, 480–498, 1990.

Lutz, R.J. Changing brand attitudes through modification of cognitive structure, *J. Consumer Res.,* 1, 49–59, 1975.

Matsumoto, Y., Kitauchi, A., Yamashita, T., Hirano, Y., Matsuda, H., Takaoka, K., and Asahara, M. Japanese morphological analysis system ChaSen, version 2.2.1, 2000. Information available online at: http://chasen.naist.jp/hiki/ChaSen/. Accessed June 30, 2008.

McGuire, W.J. Attitudes and attitude change, in *The Handbook of Social Psychology,* 3rd ed., Lindzey, G. and Aronson, E., Eds., Random House, New York, 1985, pp. 233–346.

Petty, R.E. and Cacioppo, J.T. *Communication and Persuasion: Central and Peripheral Routes to Persuasion,* Springer-Verlag, New York, 1986.

Yada, K. and Matsumura, N. Knowledge discovery from the structure of persuasive communication, *Proceedings of 2006 IEEE Conference on System, Man and Cybernetics,* IEEE Press, 1741–1746, 2006.

12 Association Bundle-Based Market Basket Analysis

Wenxue Huang, Milorad Krneta,
Limin Lin, and Jianhong Wu

CONTENTS

12.1   INTRODUCTION

Market basket analysis (MBA) discovers association patterns in retail transaction data. Marketing applications, such as the *product recommendation* and the *bundling product for promotion*, use the discovered patterns to customize strategies. This type of application, referred as to *MBA-based applications* in this chapter, can have very different formats. For example, the process of product recommendation takes the format of *query with condition*, which has certain given products and searches for products associated with these given products. But in the process of bundling products, the format is basically *query without condition*, which has no given product and searches for combinations to increase profits via among-product associations.

Different applications have different requirements for the exploration of structures to display the association relationships in patterns. They may require different *number of association relationships*, and these associations may be *between-items* or *between-sets*; *symmetric* or *asymmetric*. For example, in applications of product recommendation, the issue involves the association between the given products and others. Thus the required structure needs to display an association relationship, and the relationship is between two sets, and is asymmetric with antecedent (given products) and consequent (identified products). On the other hand, in applications of bundling productions, the issue involves among all products associations. As such, one association relationship is usually not enough; an ideal structure should reveal multiple associations, such as *between-every-two-items* associations or *between-every two-subsets* associations.

Unfortunately, only one association pattern—the association rule (AR)—has received much attention in MBA. AR was first introduced by Agrawal et al.[1] in 1993, and an association rule often expressed in the form $\{x_1,\dots,x_m\} \Rightarrow \{y_1,\dots,y_n\}$ consists of two sets of items, $\{x_1,\dots,x_m\}, m \geq 1$ and $\{y_1,\dots,y_n\}, n \geq 1$, satisfying the following two conditions, given s as the *support threshold* and c the *confidence threshold*:

$$\text{Condition 1: } Pr(x_1,\ldots,x_m,y_1,\ldots,y_n) \geq s,$$

$$\text{Condition 2: } Pr(y_1,\ldots,y_n \mid x_1,\ldots,x_m) \geq c.$$

The AR pattern is designed for *enhancing database with functionalities to process queries*. Five examples were presented in the pioneering work,[1] though few discussions were made on the structure of AR and its applications—perhaps because this structure is easy to understand and match the query applications intuitively well.

However, for applications other than query, AR patterns may not be a good solution. One obvious example is the application of bundling products described previously: AR pattern displays one association relationship between an antecedent set and a consequent set, whereas bundling products requires associations evaluated between every two items or every two subsets. Even with the query applications, further development beyond AR seems to be required. For example, in four of the five examples provided in the work by Agrawal,[1] the between-set association and the between-items association were somehow not fully differentiated; in particular, the between-sets association was used to support reasoning on the between-items relationship. We will return to this point later.

We believe that detailed description and careful exploration of the structure of patterns are needed to resolve some of these problems of developing applications of an existing pattern or identifying new patterns for interesting applications. For this purpose, in this chapter, we first examine pattern structures of AR and use some identified features to explore appropriate applications. We then discuss some new structures to design patterns for applications to which AR may not be suitable. We focus on two patterns, the *pair homogeneity-based association bundles* and the *complete homogeneity-based association bundles* and illustrate their applications to MBA. We develop a new association measure, *weighted association strength*, to use these patterns in a meaningful way. We also provide supporting algorithms and discuss our experimental results.

This chapter is organized as follows. In Section 12.2, the pattern structures of AR are investigated and their appropriate applications are studied. Two new association patterns are presented in Section 12.3, and their applications are discussed in Section 12.4. The supporting algorithms are described in the Section 12.5, and some experimental results are reported in Section 12.6. We conclude with a few remarks in Section 12.7.

12.2 AR PATTERN—STRUCTURES AND APPLICATIONS

In this section, we study pattern structures of AR and discuss their potential applications. We hope to make the following points.

1. AR applications are determined by AR structures.
2. AR-based applications without reference to AR structure may be potentially misleading.

3. AR can only solve certain application problems.
4. New association patterns are required for applications that cannot be solved by AR.

We first briefly review AR mining using an example provided by Agrawal.[2] Figure 12.1a describes the data set that contains four records in which each record contains items from the set $I = \{1,2,3,4,5\}$. AR mining discovers all possible pairs of item sets $X \subset I$ and $Y \subset I$, $S \cap Y = \varnothing$, where X is the rule antecedent and Y is the rule consequent, such that for the given support threshold s and the confidence threshold c, the concurrence probability of X and Y is greater than or equal to s, and the conditional probability of Y over X is $\geq c$. Here the probability of X is defined as the ratio of the number of records containing X over the total number of records, and the conditional probability of Y over X is the ratio of the probability of the union X and Y over the probability of X.

The two-stage approach is often used for association rule mining. The first stage is to identify the frequent item sets (FIS), which are item sets that have the probability greater than or equal to the support thresholds. The a-priori algorithm[2] is a classical algorithm for the frequent item set identification. It first identifies the size-2 FIS, then the size-3 FIS based on the size-2 FIS and so on. The FIS for the considered example is shown in Figure 12.1b. Note that the process of finding frequent item sets in a large

(a) Database

TID	Items
100	1 3 4
200	2 3 5
300	1 2 3 5
400	2 5

(b) Frequent Item Sets

size	FIS (s=1/2)
2	{1, 3} , Prob(1,3)=1/2 {2, 3}, Prob(2,3)=1/2 {2, 5}, Prob(2,5)=3/4 {3, 5}, Prob(3,5)=1/2
3	{2, 3, 5}, Prob(2,3,5)=1/2

(c) Association Rules

FIS	Association Rules (c= 23/48)
{1, 3}	1 <= 3, Prob(1|3)=2/3 3 <= 1, Prob(3|1)=1
{2, 3}	2 <= 3, Prob(2|3)=2/3 3 <= 2, Prob(3|2)=2/3
{2, 5}	2 <= 5, Prob(2|5)=1 5 <= 2, Prob(5|2)=1
{3, 5}	3<= 5, Prob(3|5)=2/3 5 <= 3, Prob(5|3)=2/3
{2, 3, 5}	2 <= {3, 5}, Prob(2 | 5,3)=1 3 <= {2, 5}, Prob(3 | 2,5)=2/3 5 <={2, 3}, Prob(5 | 2,3)=1

FIGURE 12.1 An example of association rule mining.

database is computationally very expensive, because it involves searching a lattice that, in the worst case, grows exponentially with respect to the number of items. During the last decade, much has been done in resolving this problem, and a variety of algorithms have been introduced to render the search feasible by exploiting various properties of the lattice (Equivalence Class Transformation [ECLAT],[15] frequent pattern [FP]-growth,[5] Charm,[6] Closet[12]). The second stage is to generate rules based on the identified frequent item sets. Each frequent item set S is divided into two parts, X and Y, so that X and Y make an association rule $X \Rightarrow Y$ if the conditional probability Y over X is greater than or equal to the threshold c (see Figure 12.1c).

The pattern structures of AR have three features.

1. There is one association relationship displayed.
2. The association is displayed between two sets.
3. The association is asymmetric.

In the following two subsections, we discuss the MBA applications of AR with reference to the above structures.

12.2.1 ASYMMETRIC FEATURE AND THE "LOYALTY" RELATIONSHIP

AR displays an asymmetric relationship between two sets. What does this asymmetric feature imply comparing with the concept of statistical correlation? The applications listed by Agrawal shows that the asymmetric relationship they discussed is strongly related to statistical correlation, because "the occurrence of one set having effect on another set" is exactly the scenario described by statistical correlation. However, the statistical correlation between two sets X and Y is usually a symmetric relationship. It states that if the set X is positively/negatively correlated with the set Y, then the set Y is also positively/negatively correlated with the set X, with the same strength. It is then natural to ask why an asymmetric relationship is used in an association rule. It seems to us that a "loyalty" type of relationship, which is actually a subset of the positive correlation, is what the authors presented by using the asymmetric structure when they developed the association rule pattern. This observation is supported by comparing two measures: the conditional probability and the lift. The conditional probability measures the asymmetric relationship, whereas the lift measures the (symmetric) statistical correlation. The two measures are related in the following two aspects.

1. If the conditional probability $Pr(Y|X)$ equals 1 and $Pr(X)$ and $Pr(Y)$ are within $(0,1)$, then the $lift(X,Y)$ is greater than 1, which means that X and Y must be positively correlated with each other.
2. If the conditional probability $Pr(Y|X)$ is less than 1, then the $lift(X,Y)$ can be greater than or equal to or less than 1, which means that X and Y can be positively correlated, independent, or negatively correlated with each other.

A set Y is said to be "loyal" to the set X, if the set X occurs whenever the set Y also occurs (i.e., $Pr(Y|X) = 1$. If $Pr(Y|X) = 1$), based on (F1), then the two sets X and Y

are positively correlated and hence the occurrence of X can affect the occurrence of Y and vice versa. Furthermore, if the loyalty of Y to X can be kept in a perfect "one-on-one"' form—one record increase of Y is followed by one record increase of X—then the effect of any change in X on Y can be quantified. The loyalty relationship thus makes association rules easy to understand and use.

Note that a transaction database is static; it only tells what has happened before. Because no dynamic data are available to tell about the effect of changing X on Y, decisions must be made based on the knowledge presented by the static data. For example, if X and Y are positively correlated, an actionable decision is to increase/ decrease the occurrence of X and to expect corresponding increasing/decreasing on Y and vice versa. Therefore ARs are designed to identify loyalty type of positive correlations. In such applications, a predefined condition must be met—the confidence threshold c for the conditional probability must be equal to or close enough to 1. Under such a condition, the loyalty and thus the positive correlation are guaranteed. If this condition is violated, based on (F2) described previously, the two sets X and Y may even have negative correlation.

There are two natural questions about AR: What if the data do not have any loyalty type correlation and association patterns are in need? What if the important positive correlations, either loyalty type or not, are of interest?

The first case, which arises quite often in the real-world MBA data, often results in an empty set of association rules. However, by definition, association rules can always be produced by lowering the confidence threshold c, though this method risks presenting negatively correlated item sets. A common remedy for the negative correlation is to use the correlation measure "Lift," though, in our opinion, this is not a direct way to solve the problem. If there is no loyalty type of positive correlation, then the target of MBA should switch to the second case described previously, in which important positive correlations should be investigated regardless of whether they are of loyalty type or not. As the associations change from asymmetric to symmetric; our approach should also change, for otherwise redundancy (switches between antecedent and consequent) and noisy (negative correlation) results will be produced.

Therefore symmetric association structures should be studied as a possible solution to the above questions. Symmetric association structures have important applications in MBA. For example, when bundling a group of products for promotion, the positive correlation between items is required, even if it is not a loyalty type.

12.2.2 BETWEEN-SET FEATURES AND LIMITATIONS

An AR displays only one association relationship between two subsets. The associations between individual items from the two subsets are *not* evaluated, and the usage of an association rule thus has the following limitations.

Limitation 1. When doing reasoning based on an association rule, the items in the rule antecedent (consequent) must be treated as a united body, a *combined item*, not as individual items. One cannot reason based on an association rule that individual items, as one of the many items in the rule antecedent, are associated with any of the consequent items. For example, the Association Rule Mining (ARM) functionality 2 (p. 1, Agrawal[1]) states: "Find all rules that have 'bagels' in the antecedent. These rules may help determine what products may be impacted if the store discontinues selling bagels." This statement is not true when the rule antecedent contains item other than "bagels," in which case "bagels" possibly has no association or even negative association with the consequent items. A more accurate description could be "Find all rules that have 'bagels' *as* the antecedent" (not *in* the antecedent; here, the rule antecedent should contain only bagels). These rules may help in determining what *product groups* (not *products*; here, the consequent part is product groups) may be affected if the store discontinues selling bagels.

Limitation 2. One has to be careful about the associations from *the subsets of antecedent items* to the consequent items when the occurrence of the *entire set of antecedent items* is not deterministically given. For example, in the shelf/inventory arrangement, a typical application is to promote the consequent items by putting them together with the antecedent items. Because no conditions are imposed on the association from the individual antecedent item to the consequent, it is possible that there exists certain item x_i in the rule antecedent having a "negative promotion" on the consequent. Figure 12.1c shows such an example, the rule $S \leq 2, 3$. In this example, the itemset $\{2, 3\}$ has positive correlation with the item set $\{5\}$, $Pr(5 \mid 2, 3) = 1 > Pr(3)$; however, because $Pr(5 \mid 2) = 2/3 < Pr(5)$, the item 2 has negative correlation with the item 5. In cases such as this, if customers choose the item x_i more often than they choose the entire set of antecedent items, then an unexpected *lost* instead of promotion could happen to the consequent items.

Therefore, the between-set association structure in the association rule limits its usage in applications where *between-item* associations in a group of items are required. One example of such applications is the shelf/inventory arrangement, as discussed previously. Another example is the cross-selling among a group of items by discounting on one of them. So a natural question arises: Is there any association structure that presents the between-item associations of an item group? The next section intends to provide a partial answer to this question by developing two new patterns: the pair homogeneity-based association bundle and the complete homogeneity-based association bundle.

12.3 ASSOCIATION BUNDLES—NEW PATTERNS FOR AR

We are interested in *symmetrically structured* patterns, referred to as association bundles. A symmetric structure here refers to two features. First, the homogeneity in the pattern *displays equally on each and every* component unit. For example, in the pair homogeneity-based association bundle, the bundle component unit is the bundle item pair, and the homogeneity applies to each and every pair of bundle items. As a contrast, in an association rule, only one homogeneity relationship is displayed between the antecedent set and consequent set. Second, the *symmetric measure* is used in association bundles to evaluate association relationships, which do not distinguish antecedent and consequent. One pair of items in a pair of homogeneity-based association bundles is said to be homogeneous with other pairs, because their correlation strength is as important as other pairs. Their correlation has no antecedent and consequent. As a contrast, the two sets in an association rule are differentiated to be the antecedent and consequent by the asymmetric measure conditional probability.

We explore here two types of association bundles: the pair homogeneity-based association bundle and the complete homogeneity-based association bundle. The pair homogeneity-based association bundle was first introduced in a previous article[7] as the "association bundle." We rename it here using a more precise name to differentiate it from the new type of association bundles. Also in the previous article, we did not introduce *weight* into the association bundles.

In what follows, we first give the definitions of the two types of association bundles, and then discuss their structure features, association measures, threshold settings, and supporting algorithms in comparison with association rules.

12.3.1   PAIR HOMOGENEITY-BASED ASSOCIATION BUNDLES

12.3.1.1   Definition 3.1

Let $I = \{i_1, \ldots, i_{|I|}\}$ be the item set for database and $W_I = \{W_I(i_1), \ldots, W_I(i_{|I|})\}$ the item profits as weight. A pair homogeneity-based association bundle is an item group $B = \{i_1, \ldots, i_{|B|}\}, B \subseteq I$ where for any two items i_j and i_k of B their *weighted association strength* $WAS(i_j, i_k)$ is greater than or equal to the given threshold $T_{WAS} > 0$, that is,

$$WAS(i_j, i_k) \geq T_{WAS}, i_j, i_k \in B.$$

Here the weighted association strength $WAS(i_j, i_k)$ is defined to be the multiplication of the *joint weight* $W(i_j, i_k)$ and the *association strength* $A(i_j, i_k)$, that is,

$$WAS(i_j, i_k) = W(i_j, i_k) * A(i_j, i_k),$$

where the joint weight $W(i_j, i_k)$ for the item i_j and i_k is defined to be the sum of the weight of i_j and i_k, that is,

$$W(i_j, i_k) = W_I(i_j) + W_I(i_k),$$

and the association strength $A(i_j, i_k)$ for the item i_j and i_k is defined to be the increase of their concurrence probability brought by their positive correlation, that is,

$$A(i_j, i_k) = Pr(i_j, i_k) - Pr(i_j)Pr(i_k).$$

12.3.1.2   Definition 3.2

A *maximal pair homogeneity-based association bundle* is a pair homogeneity-based association bundle that is contained in no other pair homogeneity-based association bundles.

12.3.1.3   Association Structure

Distinct from association rules, which display the one-way association from the rule antecedent to the rule consequent, pair homogeneity-based association bundles impose a two-way association between every pair of bundle items. Therefore, although an association rule $(x_1, \ldots, x_m) \Rightarrow (y_1, \ldots, y_n)$ suggests that "if a customer buys the group of products $(x_1, \ldots, x_m)$, then he/she would also buy the group of products

$(y_1,\ldots,y_n)$ with the probability greater than or equal to c,"[6] a pair homogeneity-based association bundle $(i_1,\ldots,i_m)$ tells us that "for any pair of items (i_j, i_k) in the association bundle $(i_1,\ldots,i_m)$, the extra profit brought by the positive correlation between the items i_j and i_k is greater than or equal to T_{WAS}."

12.3.1.4 Association Measures

ARs use the conditional probability (confidence power) as the association measure (excellent discussions on association measures can be found elsewhere[9,11,13] and references therein). In our previous study on association bundles elsewhere,[7] two measures were used to evaluate the between-item association—the *between-item lift* and the *between-item conditional probabilities*. The between-item lift is used to guarantee that there is strong positive correlation between items; the two between-item conditional probabilities are used to ensure that the prediction accuracy of one item with respect to another item is high enough to be important in business.

Here, we introduce a new measure—the weighted association strength—into the bundle definition to tie more closely to real-world MBA applications. The weight is the item profit, and the association strength is adapted to the increase of the concurrence probability brought by the between-item positive correlation. In such a way, the weighted association strength has the practical meaning "the extra profit brought by the positive correlation," and an identified bundle "brings greater extra profit via positive correlations."

Note that we use the formula

$$A(i_j, i_k) = Pr(i_j, i_k) - Pr(i_j)Pr(i_k)$$

to measure the increase of the concurrence probability brought by the positive correlation. It is simple in form, but theoretically biased from the true estimation, although the difference is very small. The reason is that when the database is given (and no other information available), the occurrence of i_j is statistically not independent of i_k, which implies that the probability $Pr(i_j)$ is greater than the "actual" probability. The consequence of this bias is that the derived increase is smaller than the "actual" value.

One measure with adjustment to this bias is the following formula, which is the solution (the greater one of the two real solutions) to the following equation,

$$A(i_j, i_k) = \frac{Pr(i_j) + Pr(i_k) - 1}{2}$$
$$+ \frac{\sqrt{(Pr(i_j) + Pr(i_k) - 1)^2 - 4(Pr(i_j, i_k) - Pr(i_j)Pr(i_k))}}{2}, Pr(i_j, i_k) - A(i_j, i_k)$$
$$= (Pr(i_j) - A(i_j, i_k))(Pr(i_k) - A(i_j, i_k)),$$

where the left-hand side of the equation stands for the concurrence probability without correlation increase, and the right-hand side is the multiplication of two independent events' probability.

12.3.1.5 Threshold for Measures

In AR mining, the threshold for the conditional probability (confidence threshold) is configured by users, taking values in a fixed range [0,1]. In our previous study, a *dynamic process* for determining the threshold was introduced for association bundles. In the dynamic process, the upper and lower bounds of the threshold are not fixed; they should be determined by the data under investigation to have more meaningful and efficient computation. For example, for the measure Lift, the threshold $L(\beta)$ is defined as

$$L(\beta) = L_A + \beta(L_M - L_A), \beta \in [0,1],$$

where L_A and L_M are the mean and maximum lift of all positively correlated item pairs, and the parameter β is the *strength level threshold for lift* taking values in [0,1]. Obviously, both the upper boundary $L(1)$ and the lower boundary $L(0)$ are determined by database. By default, the threshold is $L(0)$, which is the mean of the lift determined by database.

In our study here, the threshold for the measure weighted association strength is defined using the same dynamic approach; that is,

$$T_{WAS}(\beta) = T_A + \beta(T_M - T_A), \beta \in [0,1],$$

where T_A and T_M are the mean and maximum weighted association strength for all positively correlated item pairs, and the parameter β is the *strength level threshold for weighted association strength* taking values in [0,1]. By default, the threshold is $T(0)$, which is the mean of the weighted association strength determined by database.

12.3.1.6 Supporting Algorithm

A challenge in identifying association rules is to identify the "frequent item sets," for which a series of excellent algorithms such as the ECLAT,[15] FP-growth,[5] Charm,[16] and Closet[12] have been developed.

To identify pair homogeneity-based association bundles, our previous article introduced a graph approach-based algorithm. The algorithm identifies the maximal pair homogeneity-based association bundles. The graph model maps each item into a vertex, and maps each item pair having the weighted association strength greater than or equal to the given threshold into an edge, then each maximal clique corresponds to a maximal pair homogeneity-based association bundle. Many algorithms on *maximal clique enumeration* can be applied, and our algorithm was designed to fit applications to transaction data in MBA.

Note that any subset of a maximal pair homogeneity-based association bundle is also a pair homogeneity-based association bundle, thus the smaller sized bundles can be derived from the larger ones. For example, given three as the size of interested bundles, then in addition to the identified size 3 maximal pair homogeneity-based association bundles, all size-m ($m > 3$) ones are also used to enumerate the size 3 subsets, and the final result is the union removing the redundancy.

12.4 COMPLETE HOMOGENEITY-BASED ASSOCIATION BUNDLES

12.4.1 DEFINITION 3.3

Let $I = (i_1,\ldots,i_{|I|})$ be the item set for database, and $W_I = \{W_I(i_1),\ldots,W_I(i_{|I|})\}$ the item profits as weight. A complete homogeneity-based association bundle is an item group $B = (i_1,\ldots,i_{|B|})$, $B \subseteq I$, where any two subsets S_1 and S_2 of B satisfy the condition that their weighted association strength $WAS(S_1,S_2)$ is greater than or equal to the given threshold $T_{WAS} > 0$, that is,

$$WAS(S_1,S_2) \geq T_{WAS}, S_1,S_2 \subset B.$$

Here the weighted association strength $WAS(S_1,S_2)$ is defined to be the multiplication of the joint weight $W(S_1,S_2)$ and the association strength $A(S_1,S_2)$, that is,

$$WAS(S_1,S_2) = W(S_1,S_2)A(S_1,S_2),$$

where the joint weight $W(S_1,S_2)$ for the subsets S_1 and S_2 is defined to be the sum of the weight of items in S_1 and S_2, that is,

$$W(S_1,S_2) = \sum_{i \in S_1 \cup S_2} W_I(i),$$

and the association strength $A(S_1,S_2)$ between the subsets S_1 and S_2 is defined to be the increase of the concurrence probability brought by the positive correlation between S_1 and S_2, that is,

$$A(S_1,S_2) = Pr(S_1,S_2) - Pr(S_1)Pr(S_2).$$

We further introduce two concepts, the (m_1,m_2) *homogeneity-based association bundle* and the *order-m-homogeneity-based association bundle*, to clarify the meaning of "complete" in the above definition. These two concepts are also keys to later discussions on the measure threshold setting and the supporting algorithm.

12.4.2 DEFINITION 3.4

Let $I = \{i_1,\ldots,i_{|I|}\}$ be the item set for database and $W_I = \{W_I(i_1),\ldots,W_I(i_{|I|})\}$ the item profits as weight. An item group $B = \{i_1,\ldots,i_{|B|}\}$, $B \subseteq I$, is a (m_1,m_2) homogeneity-based association bundle, $m_1 > 1$, $m_2 > 1$ being two integers with $m_1 + m_2 \leq |B|$, if for any two subsets S_1 and S_2 of B with $|S_1| = m_1$ and $|S_2| = m_2$, their weighted association strength $WAS(S_1,S_2)$ is greater than or equal to the given threshold $T_{WAS}^{(m_1,m_2)} > 0$, that is,

$$WAS(S_1,S_2) \geq T_{WAS}^{(m_1,m_2)}, S_1,S_2 \subset B.$$

Here the weighted association strength $WAS(S_1,S_2)$ is defined to be the multiplication of the joint weight $W(S_1,S_2)$ and the association strength $A(S_1,S_2)$, that is,

$$WAS(S_1,S_2) = W(S_1,S_2)A(S_1,S_2),$$

where the joint weight $W(S_1,S_2)$ for the subsets S_1 and S_2 is defined to be the sum of the weight of items in S_1 and S_2, that is,

$$W(S_1,S_2) = \sum_{i \in S_1 \cup S_2} W_I(i),$$

and the association strength $A(S_1,S_2)$ between the subsets S_1 and S_2 is defined to be the increase of the concurrence probability brought by the positive correlation between S_1 and S_2, that is,

$$A(S_1,S_2) = Pr(S_1,S_2) - Pr(S_1)Pr(S_2).$$

Therefore the complete homogeneity-based association bundle can be redefined as the (m_1,m_2) homogeneity-based association bundle for any $m_1 \geq m_2 \geq 1$ with $m_1 + m_2 \leq |B|$, and the pair homogeneity-based association bundle can be redefined as the $(1,1)$ homogeneity-based association bundle.

12.4.3 DEFINITION 3.5

The $(1,1)$ homogeneity-based association bundle is the order 2 homogeneity-based association bundle. An item group $B = \{i_1,...,i_{|B|}\}$ is an order $(m + 1)$ homogeneity-based association bundle, $2 < (m + 1) \leq |B|$, if it satisfies the following two conditions.

1. Its size-m subset is the order-m-homogeneity-based association bundle;
2. It is the (m_1, m_2) homogeneity-based association bundle, for any two integers $m_1 > 0$, $m_2 > 0$ with $m_1 + m_2 = m + 1$.

With the above definition, the complete homogeneity-based association bundle B can be redefined as the order $|B|$ homogeneity-based association bundle; and it has the property that its size-m subset is the order m homogeneity-based association bundle, for any integer $2 \leq m \leq |B|$.

12.4.4 ASSOCIATION STRUCTURE

Distinct from pair homogeneity-based association bundles, which display the two-way association between every pair of *bundle items*, complete homogeneity-based association bundles display the two-way association between every pair of *bundle subsets*. Therefore, although a pair-homogeneity based association bundle $\{i_1,...,i_m\}$ tells us that "for any pair of items (i_j,i_k) in the association bundle $\{i_1,...,i_m\}$, the extra profit brought by the positive correlation between the item i_j and i_k is greater than or equal to T_{WAS}," a complete homogeneity-based association bundle B tells us that "for any subset $S \subset B$, the extra profit brought by the positive correlations within S is greater than or equal to T."

12.4.5 ASSOCIATION MEASURES

The weighted association strength is also used in the complete homogeneity-based association bundle. But for the cases in which the two subsets being evaluated have sizes greater than one, the formula extends from individual items to item sets. The weight of two sets is the sum of the weights of all items involved, and the association strength between two sets is the increase of the concurrence probability brought by the between-set positive correlation.

12.4.6 THRESHOLD FOR MEASURES

In pair homogeneity-based association bundles, the measure weighted association strength evaluates *two individual items*; but in complete homogeneity-based association bundles, it evaluates *two sets*. Two sets have two sizes; different sizes give rise to different categories of association bundles. Because a complete homogeneity-based association bundle B must also be the (m_1, m_2) homogeneity-based association bundle for any integers $m_1 + m_2 \leq |B|$, we need to give the threshold formula $T_{WAS}^{(m_1, m_2)}$ for the (m_1, m_2) homogeneity-based association bundle.

$$T_{WAS}^{(m_1,m_2)}(\beta) = T_A^{(m_1,m_2)} + \beta\left(T_M^{(m_1,m_2)} - T_A^{(m_1,m_2)}\right), \beta \in [0,1],$$

where the $T_A^{(m_1,m_2)}$ and $T_M^{(m_1,m_2)}$ are the mean and maximum weighted association strength for all positively correlated size m_1 and size m_2 set pairs whose union makes an order $m_1 + m_2 - 1$ homogeneity-based association bundle. For example, the (1,1)-homogeneity or pair homogeneity-based association bundle has the threshold formula

$$T_{WAS}^{(1,1)}(\beta) = T_{WAS}(\beta) = T_A + \beta(T_M - T_A), \beta \in [0,1],$$

where the T_A and T_M are the mean and maximum weighted association strength for all positively correlated item pairs; and the formula for the (1,2)-homogeneity-based association bundles is

$$T_{WAS}^{(1,2)}(\beta) = T_A^{(1,2)} + \beta(T_M^{(1,2)} - T_A^{(1,2)}), \beta \in [0,1],$$

where the $T_A^{(1,2)}$ and $T_M^{(1,2)}$ are the mean and maximum weighted association strength for all positively correlated size 1 and size 2 pairs whose union makes a pair homogeneity-based association bundle.

12.4.7 SUPPORTING ALGORITHM

The algorithm for the complete homogeneity-based association bundle is similar in to the Aprior algorithm (1994). The Aprior algorithm is designed for frequent item sets. It is based on the "downward closure" property of frequent item sets, which states that a size $(k + 1)$ large item set has any of its size k subsets being the size k large item set. Here our algorithm is also based on a "downward closure" property, the property for complete homogeneity-based association bundles, which states that an order $(m + 1)$ homogeneity-based association bundle has any of its size m subset being the order m homogeneity-based association bundle.

We discussed previously in this section that the algorithm for the pair homogeneity-based association bundle produces *maximal* association bundles, which implies that the smaller sized association bundles should be derived from the larger maximal association bundles. As a comparison, the algorithm for the complete homogeneity-based association bundle produces the size k complete homogeneity-based association bundles after the kth data scan.

12.5 RANKING AND APPLICATIONS OF ASSOCIATION BUNDLES

In this section, we discuss some applications that are determined by pattern structures. We describe each structure feature of the new patterns and then discuss the corresponding applications using examples from MBA. We address the ranking problem as well, because it is a basic issue to most applications.

12.5.1 BUNDLE APPLICATIONS

12.5.1.1 Symmetric Measure

Association bundles use the symmetric measure; association rules use the asymmetric measure. As discussed previously, an asymmetric measure describes the loyalty type of positive correlation, whereas a symmetric measure describes all important positive correlations including the non-loyalty ones.

In recommendation applications such as "given the product A, suggest other products most likely sold with A," the loyalty to the product A is the most important concern. We should search the association rules and find those with the product A as the antecedent; these rules are solutions to this application. In this case, we should not use association bundles, because association bundles containing product A do not tell any loyalty.

In bundle promotion applications such as "select products into a group to sell for the most cross-selling profit," the profit coming from the across-group positive correlations is a major concern, and the loyalty is less important. We should search the pair homogeneity-based association bundles and rank them by the average profit: the top ones provide solutions to this application. In this case, association rules should be used. The reasons include that profitable non-loyalty associations may be missed; only one positive correlation is guaranteed in a rule; and other relationships in a rule may not bring any profit, or even worse, bring negative profit.

12.5.1.2 Between-Item Association

Pair homogeneity-based association bundles have the between-item association. They are suitable for applications that use one bundle item to affect other individual items in the same bundle. For example, assume $\{i,j,k\}$ is the top pair homogeneity-based association bundle and is used to build a promotion bundle. Then there exist six possible promotion actions: use the item i to affect j; use the item i to affect k; use the item j to affect i; use the item j to affect k; use the item k to affect i; or use the item k to affect j. The promotion policy in this case is flexible to make. An example could be "discount on any one item in $\{i,j,k\}$ (one is enough), and to expect the sales increase not only on the discounted one, but also on any other item in $\{i,j,k\}$." As a comparison, if the $\{i,j,k\}$ comes from an association rule $\{i,j\} \Rightarrow k$, then the only possible promotion action is to use both the item i and j to affect k. The promotion policy in this case is "to discount on both i and j to expect the increase of sales also appears on k." If the discount is put in other ways, such as only on i, then the decrease on k may happen because of the potential negative correlation between i and k.

12.5.1.3 Between-Subset Association

Complete homogeneity-based association bundles have the between-subset association; they are suitable for applications that use one or more bundle items to affect any other one or more bundle items in the same bundle.

If the promotion bundle $\{i,j,k\}$ is created based on the complete homogeneity-based association bundle, then in addition to the above six possible promotion actions, there exist six more: use the item i to affect j and k; use the item j to affect i and k; use the item k to affect i and j; use the item i and j to affect k; use the item i and k to affect j; or use the item j and k to affect i. The profit can be expected much higher than that based on pair homogeneity-based association bundles, because it encourages large baskets. Making discount on any item in $\{i,j,k\}$, other items in this set not only increase sales, but also from one basket. Thus the sales can go with higher efficiency or lower cost. This can be very useful in catalog/Internet sales for reasons such as saving the shipping cost. For instance, a catalog booklet can group items based on the complete homogeneity-based association bundle, and encourage the shoppers to buy multiple items in one order. Policies can be "Ordering two or more items can get xx discount on the most expensive one," or "Ordering n, $(n < 4)$ items can get xx discount on the most expensive $n/2$ ones."

12.5.2 BUNDLE RANKING

Association rules are usually ranked in the decreasing order of the conditional probability. Thus the top rule has the greatest loyalty relationship from the rule consequent to the rule antecedent.

Association bundles cannot be ranked by the weighted association strength, because a size n pair homogeneity-based association bundle has $n(n + 1)/2$ values for weighted association strength, and this number increases to 2^n for a complete homogeneity-based association bundle. Therefore a meaningful composite index must be developed based on these values.

We develop the *weighted ranking index* to solve this problem. The weighted ranking index is the weighted average of the extra profits from all the evaluated relationships. The weight is the concurrence probability of the related components. For the pair homogeneity-based association bundle $B_p = \{i_1, \ldots, i_{|B_p|}\}$, the weighted ranking index $WRI(B_p)$ is defined as

$$WRI(B_p) = \frac{\sum_{i \neq j, i, j \in B_p} Pr(i,j)WAS(i,j)}{\sum_{i \neq j, i, j \in B_p} Pr(i,j)},$$

where $Pr(i,j)$ is the concurrence probability of the item i and j, and $WAS(i,j)$ is the weighted association strength between i and j.

For the complete homogeneity-based association bundle $B_c = \{i_1, \ldots, i_{|B_c|}\}$, the weighted ranking index $WRI(B_c)$ is defined as

$$WRI(B_c) = \frac{\sum_{s_1 \cap s_2 = \varnothing, s_1, s_2 \in B_c} Pr(s_1, s_2)WAS(s_1, s_2)}{\sum_{s_1 \cap s_2 = \varnothing, s_1, s_2 \in B_c} Pr(s_1, s_2)},$$

where $Pr(s_1, s_2)$ is the concurrence probability of the subsets s_1 and s_2, and $WAS(s_1, s_2)$ is the weighted association between s_1 and s_2.

For the pair homogeneity-based association bundle, the practical meaning of the weighted ranking index is the "expected extra profit per pair of items brought by positive correlations"; for the complete homogeneity-based association bundle, it is "the expected extra profit per pair of subsets brought by positive correlations."

With the weighted ranking index, any sized association bundles can be ranked together. The top bundle has the greatest extra profit in average relationships.

12.6   ALGORITHMS FOR ASSOCIATION BUNDLES

12.6.1   ALGORITHM FOR PAIR HOMOGENEITY-BASED ASSOCIATION BUNDLES

We describe the algorithm PAB for maximal pair homogeneity-based association bundles. There are essentially three successive stages in our algorithm: the transaction data scan, the graph modeling, and the maximal clique enumeration. Figure 12.2 lists these stages.

Algorithm : Pair-homogeneity based Association Bundles (PAB)
Input :   Transaction data set T, strength level threshold
Output :   Maximal Pair-homogeneity based Association Bundles
Stage 1.   Data Scan
               Obtain the item profit, the item probability
               and the item pairwise joint probabilities.
Stage 2.   Graph Modeling.
               i. Calculate the threshold for weighted association strength
               ii. Create the graph G = (V,E)
Stage 3.   Maximal Clique Enumeration
               Enumerate the set of maximal cliques on the graph G

FIGURE 12.2 Algorithm for pair homogeneity-based association bundles.

In the data scan stage, we obtain the item profits, the item probabilities, and the item pairwise joint probabilities. Using the scanned information, in the graph modeling stage, we first calculate all the between-item weighted association strengths, and use the mean and the maximum weighted association strength to compute the threshold $T_{WAS}(0)$ (the strength level threshold β is 0 by default); then we create an undirected graph $G = (V, E)$, where each vertex in the vertex set V corresponds to an item, and each edge in the edge set E corresponds to an item pair that has the weighted association strength greater than or equal to $T_{WAS}(0)$. With the graph model, each maximal pair homogeneity-based association bundle is mapped into a maximal clique on the graph G. Finally, in the maximal clique enumeration stage, we identify the set of maximal cliques on G.

In these three stages, stages 1 and 2 are polynomial in time cost with respect to the number of records and the number of different items, and apparently easy to implement. In stage 3, we deal with a maximal clique enumeration problem, which is a combinatorial problem that possibly leads to computation explosion. We provide a maximal clique enumeration algorithm customized for transaction data in MBA. The algorithm is described in Appendix B.

12.6.2 COMPLETE HOMOGENEITY-BASED ASSOCIATION BUNDLES

The algorithm CAB for complete homogeneity-based association bundles make multiple scans over the data. In the first scan, we obtain the item profits, the item probabilities, and the item pairwise joint probabilities and we calculate the threshold for weighted association strength, and then we determine which item pairs are order-2-homogeneity-based association bundles. In each subsequent scan, we start with a seed set that is the complete homogeneity-based association bundle determined in the previous scan. We use this seed set to generate new potential complete homogeneity-based association bundles, called *candidate complete homogeneity-based association bundles*, and obtain the probabilities for these candidates by scanning the data. After the scan, we calculate the threshold for weighted association strength and then we determine which of the candidate bundles are complete homogeneity-based association bundles, and they become the seed for the next scan. This process continues until no new complete homogeneity-based association bundles are found.

12.6.2.1 Algorithm CAB

Figure 12.3 gives the algorithm CAB for complete homogeneity-based association bundles. We use C_k to represent the size k set of candidate complete homogeneity-based association bundles, P_k the probability for the candidate in C_k, and B_k the size k complete homogeneity-based association bundles. The table in Figure 12.3 displays the note for each symbol.

The first scan produces the set of item pairs and obtains the item weight, the item probabilities, and the item pairwise joint probabilities. The size 2 complete homogeneity-based association bundles can be determined using the candidate-chk

Symbol	Note
C_k	size-k candidate
P_k	probability for the candidate in C_k
B_k	size-k complete-homogeneity based association bundles
$J_m(b) / J_r(b)$	maximum/ real number of joins occurred to produce set b
$S_c^{(m1, m2)}$	all the possible subset pairs (S_1, S_2) of size (m_1, m_2) in set c
β	strength level threshold
$WAS(S_1, S_2)$	weighted association strength between the set S_1 and S_2
$T_{WAS}^{(m1,m2)}(\beta)$	threshold on the weighted association strength w.r.t. β

Algorithm : Complete-homogeneity based Association Bundles (CAB)
Input :   Transaction data set T, strength level threshold β
Output :   Complete-homogeneity based Association Bundles
(1) $C_2 \Leftarrow$ Init-scan (T)
(2) $P_2 \Leftarrow$ Init-scan (T,C_2)
(3) $B_2 \Leftarrow$ candidate-chk (C_2, P_2, β)
(4)   for (k = 3; $B_{k-1} \neq \phi$; k++) do
(5) $C_k \Leftarrow$ candidate-gen (B_{k-1})
(6) $P_k \Leftarrow$ scan (T,C_k)
(7) $B_k \Leftarrow$ candidate-chk ($C_k, P_1, ..., P_k, \beta$)
(8)   end
(9) $B \Leftarrow \cup_k (B_k)$
(10)   return B

Algorithm : Candidate-gen function
Input : B_{k-1} (sets in order and set elements in order)
Output : C_k
(1) $C_k \Leftarrow \phi$
(2)   for b_1 in B_{k-1} // joint
(3)   for $b_2 > b_1$ in B_{k-1} do
(4) $b \Leftarrow b_1 \cup b_2$
(5)   if $|b| = k$ do
(6)   calculate $J_m(b)$
(7)   if $J_m(b)=0$ then $C_k \Leftarrow C_k \cup \{b\}$ and $J_r(b)=1$
(8)   else
(9)   search b in C_k to get $J_r(b)$
(10)   if $J_r(b) = J_m(b)$ then $J_r(b)$++
(11)   else $C_k \Leftarrow C_k \setminus \{b\}$ // prune
(12)   end
(11)   return C_k

Algorithm : Candidate-chk function
Input : $C_k, P_1, ... P_k, \beta$
Output : B_k
(1) $B_k \Leftarrow \phi$
(2)   for ($m_1 = 1$; $m_1 \leq [k/2]$; m_1++) do   // threshold
(3) $m_2 = k - m_1$
(4) $S_c^{(m1, m2)} \Leftarrow \phi$
(5)   for each c in C_k do
(6) $S_c^{(m1, m2)} \Leftarrow \{(S_1, S_2), S_1 \cup S_2 = c, |S_1| = m_1, |S_2| = m_2\}$
(7)   end
(8) $S^{(m1, m2)} \Leftarrow S^{(m1, m2)} \cup \{S_c^{(m1, m2)}\}$
(9) $T_{WAS}^{(m1,m2)}(\beta) \Leftarrow$ threshold compute ($S^{(m1, m2)}, P_{m1}, P_{m2}, \beta$)
(10)   end
(11)   for each c in C_k // prune
(12)   for ($m_1 = 1$; $m_1 \leq [k/2]$; m_1++) do
(13)   for each (S_1, S_2) in $S_c^{(m1, m2)}$ do
(14)   if $WAS(S_1, S_2) < T_{WAS}^{(m1,m2)}(\beta)$
(15)   then c is flagged as not in B_k
(16)   end
(17)   end
(18)   if c is not flagged as not in B_k
(19)   then $B_k \Leftarrow B_k \cup \{c\}$
(20)   end
(21)   return B_k

FIGURE 12.3 Algorithms for complete homogeneity-based association bundles.

function described later. The subsequent scan, say the Kth scan, consists of two phases. First, the size $(K - 1)$ complete homogeneity-based association bundles determined in the $(K - 1)^{th}$ scan are used to generate the candidates C_k, using the candidate-gen function described later, and then the candidate probabilities P_k are obtained by data scan. Next, the size k complete homogeneity-based association bundles can be determined using the candidate-chk function.

12.6.2.2   Candidate Generation

The candidate-gen function is shown in Figure 12.3. It takes as argument B_{k-1}, the set of all size $(K - 1)$ complete homogeneity-based association bundles. It returns a superset of the set of all size k complete homogeneity-based association bundles. The function works as follows. First, in the *join* step, we sequentially generate size k set using two size $(K - 1)$ sets b_i and b_j from B_{k-1}. Let $b = b_1 \cup b_2$ denote the resulting size k set. Because all the possible two-set pairs that can join to produce b are in order, the maximum number of joins occurred before b_i and b_j to produce b can be calculated based on the relative positions of b_i and b_j in b. We use $J_m(b)$ to denote this number. If $J_m(b) = 0$, then b is produced for the first time, and it should be added to C_k. If $J_m(b) \neq 0$, then in the *prune* step, we locate b in C_k to get the real number of joins recorded in C_k for b. We use $J_r(b)$ to denote this number. If b is not in C_k, or b is in C_k, but the recorded number of joins $J_r(b)$ is not equal to the $J_m(b)$, then b should be removed from C_k; otherwise J_r should be increased by one.

12.6.2.3   Candidate Check

The candidate-chk function is shown in Figure 12.3. It takes as arguments C_k, the set of all size-k candidate complete homogeneity-based association bundles, $P_1,\dots, P_k$, the candidate probabilities for $C_1,\dots, C_k$, and β, the strength level threshold. It returns the set of size k complete homogeneity-based association bundles. We use the $S_c^{(m_1, m_2)}$ to represent the set of possible subset pair (S_1, S_2) of size (m_1, m_2), with $m_1 \geq m_2 \geq 1$, and $m_1 + m_2 = k$, generated using the candidate $c \in C_k$, and use $S^{(m_1, m_2)} = \cup_{c \in C_k} \{S_c^{(m_1, m_2)}\}$ for all the possible subset pairs of size (m_1, m_2) generated using all candidates in C_k.

The function works as follows. First, in the *threshold* step, we generate all the possible subset pair (S_1, S_2) of size (m_1, m_2), $m_1 \geq m_2 \geq 1$, $m_1 + m_2 = k$, $S_1 \cap S_2 = \emptyset$, using each candidate in C_k, and compute for each pair (S_1, S_2) the between-subset weighted association strength $WAS(S_1, S_2)$ using the probabilities retrieved from $P_1,\dots, P_k$, and then we calculate the threshold $T_{WAS}^{(m_1, m_2)}(\beta)$. Next, in the *prune* step, we remove the candidate that has at least one subset pair (S_1, S_2), $S_1 \cap S_2 = \emptyset$, $|S_1| = m_1$, $|S_2| = m_2$, $m_1 \geq 1$, $m_2 \geq 1$, $m_1 + m_2 = k$, that has the weighted association strength $WAS(S_1, S_2)$ less than the threshold $T_{WAS}^{(m_1, m_2)}(\beta)$.

12.7   EXPERIMENTAL RESULTS

We now present the experimental results of the two algorithms PAB and CAB on three real-world data sets.

Data Set	Transactions	Distinct Items	Ave. size transaction	Max. size transaction
POS	77,512	3,340	5.0	161
WebView1	515,597	1,657	6.5	164
WebView2	59,602	497	2.5	267

(a) Three real world data sets for experiment

	Data=WebView1				Data=WebView2				Data=BMS-POS			
Str. Lev. Thre.	#bundles	Time (ms) for Maximal Cliques	Time (s) for Data Scan	Total Time (s)	#bundles	Time (ms) for Maximal Cliques	Time (s) for Data Scan	Total Time (s)	#bundles	Time (ms) for Maximal Cliques	Time (s) for Data Scan	Total Time (s)
0.00	1186	3675	4	7.68	50228	34520	14	48.52	1041	671	100	100.67
0.05	594	461	4	4.46	3997	4116	14	18.12	269	60	100	100.06
0.10	291	180	4	4.18	2222	2303	14	16.30	143	30	100	100.03
0.15	260	110	4	4.11	1606	1583	14	15.58	81	20	100	100.02
0.20	177	181	4	4.18	1199	1001	14	15.00	58	21	100	100.02
0.25	115	50	4	4.05	866	661	14	14.66	41	10	100	100.01
0.30	77	60	4	4.06	671	381	14	14.38	30	10	100	100.01
0.35	60	50	4	4.05	463	210	14	14.21	24	10	100	100.01
0.40	49	30	4	4.03	309	110	14	14.11	22	10	100	100.01
0.45	33	50	4	4.05	195	50	14	14.05	21	10	100	100.01
0.50	14	40	4	4.04	113	50	14	14.05	12	50	100	100.05
0.55	12	50	4	4.05	69	20	14	14.02	11	10	100	100.01
0.60	9	81	4	4.08	33	51	14	14.05	11	10	100	100.01
0.65	7	10	4	4.01	23	10	14	14.01	11	10	100	100.01
0.70	7	10	4	4.01	11	10	14	14.01	11	50	100	100.05
0.75	6	10	4	4.01	7	10	14	14.01	11	10	100	100.01
0.80	4	10	4	4.01	5	10	14	14.01	11	10	100	100.01
0.85	4	40	4	4.04	5	10	14	14.01	11	20	100	100.02
0.90	4	40	4	4.04	5	30	14	14.03	11	10	100	100.01
0.95	4	190	4	4.19	5	10	14	14.01	11	20	100	100.02
1.00	4	60	4	4.06	5	30	14	14.03	11	90	100	100.09

(b) Algorithm result: Number of bundles and time cost on the three real world data sets.

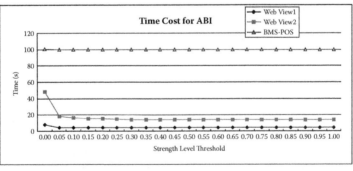

(c) Time cost plot.

FIGURE 12.4 Algorithms for complete homogeneity-based association bundles.

β	#(Complete-homogeneity based Association bundles)		
	Data=Web-View1	Data=Web-View2	Data=POS
.2	size=2,Num=77	size=2,Num=188	size=2,Num=121
	size=3,Num=46	size=3,Num=460	size=3,Num=187
	size=4,Num=19	size=4,Num=866	size=4,Num=193
	size=5,Num=3	size=5,Num=1185	size=5,Num=126
		size=6,Num=1192	size=6,Num=50
		size=7,Num=872	size=7,Num=11
		size=8,Num=450	size=8,Num=1
		size=9,Num=155	
		size=10,Num=32	
		size=11,Num=3	
.4	size=2,Num=17	size=2,Num=41	size=2,Num=23
	size=3,Num=4	size=3,Num=67	size=3,Num=13
		size=4,Num=75	size=4,Num=3
		size=5,Num=51	
		size=6,Num=19	
		size=7,Num=3	
.6	size=2,Num=6	size=2,Num=13	size=2,Num=9
	size=3,Num=1	size=3,Num=8	size=3,Num=1
		size=4,Num=2	
.8	size=2,Num=3	size=3,Num=1	size=2,Num=3
1	size=2,Num=1	size=2,Num=1	size=2,Num=1

(a) Number of identified bundles w.r.t the strength level threshold β

β	Time Cost Algorithm CAB (s)		
	WebView1	WebView2	POS
0.2	4	113	114
0.4	3	32	41
0.6	3	27	31
0.8	2	25	21
1	2	24	21

(b) Time cost for the algorithm CAB w.r.t β

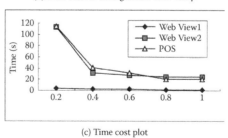

(c) Time cost plot

FIGURE 12.5 Experiment: algorithm CAB on three real-world data sets.

12.7.1 DATA

The three real-world data sets are the ones used previously[17] for comparison of AR algorithms. Figure 12.4a displays the major features of the data. Because no profit information is available in the data, we set the weight of each item identically to 1.

12.7.2 PLATFORM

We implement the two algorithms using C++. They are running on the same machine in the same environment. All the experiments are performed on an x86 997 MHz PC with 256 megabytes main memory, running Microsoft Windows XP.

12.7.3 PERFORMANCE OF THE ALGORITHM PAB

The algorithm PAB is basically the same as the algorithm ABI, which was presented for association bundle identification previously.[7] Algorithm PAB uses a different formula for association measure, and this change does not affect the algorithm performance. So we extract the results published as the performance report.[7]

Figure 12.4b and Figure 12.4c display the results. For data sets shown in Figure 12.4b, the first column is the strength level threshold, and second column is the number of bundles identified. The next three columns is the time cost. The time cost consists of two parts: the data scan and the maximal clique enumeration, and they are shown in the third and fourth columns, respectively. The fifth column is the total time cost. The plot for the total time cost against the strength level threshold is shown in Figure 12.4c.

12.7.4 PERFORMANCE OF THE ALGORITHM CAB

We display in Figure 12.5a the number of identified bundles. The strength level threshold β take values from 0.2 to 1 with increment 0.2, the complete homogeneity-based association bundles are displayed for each. The plot of the time cost against the strength level threshold is displayed in Figure 12.5b.

12.8 CONCLUSIONS

The AR is basically the only pattern ever investigated for MBA. However, because different applications may require different patterns, many important MBA applications assumed to be solved by the AR are actually misleading.

We believe that more detailed investigation on pattern structures may provide some solutions to the problems, either using an existing pattern for some applications or discovering new patterns for interesting applications. For this purpose, we discussed the structures of AR patterns and used the identified structural features to address appropriate applications. We also explored some new structures and patterns for applications that may not be solved by AR. More specifically, we examined two new patterns: the pair homogeneity-based association bundles and the complete homogeneity-based association bundles, and illustrated their applications to MBA.

ACKNOWLEDGMENT

This work was partially supported by the Collaborative Research Development Program of Natural Sciences and Engineering Research Council of Canada and by the Canada Research Chairs Program.

REFERENCES

1. Agrawal, R., Imielinski, T., and Swami, A. Mining association rules between sets of items in large databases, *Proceedings of the ACM SIGMOD International Conference on Management of Data,* 207–216, 1993.
2. Agrawal, R. and Srikant, R. Fast algorithms for mining association rules in large databases, *Proceedings of the 20th International Conference on Very Large Data Bases,* 487–499, 1994.
3. Akkoyunlu, E.A. The enumeration of maximal cliques of large graphs, *SIAM J. Comput.,* 2, 1–6, 1973.
4. Bron, C. and Kerbosch, J. Algorithm 457: finding all cliques of an undirected graph, *Commun. ACM,* 16, 575–577, 1973.
5. Han, J., Pei J., Yin, Y., Mao, R. Mining frequent patterns without candidate generation, *Data Mining Knowledge Disc.,* 8, 53–87, 2004.
6. Hipp, J., Güntzer, U., and Nakhaeizadeh, G. Algorithms for association rule mining—a general survey and comparison, *SIGKDD Explorations,* 2, 58–64, 2000.
7. Huang, W., Krneta, M., Lin, L., and Wu, J. Association bundles—a new pattern for association analysis, *Sixth IEEE International Conference on Data Mining, Data Mining Workshops,* 601–605, 2006.
8. Johnson, D.S. and Yannakakis, M. On generating all maximal independent sets, *Inform. Proc. Lett.,* 27, 119–123, 1988.
9. Liu, B., Hsu, W., Chen, S., and Ma, Y. Analyzing the subjective interestingness of association rules, *IEEE Intell. Sys.,* 15, 47–55, 2000.
10. Loukakis, E. and Tsouros C. A depth first search algorithm to generate the family of maximal independent sets of a graph lexicographially, *Computing,* 27, 249–266, 1981.
11. Omiecinski, E.R. Alternative interest measures for mining associations in databases, *IEEE Trans. Knowledge Data Eng.,* 15, 57–69, 2003.
12. Pei, J., Han, J., and Mao, R. CLOSET: an efficient algorithm for mining frequent closed itemsets, *ACM SIGMOD Workshop on Research Issues in Data Mining and Knowledge Discovery,* 21–30, 2000.
13. Tan, P., Kumar, V., and Srivastava, J. Selecting the right interestingness measure for association patterns, *Inform. Sys.,* 29, 193–331, 2004.
14. Tsukiyama, S., Ide, M., Ariyoshi, H., and Shirakawa, I. A new algorithm for generating all the maximum independent sets, *SIAM J. Comput.,* 6, 505–517, 1977.
15. Zaki, M. Scalable algorithms for association mining, *IEEE Trans. Knowledge Data Engin.,* 12, 372–390, 2000.
16. Zaki, M. and Hsiao, C. CHARM: an efficient algorithm for closed itemset mining, *Proceedings of the Second SIAM International Conference on Data Mining,* 457–473, 2002.
17. Zheng, Z., Kohavi, R., and Mason, L. Real world performance of association rule algorithms, *Proceedings of the ACM SIGKDD International Conference on Knowledge Discovery in Databases & Data Mining (KDD01),* 401–406, 2001.

13 Formal Concept Analysis with Attribute Priorities

Radim Belohlavek and Vilem Vychodil

CONTENTS

13.1 INTRODUCTION

13.1.1 CONTENT IN BRIEF

Formal concept analysis has recently been applied to data analysis, visualization, and knowledge extraction in various fields. Central to formal concept analysis is the notion of a formal concept that is a particular cluster in data. This chapter presents an extension of a basic setting of formal concept analysis. It allows a user to enter, along with the input data, his or her priorities regarding relative importance of attributes. Adding attribute priorities results in extraction of only those clusters in data that are compatible with the attribute priorities. The main effect is that the user is supplied with a smaller number of more relevant clusters and is thus not overwhelmed by a possibly large number of all formal concepts that logically exist in data. In this overview chapter, we present the approach and illustrative examples from marketing.

13.1.2 INTRODUCTION TO FORMAL CONCEPT ANALYSIS

Formal concept analysis (FCA) is a method for data analysis and knowledge discovery with growing popularity across various domains. FCA has proved to be useful in various areas such as organization of Web search results into hierarchical structure of concepts based on common topics (Carpineto & Romano, 2004; see also http://credo.fub.it/), information retrieval (Cho & Richards, 2004; Okubo & Haraguchi, 2006), hierarchical analysis of software code (Dekel & Gil, 2003; Snelting & Tip, 2000; Tonella 2003), and visualization in software engineering (Ganapathy et al., 2007; Streckenbach & Snelting, 2004), to list just a few recent application areas. Further references to applications of FCA can be found elsewhere in Ganter & Wille (1999) and Carpineto & Romano (2004), which are the main books providing an introduction to FCA. A distinguishing feature of FCA is an inherent integration of three components:

- Discovery of clusters (so-called formal concepts) in data
- Discovery of data dependencies (so-called attribute implications) in data
- Visualization of formal concepts and attribute implications in a single hierarchical diagram (so-called concept lattice)

The input data to FCA are supposed to be organized in a table such as the one in Table 13.1. The rows represent objects and the columns represent attributes. In the basic setting, attributes are assumed to be binary (presence/absence attributes, yes/no attributes). Other attributes are handled by a binarization method called conceptual scaling (Ganter & Wille, 1999). A cross in the table indicates that the object in the row has the attribute in the column; a blank indicates the opposite. Such a table is conceived as a triplet $\langle X, Y, I \rangle$, called a *formal context* in FCA. X and Y are the set of objects and the set of attributes, and I is a binary relation between X and Y representing the incidence between objects and attributes. That is, xIy denotes that object x has attribute y. In the illustrative example in Table 13.1, X consists of five objects that are particular books listed in the table, Y consists of four attributes "Textbook,"

TABLE 13.1
Books and Their Attributes

	Textbook	Research Book	Math	Engineering
Introduction to sets	X		X	
Advances in set theory		X	X	
Basics of circuits	X			X
Theory of circuits design	X	X		X
Research topics in VLSI		X		X

"Research Book," "Math," and "Engineering," and I indicates that "Introduction to Sets" is a textbook in mathematics, for example. The clusters identified in data are called formal concepts in FCA. Formal concepts are defined by particular operators, called *concept-forming operators* or arrow operators, defined as follows. For a subset A of X and a subset B of Y, put

$$A^\uparrow = \{y \in Y \mid \text{for all } x \in A: xIy\} \quad \text{and} \quad B^\downarrow = \{x \in X \mid \text{for all } y \in B: xIy\}.$$

That is, $A^\uparrow$ is the set of all attributes shared by all objects from A, and $B^\downarrow$ is the set of all objects that share all attributes from B. A *formal concept* in $\langle X, Y, I \rangle$ is a pair $\langle A, B \rangle$ of a set A of objects and a set B of attributes for which $A^\uparrow = B$ and $B^\downarrow = A$. Alternatively, a formal concept is a maximal rectangle in the table that is full of ×s, namely, the rectangle corresponding to objects from A and attributes from B. In our illustrative example,

$$\langle A, B \rangle = \langle \{\text{Advances in Set Theory, Theory of Circuits Design,}$$
$$\text{Research Topics in VLSI}\}, \{\text{Research Book}\}\rangle$$

is a formal concept in the table (note that VLSI is an acronym for very-large-scale integration). Another one is

$$\langle C, D \rangle = \langle \{\text{Theory of Circuits Design, Research Topics in VLSI}\},$$
$$\{\text{Research Book, Engineering}\}\rangle.$$

The terminology in FCA comes from traditional logic. A and B are called the extent and intent of concept $\langle A, B \rangle$ and are thought of as the collection of objects to which the concept applies and the collection of attributes that fall under the concept, respectively. This natural approach to concepts is a nice feature of FCA because people know it from everyday life. For example, people commonly say, "The concept of mammal applies to this dog" or "Attribute of warm-blooded falls under the concept of mammal." As a result, formal concepts can easily be understood and interpreted by users. The collection of all formal concepts in $\langle X, Y, I \rangle$ is denoted by $B(X, Y, I)$ and is called the *concept lattice* associated with $\langle X, Y, I \rangle$. A *subconcept-superconcept hierarchy* $\leq$ on the concept lattice $B(X, Y, I)$ is defined by

$$\langle A_1, B_1 \rangle \leq \langle A_2, B_2 \rangle \quad \text{if and only if } A_1 \subseteq A_2 \text{ (or, equivalently, } B_2 \subseteq B_1).$$

In fact, $\leq$ is a partial order under which $B(X, Y, I)$ happens to be a complete lattice. The structure of the complete lattice $B(X, Y, I)$ is described by so-called basic theorem of concept lattices. We refer to Ganter and Wille (1999) for this theorem and for mathematical foundations of FCA. Note that $\leq$ models a natural conceptual hierarchy and $\langle A_1, B_1 \rangle \leq \langle A_2, B_2 \rangle$ means that $\langle A_2, B_2 \rangle$ is a more general concept than $\langle A_1, B_1 \rangle$. In the above example, $\langle C, D \rangle \leq \langle A, B \rangle$ because $C \subseteq A$, i.e.,

$$\{\text{Theory of Circuits Design, Research Topics in VLSI}\}$$

is a subset of

$$\{\text{Advances in Set Theory, Theory of Circuits Design, Research Topics in VLSI}\},$$

In general, the meaning of a formal concept $\langle A, B \rangle$ is derived from its intent B. As an example, the above formal concept $\langle C, D \rangle$ can be regarded as the concept of "textbooks in engineering."

A concept lattice can be visualized using a particular labeled line diagram which provides a hierarchical view of the data, formal concepts, and their relationships. We present examples of concept lattices in Section 13.3.

13.2 ATTRIBUTE PRIORITIES IN FORMAL CONCEPT ANALYSIS

13.2.1 WHY WE NEED ATTRIBUTE PRIORITIES IN FORMAL CONCEPT ANALYSIS

In the basic setting of FCA, the input data consist of a table describing the objects, attributes, and their relationships. Such data and the resulting concept lattice do not capture any *background knowledge* that a user may have regarding the data. This can result in extraction of a large number of formal concepts, including those that seem artificial to the user because they are not congruent with his or her background knowledge. A particular type of background knowledge that we deal with in this chapter is relative importance of attributes. Such background knowledge is commonly used in human categorization. For instance, when categorizing books for the purpose of inclusion in a sales catalogue, one might consider the field subject of a book more important than the type of book. Accordingly, we expect to form categories of books based on the subject, such as "Engineering," "Computer Science," "Mathematics," or "Biology," and only after that, within these categories, we might want to form smaller categories based on the type, such as "Engineering/Textbook" or "Engineering/Research Book." In such a case, our background knowledge tells us that attributes describing the subject ("Engineering," "Computer Science") are more important than attributes describing the type of book ("Textbook," "Research Book"). The background knowledge depends on the purpose of categorization. For a different purpose, it can be appropriate to use different background knowledge. For instance, one could consider the type of book more important than the subject. Correspondingly, we would get categories "Textbook" and "Research Book" and their subcategories "Textbook/Engineering" and "Textbook/Computer Science." Therefore, while the input data are given (books and their attributes), the background knowledge that guides the categorization is purpose dependent. The relative importance of attributes serves as a constraint in categorization/clustering. Namely, it excludes potential clusters which do not respect the background knowledge. For instance, with subject more important than type, category "Textbook" consisting of all textbooks (irrelevant of the subject) is not relevant (is not formed in the process of categorization), because it is not congruent with background knowledge (does not satisfy the corresponding constraint saying that subject is more important than type). Contrary to that, categories "Engineering," "Engineering/Textbook," "Computer Science," and "Computer Science/Textbook" are congruent with the background knowledge. Background knowledge cannot only eliminate categories that are not suitable for a given purpose; it also can eliminate unnatural categories. As an example, not taking into account that bookbinding is less important than book subject and book type, one would end up with categories "Paperback" and

"Hardback," which, however logically correct, do not make much sense in a useful categorization of books.

13.2.2 MODELING ATTRIBUTE PRIORITIES VIA ATTRIBUTE-DEPENDENCY FORMULAS

We are going to model attribute priorities by attribute-dependency (AD) formulas (Belohlavek & Sklenar, 2005; Belohlavek & Vychodil, 2006, 2008).

An *attribute-dependency formula* over a set Y of attributes is an expression

$$A \angle B$$

where A and B are sets of attributes (i.e., subsets of Y). Let M be a set of attributes. Think of M as being an intent of a formal concept $\langle C,M \rangle$. We say that $A \angle B$ is true in M, or that M is a model of $A \angle B$, if

$$A \cap M \neq \varnothing \text{ implies } B \cap M \neq \varnothing.$$

If T is a set of AD formulas, we denote by $\text{Mod}(T)$ the collection of all models of T (i.e., all subsets M of Y such that every $A \angle B$ from T is true in M). A formal concept $\langle C,M \rangle$ satisfies $A \angle B$ if $A \angle B$ is true in M. By definition, this means that whenever the intent M contains some attribute from A, M needs to contain some attribute from B as well.

AD formulas are supposed to serve as formulas during which a user expresses and makes explicit his or her background knowledge regarding attribute priorities. As an example, consider the above table with books. Expression

$$\{\text{Textbook, Research Book}\} \angle \{\text{Mathematics, Engineering}\}$$

is an AD formula. A formal concept $\langle C,D \rangle$ satisfies this AD formula if: whenever D contains attribute Textbook or attribute Research Book, it needs to contain Mathematics or Engineering (i.e., the information regarding classification by subjects needs to already be present in D). By this AD formula, a user says that subject is more important than type of book: a classification according to a type of book (Textbook or Research Book) can only be performed after a classification according to a subject. For example, formal concept

$$\langle\{\text{Advances in Set Theory, Theory of Circuits Design, Research Topics in VLSI}\},\\ \{\text{Research Book}\}\rangle$$

does not satisfy $\{\text{Textbook, Research Book}\} \angle \{\text{Mathematics, Engineering}\}$ because $\{\text{Textbook, Research Book}\} \cap \{\text{Research Book}\} \neq \varnothing$ but $\{\text{Mathematics, Engineering}\} \cap \{\text{Research Book}\} = \varnothing$. This concept is not congruent with a user's background knowledge regarding attribute priorities and is thus not relevant to the user. On the other hand, formal concept

$$\langle\{\text{Theory of Circuits Design, Research Topics in VLSI}\},\\ \{\text{Research Book, Engineering}\}\rangle$$

satisfies the AD formula and is thus relevant to the user.

Given a set T of AD formulas that represent attribute priorities of a user, we denote by $B_T(X,Y,I)$ the set of all formal concepts of $\langle X,Y,I \rangle$ that satisfy all AD formulas from T,

$$B_T(X,Y,I) = \{\langle C,D \rangle \in B(X,Y,I) | \langle C,D \rangle \text{ satisfies every } A \angle B \text{ from } T\}.$$

The "constrained" concept lattice $B_T(X,Y,I)$ with $\leq$ is then the resulting hierarchically ordered collection of relevant formal concepts extracted from data and presented to the user.

Note that treating background knowledge in FCA differently from our approach in both the type of knowledge and the aims has been discussed elsewhere (Ganter, 1999; Stumme, 1996). Dependencies similar to AD formulas are used in Doignon and Falmagne (1999).

13.2.3 SOME RESULTS ON MATHEMATICAL AND COMPUTATIONAL TRACTABILITY

In this section, we present basic mathematical properties regarding theoretical and computational tractability of AD formulas. Because of limited scope, we limit ourselves to basic results and refer the reader to Belohlavek & Sklenar (2005) and Belohlavek & Vychodil (2008) for details and further results.

13.2.3.1 Entailment and Its Efficient Checking

Given a set T of AD formulas and an AD formula $A \angle B$, it is possible to check efficiently whether T entails $A \angle B$. The basic insight behind the procedure is that the set Mod(T) of all models of T is an interior system. Moreover, one can efficiently compute the greatest model $I_T(M)$ of T, which is included in a given set M of attributes. Finally, it can be proved that T entails $A \angle B$ if and only if $A \cap I_T(Y - B) = \emptyset$. This yields the procedure for checking entailment.

13.2.3.2 Complete System of Deduction Rules for AD Formulas

A proof system with deduction rules resembling Armstrong rules known from databases (Maier, 1983) exists with its completeness theorem. A small set of such deduction rules is:

(from empty set of premises) infer $A \angle A$,
from $A \angle B$ infer $A \angle B \cup C$,
from $A \angle B$ and $C \angle A \cup D$ infer $C \angle B \cup D$.

Completeness says that T entails $A \angle B$ if and only if $A \angle B$ can be proved from T using the above deduction rules.

13.2.3.3 Computing a Complete Nonredundant Set of AD Formulas

The procedure for efficient checking of entailment enables us to compute, given a set T of AD formulas, its non-redundant subset that entails the same AD formulas (i.e., is equivalent to T). Moreover, an algorithm has been established that computes a complete non-redundant set T of AD formulas from data $\langle X,Y,I \rangle$,

- Every AD formula from T is true in $\langle X,Y,I\rangle$ in that it is true in the set of attributes of every object from X.
- Any AD formula is true in $\langle X,Y,I\rangle$ if and only if it is entailed by T.
- One cannot remove any AD formula from T without losing the above two properties.

Such an algorithm is needed if we want to infer the background knowledge from a set of relevant concepts supplied by a user or marked by a user as relevant in a large collection of concepts.

13.3　APPLICATIONS IN MARKETING

In this section, we show how AD formulas can be used to represent customer priorities on attributes of products and how such priorities can enhance visualization and exploration of products by means of concept lattices. We demonstrate that using AD formulas, users can reduce the number of groups of products (product clusters) extracted by ordinary FCA by focusing on relevant groups (i.e., groups that are congruent with the priorities). This way, our method improves a user's ability to search, evaluate, and compare different products by means of their attributes.

We consider an example in which products are computer workstations supplied in certain configurations. The attributes are particular parameters of the configurations such as the number of CPUs, CPU speed, or maximum memory available. Having several configurations available, a user may wish to choose among the configurations based on his or her preferences. Some users may prefer total mass storage capacity over CPU speed (e.g., users interested in database applications); other users may wish to have a system with faster CPU and larger memory (e.g., for CAD applications). Constraints such as these are naturally expressed through AD formulas.

In our example, we are going to use Sun Ultra Workstations, manufactured by Sun Microsystems, which come in several different configurations. The data were taken from www.sun.com (all models are from November 2007). Using information from Sun's Web page, we have constructed a data table describing important parameters of the workstations; see Table 13.2.

TABLE 13.2
Sun Workstations

Model	Arch.		Manufacturer			CPUs		Cores			Clock			RAM			HDD			Price		
	86	sp	A	I	S	1	2	1	2	4	l	m	h	8	16	32	1	2	3	1k	2k	3k
20	X		X			X		X	X		X			X			X			X		
24	X			X		X			X	X		X		X	X			X	X			
40	X		X			X	X	X	X				X	X	X	X	X				X	
25		X			X	X		X			X			X			X			X		
45		X			X	X	X	X			X			X	X		X					X

Rows of the table (objects) represent models of Sun Ultra Workstations: 20, 24, 40, 25, and 45. We consider 22 attributes divided into 8 groups: *architecture* (*86* − Intel compatible; *sp* − UltraSparc); *manufacturer* (*A* − AMD; *I* − Intel; *S* − Sun); *number of CPUs* (*1* or *2*); *number of CPU cores* (*1*, *2*, or *4*); *clock speed* (*l* − ≤1.5 GHz; *m* − ≤2.0 GHz; *h* − >2.0 GHz); *maximum memory* (*8*, *16*, or *32* GB); *maximum mass storage* (*1*, *2*, or *3* TB); and *starting price* (*1k* − ≤\$1000; *2k* − \$1000–\$3000; *3k* − >\$3000).

The concept lattice $B(X,Y,I)$ associated with Table 13.2 contains 17 concepts. The concepts are shown in Table 13.3.

For instance, the extent of concept number 4 contains models 25 and 45, and its intent contains attributes *sp* (architecture: UltraSparc), *S* (manufacturer: Sun), *1* (1 CPU), etc. The corresponding concept lattice $B(X,Y,I)$ is depicted in Figure 13.1.

Suppose that a customer is interested in finding workstations according to the following priorities:

1. *Mass storage capacity* is more important than *price*
2. *CPU clock speed* is more important than *mass storage capacity*
3. *Processor architecture* is more important than *number of processor cores*

Priorities of this type may be imposed by, for example, a customer interested in a high-speed graphics workstation. In terms of AD formulas, we represent this particular constraint as follows:

$$\{1k, 2k, 3k\} \angle \{HDD1, HDD2, HDD3\},$$

$$\{HDD1, HDD2, HDD3\} \angle \{l, m, h\},$$

$$\{Cores1, Cores2, Cores4\} \angle \{86, sp\}$$

Of all the original concepts, 10 satisfy such constraints: 1, 2, 3, 5, 8, 9, 10, 13, 16, and 17. For instance, concept 4 does not satisfy the constraint because it specifies mass storage information but not the CPU clock speed, which is not interesting for our user, who prefers information about CPU speed over the mass storage capacity. The constrained concept lattice $B_T(X,Y,I)$ corresponding to the above set T of AD formulas is shown in Figure 13.2.

Sometimes, users can feel that certain attributes are equally important. For instance, *CPU manufacturer* and *CPU clock speed* can both be important and a user may wish to have information about both of them or none of them at the same time. From the point of view of AD formulas, we can formulate the constraint as follows:

$$\{A, I, S\} \angle \{l, m, h\},$$

$$\{l, m, h\} \angle \{A, I, S\}.$$

The AD formulas say that whenever information about the architecture is present, information about the speed must also be present and vice versa. If we use this

TABLE 13.3
Formal Concepts Associated with Data in Table 13.2

| | Extent | | | | | | | Intent | | | | | | | | | | | | | | | | | | | |
| | Model | | | | | Arch. | | Manufacturer | | | CPUs | | Cores | | | Clock | | | RAM | | | HDD | | | Price | | |
#	20	24	40	25	45	86	sp	A	I	S	1	2	1	2	4	l	m	h	8	16	32	1	2	3	1k	2k	3k
1						X	X	X	X	X	X	X	X	X	X	X	X	X	X	X	X	X	X	X	X	X	X
2					X		X			X	X	X	X				X		X	X	X	X	X	X	X		X
3				X			X			X	X		X			X			X			X				X	
4				X			X			X	X		X						X			X					
5			X			X		X			X	X		X				X	X	X	X		X			X	
6			X		X						X	X							X	X	X						
7			X	X							X				X				X							X	
8		X				X			X		X			X				X	X					X	X		
9		X	X			X					X			X				X	X					X	X		
10	X					X		X			X			X			X		X			X			X		
11	X				X						X		X				X		X			X					
12	X			X	X						X		X						X			X					
13	X		X	X		X		X			X			X					X								
14	X		X	X	X						X		X						X								
15	X	X				X					X			X					X						X		
16	X	X	X	X		X					X			X					X								
17	X	X	X	X							X		X						X								

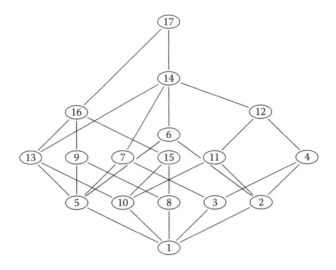

FIGURE 13.1 Concept lattice $B(X,Y,I)$ of data from Table 13.2.

constraint, we obtain 13 concepts. The concepts that do not satisfy the constraint are: 4, 9, 11, and 13. The constrained concept lattice $B_S(X,Y,I)$ corresponding to the above set S of AD formulas is shown in Figure 13.3.

AD formulas representing constraints can be constructed after the user answers a series of questions such as "Do you prefer A over B?" By showing the user just the concepts congruent with the preferences, we draw his or her attention to groups of products that are coherent with his or her expectations. In addition to that, the hierarchy of such concepts may help the user decide which configuration is better for a given purpose by comparing more specific or more general groups of configurations. During the exploration of interesting concepts, the user can eventually come up with new important constraints that were not explicitly mentioned in the first place but

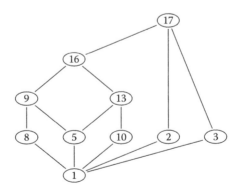

FIGURE 13.2 Constrained concept lattice $B_T(X,Y,I)$.

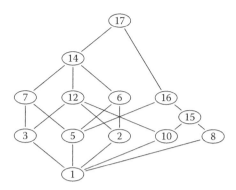

FIGURE 13.3 Constrained concept lattice $B_S(X,Y,I)$.

that were subconsciously expected by the user. This way, the exploration based on constrained concept lattices may help the user to further clarify his or her feeling of which properties are important for the job of interest.

Investigation of such interactive procedures for data exploration based on user preferences is the subject of future research.

ACKNOWLEDGMENT

Supported by grant No. 1ET101370417 of GA of CAS, by grant No. 201/05/0079 of the Czech Science Foundation, and by institutional support research plan MSM 6198959214.

REFERENCES

Belohlavek, R. and Sklenar, V. Formal concept analysis constrained by attribute-dependency formulas, in *Lecture Notes in Computer Science,* vol. 3403, Springer, Berlin, 2005, pp. 176–191.

Belohlavek, R. and Vychodil, V. Semantic entailment of attribute-dependency formulas and their non-redundant bases, in *JCIS 2006,* Kaohsiung, Taiwan, ROC, 2006, pp. 747–750.

Belohlavek, R. and Vychodil, V. 2008. Adding background knowledge to formal concept analysis via attribute dependency formulas. In *ACM Symposium on Applied Computing,* forthcoming.

Carpineto, C. and Romano, G. *Concept Data Analysis. Theory and Applications,* J. Wiley, Chichester, UK, 2004.

Cho, W.C. and Richards, W. 2004. Improvement of precision and recall for information retrieval in a narrow domain: reuse of concepts by formal concept analysis, in *IEEE/WIC/ACM International Conference on Web Intelligence* (WI04), 2004, pp. 370–376.

Dekel, U. and Gil, Y. Visualizing class interfaces with formal concept analysis, in *ACM SIGPLAN OOPSLA03*, Anaheim, CA, 2003, pp. 288–289.

Doignon, J.-P. and Falmagne, J.-C. *Knowledge Spaces*, Springer, Berlin, 1999.

Ganapathy, V., King, D., Jaeger, T., and Jha, S. Mining security-sensitive operations in legacy code using concept analysis, in *Proceedings of the 29th International Conference on Software Engineering* (ICSE 2007), 2007, pp. 458–467.

Ganter, B. Attribute exploration with background knowledge, *Theor. Comput. Sci.*, 217, 215–233, 1999.

Ganter, B. and Wille, R. *Formal Concept Analysis. Mathematical Foundations*, Springer, Berlin, 1999.

Maier. D. *The Theory of Relational Databases*, Computer Science Press, Rockville, MD, 1983.

Okubo Y. and Haraguchi, M. Finding conceptual document clusters with improved top-n formal concept search, in *IEEE/WIC/ACM International Conference on Web Intelligence* (WI'06), 2006, Hong Kong, pp. 347–351.

Snelting G. and Tip, F. Understanding class hierarchies using concept analysis, *ACM Trans. Program. Lang. Sys.*, 22, 540–582, 2000.

Streckenbach, M. and Snelting, G. Refactoring class hierarchies with KABA, in *ACM SIGPLAN OOPSLA 2004*, 2004, pp. 315–330.

Stumme, G. 1996. Attribute exploration with background implications and exceptions, in *Data Analysis and Information Systems. Statistical and Conceptual Approaches*, Bock, H.-H. and Polasek, W., Eds., Springer, Piscataway, NJ, pp. 457–469.

Tonella, P. 2003. Using a concept lattice of decomposition slices for program understanding and impact analysis, *IEEE Trans. Software Engin.*, 29, 495–509, 2003.

14 Literature Categorization System for Automated Database Retrieval of Scientific Articles Based on Dedicated Taxonomy

Lukáš Pichl, Manabu Suzuki, Masaki Murata,
Daiji Kato, Izumi Murakami, and Akira Sasaki

CONTENTS

14.1 TAXONOMY IN DEDICATED SEARCH ENGINES

Data structuring has grown increasingly complex in the age of information technology,[1–6] when virtually all fields of science are recognized as interconnected. On the side of human-based information retrieval, the inflation of information available via electronic systems resulted in enormous quantitative load of relatively routine content-filtering tasks for human to perform, a price to pay for the efficiency of content access and delivery. Search engines have been developed in response to this problem; being universal and common are now the main keywords, as the algorithms developed for the most successful public systems include learning layer into search and contents provision. While such inbuilt evolutionary elements are crucial for public or commercial success of the search engines, in fact featuring soft functional separation, these generally degrade search precision in highly specific tasks, such as retrieval of scientific articles on a narrow subject, in case of which common methods prove extremely inefficient (delivery failure for tasks where user input is less valued than system output).

Innovative commerce leaders are busy with developing new generations of design systems, or more commonly, with assembling and implementing new associations within existing constructs or systems. To this aim, it is indispensable to follow new developments in science. The major obstacle in our viewpoint is the bureaucratic tendency common to most human organizations, namely to capture own languages (scientific dialects) to describe some partial discipline as innovative, novel, or even unique. Such delimiting feature makes the task to synchronize with new scientific developments relatively difficult for business people, especially since new word collocations have context dependent meaning while their context framework itself is still establishing. Therefore judging originality and potential business value of new organizational schemes is not only a quantitative task but also a piece of art. Business people working on marketing and design thus need to evaluate keywords and documents in science, decipher their major relations with respect to applicability, and set up a framework rigorous enough to ask for expert judgment. For instance, a manufacturing firm in car industry may seek information on hydrogen fuel or new biotechnological approaches to produce ethanol; robotics company may seek a breakthrough in computational linguistics or neural network architecture, food companies track new developments in agriculture, and so forth. The central task for this chapter is therefore to recognize innovation and new developments based on text base with newly forming (or highly specialized) vocabulary, typically by means of machine learning and categorization algorithms.

Dynamic search engine algorithms built atop learning and evolution are in sharp contrast with academic view on historical information science, in particular library science. It is important to recognize how the entire scientific method is based on categorization, which is rooted within medieval trivium, and demonstrated in categorization systems approached by means of library science. In this context, taxonomy is the key – fixed tagging system with sufficiently deep hierarchy framing data-insert and data-search algorithms, as being common in the classical computer science notion of tree structures. Referring to the sphere of public search engines, the failure to synchronize content insert operation (linking a cached copy for previous act of web page upload) with content categorization (assignment of unique label or multiple tags corresponding to fixed taxa) motivates interesting questions on the level of consciousness of contents provider (or skill of the contents categorizer, whether human or machine). It is common that information value is degraded both for broad-context data (extensive set of tags deep in the categorization tree, or string prefix explicated to lower tree-depth level) and narrow-context data (small set of labels deeply in the categorization tree). Pursuing such contents annotation dilemma from the level of the document (multimedia contents) towards the enumerated text level brings up interesting linguistic parallels, in particular selection of words with broad or narrow information content (cf. document content categorization), as if the document level and text level were (as indeed are) complementary projections of mental (language) representation level. That is schematically how taxonomy of documents relates to semantics of words, and the tree structure of content labels reflects on multi-graph structure of natural language. The borderline between the implicit and explicit is not always visible; while this fact is less than obvious issue in natural sciences, for humanities, such as literature studies or philosophy, it provides an educational and conceptual framework for genres and schools of thought. A rigid taxonomy system that has sufficient complexity is often paralleled by social-based folk taxonomy (i.e. multilectal) version, this phenomenon is a consequence of communication economies, communication structure, and also social hierarchical system of doing science and categorizing scientists. In such environment, folksonomies were adopted as strategy, meaning a collaborative categorization scheme based on freely chosen tags under some social selection scrutiny system. In brief, within the academic system rigid scientific taxonomies remain on long time scale, while the rapidly evolving folksonomies are used to deal with rigid problems on short time scale, both possibly converging to a unified socio-computing system, that elevates integral knowledge representation, leaves it invariant, or even degrades knowledge system. Static knowledge equilibrium was not the case, it appears, in history, when civilizations with developed scientific taxonomies sometimes ceased, succumbing to brute-force methods and invasions of primitivism, which can now be enumerated and simulated. Such cultural oscillations may correspond to gradual shift between conscious and unconscious levels, which has certain analogs in the evolution of taxonomies, due to the method of applicable claiming range of word meaning (or claiming the range of knowledge comprehension, for the sake of intellectual property or historical legacy). Namely, when key notions (or elements of expertise) become void, for instance disregarded as too subtle, devalued by over-emphasizing, marketed out in exchange for cheaper substitutes, the meaning of acronyms lost through phonetic vocabularization, expertise destroyed on purpose, and so forth, a replacement or functional complement may arise from surrounding network of mutual relations; however, it often tends to be coarser, less sophisticated, or even minimalist. That is why understanding of taxonomies in the context of knowledge representation is important, namely for design of their potential in knowledge growth and science evolution. Importantly at this point, a customizable taxonomy allows for crisp data filtering from innovative points of view, and thus enables chance cognition; furthermore, taxonomy optimized to prescribed boundary conditions is then a powerful tool for knowledge formation and chance construction.

Within the taxonomy scene above, in this chapter we study document retrieval of scientific papers that contain numerical data relevant for a fixed-purpose database as a case study. The database system is called AMDIS, and contains numerical data of collision cross sections for the processes of excitation, ionization, and dissociation occurring as a result of electron impact on atom or molecule. The system is maintained by the National Institute for Fusion Science (NIFS). Although majority of relevant articles is published in about five major journals, there exist relevant documents retrieved elsewhere in numbers as low as one or two per journal. The articles are either of theoretical or experimental type; theory texts sometimes give formalism and computational methods without any relevant numerical data. Many of the journals use the PACS (Physics and Astronomy Categorization Scheme) system.[7] The taxonomy of PACS is supposed to be strictly hierarchical; PACS codes (in fact alphanumeric strings including dot and plus delimiters) are either aggregate (internal tree node) or resolved (leaf node); every scientific paper in a journal following PACS categorization has one or more PACS tags assigned, usually by choice of author. Taking a list of 147 articles published in the Physical Review, Series A, journal of American Physical Society, recommended for evaluation by human expert scientist, 139 items had at least one of the following string tags (related keywords are shown in the brackets):

34.80.Kw (Electron-ion scattering; excitation and ionization)
34.80.Dp (Atomic excitation and ionization by electron impact)
32.80.Dz (Autoionization),

which demonstrates the strength of appropriate taxonomy system, and yields recall rate of 95%. On the other hand, article search using the above three tags results in 985 papers for one-year volume of the journal containing (after standard data preprocessing) 22,147 articles, meaning only a minor fraction is found relevant. Such a sample excurse shows that PACS categorization system alone is incapable of resolving papers relevant to the specific NIFS AMDIS database. One clue to the complexity of the problem are the keywords (or brief sentences) accompanying each PACS annotation: these appear as a guide to scientists rather than a semantic definition. Some of the keywords, whether alone or as a part of longer phrases, occur in auxiliary wording of multiple PACS tags, which provides an instance of knowledge overlap layer between semantics and taxonomy. The keyword-based label fixation concerns especially with terminological selection of *processes* that occur in collisions of electron incident on target atoms or molecules. Because the project database is dedicated to the problem of computer simulations of plasma fusion, there exists another standpoint: chemical *materials*. Particular atomic and molecular species are scarce in the wording of PACS categorizing system; furthermore, these are materials common in thermonuclear fusion reactors, namely hydrogen (H), deuterium (D) and tritium (T) as the fuel, helium (He) as the product, and then various chemical elements, e.g. carbon (C) or tungsten (wolfram, W) from reactor wall material, chemical elements left over as air remnants, oxygen (O), nitrogen (N), impurities from diagnostic probes such as lithium (Li), and so forth. Any chemically admissible combination of the above elements (atom or molecule) in an energetically stable charge state (positive ions formed by electron removal, negative ions formed by electron attachment) is relevant for the database. This fact could apparently be represented in the form of pattern recognition rule: match atoms or molecules on specific list. Such a rule, however, still requires some amendments, e.g. "and not too large," in order to apply widely across comprehensive science bibliography database. The aforementioned addition of broad rule filters out organic molecules (notice that H and C atoms are contained also in hydrocarbons or polymer components), which are not likely to be formed or found within fusion reactors. With the advance of nano-science in material technology, other plausible amendments may require in the future exclusion of organic molecules adsorbed on nano-layer surfaces, and so forth, until the original taxonomy (or the database, or both) obsoletes. Finally we notice that even the PACS scheme is regularly updated (up to five per cent of modified nodes per revision), which allows for nontrivial correspondence between various time snapshots of the categorization structure.

The ultimate applicability scales up with scientist participant understanding and community etiquette.

The above outline of the taxonomy subsystem dedicated to NIFS AMDIS database motivates inference that neither the popularity-based search engines, such as GOOGLE, or standard taxonomy based system, such as online databases (or local disk copy of article abstracts) have categorizers (or search tags) combinable into a usable matching rule. This is obvious in the former case and rather intuitive in the latter case, if the reader recalls layout of query interfaces at online bibliography databases, typically restrained to author, institution, title, abstract, keyword, few Boolean operators, and some wildcard symbols. While theorists come up with regular expression as ultimate answer, practitioners have yet to determine admissible counting for links of indirection. It is, however, possible to apply a rule-based filtering within our article retrieval system, as given below.

In what follows, we motivate a modular algorithm maximizing recall on the expense of precision, as the information retrieval measure in screening of article abstracts; while the lack of explicit taxonomy format is common in standard retrieval engines, the additional suppression of precision allows to overcome common limits on ultimate recall in machine learning algorithms, yielding increase of typical ceiling values from 70% to 90% or more. Such increase of recall in case of dedicated search is facilitated by taxonomy-tag recognition engine integrated into the abstract analysis engine for this purpose (chemical species, electronic states, etc.). Finally, a rule-based filtering module is applied to the compact areas of full text article that are rich in taxonomy tags (namely the text within captions of Figures and Tables), increasing the precision of article retrieval while preserving the achieved recall.

14.2   ABSTRACT SEARCH ENGINE WITH XML TAGGER

The first phase of the automated database retrieval of scientific articles relevant to computer simulations of fusion *edge* plasma (in which atoms and molecules and their ions may exist) consists in listing potentially relevant sources through breath-first screening of published abstracts. To that aim, we have previously developed Joint Search Engine,[8] an online connection interface that can send queries simultaneously to multiple online bibliography databases. The system has implemented a module for recognition of tags specific to a subset (and dialect) of chemical terminology, and assigns tags specific to electronic states of atoms and molecules.

At this point, let us illustrate certain specific features of custom taxonomies using several examples. First, most search engines and algorithms for information retrieval omit dummy words, such as the preposition "in" or the verb "be"; raising the case of the first letter, we obtain "In" for Indium, and "Be" for Beryllium. Resolving letter capitalization decreases the frequency of encountering the ambiguity, however, sentence fragments such as "In this respect..." or "Be more ..." still require a conjunction with an extra rule so as to filter out the sequences *not* containing chemical elements or electronic state designation as *immediate suffix*. Another feature common especially in denoting electronic states is the functional annotation by means of superscript and subscript fonts. Such formatting is sometimes omitted for the sake of inline expression simplicity, which further complicates disambiguation.

Furthermore, it is common to designate angular momentum states with capital letters S (0), P (1), D (2), F (3)… that are same as chemical symbols of Sulfur, Phosphor, Deuterium, Fluor, and so forth. In these cases, formatting (e.g. italics for electronic states) is needed to avert context-dependent ambiguity.

Since the abstract search engine, Joint Search, was described in previous publication[3], we restrict to summarizing its main features here, and focus on the newly added extraction module for chemical and electronic state terminology, i.e. the special purpose tagging feature integrated within the searching tool.[9] In order to analyze the abstracts from online publisher databases, it is (1) necessary to parameterize html request with data for search forms in case of each abstract source website, and (2) to develop string-matching rules for the analysis of resulting html page. Both phases of subsequent article retrieval can be reduced to processing a comprehensive pool of meta-annotated abstracts from a central database. At present, it is the INSPEC abstracting system; article abstracts from a variety of relevant (and subscribed) journals are available for analysis as a local copy for the NIFS AMDIS project. Let us note that INSPEC article annotations have been available at present in the form of an excel file and/or as an XML-labeled text file. The former format may be abandoned in future editions of INSPEC, which illustrates the trend towards annotation of scientific results in the form suitable not only for human knowledge sharing but also for broader processing by machine learning algorithms.

The Joint Search system[3] is an online interface to other search interfaces, a meta-search system. The search requests are sent to http://scitation.aip.org/vsearch/servlet/VerityServlet?KEY=ALL, and http://www.iop.org/EJ/search/. The retrieved answer pages from AIP and IOP are processed by PHP scripts, which discard redundant formatting features and extract bibliography information.

The terminology extraction module, i.e. the tagger program, is applied in the form of a Perl-written common gateway interface, CGI, to colorize all matched terms in the output, as shown in Figure 14.1 (upper panel for article titles, lower panel for article abstracts). The meta-search engine is depicted in Figure 14.2. Queries are translated to selected databases, and sent over the html port 80 along with target URLs. The Perl script deals with nuances such as occurrence of synonyms, e.g. iron, FERRUM, Fe for the chemical elements, or He-like Lithium, Li II or Li+ for the Lithium ion in charge state plus one. We have previously published a modification of the Joint Search 1, the Evolutionary Database, which retrieves and stores data by means of similar interface prototype. The search results along with the assigned (colorized) tags serve as the input for abstract relevance pre-assessment by methods developed recently.[6] In particular, the method tested in Ref. 6 is based on the Learning Vector Quantization as one of the elementary machine learning algorithms. If applied to the raw html text without preprocessing specific for given taxonomy, it yields recall of about 70% (with precision optimized at the same time, its values falling within the range 50%–70%). We note that recognition of specific terminology, and preference of recall to precision in the ratio of 5:1 increases the recall over 90% with precision remaining above 20%.[6]

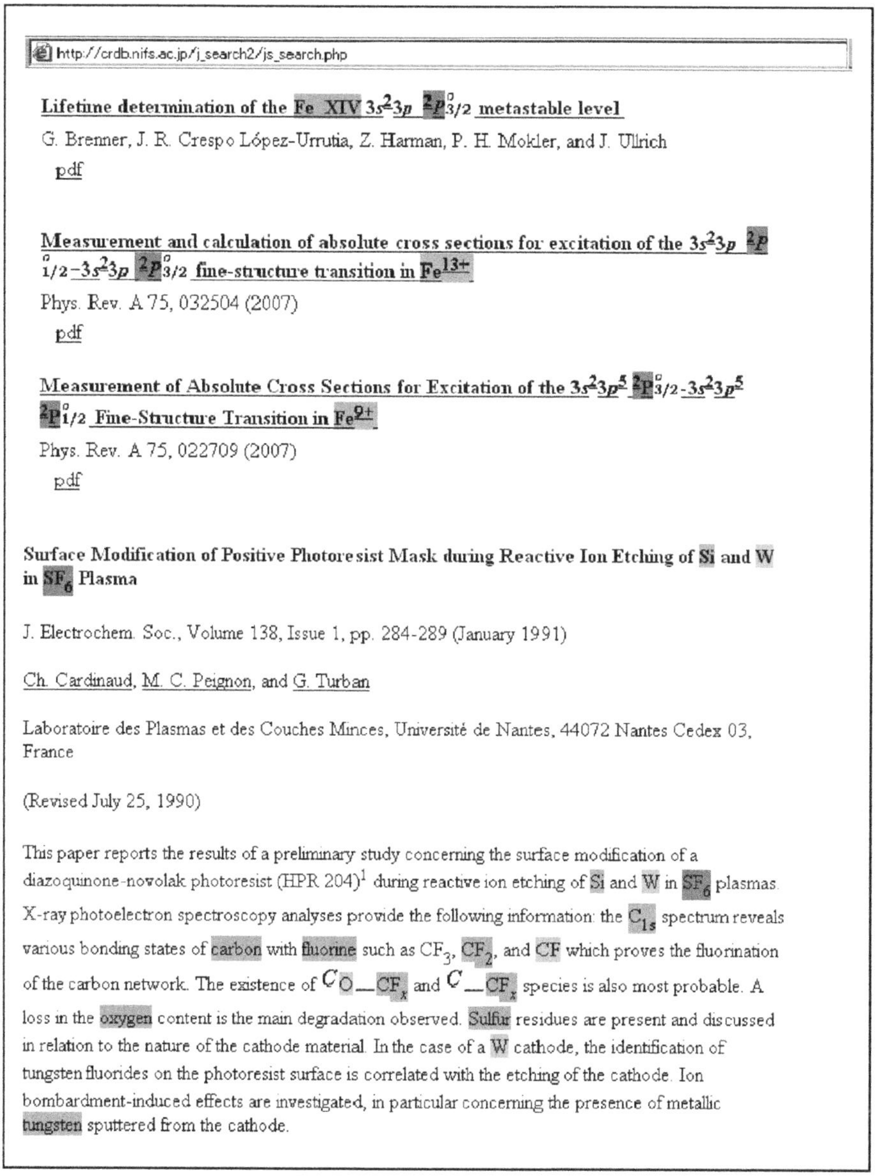

---

http://crdb.nifs.ac.jp/j_search2/js_search.php

Lifetime determination of the Fe XIV $3s^2 3p\ ^2P^o_{3/2}$ metastable level

G. Brenner, J. R. Crespo López-Urrutia, Z. Harman, P. H. Mokler, and J. Ullrich

  pdf

Measurement and calculation of absolute cross sections for excitation of the $3s^2 3p\ ^2P^o_{1/2} - 3s^2 3p\ ^2P^o_{3/2}$ fine-structure transition in Fe^{13+}

Phys. Rev. A 75, 032504 (2007)

  pdf

Measurement of Absolute Cross Sections for Excitation of the $3s^2 3p^5\ ^2P^o_{3/2} - 3s^2 3p^5\ ^2P^o_{1/2}$ Fine-Structure Transition in Fe^{9+}

Phys. Rev. A 75, 022709 (2007)

  pdf

Surface Modification of Positive Photoresist Mask during Reactive Ion Etching of Si and W in SF_6 Plasma

J. Electrochem. Soc., Volume 138, Issue 1, pp. 284-289 (January 1991)

Ch. Cardinaud, M. C. Peignon, and G. Turban

Laboratoire des Plasmas et des Couches Minces, Université de Nantes, 44072 Nantes Cedex 03, France

(Revised July 25, 1990)

This paper reports the results of a preliminary study concerning the surface modification of a diazoquinone-novolak photoresist (HPR 204)[1] during reactive ion etching of Si and W in SF_6 plasmas. X-ray photoelectron spectroscopy analyses provide the following information: the C_{1s} spectrum reveals various bonding states of carbon with fluorine such as CF_3, CF_2, and CF which proves the fluorination of the carbon network. The existence of $C_O - CF_x$ and $C - CF_x$ species is also most probable. A loss in the oxygen content is the main degradation observed. Sulfur residues are present and discussed in relation to the nature of the cathode material. In the case of a W cathode, the identification of tungsten fluorides on the photoresist surface is correlated with the etching of the cathode. Ion bombardment-induced effects are investigated, in particular concerning the presence of metallic tungsten sputtered from the cathode.

FIGURE 14.1 Recognition of electronic states, chemical elements, and molecular symbols within an abstract search engine: tag frames assigned within custom taxonomy system are shown in shading.

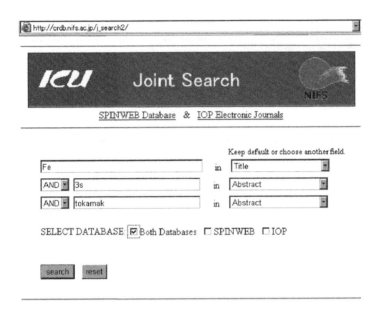

FIGURE 14.2 Meta-search interface with inbuilt tagging module, "Joint Search 2," for online bibliography databases.

14.3 RULE-BASED FILTERING

The next step of the information retrieval concerns with the numerical data themselves, and may not be solely achieved based on the analysis of abstracts.[8] The broad purpose is to increase the precision of relevance assessment by means of content filtering. In particular, the textual captions of all figures and tables in the manuscript are together analyzed for simultaneous occurrence of (1) processes and (2) atomic/chemical species; the article is recognized as relevant in case such simultaneous hit occurs at least once. The *precision* of the two stages combined in the automated retrieval (newly published articles) reaches over 90%. This result was confirmed in case of a sample data set, which consisted of 230 articles, mostly from the Physical Review A journal (PRA), Journal of Physics B, and articles published by EDP sciences. Because of the low number of irrelevant articles in the original training set, we have extended the evaluation experiment to include one PRA volume with 22,147 abstracts available. The sample distribution of PACS numbers for the relevant articles is listed in Table 14.1, indicative of highly specific taxonomy for the sample. Since numerical data are presented as a rule in the form of tables or can be deduced from figures, and because text of all captions is required to be compact, specific, and highly informative, it is claimed here that the ultimate precision of rule-based filtering for relevance assessment on existence of numerical data in scientific articles is substantially limited by available format conversion and reduction tools (pdf to text transform, for instance) rather than by any aspect of computational linguistics or particular form of rule-based filtering logic.

TABLE 14.1
Categorization Symbols of 230 Representative Articles Included at the NIFS Database

02.70.-c: 1	31.15.Ar: 1	32.30.Rj: 9	32.60.+i: 1	32.70.-n: 2
32.70.Cs: 1	32.70.Fw: 2	32.80.Cy: 2	32.80.Dz: 14	32.80.Hd: 3
34.10.+x: 5	34.50.Fa: 7	34.80.-i: 2	34.80.Bm: 1	34.80.Dp: 29
34.80.Ht: 1	34.80.Kw: 124	34.80.Lx: 1	34.80.Nz: 2	34.90.+q: 1
42.55.Vc: 1	52.20.-j: 1	52.20.Fs: 3	52.20.Hv: 1	52.25.Kn: 3
52.25.Vy: 2	52.70.La: 1	95.30.Ky: 1	97.10.Ld: 1	97.60.Jd: 1

Discontinued or nonassigned physics and astronomy categorization scheme: 6

14.4   COMPARISON WITH OTHER ARTICLE SEARCH ENGINES

As discussed above, maintenance of dedicated database belongs to projects common in various areas of science, for instance the PubMed bibliography database in biology.[10] While the PubMed project is based on coordinated submission of articles, endorsed by editors of the participating journals under the auspices of National Library of Medicine (relevance by design), the present project focuses upon automated relevance assessment and construction. Naturally, technical solutions in database maintenance fields tend to include a mixture of data provision and active data search elements, e.g. the DBLP system (originally DataBase systems and Logic Programming)[11]. We are not, however, aware of a project as focused as the present one, except for GENIE, a **Gen**eral **I**nternet Search **E**ngine for Atomic Data.[11] GENIE is a specific database query tool provided by the Nuclear Data Section, backed by international association based in Vienna, which integrates the AMDIS database at NIFS with other participating institutions. The search interface and sample result page of GENIE (edited for sake of space) are shown in Figure 14.3.

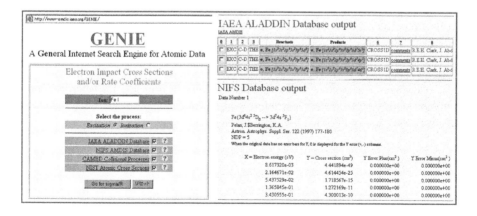

FIGURE 14.3 Portal of Genie search engine: query interface (left panel) and sample output (right panel).

GENIE's search output (right panel in Figure 14.3) combines the results from the IAEA Database, CAMDB (output not shown in Figure 14.3) and NIFS database. Unlike Joint Search 2, the results appear not semantically analyzed; retrieved pages are instead divided by line delimiters and merged into one common HTML file. GENIE thus has no categorization modules available on output for recognition of specific terminology on user side. The result, on the other hand, includes numerical data (or provides links to numerical data tables), each formatted according to the standards of the particular participating database. Therefore the main difference seen between GENIE and the present system based on Joint Search 2 is the ability to retrieve, categorize, annotate and finally relevance-assess (in the sense of taxonomy-based formulation above) research papers through integrated framework.

14.5   LESSONS LEARNED AND FUTURE PROSPECTS

We have presented a specialized search engine for retrieval of journal articles relevant to a dedicated scientific database with a narrow focus. The Joint Search tool sends in parallel queries to two major online databases, retrieves and analyzes the results, and consequently categorizes the relevant part of HTML output for terminology specific to edge plasma processes. The extracted terminology is distinguished by color fields, which represent XML tags assigned by the system to the original text, within the environment of search engine. The present terminology extraction facilitates relevance assessment of journal articles so as to decide whether to include them in particularly specialized database or not.

Since the majority of meta-databases of scientific bibliography data rely on coordinated submission efforts by journal editors and publishers, and their respective search tools (database query interfaces) are standardized according to the tools of traditional library science, there are few interfaces to perform comprehensive and customized searches. Although typical "advanced" query tools offer Boolean operators or wildcards (duplicating or opening the features of the underlying software implementation), they do not usually allow definition of custom vocabularies (e.g. by uploading list of chemical elements) or prototyping syntactic relations. The specialized project reported in this chapter can therefore be understood as a pioneering study; moreover, the linguistic formulation in terms of dedicated taxonomy is common enough to guarantee numerous applications (or interface ports) to article retrieval systems specialized for particular areas in life science, material sciences, technology, and elsewhere. The meta-search formulation allows in principle for heterogeneous implementation of dedicated article retrieval systems atop one underlying database instance, such as the INSPEC bibliography system.[13]

REFERENCES

1. Jensen, L.J., Saric, J., and Bork, P. Literature mining for the biologist: from information retrieval to biological discovery, *Nat. Rev. Genet.*, 7, 119–129, 2006.
2. Hu, Z.Z., Narayanaswamy, M., Ravikumar, K.E., Vijay-Shanker, K., and Wu, C.H. Literature mining and database annotation of protein phosphorylation using a rule-based system, *Bioinformatics,* 21, 2759–2765, 2005.

3. Tsujii, J. and Ananiadou, S. Thesaurus or logical ontology, which one do we need for text mining? *Lang. Resources Eval.,* 39, 77–90, 2005.

4. Mima, H., Ananiadou, S., and Matsushima, K. Terminology-based knowledge mining for new knowledge discovery, *ACM Trans. Asian Lang. Inform. Proc.*, 5, 74–88, 2006.

5. Okazaki, N. and Ananiadou, S. Building an abbreviation dictionary using a term recognition approach, *Bioinformatics,* 22, 3089–3095, 2006.

6. Kashiwagi, H., Watanabe, C., Sasaki, A., and Joe, K. Text classification for constructing an atomic and molecular journal database by LVQ, *Proceedings of International Conference on Parallel and Distributed Processing Techniques and Applications*, 2005, 481–487.

7. PACS, Physics and Astronomy Classification Scheme by American Institute of Physics. Available online at: http://www.aip.org/pacs/. Accessed August 26, 2007.

8. Pichl, L., Suzuki, M., Joe, K., and Sasaki, A. Networked mining of atomic and molecular data from electronic journal databases on the Internet, *Lect. Notes Computer Sci.,* 3433, 159–170, 2005.

9. Murata, M., Kanamaru, T., and Isahara, H. Automatic synonym acquisition based on matching of definition sentences in multiple dictionaries, *Lect. Notes Computer Sci.,* 3406, 293–304, 2005.

10. PubMed, U.S. National Library of Medicine. Available online at www.ncbi.nlm.nih.gov/entrez/. Accessed August 26, 2007.

11. Digital Bibliography and Library Project, DBLP URL (2007/8/26): http://dblp.uni-trier.de/.

12. Humbert, D.P., Nichols, A.L., and Schwerer, O. IAEA Nuclear Data Section: provision of atomic and nuclear databases for user applications, *Appl. Radiat. Isotopes,* 60, 311–316, 2004; also General Internet Search Engine for Atomic Data, IAEA, available online at: http://www-amdis.iaea.org/GENIE/. Accessed August 26, 2007.

13. Inspec (The Database for Physics, Electronics and Computing). Available online at www.ovid.com/site/products/ovidguide/inspdb.htm. Accessed August 26, 2007.

15 A Data-Mining Framework for Designing Personalized E-Commerce Support Tools

Timothy Maciag, Dominik Ślęzak,
Daryl H. Hepting, and Robert J. Hilderman

CONTENTS

15.1 CONSUMER DECISION MAKING, E-COMMERCE, AND USER-CENTERED DESIGN

Imagine you are browsing an e-commerce site, such as Amazon, Chapters-Indigo. ca, or JCPenney.com, with the goal of searching for and comparing products you are interested in purchasing, such as household cleaning products, books, CDs, or clothing. Depending on the specific goal of your shopping activity (browse, search, compare, purchase), you may wish to conduct a more in-depth product search/comparison or you may choose to conduct a broader, loosely based search/product comparison to arrive at a final purchase decision. In one instance, you wish to systematically evaluate *all* products in relation to *all* corresponding features (attributes) in terms of your preference set. This type of consumer decision-making strategy stems from *rational choice theory*[1] and is referred to as *compensatory* analysis: when a decision maker fully rationalizes a decision in relation to a predefined set of preferences (expert or nonexpert).[1–4] In another instance, you wish to evaluate products using only a small but important subset of product features that you highly value, while omitting all others. This type of consumer decision-making strategy is referred to as noncompensatory analysis, which stems from Simon's concept of bounded rationality[3,4]—the idea that there are limitations in the human capacity for reaching fully rationalized decisions—and further elaborated by Bettman[18] and Luce et al.[19] In noncompensatory analyses, a decision maker will arrive at a final decision based on ad hoc information derived from a variety of factors, including predefined or "on the spot" (e.g., emotionally based) preference sets, among others.[1,3,5,6,19]

As indicated by the increasing number of people who connect to the Web each day to conduct their shopping activities, such as browsing for products in Web-based catalogues, searching for product information using Web-based tools, and finalizing purchasing decisions online, it is clear that the Web is continually changing the way people think about their everyday needs and tasks.[7,16,31] This increase in e-commerce activities has brought many challenges to e-businesses, one of which includes how to enhance consumer online shopping experiences to ensure their satisfaction. More often than not, consumers are left to their own expertise when formulating online purchasing decisions. Designing a more adequate and effective online support framework that would aid consumers in formulating *better* purchasing decisions by incorporating support for compensatory and noncompensatory analyses is one possible approach to improve design. A more effective support framework in such regards could have the potential to increase consumer satisfaction, increase consumer/company loyalty, and boost overall sales. As an underlying foundation to such a framework, personalization and customization of the user interface could be considered.

For example, the Web retailer Amazon provides personalized/customizable user interfaces by providing its customers with up-to-date product recommendations based on previous transaction histories and product rankings. Although this type of framework is a step in the right direction, there still exist opportunities for improvement as many times, for product recommendations to prove meaningful, one *may* have to input substantial amounts of information, thus skewing the consumers' focus from their shopping activities and placing it undesirably on the interface itself. In this regard, Norman[20,21] describes the concept of the invisible computer, in which the computer system, in essence, becomes *invisible* and the task is all that remains. It relates to one of the pitfalls of user interface design, and in our opinion, of the Amazon framework—how the interface may act as an obstacle between the user, the system, and the shopping tasks to be achieved. Furthermore, Raskin[22] defines his laws of user interface design, two of which include that the computer should not waste the user's time or require the user to do more work than necessary and that users set the pace of an interaction, both of which many of the current online support frameworks reject. If we detract the users' cognitive efforts away from their primary task goals (e.g., shopping), the user interface is flawed.[20]

Our proposed framework builds on the concepts of personalization/customization and aims to incorporate Norman's and Raskin's ideas. Specifically, our goal is to design a support framework that shifts the consumers' focus away from the user interface, placing it solely on their shopping activities. We hypothesize that incorporating decision-making aids that assist consumers in conducting both compensatory and noncompensatory decision analyses is a critical element of such a design. This type of support framework would hold true to both Norman's and Raskin's theoretical viewpoints and, hypothetically, consumer satisfaction would be increased, as with little effort consumers would obtain a personalized user interface, one that would place their focus where it belongs and one that would more adequately support their decision-making tasks.[7]

15.2 METHODS

There exist a multitude of methods that could be used in designing more effective, comprehensible, and satisfying[8] support frameworks with the above-described goals in mind—including fuzzy sets,[32] clustering,[33] and neural networks.[34] For the purposes of this chapter, we focus only on those methods that relate to our research specifically—association mining and rough set theory.

15.2.1 DATA MINING

Mobasher et al.,[28] Holland et al.,[29] and Eirinaki and Vazirgiannis[30] discuss the prospect of data mining and Web usage mining methods, such as mining frequent item sets that meet minimum support and confidence thresholds and that generate association rules to obtain useful consumer patterns with the goal of personalizing user interfaces in such environments. Common algorithms for such tasks include Apriori[10] and Eclat[11,23] (breadth-first and depth-first prefix tree search, respectively). The general framework for personalization may include highlighting certain aspects of the problem domain, such as which items do users frequently purchase together or which product pages do users frequently view per online shopping session. A series of rules would be generated in the form of if-then statements describing various associative patterns among the data given certain probabilistic thresholds (e.g., *if* product A is purchased with product B and C 90% of the time, *then* product A should be highlighted in some fashion with products B and C).

15.2.2 ROUGH SETS

Greco et al.[12,13] discuss the prospect of rough sets, specifically the dominance-based rough set approach (DRSA), to formulate associative patterns in the form of decision rules. These patterns can be used in consumer profiling tasks, similar to the data mining techniques previously mentioned. DRSA is an extension of the classical rough set approach (CRSA), proposed by Pawlak[9] in the early 1980s. CRSA provides methods for data reduction through analysis of data equalities. In CRSA, positive, negative, and boundary regions are defined based on a given knowledge system or decision table, where objects, their feature values, and decision attributes are represented in tabular format. For instance, consider a decision system $D = (U, R)$, where U comprises all objects in a knowledge space and R is an equivalence relation over U. $X \subseteq U$ may be approximated by groups of mutually indiscernible objects in respect to R.

As such, those groups fully included in X comprise the positive region, those groups fully disjoint with X comprise the negative region, and all remaining groups the boundary region. An analysis of feature reduction may be conducted to derive minimal subsets, referred to as decision reducts, of those features necessary to distinguish between other objects in the decision system, with corresponding *decision rules* that describe these minimal boundary regions.

DRSA is similar to CRSA; however, DRSA is based on inequalities (dominance relations), as opposed to equalities (indiscernibility relations), as in CRSA. Consider a decision system, $D = (U, R)$, where U comprises all objects in the knowledge space. Here, objects in D are composed of gain ($\uparrow$) or cost ($\downarrow$) features in which gain features include those object features where higher or increasing values are preferred and where cost features include those object features where lower or decreasing values are preferred. R represents a dominance relation over U where objects in D are either equal to, more preferred (=) or equal to, or less preferred (=) based on respective decision class designations.[13] Similarly, as in CRSA, decision rules are generated based on the formulated decision reducts. Decision reducts in CRSA describe equality relations among the data, whereas the decision reducts in DRSA describe the inequality relations among the data.

15.2.3   AN ILLUSTRATIVE EXAMPLE OF CRSA AND DRSA

To better understand the differences between CRSA and DRSA and how each functions, consider a decision system comprised of environmentally friendly cleaning products (Table 15.1). Illustrated are five contrived cleaning products, each with values for three environmental features—skin irritation (skin), air pollution percentage (air), and recyclable packaging (rec)—and one decision attribute, the Environmental Protection Agency (EPA) rating. For the purposes of this example, we consider preferred products as those that have lower skin irritation, have lower air pollution percentage, use recyclable packaging, and have a higher contrived EPA rating.

CRSA refers to positive regions based on each of specific EPA ratings: Pos(4) = {a, e}, Pos(3) = {b}, Pos(2) = {c}, Pos(1) = {d}. CRSA feature reduction methods could be then applied. For the actual CRSA-based algorithmic framework, we refer to previous work.[26] Here, for illustration purposes only, let us informally follow a

TABLE 15.1
Decision Table with Cleaning Products

	Skin Irritation	Air %	Recyclable Packaging	Environmental Protection Agency Rating
a	None	$\leq 1\%$	Yes	4
b	None	$\leq 3\%$	Yes	3
c	Medium	$\leq 5\%$	No	2
d	Strong	$\leq 10\%$	No	1
e	Mild	$\leq 1\%$	Yes	4

simple greedy heuristic trying to remove attributes step by step, subject to keeping the positive regions unchanged. First, assume that we evaluate removal of the feature *skin*. Because we are still able to discern products with different EPA ratings based on their values for *air* and *rec*, we can safely remove *skin* from the table. Second, given the feature *skin* already removed, let us consider *air*. Now, however, with only *rec* remaining, we would be no longer able to discern products with different EPA ratings, since *a*, *b*, and *e* have the same value for *rec* yet have conflicting EPA ratings. Given the inability to remove *air*, backtracking, we finish with trying to remove *rec*. If we had only *air* left, we would still be able to satisfactorily discern products with conflicting EPA ratings. Thus the feature *air* comprises a reduct. The corresponding decision rules would be as follows: [{*if air = ≤ 1% then EPA Rating = 4*}, {*if air = ≤ 3% then EPA Rating = 3*}, {*if air = ≤ 5% then EPA Rating = 2*}, {*if air = ≤ 10% then EPA Rating = 1*}].

DRSA generates positive regions using inequality relations. For example, the positive regions corresponding to Table 15.1 include: $Pos (\leq 2) = \{c, d\}$, $Pos (\leq 3) = \{b, c, d\}$, $Pos(\geq 2) = \{a, b, c, e\}$, $Pos(\geq 3) = \{a, b, e\}$, $Pos(\geq 4) = \{a, e\}$. As before, DRSA feature reduction methods can be applied. However, when observing information in Table 15.1, it turns out that all features are required to describe the inequalities among EPA ratings.[7] A sample subset of the corresponding decision rules generated would include: [{*if skin ≤ none & air ≤ 1% & rec ≥ yes then EPA Rating ≤ 4*}, {*if skin ≤ mild & air ≤ 1% & rec ≤ yes then EPA Rating ≤ 4*}, {*if skin ≤ medium & air ≤ 5% & rec ≤ yes then EPA Rating ≥ 2*}, {*if skin ≤ mild & air ≤ 5% & rec ≤ yes then EPA Rating ≥ 3*}].

The general idea of using CRSA or DRSA in this way in designing a support framework for personalization of user interfaces would be to use the formulated decision rules to develop consumer profiles. For example, we may be interested in clustering consumers based on their feature preferences and product selections. Here, the decision rules generated could form the basis for the consumer profiling (e.g., if feature A and feature B comprise decision reduct features and are ranked highly by a new consumer, then this consumer belongs to this specified consumer cluster). Using CRSA or DRSA could reduce the amount of information we would need to solicit from consumers, which would enable personalized enhancements to be deployed more quickly, which may enable consumers to focus more on their shopping tasks instead of on the interface.

The choice between CRSA and DRSA depends on the nature and interpretation of the data. CRSA is good at non–preference-based cases. DRSA is ideal when preference order matters (e.g., for Likert scale/preference rankings).[8] Discretization methods[26] may be employed in CRSA to emulate preference order by assigning features with new, discretized values (e.g., in ascending/descending order of importance). However, DRSA may be still preferred as it does not require such an additional preprocessing step. Also, strictly using equalities or inequalities may not always be accepted. In the described example, observing inequalities in the case of *skin irritation* could be preferred, as feature values have defined levels of degree, whereas inequality relations become less useful in cases where feature values do not have defined levels, such as in the case of *recyclable packaging*. When using original DRSA, it is required to determine which features designate cost or gain values accordingly (i.e., we may say that *recyclable packaging* is a gain feature, with "no" being treated as less than "yes"). Future work will include an analysis of a hybrid CRSA-DRSA framework, which will enable a choice of observing equalities/inequalities relationships on a feature-to-feature basis.

15.3   FRAMEWORK, ANALYSIS, AND EVALUATION

In the early stages of our research, we drafted a theoretical framework to construct personalized user interfaces using a hybridized procedure comprising CRSA and the Eclat association mining algorithm.[2] Our primary goal was to evaluate the possibility of data reduction—reducing the amount of consumer input required to gain enough information about consumers preferences and purchasing habits to design personalized user interfaces. To obtain data for our analyses, we conducted a usability evaluation of an online support tool designed by the U.S. EPA that enabled product comparisons of 29 environmentally preferable cleaning products, each distinguished by eight environmental and health-related attributes (Table 15.2).[14] We selected the U.S. EPA tool given the increased interest in environmental and health concerns in Canadian society[17] as well as the convenient availability of the system. To conduct a comparative evaluation, we developed an additional support tool using the same data based on a system developed by Hepting called *cogito*.[14] For our evaluation, 56 participants were recruited from the University of Regina Computer Science Participant Pool[15] and asked to complete a number of activities, one of which was to fill out a questionnaire that solicited valuable information about the participants' shopping habits and preferences. As part of the questionnaire, participants were asked to rank each feature based on perceived importance using a 4-point scale: unimportant (1), somewhat important (2), important (3), and very important (4). As well, participants

---

TABLE 15.2
U.S. Environmental Protection Agency Feature Set (Including Abbreviations)

Feature (Abbreviation)	Values (Integer Designation)
Skin irritation (skin)	Exempt (0), negligible-slight (1), slight (2), medium (3), strong (4), not reported (5)
Food chain exposure (fce)	Exempt (0), ≤5000 (1), ≤10,000 (2), ≤15,000 (3), ≥15,000 (4), not reported (5)
Air pollution potential (air)	0% (0), ≤1% (1), ≤5% (2), ≤15% (3), ≤30% (4), ≥30% (5), not reported (6)
Fragrance (frag)	No (0), yes (1)
Dye (dye)	No (0), yes (1)
Concentrated packaging (con)	Yes (0), no (1)
Recyclable paper packaging (rec)	Yes (0), N/A (1)
Minimize exposure to concentrated packaging (exp)	No (0), no/small sizes (1), yes (2)

The integer values assigned represent the scaling used in the analyses. Lower integer values are preferred.

were asked to select 1 of the 29 cleaning products they would consider purchasing for personal applications. Of the 56 participants, 42 fully completed the questionnaire; thus these 42 encompassed the test data. Acquiring more data, based on a larger, more diversified participant pool, and with more advanced handling of uncompleted questionnaires is one of our nearest future research activities.

15.3.1   CRSA-Eclat Framework

The first task in our analysis was to cluster the 29 products with the goal of deriving groupings of participants based on similar cleaning product selections that would later represent our decision variable for the CRSA and DRSA analyses.[2,3,7] We conducted a survey of four clustering distance metrics, including Euclidean, maximum, Pearson, and Spearman. In all cases, the evaluation of the different clustering distance metrics provided unique results.[2] To assist in choosing the most appropriate clustering distance metric, we used Hubert's Γ statistic,[24,25] specifically Hubert's knees—where sharp knee bends help to subjectively observe how many clusters to use. We found that the maximum distance metric provided the most distinctive Hubert knee, thus was chosen as the final clustering result. Table 15.3 describes the cluster dispersion.

Based on the clustering results obtained and product selections given by each participant we assigned participants to the corresponding product clusters. The participants' assigned cluster membership values became the decision variables in our analyses. For example, if a participant selected product 23, the participant's decision variable would equal 2 (Table 15.3). Some participants responded with multiple product selections. In these cases, the participants were assigned to the product cluster corresponding to the one that covered the majority of their selections. For example, if a participant responded with five product selections, three of which belonged to a given cluster, the participant was assigned to that product cluster accordingly. If a participant answered with multiple product selections that were evenly distributed among product clusters (e.g., two products, each in different product clusters), he or she was randomly assigned to one of the product clusters accordingly. Some participants did not select any products and were omitted in further steps.

We constructed a decision system comprised of the 42 participants as objects, their nondiscretized feature rankings (4-point importance scaling, Likert scale), and discretized feature rankings—features ranked as important or higher were discretized

TABLE 15.3
Results of Product Clustering Using
the Maximum Distance

Cluster	Products
1	15, 24, 25, 29, 7, 27, 18, 26, 28
2	23, 16, 11, 8, 9
3	10, 2, 1, 5, 4, 6
4	17, 19, 14, 13, 20, 22, 21, 3, 12

TABLE 15.4

Classical Rough Set Approach–

Generated Decision Reducts

Size	Reduct
2	dye, con
2	fce, rec
2	fce, con
2	skin, exp
2	fce, exp
2	air, con
3	frag, dye, exp
2	rec, fce(d)
2	con, dye(d)

Features denoted with a "(d)" refer to those using the discretized scaling.

against features ranked as somewhat important or lower to represent a form of preference ordering. We conducted a CRSA reduction analysis using the Rough Set Exploration System,[26] along with its genetic algorithm functionality to formulate the top 10 smallest reducts. Table 15.4 provides the results of the analysis. The general concept of our framework for personalization is to use the decision rules and decision reducts generated to construct a very brief consumer profiling survey to cluster consumers based on their preferences regarding the reduct features, in which a personalized user interface would await them on their responses (e.g., for the first reduct in Table 15.4, if the consumer ranks the features dye and con as unimportant, we could assign him/her to a specified cluster). To test this idea, we performed a train-and-test analysis using a 10-fold cross-validation technique and found a global classification accuracy of 87.5% with 100% coverage.

Given the results obtained, our hypothesis that CRSA could successfully be used to reduce the consumer input required at the initial stages of the personalization design framework proved encouraging. It was observed that 2 of the 16 feature rankings (discretized and nondiscretized) may be enough to satisfactorily discern consumer clusters. It significantly reduces the amount of initial consumer input required to group new consumers accordingly, because we would only need to solicit their preferences for a few reduct features as opposed to all.

We next wanted to examine associations among participant feature rankings and product features to further develop our personalization framework. By observing these associations, we could theoretically highlight strong associative patterns with the end goal of incorporating enhanced functionality in the design of the user interface to support compensatory and noncompensatory decision-making strategies.[7] We chose to use the Eclat algorithm to analyze the associative patterns among the data. It is important to note that all features were used in this part of the analysis and not only the features represented in decision reducts since at this stage we were interested in visualizing the features consumers ranked highly among all (or a subset of) the clusters, not only the features that are enough to *discern* between clusters. For example, it may be that consumers in one cluster highly ranked air pollution potential and consumers in another cluster highly ranked air pollution potential and food chain exposure. Then, in a reduct, we might observe only food chain exposure, with air pollution potential having no additional influence on the clusters' discernibility. The Eclat-based analysis using only the decision reducts is left for further study.

We hypothesize that the knowledge obtained from our analyses would enable incorporation of decision aids in the user interface that would highlight certain products and product features to better equip consumers with the enhanced functionality and design to more effectively conduct compensatory or noncompensatory product analyses.[7] For the Eclat analysis, we used a support and confidence threshold of 75%, also observing associative patterns that were relatively close to the 75% threshold. Table 15.5 describes the strong associations among products residing in respective clusters. Table 15.6 describes associations for the participant feature rankings. Using the results, we may highlight certain aspects of the data to help guide the consumers and make them more productive decision makers. For example, in Table 15.5, since the majority of products in cluster 3 are manufactured in concentrated form

TABLE 15.5
Results of the Eclat Procedure for Product Analysis

Cluster	Associated Feature Sets (Product Features)	Confidence
All Products	frag = no	86%
1	rec = N/A, dye = no, frag = no, fce = exempt	78%
	dye = no, frag = no, fce = exempt	89%
	fce = exempt	100%
	frag = no	89%
	dye = no	89%
	rec = N/A	78%
2	frag = no, fce = not reported	83%
3	rec = yes, exp = no, con = yes	83%
	exp = no, con = yes	100%
	rec = yes	83%
4	dye = no, frag = no	78%
	fce = exempt, frag = no	78%
	frag = no	89%
	fce = exempt	78%
	dye = no	78%
	dye = no, fce = exempt, frag = no	67%

Italicized associations refer to interesting results below the minimum confidence threshold.

TABLE 15.6
Results of the Eclat Procedure for the Participant
Feature Ranking Analysis

Cluster	Type	Associated Feature Sets (Feature Rankings)	Confidence
All Participants	D	air = important, skin = important	88%
	D	skin = important	95%
	D	air = important	93%
1	—	*no participants assigned*	—
2	—	*only 1 participant assigned*	—
3	D	{exp, rec, con, dye} = not important, {frag, air, skin} = important	100%
	ND	{rec, con} = somewhat important, air = very important	100%
4	*D*	*{rec, air, skin} = important*	*74%*
	D	{air, skin} = important	93%
	D	skin = important	97%
	D	air = important	95%
	D	rec = important	77%
	ND	*skin = very important*	*72%*

"N" denotes discretized rankings, whereas "ND" denotes the nondiscretized rankings. Italicized associations refer to interesting results below the minimum confidence threshold.

and recyclable packaging (83%), this feature may be preincluded in the consumers' search processes because it is highly probable that they may have such a preference. Also, in Table 15.6, because the majority of consumers in cluster 4 ranked recyclable packaging, air pollution potential, and skin irritation as important (74%), these features could be highlighted in both the consumers' search processes and the resulting product descriptions.

The CRSA-Eclat analysis proved quite interesting and very encouraging. However, we also wanted to evaluate DRSA, as it may provide a more realistic depiction of preferences/similarities. Indeed, the analysis in terms of inequalities may (depending on the data) be considered more natural with respect to the consumer decision-making process.[4]

15.3.2 DRSA FRAMEWORK

Because DRSA considers preference order, we deemed it necessary to develop a procedure to order the product clusters from *best* to *worst* (i.e., we needed to determine if one cluster was comprised of *better* products than another). Ordering the product clusters in such fashion has the potential to be quite complicated as it may be difficult to derive which products are truly better than others, as certain features may have more bearing on a consumer's decision formulation given their preference sets. Given this inconsistency, a broad analysis of the products was considered. As such, we ordered the product clusters by evaluating each product feature as equal using the following procedure: (1) calculate mean values for each product feature in relation to products specific to product cluster, (2) add the mean value for each cost ($\downarrow$) feature and subtract the mean value for each gain ($\uparrow$) feature, and (3) reorder products in relation to the product clusters accordingly. The clusters were reordered based on results in Table 15.3: cluster 4 (new cluster 1) $\leq$ cluster 1 (new cluster 2) $\leq$ cluster 3 (new cluster 3) $\leq$ cluster 2 (new cluster 4). The DRSA analysis was similar to the case of CRSA-Eclat, however somewhat more simplified because the discretization step was omitted. To conduct the DRSA analysis we used the JAMM[27] software application developed by the Laboratory of Intelligent Decision Support Systems at Poznan University of Technology. We first conducted the DRSA feature reduction with results described in Table 15.7. Similarly as for CRSA-Eclat, the general concept of our approach to personalization would be to use the decision rules and decision reducts generated to construct a brief consumer profiling survey to cluster consumers based on their preferences of the decision reduct features where a personalized user interface would await them on their responses (e.g., if a consumer ranks the features air, dye, rec, and exp a certain way [refer to the first reduct in Table 15.7], e.g., if "air $\leq$ 1%" and "dye $\leq$ yes" and "rec $\leq$ yes" and "exp $\leq$ no", we could assign him or her to one of the specified clusters). On the other hand, let us note that it may be more difficult to cluster consumers since DRSA uses inequality relations (e.g., consider this contrived example: if consumers rank "air" as important or greater, "dye" as unimportant or less, "rec" as very important or less, and "exp" as important or less, then they may belong in consumer cluster 2 or greater (cluster 2, 3, or 4).)

As in our original evaluation of CRSA-Eclat, a 10-fold cross-validation method was used to test the DRSA reducts and their classification accuracy. An average global classification accuracy of 85.7% with 100% coverage was found. These results were only slightly lower than those obtained in our original evaluation using CRSA-Eclat (87.5% and 100%). We also conducted an analysis of possible associations

---

TABLE 15.7
Dominance-Based Rough Set Approach–Generated Decision Reducts

Size	Reduct
4	air, dye, rec, exp
4	fce, air, dye, rec
4	frag, dye, rec, exp
4	fce, frag, dye, rec
2	dye, con, rec

TABLE 15.8

Results of the DRSA Association Mining Procedure for Product Analysis

Cluster	Associated Feature Sets (Product Features)	Confidence
≤2	air ≥ 15%	78%
≤3	skin ≥ medium	80%
≥3	*air ≤ 1%*	*73%*
≥4	skin ≤ slight, air ≤ 1%	78%
	fce ≤ 10,000, air ≤ 1%	78%
	skin ≤slight, fce ≤ 10,000, air ≤5%	100%
	skin ≤slight, fce ≤ 10,000, rec ≤ yes	*67%*
	skin ≤slight, air ≤5%, dye ≤ no	78%
	fce ≤ 10,000, air ≤5%, rec ≤yes	*67%*

Italicized associations refer to interesting results below the minimum confidence threshold.

among product features and rankings. As in Eclat-based evaluation, we used all of the features. JAMM enables association mining to be conducted using an Apriori algorithm implementation (breath-first prefix tree search) with inequality relations, keeping it consistent with DRSA methods. This differs from the Eclat procedure we used, which derived association rules using equalities, being more consistent with CRSA methods. Similar to our original evaluation using Eclat, we analyzed associations meeting a 75% support/confidence threshold, observing associations close to this threshold. Results of the DRSA (JAMM) association mining analyses are described in Table 15.8 and Table 15.9. When comparing results of the CRSA reduction with the DRSA reduction, it is interesting to note that reducts are smaller when using CRSA. When using DRSA, the larger-sized reducts and slightly lower classification accuracy may likely be due to the inherent complexity of DRSA in relation to CRSA (observing inequalities versus equalities). Thus, it may be more difficult in DRSA to approximate decision outcomes as opposed to CRSA.

15.3.3 Discussion

Our proposed framework to design personalized user interfaces in e-commerce environments can be split into two phases: a consumer clustering/profiling phase and an association mining phase. Of importance to the consumer clustering/profiling phase is the feature reduction supported by both CRSA and DRSA. Here, we attempt to reduce the amount of initial consumer input required to provide meaningful personalized user interfaces. Feature reduction theoretically enables a personalized interface to be deployed more quickly, complete with product recommendations and feature highlighting, which may enable consumers to focus on their primary activity of searching for items of interest specific to their values. Observing the results

TABLE 15.9

Results of the DRSA Association Mining Procedure for Feature Ranking Analysis

Cluster	Associated Feature Sets (Product Features)	Confidence
≤3	*{skin ≤3, exp ≤1}*	66%
	or {fce ≤2, dye ≤2, exp ≤1}, or	
	{dye ≤2, con ≤2, exp ≤1}	
	or {dye ≤2, rec ≤2, exp ≤1}	
≥2	{skin ≥2} or {fce ≥1} or {air ≥1}	100%
	or {frag ≥1} or	
	{dye ≥1} or {con ≥1} or {rec ≥1}	
	or {exp ≥1}	
≥3	frag ≥2	78%
	con ≥2	98%
	exp ≥2	85%
≥4	rec ≥3	77%

Integers refer to the ranking scaling (1: unimportant; 2: somewhat important; 3: important; 4: very important). Italicized associations refer to interesting results below the minimum confidence threshold.

in Table 15.4 and Table 15.7, the decision reducts generated by CRSA are noticeably smaller than those generated by DRSA. This may be due to the more complex nature (richer decision characteristics) of DRSA. In either case, analysis with real users is needed to truly realize which approach is most successful.

The second phase in our framework included observing the associative patterns among products' feature rankings (respective to the derived clusters). We hypothesize that the knowledge obtained from such an analysis is useful in designing interface enhancements in terms of search functionality (compensatory and noncompensatory) and in the organization of products and product features on the user interface. This way, we may support compensatory analyses by highlighting product features in relation to cluster designations (e.g., we may preinclude certain features common to individual product clusters and enable consumers, if they choose, to focus as well on the other features [feature values], not common to the products within the cluster). Furthermore, we may support noncompensatory analyses by highlighting those features ranked highly among users in specific consumer clusters. In this sense, we could direct the consumers' attention, enabling them to focus on those products (product features) that they truly care about.

When analyzing the second phase of our analyses, it is interesting to observe the differences among the results obtained when evaluating the different techniques. In our initial approach, which used Eclat to generate associative patterns, results (Table 15.5 and Table 15.6) provided a more cluster-specific view of the associative patterns among product features and participant feature rankings (e.g., consumers in cluster 4 value these features). Alternatively, when using JAMM[27] to generate associative patterns, results (Table 15.8 and Table 15.9) provided a more global view of the associative patterns among all clusters in relation to product features and participant feature rankings, thus providing an overview of various cross-cluster similarities (e.g., consumers in clusters 2, 3, and 4 value these features). Again, more testing is required to fully evaluate either of the techniques.

It may also be worth considering the decision reducts more closely to fully analyze the importance of the features. Specifically, we could further analyze the rules that are generated by the reducts to evaluate whether or not they provide useful information in terms of associative patterns among the data. However, we need to remember that such rules are not going to be based on all the features.

15.4 CONCLUSION

We provided an overview of research conducted to derive a model of a framework to personalize user interfaces for online shopping support tools. We discussed how rough set methods as well as association mining could be used to set the foundations for such a framework. We described the concepts of compensatory and noncompensatory decision-making analyses and how, through understanding such decision-making analyses, the design of the user interface could be enhanced by incorporating personalized features to better aid consumers in conducting their shopping activities. Our proposed framework was comprised of two phases: a consumer clustering/profiling phase aimed at grouping consumers with similar preferences as effectively and efficiently as possible, and an association mining phase aimed at deriving associative patterns among product features and consumer feature rankings respective to each individual and all consumer clusters. The applied techniques provided interesting results, though further user testing is required to fully realize the success of either technique in a real application setting. Future work will include a survey to obtain additional information with a hope of improving the data quality, as well as more advanced implementation and evaluation of described methods.

ACKNOWLEDGMENTS

We wish to thank Dr. Roman Slowinski of the Institute of Computing Science at Poznan University of Technology for his invaluable assistance in understanding DRSA. As well, the first, third, and fourth authors would like to acknowledge the support of the Centre for Sustainable Communities and the Natural Sciences and Engineering Research Council (NSERC) of Canada.

REFERENCES

1. Bettman, J.R., Luce, M.F., and Payne, J. W. Constructive consumer choice processes, *J. Cons. Res.,* 25, 187–217, 1998.
2. Maciag, T., Hepting, D.H., and Ślęzak, D. Consumer modeling in support of interface design, *IEEE Int. Conf. Hybrid Info. Technol.,* 2, 153–160, 2006.
3. Maciag, T., Hepting, D., Ślęzak, H. D., and Hilderman, R. J. Mining associations for interface design, *Int. Conf. Rough Sets Knowl. Technol.,* 109–117, 2007.

4. Simon, H.A. A behavioral model of rational choice, *Economics,* 69, 99–118, 1955.
5. Hsee, C.K. and Leclerc, F. Will products look more attractive when presented separately or together? *J. Cons. Res.,* 25, 175–186, 2008.
6. Norman, D.A. *Emotional Design,* Basic Books, 2003.
7. Maciag, T., Hepting, D.H., Hilderman, R.J., and Ślęzak, D. Evaluation of a dominance-based rough set approach to interface design, in *Proc. Int. Conf. Frontiers Convergence Biosci. Info. Technol.,* 2007.
8. Rosson, M.B. and Carroll, J.M. *Usability Engineering: Scenario-Based Development of Human-Computer Interaction,* Academic Press, 2002.
9. Pawlak, Z. *Rough Sets, Theoretical Aspects of Reasoning About Data,* Kluwer, 1991.
10. Ceglar, A. and Roddick, J.F. Association mining, *ACM Comp. Surveys,* 38, 2006.
11. Zaki, M.J. Scalable algorithms for association mining, *Trans. Knowledge Data Eng.,* 12, 2000.
12. Greco, S., Matarazzo, B., and Slowinski, R. Rough set approach to customer satisfaction analysis, *Rough Sets Curr. Trends Comp.,* 284–295, 2006.
13. Greco, S., Matarazzo, B., and Slowinski, R. Rough set theory for multicriteria decision analysis, *Eur. J. Oper. Res.,* 1–47, 2001.
14. Maciag, T. *Supporting Sustainable Decision-Making: Evaluation of Previous Support Tools with New Designs,* VDM Verlag Dr. Muller, 2007.
15. Hepting, D.H. Ethics and usability testing in computer science education, *ACM Special Interest Group Comp. Sc. Ed. (SIGCSE)* 38, 76–80, 2006.
16. Jedetski, J., Adelman, L., and Yeo, C. How web site decision technology affects consumer, *Internet Comp.,* 72–79, 2002.
17. Boyd, D.R. *Sustainability Within A Generation: A New Vision for Canada,* 2004.
18. Bettman, J. *An Information Processing Theory of Consumer Choice,* Addison-Wesley, 1979.
19. Luce, M.F., Payne, J.W., and Bettman, J.R. Emotional trade-off difficulty and choice, *J. Marketing Res.,* 36, 143–159, 1999.
20. Norman, D.A. *The Invisible Computer,* MIT Press, 1998.
21. Norman, D.A. *The Psychology of Everyday Things,* Basic Books Inc., 1988.
22. Raskin, J. *The Humane Interface,* Addison-Wesley, 2000.
23. Borgelt, C. *Implementations of Apriori and Eclat,* Workshop on Frequent Item Set Mining Implementations (FIMI), 2003.
24. Bezdek, J.C. and Pal, N.R. Some new indexes of cluster validity, *Trans. Sys. Man, Cybernetics,* 28, 301–315, 1998.
25. Halkidi, M., Batistakis, Y., and Vazirgiannis, M. Cluster validity methods: part 1, *Special Interest Group Manage. Data (SIGMOD),* 31, 40–45, 2002.
26. Bazan, J. and Szczuka, M. The rough set exploration system, *Trans. Rough Sets,* 3, 37–56, 2005.
27. Laboratory of Intelligent Decision Support Systems at Poznan University of Technology, JAMM software. Available online at: http://www-idss.cs.put.poznan.pl/site/jamm.html. Accessed Fall 2007.
28. Mobasher, B., Dai, H., Luo, T., and Nakagawa, M. Effective personalization based on association rule discovery from web usage mining, *Web Info. Data Manage.,* 9–15, 2001.
29. Holland, S., Ester, M., and KieBling, W. Preference mining: a novel approach on mining user preferences for personalized applications, *Prin. Pract. Knowledge Discovery Databases (PKDD),* 204–216, 2003.
30. Eirinaki, M. and Vazirgiannis, M. Web mining for web personalization, *ACM Trans. Internet Technol.,* 3, 1–27, 2003.
31. Ha, S.H. Helping online customers decide through web personalization, *IEEE Intell. Syst.,* 34–43, 2002.

32. Zhou, B., Hui, S.C., and Fong, A.C.M. An effective approach for periodic web personalization, *IEEE/WIC/ACM Int. Conf. Web Intell.*, 284–292, 2006.

33. Schickel-Zuber, V. and Faltings, B. Using hierarchical clustering for learning the ontologies used in recommendation systems, *Knowl. Discov. Databases,* 599–608, 2007.

34. Awad, M.A. and Khan, L.R. Web navigation prediction using multiple evidence combination and domain knowledge, *IEEE Trans. Syst. Man Cybernetics,* 37, 1054–1062, 2007.

16 An Adjacency Matrix Approach for Extracting User Sentiments

Bin Shi and Kuiyu Chang

CONTENTS

16.1   BACKGROUND

The Internet has become the universal information source, allowing people from all over the world to share their personal experiences through participation in online forums, wiki pages, blogs, etc. This sharing invariably includes user opinions about products, services, persons, and organizations, among many other things. The sharing of personal experiences regarding a product or service has become the epitome of user empowerment. Internet sites such as Amazon.com (pioneer in online book reviews) and eBay.com (first to popularize buyer/seller ratings) have propelled into the leagues of major online shopping brands simply because they understand how important user reviews/opinions affect people's buying decisions. Smaller sites specializing in a particular product genre have also blossomed. For example, instead of walking into a retail store to make an impulsive digital camera purchase, people have learned to educate themselves by visiting camera review sites such as dpreview.com, steves-digicams.com, and others, before making the plunge to actually buy a digital camera. Naturally, first-hand evaluations or comments from customers who have used a product are extremely valuable. More so a large number of customer opinions/reviews can be assembled and summarized in a neat fashion. However, it is not easy to compare similar products by manually reading online posts/comments that could add up to the hundreds for some popular brand or model. Unfortunately, automatic approaches for analyzing consumer opinions suffer from the succinctness of typical online comments, which cannot be accurately represented using classical vector space models (VSM).[9] We thus propose a novel approach to represent individual sentence segments using a word adjacency matrix, which will greatly facilitate the automatic sentiment analysis of hundreds and thousands of user opinions, ultimately simplifying the task of data collection for market analysts and consumers alike.

16.1.1   WHY USE AN ADJACENCY MATRIX TO REPRESENT A SENTENCE?

Despite throwing away the sequence information of words, the venerable bag-of-words vector space model text representation and its variants have demonstrated remarkable accuracy and robustness in many document retrieval tasks.[19,20] This is partly because what is lost in word sequence information is made up for by the sheer volume of words available in a typical document. Moreover, word sequence and context play an important role in sentence segment sentiment classification. Further, the number of words/features in a sentence is one to two orders of magnitude less than a document, which means that subtle changes in term sequences would completely alter the sentence semantics. Thus the vector representing a sentence is extremely sparse.[10]

Bag-of-words models have been shown to consistently underperform in sentence retrieval tasks such as sentiment classification and event detection,[2] because the limited features and context embedded in the ordering of terms in a sentence are largely lost in a VSM representation.

Hence we propose using an adjacency word matrix to capture the semantics of a sentence. Each row and column of the matrix denote the source and target terms, respectively. If a target term w_j (e.g., "love") occurs anywhere after a source term w_i (e.g., "I") in a sentence, the corresponding matrix entry $m_{ij} = 1$; otherwise, the entry is zero. Clearly, using a word matrix does not make much sense for typical documents, because the ordering words outside a sentence context is largely meaningless. Thus, until now, nobody has considered representing documents using a word matrix. However, a word adjacency matrix is extremely useful for representing sentences, which typically yield sparse word adjacency matrices that can be heavily pruned to avoid incurring an exponential amount of storage for each sentence.

The matrix representation was actually motivated by our need to accurately classify online products and services review sentiments.[14] We therefore first evaluate it on Chinese sentence sentiment classification and later apply it to English sentence news event categorization, which shows that our approach works equally well across languages.

16.2   RELATED WORK

16.2.1   SENTENCE CLASSIFICATION AND RETRIEVAL

As stated elsewhere,[10] analysis at the sentence level will result in an extremely sparse vector representation compared with a document. Several sentence-level analysis approaches involving the use of additional context information have been proposed.

Tamura et al.[16] proposed a method to classify multi-sentence questions for question-answering systems. They reformulated the problem as that of selecting the "core" sentence from a multisentence question, followed by classification of the "core" sentence. An SVM classifier was used to select the "core" sentence. To improve the context, each sentence is represented by a vector that includes features from it and sentences appearing before and after. Although the feasibility of this method has been demonstrated for question-answering systems, it is not always applicable to other domains. For example, in review sentiment analysis, each sentence may contain completely different opinions, making a concatenation meaningless. Intuitively, to determine if a sentence in a review is an opinion sentence, involving adjacent sentences in the review can only interfere with this goal.

Another approach to add contextual information that includes the sentence position was proposed previously.[10] The authors defined four sentence types for medical abstracts: "introduction," "method," "result," and "conclusion." The sentence type is classified according to its content and relative position in the abstract. Experimental results show that the approach helped improve SVM's performances on classifying partial sentences. We have yet to apply position information in our classification of sentence types; it could be studied in future work.

Improving on McKnight's work, Yamamoto et al.[18] included additional syntactic features. Sentence types discussed elsewhere,[10] such as "introduction" was split into "background" and "purpose." The relative position of a sentence was reformulated as two numbers, one that counts from the beginning, and other syntactic attributes such as a term's affinity to certain sentence types, co-occurrences, and the presence of special auxiliary verbs were added to enhance the classification. We feel that the approach has become too specialized with the addition of these syntactic features, some of which are specific to English. We might eventually incorporate some of these syntactic rules to go the last mile of improvement, but for now that will be part of future work.

Unlike methods that use external information of a sentence to enhance sentence classification,[10,18] van Zaanen et al.[8] extract implicit information within the sentence itself using a learning information extraction approach. Sentence structure patterns are extracted from the training set and used to form a sentence classification regular expression. In particular, alignment-based learning is applied to extract sentence structure patterns and their respective frequencies for each sentence category. Regular expressions are constructed from these patterns and applied to a new sentence to look for matches. The category that yields the highest number of matches is then assigned to the sentence. Despite the sophistication, it appears that the classical trie-based approach would easily beat this method, as shown by Zaanen et al.[4] The good thing about this approach is that the extracted rules can be validated by humans, and easily applied to a new sentence.

Also related to the question sentence classification domain, several benchmark experiments were conducted by Augusto and Pizzato.[3] In that article, they compared SVM with the trie-based[4] approach and found SVM to be as good as or better than the latter in most cases.

In a different domain, the structural information of a sentence has been shown to be helpful for sentence classification and retrieval using machine learning techniques by Hachey and Grover.[5] They compared the classification performances on rhetorical sentences from the legal domain of five machine learning methods. Each sentence included contextual and lingual features such as length, location, and thematic words. The comparison indicated that SVM using a bag of words combined with a maximum entropy sequence tagger achieved the best results.

16.2.2 SENTIMENT ORIENTATION CLASSIFICATION

Many sentiment classification approaches at the document level have been proposed. Generally, they can be divided into two groups: ML (machine learning) and non-ML approaches.

One typical non-ML approach[17,22] computes a document's semantic orientation (SO) value using several heuristics. First, a pair of extremely positive and negative opinion words is selected as a reference (e.g., classical, disappoint). Next, five categories of two-word opinion phrases are manually defined. For each found opinion phrase in a movie review, the number of search engine returned pages containing both the opinion phrase and "classical" or "disappoint" are noted, respectively. The SO value of the opinion phrase is then computed as a weighted sum of the number of positive and negative hits. After the SO values of all opinion phrases in the movie review have been computed, an average SO value is tallied for the entire movie review and compared to a predefined threshold to determine whether the movie review is positive or negative.

This approach, although interesting, can only determine if a review is overall positive or negative, with no sentiment indication about specific aspects/features (e.g., length, story, music) of the movie/product. Moreover, Ye et al.[21] showed that the heuristic-based method cannot compete with a machine learning approach (SVM) using a bag of words.

Another kind of non-ML sentiment classification approach[6,7,14] that focuses on sentence level classification is the concept lexicon-based method. They all work more or less the same, as described in the following section. Two polarized (positive and negative) sets of "seed" opinion words are manually collected. Each set of words is then automatically expanded with synonyms and antonyms from a semantic lexicon. A sentence orientation is then determined by a simple tally of the number of matching words from the two sets.

A sentence-level opinion orientation identification and feature mining method was proposed previously,[6] which finds association rules[1] of frequent product features. A concept dictionary such as WordNet[11] was used to generate positive and negative opinion/sentiment word sets. To find the orientation of a sentence, opinion sentences are first extracted from the review, after which their orientations are determined. An opinion sentence is a sentence containing at least one known feature word and one known opinion word. From the dictionary of generated positive and negative opinion words, an opinion sentence's orientation is assumed to be the orientation of the adjective "nearest" the product feature word, while taking into account the reversal effect of nearby negation words such as "not." From a grammatical perspective, any nearby negation word will invert a word's orientation. Sometimes, a conjunction such as "but" may completely reverse a sentiment. Word distance and a simple threshold are used to quantify "nearness."

There are several drawbacks to this approach. First, opinion orientation should not be classified into only two categories, positive and negative. Sometimes, neutral sentiments are also expressed. In Liu's approach, only adjectives were considered opinion words. Moreover, experiments[12] indicated that most sentiments are expressed through verbs, adjectives, and adverbs. For example, the verb "like" can be construed as expressing a positive opinion. Another disadvantage of this approach is that it lacks the ability to extract implicit opinion about a feature because it only processes sentences containing at least one feature word. An improvement over previous work[6] was presented[7] that considered short sentences, expanded opinion words to include verbs and adjectives, and also made an effort to extract implicit features.

With regard to ML techniques for sentiment classification, Pang et al.[13] benchmarked three classifiers, naive Bayes, maximum entropy, and SVM on document-level sentiment classification and found SVM to give the best overall performance. They noticed that some of the errors are due to SVM treating text as a bag of words.

Based on these related works, the SVM-based approach appears to be the most flexible and dynamic choice for sentence classification. It can be improved further with the addition of contextual information. Thus in our approach, we will use a SVM classifier for sentiment analysis.

16.3   MATRIX REPRESENTATION

In this section, we present our simple adjacency matrix representation model for sentences. We also show the completeness property of the matrix model.

16.3.1 MODEL

16.3.1.1 Definition 1

(Dictionary) Let w be a set of N distinct terms, $w = \{w_1, \ldots, w_i, \ldots, w_N\}$, where w_i denotes the i-th term.

16.3.1.2 Definition 2

(Sentence) A sentence s is a sequence of m terms, $s = [s_1, \ldots, s_i, \ldots, s_m]$, where $s_i \in w$.

16.3.1.3 Definition 3

(t-order adjacency matrix) Given a sentence s with m terms, its t-order adjacency matrix $M^t = [m^t_{ij}]_{N \times N}$, where each entry is defined as:

$$m^t_{ij} = \begin{cases} 1, & if \quad \exists u, v = u + t, s_u = s_v \\ 0, & otherwise \end{cases}$$

The 0-order adjacency matrix values are all zeros except for those terms contained in the sentence; for example, $M_0 = \mathrm{diag}[m_1, \ldots, m_i, \ldots, m_N]$, where $m_i = 1$ if $w_i \in s$. The vector formed by the diagonal entries of M_0 degenerates to the VSM vector.

The 1-order adjacency matrix representation for a sentence simply measures the immediate co-occurrence of two terms w_i and w_j (i.e., $m^1_{ij} = 1$ if w_j occurs immediately after w_i in the sentence). In fact, M^{t+1} can be iteratively computed from M_t using the simple graph transitivity property, as follows:

$$m^{t+1}_{ij} = \sum_{k \geq i}^{N} m^t_{ik} m^1_{kj}, \quad \forall i \leq j, \ t > 0$$

For a sentence with m terms, up to the $(m-1)$-order adjacency matrix can be computed. We thus propose the following.

16.3.1.4 Proposition 1 (Matrix Representation)

A sentence s containing m terms can be represented by its $(m-1)$-order adjacency matrix. Figure 16.1 shows an example of our matrix representation of the four-word sentence "I like this phone." For simplicity, only the 4×4 sub-matrix of the full $N \times N$ matrix is displayed, whereas all other terms are zero.

16.3.2 ADVANTAGES OF MATRIX REPRESENTATION

As mentioned, one serious problem with VSM for sentences is its data sparseness. Given a sentence comprising m unique terms, the density of its VSM vector is m/N, whereas the density of its $(m-1)$-order adjacency matrix is $m(m-1)/2N'$, where $N' = N^2$ for a full adjacency matrix. Consider the inequality $m(m-1)/2N' > m/N$; if we can heavily prune the infrequent entries of the adjacency matrix, such that $N' = N$ instead of the full $N' = N^2$, we obtain the limit $m > 3$.

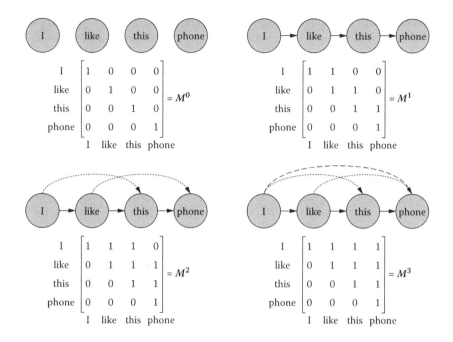

FIGURE 16.1 Matrix representation of a sentence with four words.

Another implicit advantage of the matrix representation is that in theory, the sentence sequence can be completely recovered from the adjacency matrix of order $m - 1$ provided that there are no duplicate terms, as described in the proposition below.

16.3.2.1   Proposition 2 (Matrix Completeness Property)

A sentence s containing m non-repeating terms can be completely recovered from its $(m - 1)$-order adjacency matrix. This means that the matrix completely captures the ordering semantics of the sentence. The recovery is straightforward, outlined below in lieu of a formal proof.

1. Sum all rows of the $(m - 1)$-order adjacency matrix to obtain a $1 \times m$ row vector.
2. Count the non-zero entries for each column of the row vector.
3. Rank each word according to the count obtained in the previous step.
4. Order the words in ascending order according to their rank in the previous step; this is the original ordering of the words.

For example, for the adjacency matrix of Figure 16.1, the count of non-zero entries for "phone" is 4, "this" is 3, "like" is 2, and "I" is 1. By ranking the words in ascending order, the recovered sequence is "I like this phone."

Notice that this recovery procedure applies only to sentences without duplicate terms. For these types of sentences, the ordering of the duplicate word cannot be uniquely determined. Although the matrix representation is $N \times N$, in practice we have to scan convert it to a $N^2 \times 1$ vector by converting each row into a column.

16.4 EXPERIMENT SETUP

16.4.1 DATA SETS

Two sentence classification data sets, "basketball" (English) and "cell phone" (Chinese), were used to evaluate the suitability of our matrix representation across language boundaries.

The basketball data set contains 2340 English sentence segments of three classes: "postype" indicating current win, "histype" indicating historical win, and "negtype" for irrelevant sentence, distributed as shown in Table 16.1. Porter stemming was applied and a simple flat SVM classifier was used on varying amounts of training data. The goal is to observe how the performance changes with increasing availability of training data.

The cell phone data set includes 2000 online reviews randomly selected from our crawled Chinese cell phone online review corpus. Each review has been pre-processed into sentence segments, with distribution as shown in Table 16.2. These sentence segments are grouped into three categories, "positive" expressing positive opinion, "negative" expressing negative opinion, and "non-opinion," which includes neutral opinion (e.g., "OK") and non-opinion. Notice that because of the small number of neutral training opinion segments, no decent training can be achieved; thus neutral opinion segments are treated as non-opinion segments.

Even at the sentence segment resolution, some segments may still contain more than one opinion, as listed in Table 16.2. These types of segments can only hurt an SVM classifier and are therefore discarded for the machine learning approach.

Clearly, the two data sets are highly skewed and unbalanced in terms of class distribution, which is nevertheless quite representative of real-life classification problems.

16.4.1.1 Sentence Representation Evaluation Schemes

We evaluate several sentence representation approaches, listed below as Single (VSM), NGram2 (Bigram), and Matrix.

Trigrams are not evaluated as it will only increase the data sparseness for the already sparse sentence segments. Likewise, we do not restrict the order of the matrix (i.e., we use the full $(m - 1)$-order adjacency matrix).

TABLE 16.1
Basketball Match Data Set Distribution

	Postype	Histype	Negtype
count	189	117	2034

TABLE 16.2
Cell Phone Review Data Set Distribution

	Positive	Negative	Non-Opinion	Multiple	Total
Count	1141	1051	4511	60	6763

16.4.1.2 Atomic Unit Evaluation Schemes

There are three common ways to extract the atomic unit of a sentence, namely Unigram (single character or letter), Word, and part-of-speech tagged word. As it stands, the sentence segment vector is already extremely sparse, and representing a segment using part-of-speech tagged word will make it even worse (each word will have several different representations, vastly increasing the vocabulary size). Thus we will not consider the part-of-speech tagged word representation.

In English, Unigram refers to a single letter/character, which is quite useless, so we will only evaluate the English basketball content at the Word representation level. On the other hand, a single Chinese character or Unigram contains enough information, so it will be investigated along with Word representation for the cell phone review data set. To make the definition unambiguous, in Figure 16.2, a simple English sentence "I like it" and its Chinese equivalent are used to illustrate the three kinds of atomic units for each language.

16.4.1.2.1 Term Weighting Evaluation Schemes

Binary (term presence), term frequency, and term frequency inverse document frequency[15] are three common weighting schemes that are evaluated in our experiments. For most problems, the term frequency inverse document frequency weighting seems to work very well. In fact, there is no significant difference between the three when it comes to the sentence segment because the probability of a word repeating itself is very low in a sentence context.

16.4.1.2.2 Evaluation Metrics

We look at a number of different metrics for assessing the quality of a classifier. The accuracy metric evaluates overall performances as:

$$\text{Accuracy} = \#\text{correctly classified samples}/\#\text{samples}$$

Original: I like it. 　　　　　　我喜欢它。
POS tagged: I/p like/v it/p ./w 　我/p 喜欢/v 它/p 。/w
p = Pronoun, v = Verb, w = Punctuation

2nd Element	Unigram	Word	Word-with-POS
English	I	like	like/v
Chinese	喜	喜欢	喜欢/v

FIGURE 16.2 Three atomic representations in English and Chinese.

To analyze the detailed performance of specific categories, we computed their Precision, Recall, and F − Measure, defined as follows.

$$\text{Precision} = \#\text{classified true positive}/\#\text{classified positive}$$

$$\text{Recall} = \#\text{classified true positive}/\#\text{true positive}$$

$$\text{F −Measure} = 2 \times \text{Precision} \times \text{Recall}/(\text{Precision} + \text{Recall})$$

16.5   EXPERIMENT RESULTS

For each of the two atomic unit representation schemes, three choices of sentence representations are possible—Matrix, NGram2, and Single—which can be weighted using three schemes—binary, term frequency, and term frequency inverse document frequency. Thus, in theory, there are $2 \times 3 \times 3 = 18$ possible permutations. Moreover, because our goal is to find the best sentence representation, only the best results from each of the 3 sentence representations will be shown.

For each representation scheme, we plot the metric value versus an increasing percentage of cross-validated training data. For example, at 10% of cross-validated training data, 90% of the entire data set is used for testing averaged over 10 different partitions of the 90% data. For other percentages, we maximize the amount of non-overlapping data while sampling. For example, at 60% training, we sample two different chunks of 60% training data with 20% overlap.

16.5.1   OVERALL ACCURACY

Figure 16.3 shows the cross-validated accuracy metric for various segment representations. In the three sub-diagrams, it is easy to see that Matrix outperforms the other two sentence representation methods. Comparing the Matrix results of Figure 16.3b and 16.3c, it appears that Unigram is about 2% better than Word, and Matrix is about 4% better than Single. As shown in Figure 16.3a, the results for Matrix and Single experience substantial fluctuations, which highlight the inconsistency of the basketball data set (the annotations can be quite subjective at times).

The accuracy metric evaluates overall sentence representation classification performance, regardless of the class distribution, and thus could be biased by a large negative class. In practice, minor categories in the data set are usually more interesting; this includes the "postype" and "histype" sentences for the basketball data set and "positive" and "negative" opinion segments for the cell phone review data set. Hence, besides overall performance, we need to further evaluate the performance of the representation schemes on each "major" and "minor" category.

16.5.2   F-MEASURE OF MAJOR CATEGORIES

Figure 16.4 plots the F-measure values for the "major" categories (i.e., "negtype" for basketball and "nonopinion" for cell phone). For the basketball data set, Matrix performs better than NGram2, especially when the training data fraction exceeds 60%. It is just slightly (0.5%) worse than Single, otherwise. Further, as training

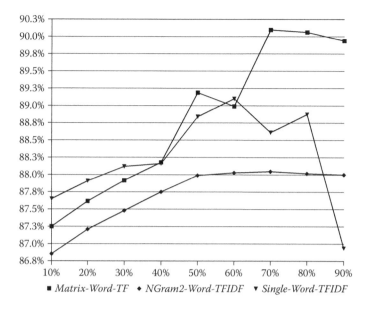

FIGURE 16.3a Basketball (English word atomic unit) overall accuracy.

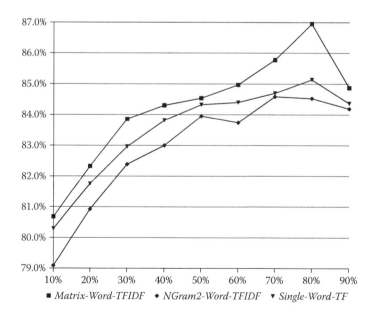

FIGURE 16.3b Cell phone (Chinese word atomic unit) overall accuracy.

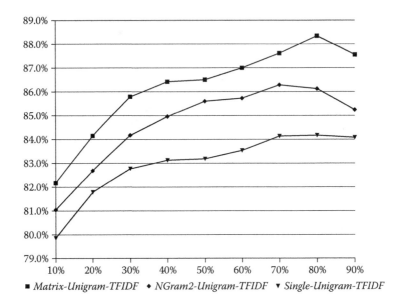

FIGURE 16.3c Cell phone (Chinese unigram atomic unit) overall accuracy.

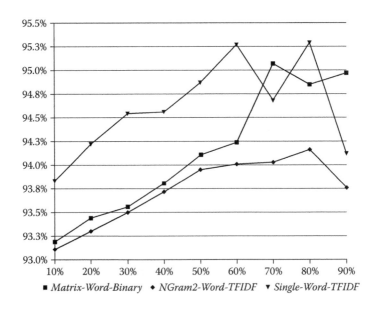

FIGURE 16.4a Basketball (English word atomic unit) F-measure for negative class (majority).

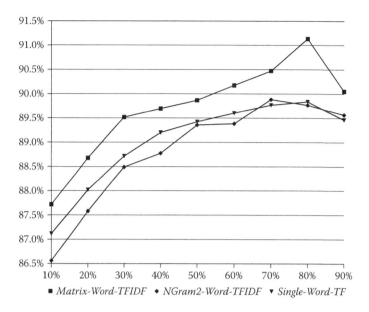

FIGURE 16.4b Cell phone (Chinese word atomic unit) F-measure for non-opinion class (majority).

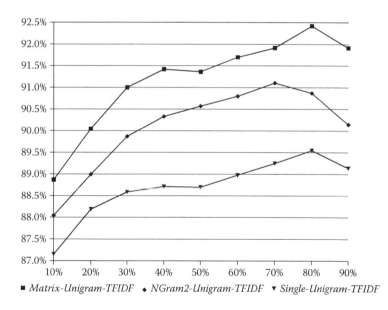

FIGURE 16.4c Cell phone (Chinese unigram atomic unit) F-measure for non-opinion class (majority).

data increase to more than 70%, Matrix performs better and more consistently than Single, as shown in Figure 16.4a.

For the cell phone data set, Matrix consistently give the best result that is on average 1.5% better than Single. Therefore, it can be said that, overall, Matrix beats Single and NGram2 in the major category's F-Measure for both Chinese and English data sets.

As with the accuracy plots, Matrix and Single exhibit substantial instability with respect to increasing training data. We also found that Unigram is about 1% better than Word for the cell phone data set, which could be attributed to the low quality of word segmentation.

16.5.3 F-MEASURE OF MINOR CATEGORIES

As demonstrated in Figure 16.5, the F-measures for minor categories are not stable across the two data sets. In fact, it is hard to tell which one is the overall best, Matrix or Single. Matrix beats NGram2 in five of the six subfigures (except Figure 16.5a). With the "Unigram" atomic unit scheme, shown in Figure 16.5.c and Figure 16.5.f, Matrix is always the best and leads Single by 2%.

By comparing the peak F-measure values of the two data sets using the same representation scheme, such as Single's 57% for "postype" class of basketball (Figure 16.5a) and Single's 80% for "positive" class of cell phone (Figure 16.5c), or Single's 50% for "histype" class of basketball (Figure 16.5d) and Single's 72.5% for "negative" class of cell phone (Figure 16.5e), we observe that the maximum F-measure values of the basketball data set are more than 20% less than the ones for

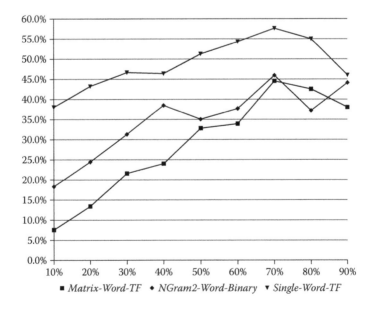

FIGURE 16.5a Basketball (English word atomic unit) F-measure for postype class (minority).

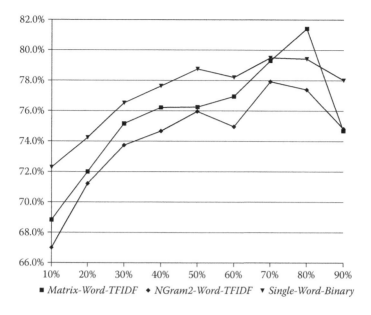

FIGURE 16.5b Cell phone (Chinese word atomic unit) F-measure for positive class (minority).

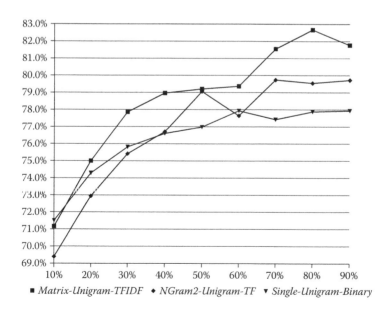

FIGURE 16.5c Cell phone (Chinese unigram atomic unit) F-measure for positive class (minority).

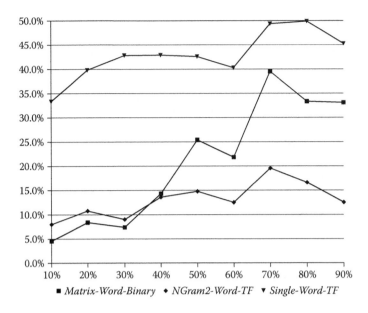

FIGURE 16.5d Basketball (English word atomic unit) F-measure for histype class (minority).

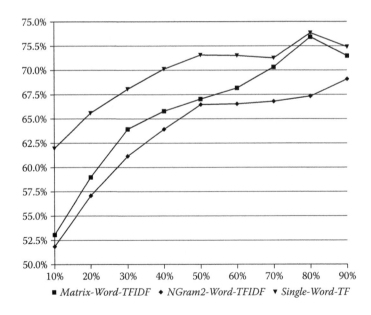

FIGURE 16.5e Cell phone (Chinese word atomic unit) F-measure for negative class (minority).

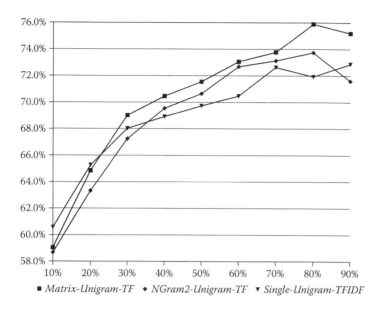

■ *Matrix-Unigram-TF*   ◆ *NGram2-Unigram-TF*   ▼ *Single-Unigram-TFIDF*

FIGURE 16.5f Cell phone (Chinese unigram atomic unit) F-measure for negative class (minority).

the cell phone data set, even using the same representation method. This observation, in some degree, confirms the low quality of our basketball data set.

Another observation is that Matrix remains the best representation for Unigram (Figure 16.5c and Figure 16.5f), outperforming all other representations by 2%.

Thus we conclude that, for Chinese sentence classification, the Matrix representation method with Unigram atomic unit is the best approach.

Because F-measure is derived from Precision and Recall, to identify what is causing the inconsistent results in the minor categories results, we take a closer look at its Precision and Recall curves. To summarize, by sacrificing some Precision, Matrix achieves a much larger increase in Recall and thus performs the best.

16.5.3.1 Precision of Minor Categories

The precision values for the minor categories are shown in Figure 16.6. Note that Matrix always performs best in minor categories, regardless of the distribution of the minor categories. Also, NGram2 almost beats Single (except Figure 16.6d). This implies that involving contextual and structural information will benefit sentence classification.

Quantitatively, the precision of Matrix is 12% better than Single. Also, for the basketball data set, more than 30% improvement in precision is achieved by using Matrix instead of Single.

16.5.3.2 Recall of Minor Categories

From Figure 16.7, we can understand why Matrix performs badly on the F-measure of minor categories; Matrix's recall is almost always the worst among the three, off by 25%

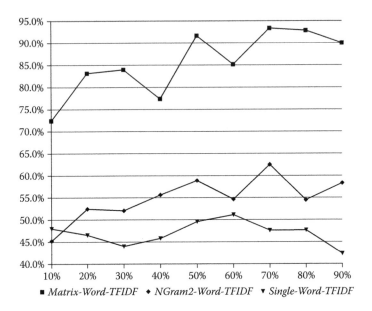

FIGURE 16.6a Basketball (English word atomic unit) precision for postype class (minority).

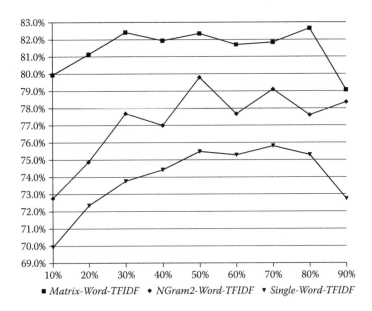

FIGURE 16.6b Cell phone (Chinese word atomic unit) precision for positive class (minority).

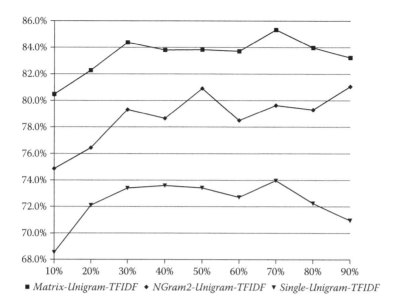

FIGURE 16.6c Cell phone (Chinese unigram atomic unit) precision for positive class (minority).

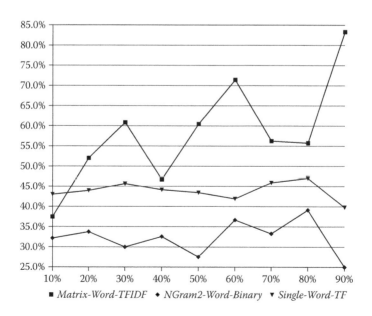

FIGURE 16.6d Basketball (English word atomic unit) precision for histype class (minority).

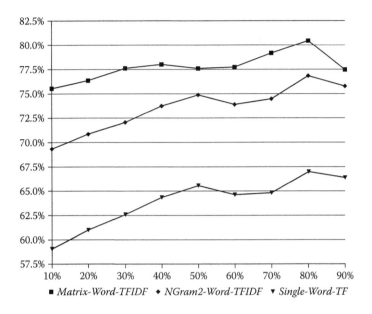

FIGURE 16.6e Cell phone (Chinese word atomic unit) precision for negative class (minority).

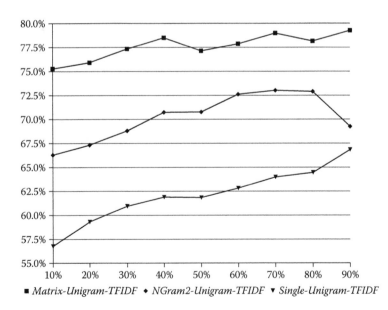

FIGURE 16.6f Cell phone (Chinese unigram atomic unit) precision for negative class (minority).

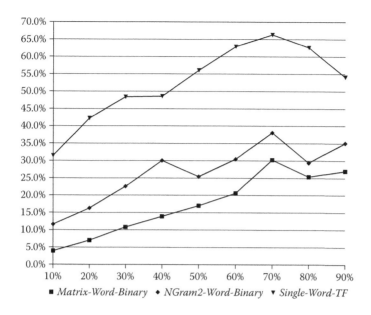

FIGURE 16.7a Basketball (English word atomic unit) recall for postype class (minority).

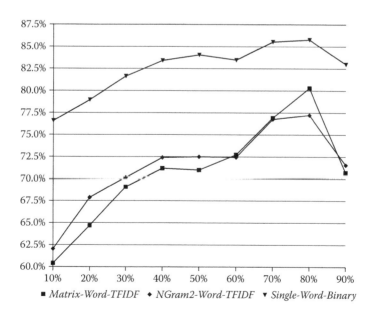

FIGURE 16.7b Cell phone (Chinese word atomic unit) recall for positive class (minority).

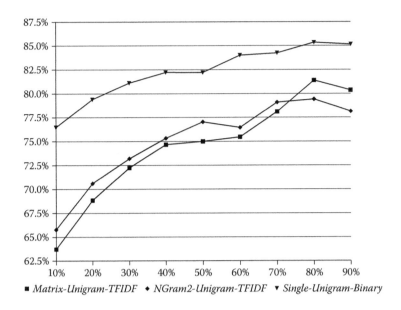

FIGURE 16.7c Cell phone (Chinese unigram atomic unit) recall for positive class (minority).

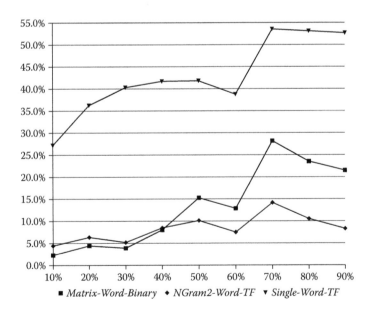

FIGURE 16.7d Basketball (English word atomic unit) recall for histype class (minority).

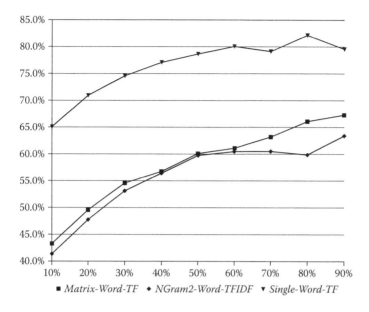

FIGURE 16.7e Cell phone (Chinese word atomic unit) recall for negative class (minority).

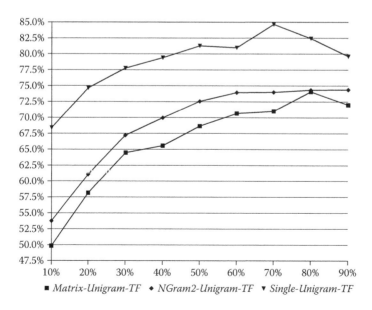

FIGURE 16.7f Cell phone (Chinese unigram atomic unit) recall for negative class (minority).

and 10% compared to Single for the basketball and cell phone data set, respectively. This degradation overshadows Matrix's otherwise excellent precision performances.

Ideally, a classifier needs to perform well in both Precision and Recall, but for real-life classification tasks where minor categories are more important, precision can take more importance. This is especially true for review mining, where users want all shown classified reviews to be accurate, but not necessarily comprehensive and complete. Hence, for minor category classification, Matrix remains the best choice despite its low F-measure scores.

16.6   DISCUSSION

Several observations can be drawn from the experimental results across two different languages. Overall, Matrix appears to be the best sentence representation with respect to classification, yielding on average 2% better accuracy than Single, as demonstrated in Figure 16.3. Matrix also beats NGram2 and Single for the specific category performance. For the major categories, Matrix's performance is stable and ranks among the top performers, as illustrated in Figure 16.4. For minor categories, which are the focus of our research, Matrix achieves the highest precision, as shown in Figure 16.6. Even on a poorly annotated data set such as the basketball data set, Matrix was able to outperform the other two classical text representations.

Notice that the superiority of Matrix holds true for both English and Chinese data sets and also over different types of writing style. The basketball data set is extracted from formal reports, whereas the cell phone data set comprises user reviews that are more colloquial and short. We are quite confident that the Matrix sentence segment representation will work well for other domains and languages.

All of our experiments were conducted at the sentence resolution, which results in a very sparse representation. The Matrix representation was able to partially overcome this sparseness problem by completely capturing the sequence information of all terms in the sentence, which are otherwise discarded by the classical Single representation. For the basketball test data set (1169 test segments, 50% of all), the density of non-zero entries is 0.47% for VSM (Single) and 0.043% for Matrix representation. Similarly, for the cell phone test data set (1000 test reviews, accounting for 50% of total size), the densities are 0.19% for Single and 0.03% for Matrix, respectively. Despite having 10 times sparser representation, the Matrix approach was able to outperform the vector space representation. This goes a long way to show the superiority of our Matrix method. With additional pruning, our Matrix approach could perform even better.

Traditionally, word segmentation plays an important part in the preprocessing of Chinese languages. Moreover, current Chinese word segmentation approaches cannot always get the job done right, resulting in errors at the later stages of processing. However, our experiment results indicate that the Chinese word segmentation procedure could be skipped entirely if we used a Matrix representation. As shown in Figure 16.3, Figure 16.4, and Figure 16.5, Matrix combined with Unigram actually outperformed the corresponding Matrix with Word representation.

16.7 CONCLUSION AND FUTURE WORK

In this chapter, we proved that involving contextual information in a proper way could improve classification result and potentially overcome data sparseness problem at the sentence level. Also we presented a new approach that uses context information wisely which outperforms existing NGram and VSM approaches across different language; this is all in spite of the matrix representation's being an order of magnitude higher in terms of sparsity! Lastly, Chinese NLP tasks at the sentence level may benefit significantly from the Matrix representation by bypassing the often problematic word segmentation procedure.

Future work includes devising systematic strategies to prune the extremely sparse Matrix representation to further improve its performance. The completeness property of the matrix representation is not formally proved. In addition, we need to learn how to deal with duplicate characters in a sentence segment, which are somewhat common in the Chinese language. We also need to determine whether duplicate entries reduce the accuracy of our representation.

REFERENCES

1. Agrawal, R. and Srikant, R. Fast algorithms for mining association rules, in *Proceedings of the 20th International Conference on Very Large Data Bases, VLDB,* 1994, 487–499.
2. Allan, J., Lavrenko, V., and Jin, H. First story detection in TDT is hard, in *9th ACM CIKM Conference,* 2000, 374–381.
3. Augusto, L. and Pizzato, S. Using a trie-based structure for question analysis, in *Proceedings of the Australasian Language Technology Workshop*, Macquarie University, Sydney, Australia, December 2004, 25–31.
4. Clément, J., Flajolet, P., and Vallée, B. The analysis of hybrid trie structures, in *Proceedings of the Ninth Annual ACM-SIAM Symposium on Discrete Algorithms*, San Francisco, 1998, 531–539.
5. Hachey, B. and Grover, C. Sentence classification experiments for legal text summarization, in *Proceedings of the 17th Annual Conference on Legal Knowledge and Information Systems*, Berlin, Germany, 2004.
6. Hu, M. and Liu, B. Mining and summarizing customer reviews, in *Proceedings of the ACM SIGKDD International Conference on Knowledge Discovery & Data Mining*, Seattle, WA, August 2004.
7. Liu, B., Hu, M., and Cheng, J. Opinion observer: analyzing and comparing opinions on the Web, in *Proceedings of the 14th International World Wide Web Conference*, Chiba, Japan, May 2005.
8. Pizzato, L.A., van Zaanen, M., and Moll, D. Classifying sentences using induced structure, in *Proceedings of the 12th Edition of the Symposium on String Processing and Information Retrieval*, Buenos Aires, November 2005, pages 139–150.
9. McCallum, A. and Nigam, K. A Comparison of event models for naive Bayes text classification, In AAAI workshop on learning for text categorization, Madison, July, 1998.
10. McKnight, L. and Srinivasan, P. Categorization of sentence types in medical abstracts, in *AMIA Symp.,* 2003, 440–444.
11. Miller, G.A., Beckwith, R., Fellbaum, C., Gross, D., and Miller, K. Introduction to WordNet: an on-line lexical database, *J Lexicography,* 3, 235–244, 1990.

12. Na, J.C., Sui, H., Khoo, C., Chan, S., and Zhou, Y. Effectiveness of simple linguistic processing in automatic sentiment classification of product reviews, in *Proceedings of the Eighth International ISKO Conference,* Wurzburg, Germany, 2004.

13. Pang, Bo, L., Lillian, and Vaithyanathan, S. Thumbs up? Sentiment classification using machine learning techniques, in *Proceedings of the Conference on Empirical Methods in Natural Language Processing*, 2002, 79–86.

14. Shi, B. and Chang, K. Mining Chinese review, in *Sixth IEEE International Conference on Data Mining—Workshops (ICDMW'06),* Hong Kong, December 2006, 85–589.

15. Sui, H., Khoo, C., and Chan, S. Sentiment classification of product reviews using svm and decision tree induction, in *Proceedings of State of the Art Implementation of Classification Research in Information Technologies: 14th Annual ASIST SIG CR Workshop,* American Society for Information Science & Technology, 2003.

16. Tamura, A., Takamura, H., and Okumura, M. Classification of multiple sentence questions, in *Proceedings of the 2nd International Joint Conference on Natural Language Processing*, Jeju Island, Korea, October 2005.

17. Turney, P.D. Thumbs up or thumbs down? Semantic orientation applied to unsupervised classification of reviews, in *Proceedings of the Association for Computational Linguistics 40th Anniversary Meeting*, New Brunswick, NJ, 2002.

18. Yamamoto, Y. and Takagi, T. A sentence classification system for multi biomedical literature summarization, in *Proceedings of the 21st International Conference on Data Engineering Workshops,* 2005.

19. Yang, Y. and Liu, X. A re-examination of text categorization methods, in *Proceedings of the 22nd Annual International ACM SIGIR Conference on Research Development and Information Retrieval,* Berkeley, CA, August 1999, 42–49.

20. Yang, Y. and Pedersen, J.O. A comparative study on feature selection in text categorization, in *14th International Conference on Machine Learning,* Nashville, TN, 1997, 412–420.

21. Ye, Q., Lin, B., and Jun Li, Y. Sentiment classification for Chinese reviews: a comparison between SVM and semantic approaches, in *Proceedings of the 4th International Conference on Machine Learning and Cybernetics,* Guangzhou, August 2005.

22. Ye, Q., Shi, W., and Li, Y. Sentiment classification for movie reviews in Chinese by improved semantic oriented approach, in *Proc. 39th Annu. Hawaii Int. Conf. Syst. Sci.,* 3, 53.2, 2006.

17 Visualizing RFID Tag Data in a Library for Detecting Latent Interest of Users

Yukio Ohsawa, Takuma Hosoda, and Takeshi Ui

CONTENTS

17.1   INTRODUCTION

Marketing researchers' interest in Radio Frequency Identification (RFID) tags is growing rapidly.[1] The ability to record the selection behaviors of customers in a retail store before they decide to buy or not to buy enables us to understand their latent interests more deeply than any previous data on the position of sales (POS). The information that a customer's interest in an item is strong enough to pick it out but not enough to buy it has not been dealt with because we deal only with POS data. For example, suppose there is a cheese that a supermarket manager wants his or her customers to eat. This cheese, however, costs 2500 JPY (approximately $20 US). Many customers walking around the store may pick the cheese up, but most will not buy it when they look at the price. As a result, this cheese hardly ever appears in the POS data. However, if we can record the picking behaviors of customers, the data include useful information (e.g., 10 of 1000 customers selected the

277

cheese but did not buy it). Introducing the RFID tags, we may be able to know if the price of this cheese should be discounted, because RFID tags can sense selection actions of customers.

Encouraged by this sensitivity of RFID tags, the data from RFID tags were dealt with from the aspect of data-based marketing.[2-4] Applying the methods of data mining, we may be able to acquire a deeper level of knowledge about consumers and customers than we did with POS data.

A customer's identification (ID) (i.e., the information identifying each customer) tends to be missed when RFID tags are attached to items in a retail store because of privacy concerns.[5] This has been regarded as an obstacle in predicting a customer's attitude about each item. In this chapter, we consider the circumstance in which RFID tags are used. Although individual customers cannot be distinguished, we can obtain data about the group behavior of customers. By applying the concept of chance discovery (i.e., to discover an event significant for decision making), in Section 17.2, we first show how an expensive cheese can be meaningful even if we do not discount its price. Based on this idea, we experimentally show that the data on the group behavior of customers in the real space are recorded with ID-less RFID tags and that the visualization of the data with KeyGraph, a data visualization tool for chance discovery, aids the discovery of new values in the market. This expectation is validated by experiments in a library.

17.2   CHANCE DISCOVERY AS A HIGHLIGHTED APPLICATION OF RFID TAGS

17.2.1 $20 CHEESE: A CHANCE IN A SUPERMARKET

In *chance discovery*, a chance means an event that plays a significant role in human decision making.[6] For example, let us consider the expensive cheese in Chapter 1 again. Suppose a customer often goes to the supermarket close to his house, and mostly buys liquor. The supermarket keeper likes her to buy things to eat, also. However, an established lifestyle is hard to change. One day, he finds a very nice-looking cheese close to the liquor shelf from which he usually buys beer and wine. The cheese looks good to have with the wine, but . . . he picks up the cheese and returns it to the shelf, because it is expensive at $20. Yet he goes to the shelf containing cheese and snacks, because he is now interested in something to eat that tastes like cheese. Since then, he has bought things to eat there. Although the $20 cheese was not bought, it led the customer to a new purchase decision.

See the left side of Figure 17.1 for the conceptual sketch of this scenario. The $20 cheese is apparently a chance, because the event of picking the cheese made a strong influence on his decision. As well, the supermarket manager may decide to keep the expensive cheese on the same shelf rather than to move it elsewhere or discount its price. Changing the lifestyle of a customer provides more benefit for the manager than having the customer buy an expensive item once. Thus we can expect to enable chance discovery by introducing RFID tags data and visualizing the data in the way shown in Figure 17.1.

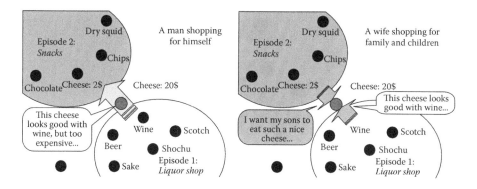

FIGURE 17.1 Chance discovery in a supermarket: The expensive cheese plays a role.

Another case may be as on the right-hand side of Figure 17.1, where a wife buys $2 of cheese or some other snacks for her children every day but finds that the $20 cheese looks so nice that she wishes her children could eat it. The reason for picking out the cheese is different from the woman above, and this time she may buy the expensive cheese, believing the cheese will be good for she and her husband to drink wine with. The $20 cheese has not been bought frequently so far, but its priceless value will be noticed if the wife thinks about her own family's lifestyle.

We call a map as in Figure 17.1 a scenario map,[7,8] because this map aids the user in designing a valuable future scenario. This effect is expected to work better if other customers come, see, touch, and talk about the cheese, as mentioned in the next section.

17.2.2 A Chance in the Real Space, and for a Community

The customer in the left-hand example of Figure 17.1 took the cheese from the shelf, and may have smelled the cheese and felt the weight and the softness. He estimated how good the product is, but finally decided not to buy it. It is noteworthy that the customer was in the same part of the store as the $20 cheese. This is why it is important to detect the customer's interaction with the sold item in the real space.

We can also point out another effect of the real space to the customer. Let us define a community as a group of people who communicate. When each member of the community embraces a scenario (a series of actions and events that occur under a coherent context) planned in the mind, he or she may talk to other members about the scenario, or realize the scenario by real actions. Another member who hears about this scenario or looks at the actions may like to use it in the future if he or she feels empathy, as in Figure 17.2. This effect is not rare when we go into a prosperous supermarket where there are other customers. Even though one may not talk to other customers, their behaviors can be seen; this is a nonverbal communication from which one can import other customers' purchase/consumption scenarios and create new actions.

On the basis of the discussion above, we formulate a hypothesis that the scenario map in Figure 17.1 or Figure 17.2 can represent the behaviors of people in a

FIGURE 17.2 The female shopper is just giving up buying the expensive cheese due to the high price, but someone encourages her to buy a cheaper cheese by moving to another shelf.

community, not only an individual customer's actions, and of a customer choosing products in a real space rather than on a shopping Web site. Also, the definition of a community can be relaxed to a group of people who implicitly communicate (i.e., who see each other's behaviors). If a person regards another person's choice to be similar to his own recent choice, then he may feel empathy with the other person and import her scenario into his own.

If we take customers' data as follows, we can obtain a scenario map as in Figure 17.1 and Figure 17.2, including rarely purchased items such as $20 cheese. On this map, if the group of customers behaves like a community, or if customers interact with sold items in the real space, we can expect each customer to be interested in item X as the extension of his or her recent purchase history, even if X has been bought in low frequency in the past.

> On February 1, Mr. X picked out the set {beer, wine, cheese $20}
> On February 2, Mr. X picked out the set {wine, cheese $2, chips}
> On February 1, Ms. Y picked out the set {beer, cheese $20}
> On February 2, Ms. Y picked out the set {beer, wine, cheese $2}

17.3 INTRODUCING RFID TAGS IN A LIBRARY

In this chapter, we show the data on a customer's picking of books with RFID tags. The reason we chose a library as the test field in this study is threefold.

1. Each book has a high-dimensional and understandable value set (see Section 17.3.2).
2. A large number of items (i.e., books) can be put on the shelves; we can store 50 books on a shelf of 1-meter width.
3. People often exhibit pick-and-return behaviors when they touch a bookshelf.

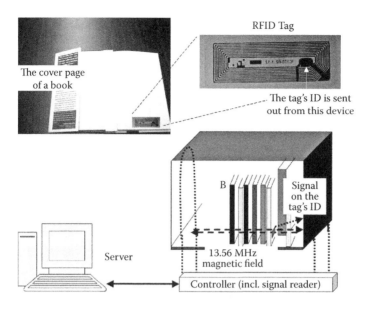

FIGURE 17.3 The overview of the library system with an RFID tag in each book.

17.3.1 THE RFID SYSTEM

In our experimental library, one RFID tag was put on the back of the cover page of each book.[9] As in Figure 17.3, the system here used a 13.56-MHz magnetic field to feed power to the passive RFID tags. The controller under the shelf managed this field, read the data obtained from the tag identification signals sent from the RFID tags (attached to the books), and forwarded them to the server. Via this server, the picking data of people who use this library are recorded in the database. From this setting, we should keep in mind the following (1) The reach length of the 13.56-MHz magnetic field is 30–50 cm. The system judges that the book left the shelf if the book is farther from the shelf than 50 cm but may take it as sitting still if a user just picks out the book within 30 cm of the shelf. (2) The switching of the magnetic field is managed by the controllers to be circulated throughout all shelves every 30 seconds. This means a picking of fewer than 30 seconds may be ignored. (3) The passive tags do not have a power source, so they are light enough for the user to feel no difference from his or her daily experience with books.

As a result of (1) and (2), the user's looking at the picked book or feeling the book's weight is detected, whereas just picking it out for a moment is hardly included in the data. The shelves in the library are separated as in Figure 17.4. There are six stacks, and each stack has three levels (upper, middle, and lower). Note the Chinese characters are used for representing upper, middle, and lower. Each level is separated into four shelf boxes (shelves, hereafter) A, B, C, and D. As a result, each shelf in the stack is called "1-A-Upper" ("Upper" is written in Chinese in the figures) if it is in box A of the upper level of the first stack. Library patrons are allowed to walk around freely, to talk to each other, and to take the seats nearby to read books they pick.

FIGURE 17.4 The view of bookshelves in the library.

17.3.2   THE DATA FORMAT OF USERS' PICKING BOOKS WITH RFID

The data in Table 17.1 are recorded as a result of the exercise in 17.3.1. Each line
has information about the book picked/returned at each moment, such as the title,
authors, and the shelf the book belongs to. Note that there are no delimiters of baskets
as POS data have, because we do not have information to distinguish between library
users. That is, each line of Table 17.1 means a book that was picked or returned by
"somebody" who visited.

TABLE 17.1

The Data Format of RFID Tags on Books in the Library

Pick (1) and return(0)	Date and time	Shelf		ISBN	Title	Author
1	2006/11/6 1432	4-A-下	4	4-7673-0803-8	小売･サービス業勝ち残る店は	安田龍平 編著
1	2006/11/6 1433	2-A-上	177	4-532-13247-9	ゼミナール経営学入門	伊丹敬之, 加護
1	2006/11/6 1433	1-A-上	1351	4-478-50210-2	マーケティング原理	フィリップ･コトラー
0	2006/11/6 1433	2-C-上	1570	4-8201-1736-X	組織設計のマネジメント	ジェイ Rガルブレ
1	2006/11/6 1433	2-C-上	1570	4-8201-1736-X	組織設計のマネジメント	ジェイ Rガルブレ
1	2006/11/6 1433	6-C-中	1151	4-502-59260-9	「人間力」で仕事が変わる	鈴野智子 著
0	2006/11/6 1433	6-C-上	1977	4-901318-34-9	堀江貴文のお金をつかめ!	大谷哲郎&ホリエ
0	2006/11/6 1434	1-A-上	1351	4-478-50210-2	マーケティング原理	フィリップ･コトラー

17.4   EXPERIMENT STEP (I): PICKING FROM SHELVES AND DATA VISUALIZATION

17.4.1   THE EXPERIMENT SETTING AND BASIC DATA

We had 20 subjects who used the library for 120 minutes. They were instructed to read the books and were encouraged to write down their impression of each book they picked. This was so they would look in each picked book and keep a book more than 30 seconds more than 50 cm from the shelves. We also aimed to check the subjects' intentions by this questionnaire (e.g., whether they meant to read or were just attracted by the book cover).

The 20 subjects were split into groups of three to four members. The subjects in each group were allowed to talk to each other, but no intergroup communications were allowed. This setting created a situation similar to a bookstore, where two to three people may come together and talk (although they should not). The shelves in stack No. 6 (the right part of Figure 17.5) were the most popular when we counted the frequency for all times. The shelves in stacks No. 3 and No. 4 were much less popular. The most elementary data analysis may conclude that the books on these shelves should be removed. Books on 2-B might be also judged in the same way.

17.4.2   MOVEMENT FROM/TO SHELVES

In Figure 17.6, we see the change of picked shelves every 40 minutes of the 120-minute experiment. These graphs were drawn by the drawing function of Microsoft Excel 5.0. The horizontal axis means the stack number, and the vertical axis means the shelf box in each stack. The dots mean the shelves from/to which the

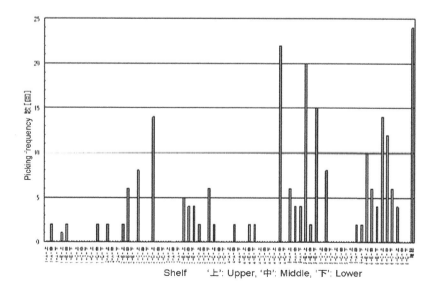

FIGURE 17.5 The picking frequencies of books on each shelf.

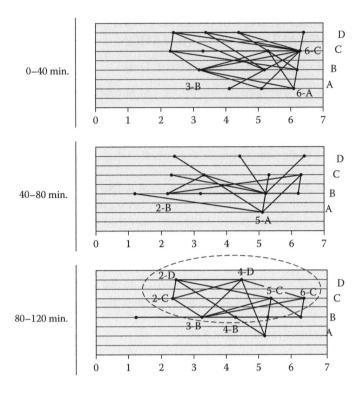

FIGURE 17.6 The emergence of a shelf-cluster after 80 min.

subjects picked/returned books. The lines show the sequential occurrence of these shelves in the data as in Table 17.1. That is, a pair of nodes connected by a line in Figure 17.6 means that the books in these shelves were touched in a short time (fewer than 30 seconds before or after the other). We find the following behavior of subjects.

Stage 1. Users started from stack No. 6. They took the most books from shelf 6-C and moved to other shelves in a short time.

Stage 2. Users' attention changed to No. 5. They moved further to the other shelves. Some seem to have picked a few books from No. 2.

Stage 3. There is no more central target such as No. 5 and No. 6 that we found in the earlier stages. The subjects are checking books in the cluster of shelves including 2-C, 2-D, 3-B, 4-B, and 4-D, and are still interested also in 5-C and 6-C.

Shelf 5-A is playing the role of a *bridge* here (i.e., users move to form a new cluster after using 5-A, like the customer taking the $20 cheese) in the left of Figure 17.1 shifts to the shelf of snacks. This shelf had books on marketing. Before this movement, the subjects' targets of picking were ranging across areas without a coherent context, because they just started from the shelves close to the place they started walking. After this,

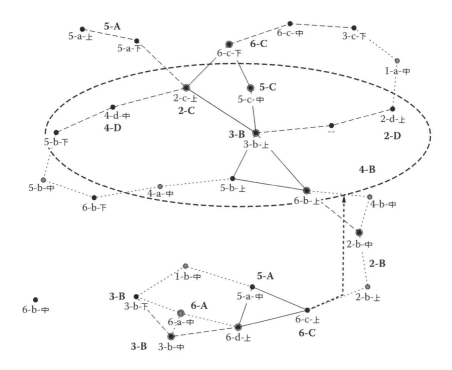

FIGURE 17.7 The emergence of a shelf-cluster after 80 min, by KeyGraph.

in Stage 3, the subjects started to read from shelves relevant to the business methods based on established theories, such as marketing and strategic organizations.

Then we visualized the same data with KeyGraph (Appendix A).[7,8] KeyGraph shows *islands* (co-occurrence clusters of frequent events that are visualized by black nodes) and *bridges* (events visualized by red nodes, which may be rare in the data but co-occur with items in multiple islands). Here, every three books picked sequentially by any members of the subjects were counted as one basket. As a result, the shelves in 2-B are found to bridge the starting shelves and the new cluster, as in the upper area of Figure 17.7. Items in this new cluster correspond to ones in the new cluster in Figure 17.6. The 2-B-Upper shelf on the bridge, however, disappeared when the new cluster was formed according to Figure 17.6. Thus 2-B-Upper was the least outstanding.

On the other hand, as in Figure 17.7, KeyGraph visualized 2-B including a scientific book titled *What Is a Complex System?* that they picked just a few times and moved to the new cluster where science and business topics are merged. Hence, the detection of bridging effect was similar to the $20 cheese in Figure 17.1 and Figure 17.2.

17.5   EXPERIMENT STEP (II): PICKING OF BOOKS ON KEYGRAPH

The values of the "title" variable in Table 17.1 were taken for data in this section, and here we use only KeyGraph for visualization because we desired to find items that were not frequent in the collected data but may work as the $20 cheese did.

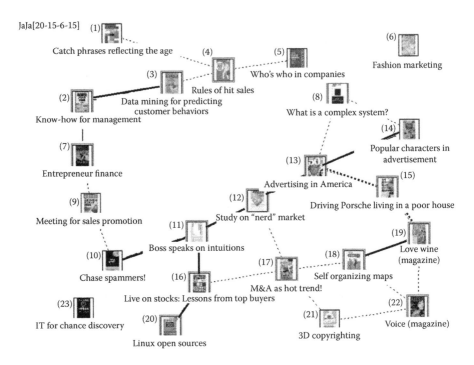

FIGURE 17.8 KeyGraph visualizing the titles of books which were picked in experiment I.

The scenario map resulted as in Figure 17.8: the angular nodes (with cover pictures) with black frames show frequent books in the data as in Table 17.1, and the black lines show the co-occurrence (being picked at close time) of these popular books. Each connected graph of these black nodes and lines show an *island* (i.e., a popular cluster of books), and the nodes with red frames show rare items that are *bridges* connecting multiple islands via dotted lines. Each red line shows the co-occurrence of a rare item with islands in a neighborhood island. See Appendix A for more on KeyGraph.

Then the two steps below were executed.

Step 1. We hired 11 subjects among the 20 who did the picking in the previous section. Here, the 23 books appearing in the graph of Figure 17.8 obtained by KeyGraph were put on a table, and each subject was instructed to pick and read books as they liked for 30 minutes. At any moment during this experiment, at least one subject was engaged in the experiment.

Step 2. We recorded the sequences of books that each subject picked. Then, after the 30 minutes of Step 1, the next task of the subject was to look at the graph and to choose and mark books he or she wanted to read with dotted circles.

The results were as shown in Figure 17.9, Figure 17.10, and Figure 17.11. Here, we depict dotted arrows on the graph, according to the order in which each subject picked books on the table in Step 1. The large solid (e.g., item 23 in Figure 17.9) and

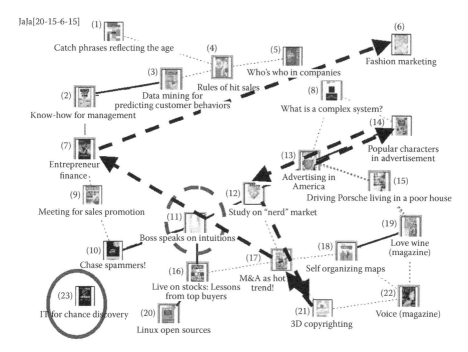

FIGURE 17.9 Subject 1: the sequential order of books picked in the new experiment.

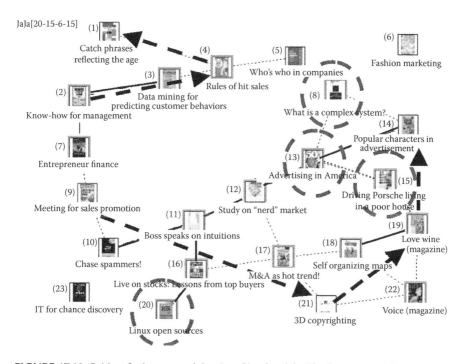

FIGURE 17.10 Subject 2: the sequential order of books picked in the new experiment.

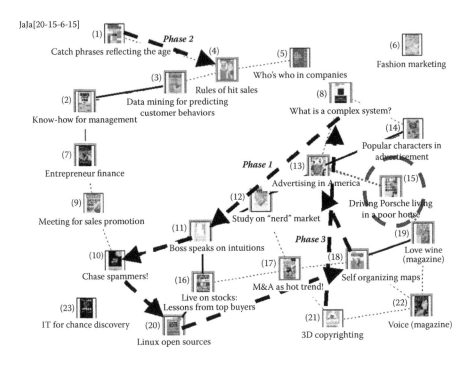

FIGURE 17.11 Subject 3: the sequential order of books picked in the experiment.

dotted circles (e.g., item 11 in Figure 17.9) in the figure, respectively, show books the subject had read in the experiment step (I) (i.e., before the new experiment [II]), and those the same subject chose in Step 2 here. Let us show the results by looking at 3 subjects among the 11.

> *Subject* 1. As in Figure 17.9, subject 1 started from item 13 and traced the links in KeyGraph back and forward, although he was not looking at Figure 17.8 in Step 1, the output from KeyGraph, until he reached item 17. The books in this path were related to marketing strategies. Then he jumped to item 7, *Entrepreneur Finance,* which is about creating a new company and managing its finances, six links away from item 17. Finally, he jumped to item 6, *Fashion Marketing*, which is isolated from all other nodes. After this, at Step 2, this subject said he became interested in item 11. He mentioned he thought the content of this book (*Boss Speaks on Intuition*) provided a common basis for readers of the books he had browsed so far, because a new company needs talented "bosses" who catch trends and explain their understanding of the market clearly. We can also regard item 11 as a neighbor of 12, which is the end of the first continuous path he traced.
>
> *Subject* 2. As shown in Figure 17.10, subject 2 started Step 1 from item 9 and jumped five links to 21. However, after this, he traced the paths in the

figure, skipping approximately three links per step, except once when he jumped from item 14 to item 2. From item 2, this subject traced to item 1 via item 4. Items 8 (*red*), 13, and 15 (*red*), which he preferred at the end of Step 2 of the experiment (looking at KeyGraph), are found close to the end of the first path he traced in Step 1.

Subject 3. As shown in Figure 17.11, the subject started Step 1 from item 8 (*red*) and traced the paths in KeyGraph with skipping approximately three links per step until he reached items 18 and 13. Then he jumped to item 2 and followed the path, until he jumped from item 1 to item 21. After the browsing in Step 1 without looking at the output figure of KeyGraph, he mentioned, with looking at KeyGraph in Step 2, that he was interested in reading all the books initially but his interest finally was focused on item 15 (*red*), which he had not picked, but that he felt connected to items 18 and 13 at the end of the first path he traced. This subject converged to the red nodes at the end of each period he traced the paths on the graph.

From these few examples, we can hypothesize that the following tendencies are underlying the behaviors of the subjects.

1. *Tracking co-occurrence links*: In Step 1 of experiment II, subjects at first tend to wander around the islands in KeyGraph (i.e., books that were picked in the data collection phase, experiment I with RFID tags in Section 17.4). That is, they tend to pay attention to popular items in the initial phase of experiment II.

2. *Returning to the early-stage interest:* When subjects browse without looking at any referential information based on real data, they start from popular items that frequently appear in the data obtained from RFID tags in experiment I and then shift their attention to items that are less popular but are close to the end of a connected path in the early stage of browsing in Step 1 of experiment II. About this behavior, subjects tend to mention that they noticed their own interests that had been latent before the experiment.

3. *Seeing novel bridge of popular trends:* When a subject looks at KeyGraph's output, which visualizes the map summarizing the behaviors of all subjects including oneself, the subject tends to be interested in books he or she never picked. These books of new interest tend to exist on bridges connecting islands of popular book items by higher probability. Also, the subject tends to remark that the books connecting his or her multiple interests are highly attractive.

We evaluated these hypotheses using three methods. First, we checked all sequential selection of books for each subject. That is, we counted set *A* of book pairs taken for two sequential times and set *B* of pairs linked within three links in KeyGraph. As a result, the subjects' average of |*A and B*| / |*A*| was 0.54 and its standard deviation was 0.54. This means Hypothesis 1 does not stand as reliable knowledge about subjects' behaviors. Second, we looked at the behavior of each of the 11 subjects, and counted the two sets,

> *Set C*: Items that are within three links in KeyGraph from the end of each traced connected path in Step 1 of experiment II. Here, we defined a connected path as a sequence of items (books) the subject picked without skipping more than three links. A single item isolated from any connected path is regarded as a connected path, according to this definition.
>
> *Set D*: Items he or she marked in Step 2 of experiment II.

As a result, the value of |C *and D*| / |D| took an average of 0.90 and standard deviation of 0.23 for the 10 subjects who marked one or more items at Step 2 of experiment II as books he or she liked to read. Thus Hypothesis 2 came to be validated as reliable.

Third, to validate the third hypotheses, we counted set *E* of books taken for Step 2 of experiment II, and set *F* of red (bridge) items in KeyGraph. As a result, the subjects' average of |E *and F*| / |E| was 0.63 and its standard deviation was 0.34. We can regard this hypothesis as reliable, because only 30% among all visualized items by KeyGraph were red nodes in Figure 17.8.

For more understanding of structural transition, we compared the snapshots of the frequently appearing items in the behaviors of the 11 subjects. As in Figure 17.12,

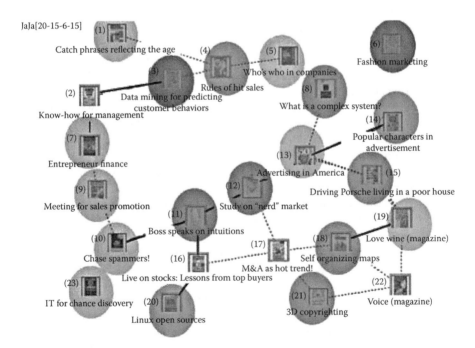

FIGURE 17.12 Phase (a). The highlights in the early half of browsing without looking at the KeyGraph figure.

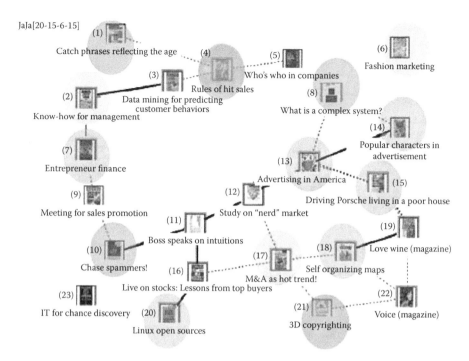

JaJa[20-15-6-15]

(1) Catch phrases reflecting the age

(4)

(5) Who's who in companies

(6) Fashion marketing

(3) Rules of hit sales

(2) Data mining for predicting customer behaviors

Know-how for management

(8) What is a complex system?

(7) Entrepreneur finance

(14) Popular characters in advertisement

(13) Advertising in America

(9) Meeting for sales promotion

(12) Study on "nerd" market

(11)

(15) Driving Porsche living in a poor house

(19)

(10) Chase spammers!

Boss speaks on intuitions

(17) M&A as hot trend!

(18) Self organizing maps

Love wine (magazine)

(16) Live on stocks: Lessons from top buyers

(23) IT for chance discovery

(20) Linux open sources

(21) 3D copyrighting

(22) Voice (magazine)

FIGURE 17.13 Phase (b). The highlights in the latter half of browsing without looking at the KeyGraph figure.

Figure 17.13, and Figure 17.14, we visualized the frequencies of each item in Figure 17.8 by the density of colors, for three periods: (a) the early half and (b) the latter half of Step 1 of experiment I, and (c) the time the subject looked at KeyGraph in Step 2. Here, we understand Hypotheses 2 and 3 stands above. That is, the *bridges* (items 13, 15, and 17, for example) become more outstanding from phase (a) to (b), whereas the colors of items on the islands (items 3, 12, 18, 19, and so on) are weakened. After (b), we find the strong colors are focused even farther from the items close to the bridge (items 13, 15, 19, and 17: note that a bridge may be a path including popular items and a rare item between them). Also, we find some items such as items 11 and 12 recover at phase (c).

We can point out that tendencies in Hypotheses 2 and 3 are the results of the subjects' behaviors of reading in the real space of the book shelf. That is, they are attracted by some titles and pick up those books. Then they read the content by opening and looking in the book. Here, some words (e.g., "market" and "America" found by opening book (3), and "new business." in book (21) are recorded into the subjects' minds. Then, they tend to feel some underlying context among their favorite books, and such a context is represented by the titles of red nodes such as book (17) which exist between clusters of popular books, which Hypothesis 3 means. However, the initial attention they paid to the titles, which first attracted the subject, may remain and revive after all.

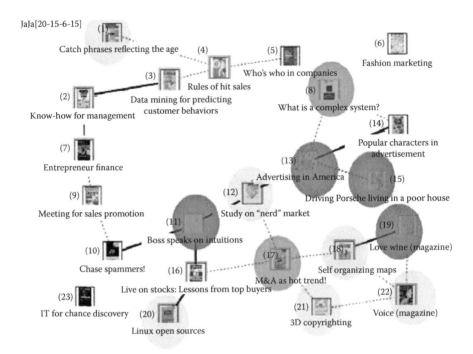

FIGURE 17.14 Phase (c). The highlights with looking at the KeyGraph figure, after browsing.

These behaviors are recorded as data sets obtained with RFID tags embedded in books and antennas in the book shelves. If we take only the sales data in a bookstore, or browsing data on the Web, such a dynamic transition of customers' interests cannot be understood. We can also say that visualization using KeyGraph worked well, because the shift of subjects' interest was discovered to move from the islands of popular items to rare items on the bridges between the islands.

17.6 CONCLUSION

An expectation of RFID tags applied to marketing is to detect items which may not be bought (i.e., do not appear in the sales data) frequently but are touched and picked from customers' latent interest. We aimed in this chapter to discover such "chances," which here means items that are not outstanding but may influence the near-future behavior of customers by introducing the visualization method KeyGraph to the data collected with RFID tags.

The results imply that our aim may come true, in that the visualization of the data on RFID tags is useful in predicting and navigating customers (the visitors browsing books in this chapter) to a niche but potentially popular market. Although we may not be able to distinguish customers because of their will to protect their privacy,[5] the experiment here, where each customer is anonymous, encourages us to introduce RFID tags to real spaces such as apparel stores and supermarkets.

REFERENCES

1. Lace, S. Radio frequency identification technology in retail. Briefing for the 5 February 2004 summit at the National Consumer Council. Available online at: http://www.ncc.org.uknccpdf/poldocs/NCC05/b_rfid.pdf.
2. Gonzalez, H., Han, J., and Li, X. Mining compressed, commodity workflows from massive RFID data sets, *Proceedings of the 15th ACM International Conference on Information and Knowledge Management,* 162–171, 2006.
3. Murakami, E. and Terano, T. *Fairy Wing: Distributed Information Service with RFID Tags, Multi-Agent for Mass User Support,* Springer, Heidelberg, 2004.
4. Hsu, H.-H., Cheng, Z., Huang, T., and Han, Q. Behavior analysis with combined RFID and video information, *The 3rd International Conference on Ubiquitous Intelligence and Computing (UIC-06),* China, September 2006.
5. Landwehr, C.E. Conference report on RFID privacy workshop, concerns, consensus, and questions, *IEEE Security Privacy,* March/April, 34–36, 2004.
6. Ohsawa, Y. and McBurney, P. *Chance Discovery,* Springer, Heidelberg, 2003.
7. Minami, T. RFID in marketing library marketing with RFID for supporting learning patrons, *International Conference on Multimedia and Information,* Spain, November 2006.
8. Horie, K. and Ohsawa, Y. Product designed on scenario maps using Pictorial KeyGraph, *WSEAS Trans. Info. Sci. Appl.,* 3, 1324–1331, 2006.
9. Ohsawa, Y. Scenario maps on situational switch model, applied to blood-test data for hepatitis C patients, in *Chance Discoveries in Real World Decision Making,* Ohsawa, Y. and Tsumoto, S., Eds., Springer, Berlin, 2006. pp. 69–82. 415–438.

Appendix A: KeyGraph and Pictorial KeyGraph

CONTENTS

The visualization method introduced here is called Pictorial KeyGraph, an extension of KeyGraph that embeds pictures of real entities in the data. Let us show the outlines of KeyGraph and Pictorial KeyGraph, which are employed in some chapters of this book.

A.1 THE BASIC KEYGRAPH

KeyGraph is a tool for visualizing the map of event relations in the environment to aid in the process of chance discovery, from a given data set. By visualizing the map where the words appear connected in a graph, one can see the overview of participants' interest. Suppose a textlike dataset (string sequence) D is given, describing an event (e.g., the purchase of an item) sequence sorted by time, where each line (e.g., the item set bought by one customer at a time) ends at the moment of a major change. For example, let a data set D be:

$$D = a1, a2, a4, a5 \ldots.$$
$$a4, a5, a3, \ldots.$$
$$\ldots a4, a5 .$$
$$a1, a2, a5, \ldots, a10.$$
$$a1, a2, a4, \ldots, \ldots, a10. \tag{A.1.1}$$

On data D, KeyGraph runs the following procedure, where $M0$, $M1$, $M2$ are set by the user.

> *KeyGraph-Step 1:* Clusters of frequent items (events among the $M0$ most frequent in D) are made by connecting the $M1$ highest co-occurrence pairs. Each cluster is called an *island*. Items in islands are depicted with black nodes, and each pair of these items (often occurring in many of the same lines) are linked via a solid line. That is, each connected graph here forms an

(1) Obtain the co-occurence network

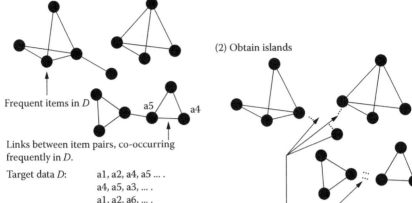

Frequent items in D

Links between item pairs, co-occurring
frequently in D.

Target data D: a1, a2, a4, a5 .... .
                        a4, a5, a3, ...
                        a1, a2, a6, ...
                        ... a4, a5.
                        ... .

(2) Obtain islands

Separate into fundamental clusters,
i.e., islands.

(3) Obtain bridges, on which chances may exist

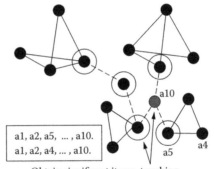

a1, a2, a5, ... , a10.
a1, a2, a4, ... , a10.

Obtain significant items, touching
many node cluster (green nodes)
bridges of frequent co-occurrence. If
the node is rarer than black nodes, it is
a new node put as a red one.

FIGURE A.1 Basic KeyGraph.

island, implying a common context underlying the belonging events/items.
See (1) and (2) of Figure A.1.

KeyGraph-Step 2: Items that may not be as frequent as the nodes in islands,
but whose co-occurrence with items two or more islands is among the $M2$
highest item-island co-occurrence, are *hubs*. A path of links connecting
islands via hubs is called a *bridge*. If a hub is rarer than the black nodes
in islands, it is colored in a different color (e.g., red). We can regard such a
new hub as a candidate of *chance* (i.e., items significant with respect to the
structure of item relations). This step is in Figure A.1 (3).

As a result, the output of KeyGraph as shown in (3) of Figure A.1 includes islands and bridges, and this is expected to work as a scenario map introduced in Section A.1. For example, a4 and a5 may be "beer,"and "wine," and also may be "cheese:20$" in Figure 1.7.

A.2   PICTORIAL KEYGRAPH

In the case of a sales (position of sales: POS) data the lines in Equation A.1.1 correspond to baskets. And in the case of a document, each sentence corresponds to a basket and each word corresponds to an item. In previous works by Ohsawa and Usui (reference 11, Chapter 1) and Horie and Ohsawa (reference 12, Chapter 1), we found that embedding real entities or the pictures corresponding to real entities of items in the corresponding nodes in a graph is supportive to the user's understanding of the visualized graph.

In the case of Ohsawa and Usui, the graph from KeyGraph was complex and the professional marketing staff of the textile development and sales company could not discover a "chance" product on the graph. Then the real textile pieces corresponding to the nodes in the output graph were put on the printed-out graph. As a result, the participants smoothly discovered a promising textile, because they could imagine real customers behind the graph. In addition, in Horie and Ohsawa, the pictures of

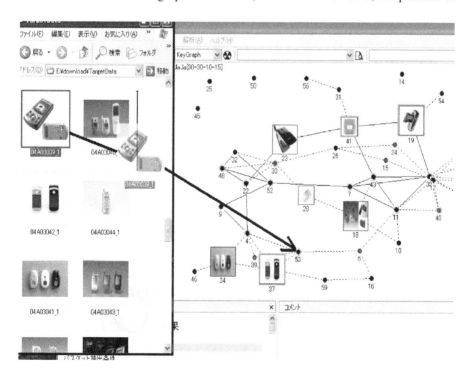

FIGURE A.2 Pictorial KeyGraph (on Polaris; reference 7, Chapter 1). Pictures of items 18,19, etc. are already pasted in the corresponding nodes. The user is now pasting the picture of item 53.

film scratches were put on nodes in a graph obtained by KeyGraph and applied to users' claims of the film-scratch checking machine. In this case, the developers of the machine acquired ideas about new products.

In Pictorial KeyGraph, nodes are simply replaced by pictures of corresponding real entities in D. This replacement has been executed by a user dragging picture icons from a PC desktop to an output window of KeyGraph (Figure A.2).

This manual operation aids users' thoughts, although automated pasting of pictures for all nodes is also possible.

Appendix B: A Maximal Cliques Enumeration Algorithm for MBA Transaction Data[*]

CONTENTS

We incorporate full consideration of two distinct features of market basket analysis (MBA) transaction data into the algorithm design. The first feature is that the total number of different items can be large; the second feature is that the number of associated items for each item, in comparison with the total number of different items, is relatively small when the strength level threshold ranges in [0,1]. In terms of the modeled graph $G = (V,E)$, the first feature is that the number of vertices $|V|$ can be large; the second feature is that, in comparison with the whole graph G, the induced subgraph of G on each vertex is considerably small. As an example, the graph modeled for the data set WebView2 using significance level $\alpha = 0$, as shown in Figure B.3, has 3324 vertices. However, the number of edges is 55,126, thus the density of edges over vertices for this graph is 20, far less than the total number of vertices 3324.

Our selection and development of maximal clique enumeration algorithms are heavily influenced by the aforementioned two features. Among the dozens of published algorithms,[3,4,8,10,14] the depth-first dynamic algorithm in Tsukiyama et al.[14]

---

[*] This Appendix explains the details of some of the concepts used in Chapter 12, and the citation numbers herein correspond to the references in Chapter 12.

(denoted as MIS) has the $O(n + m)$ space cost and $O(nm\mu)$ time cost, where $n = |V|$, $m = |E|$, and μ is the number of maximal cliques. The algorithm MIS is suitable for relatively large graphs,[8] because it dynamically enumerates distinct maximal cliques one at a time and writes the identified maximal clique onto the hard disk right away; thus the runtime memory cost is only the very small space for each tree path. Therefore the algorithm MIS is a good solution for MBA in terms of the first feature of MBA transaction data. However, the algorithm MIS has the time delay $O(|V|)$ between the successive enumerations of maximal cliques. As shown in the experimental results in Figure B.3, the time cost increases very quickly with respect to the number of vertices, $|V|$, hence some modifications become necessary to implement association bundle identification (ABI).

We use the idea of the depth-first dynamic tree approach to develop an algorithm similar to MIS, but also employ the second feature of MBA transaction data. Denote our proposed algorithm by MCE. The two major differences between the algorithm MCE and the algorithm MIS are: MCE maps each maximal clique into a distinct root-to-leaf tree path, whereas MIS maps each maximal clique into a leaf node; and each tree path in MCE has a height limited by the size of maximal clique, whereas each tree path in MIS has the fixed height $|V|$. Because of these differences, MCE has a time delay not fixed by $|V|$, but determined by the size of subgraphs induced on vertices of individual maximal clique. Therefore MCE performs better than MIS when the subgraphs induced on each vertex are considerably smaller than the whole graph, which is exactly the case for MBA transaction data.

Because tree structure is the key concept to explain the idea of algorithm MCE, we describe how we add features to our tree one by one and then present the major steps of MCE. We start with a short review of the backtracking method which is basic to our algorithm.

B.1   THE BACKTRACKING METHOD

Given an undirected graph $G = (V,E)$, let $MCS = (G)$ denote the set of maximal cliques on G and $MCS(v|G)$ the subset of $MCS(G)$ that contains the vertex v. The basic idea of the backtracking method for maximal clique enumeration can be described using the following formulas.

$$MCS(G) = \bigcup_{v \in V} MCS(v \mid G) = \bigcup_{v \in V} MCS(v \mid G(v \mid G)),$$

$$MCS(v \mid G(v \mid G)) = \{v\} \cup MCS(G(v \mid G) \ \{v\}).$$

Here the expression $G(v|G)$ denotes the *induced graph* of G on v, that is,

$$G(v \mid G) = (Ext(v \mid G), E(Ext(v \mid G))),$$

where

$$Ext(v \mid G) = \{v\} \cup \{u \mid u \in V, < u, v > \in E\}$$

and

$$E(Ext(v \mid G)) = \{< x, y > \mid < x, y > \in E, x, y \in Ext(v \mid G)\}.$$

Furthermore, the expression $G(v|G) \{v\}$ denotes the induced graph of $G(v|G)$ on the vertex set of $G(v|G)$ not containing v, that is,

$$G(v \mid G) \{v\} = (Ext(v \mid G) \{v\}, E(Ext(v \mid G) \{v\})),$$

where

$$Ext(v \mid G) \{v\} = \{u \mid u \in V, < u, v > \in E\},$$

and

$$E(Ext(v \mid G) \{v\}) = \{< x, y > \mid < x, y > \in E, x, y \in Ext(v \mid G) \{v\}\}.$$

B.2   BACKTRACKING TREES

A *backtracking tree* is constructed using the backtracking method described previously. As illustrated in the example provided in Figure B.1, a backtracking tree has a virtual root node representing the input graph G. Each son node of the root node represents the subgraph $G(v|G)$ $v, v \in V$, where the vertex v is called the *node vertex* and $G(v|G)$ v the *node graph*. The son nodes in the following levels of the tree are created in the same way as those for the root node, until empty graphs are reached (the leaf nodes). The set of node vertices along each path from root to leaf consists of a maximal clique, and the union of all the paths consists of the set of maximal cliques on the input graph G. However, as shown in Figure B.1, the path in a backtracking tree is not distinct.

B.3   SEQUENTIALLY ORDERED BACKTRACKING TREE

In a *sequentially ordered backtracking tree*, the duplication of maximal cliques is removed based on a sequentially ordered vertex removing. Let the vertices of graph G be ordered $v_1, v_2, \ldots, v_{|v|}$, and denote the set of maximal cliques over the first vertex v_1 by $MCS(v|G)$. If we first remove the vertex v_1 from G to obtain a reduced graph $G(v_1)$ and then get the set of maximal cliques on the vertex v_2 with respect to the reduced graph $G\{v_1\}$ (denoted by $MCS(v_2|G \{v_1\})$), then it is obvious that the two sets of maximal cliques $MCS(v_1|G)$ and $MCS(v_2|G \{v_1\})$ have no intersection. Therefore the sequentially ordered backtracking tree creates no duplicate paths. However, a byproduct of this process is that not all the paths in the sequentially ordered backtracking tree contribute to maximal cliques; some paths are cliques, but not maximal cliques. For example, the maximal cliques containing both v_1 and v_2 are contained in $MCS(v_1|G)$; they do not show up in $MCS(v_2|G \{v_1\})$, but each of

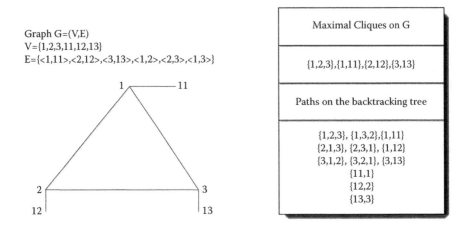

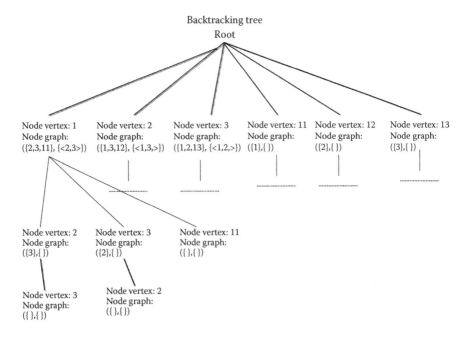

FIGURE B.1 An illustrative example for the backtracking tree.

them has "the part without v_1" showing up in $MCS(v_2|G \{v_1\})$. We format this property as follows.

B.3.1 Proposition B.1

Given a graph G, it holds that

$$MCS(G) = MCS(v\_1|G) + MCS(v_2 \mid G \ v_1)$$

$$-\{c \mid c \in MCS(v_2 \mid G \ v_1), c \cup \{v_1\} \text{ is a clique }\}$$

$$+MCS(v_3 \mid G \ \{v_1, v_2\}) - \{c \mid c \in MCS(v_3 \mid G \ \{v_1, v_2\}),$$

$$\text{and } c \cup \{v_1\} \text{ or } c \cup \{v_2\} \text{ is a clique }\}$$

$$+\cdots+\{< v_{|V|-1}, v_{|V|} >|< v_{|V|-1}, v_{|V|} >\in E,$$

$$\text{and } \forall w \in \{v_1, \ldots, v_{|V|-2}\}, \{w, v_{|V|-1}, v_{|V|}\} \text{ is not a clique }\}$$

Here the sign + is used for the union of two non-intersect sets and − is used for the subtraction of a set from its super set.

B.4   IDENTIFY NON-MAXIMAL CLIQUES USING ABSENT VERTICES

We now have a sequentially ordered backtracking tree in which paths are distinct, but a path mapping to maximal clique may have its "subpart" showing up as a path in later branches. We identify these paths that map to the non-maximal cliques using the *absent vertices*. Absent vertices $A(d)$ are defined on each node d, and there are two sources for absent vertices. The first is from those removed vertices incurred when creating son nodes from father nodes, denoted by $A_1(d)$. The second source is from those absent vertices inherited from the father node, denoted by $A_2(d)$. To give a formal expression, let d' be a tree node having the node graph $G(d') = V(d'), E(d')$, and $v_1 \in V(d')$ the node vertex for the ith son node d_i of d', $i = 1, \ldots, |V(d')| - 1$; then the absent vertices $A(d')$ for the node d_i are $A(d_i) = A_1(d_i) + A_2(d_i)$, where

$$A_1(d_i) = \{v_{j_1}, \ldots, v_{j_{|A_1(d_i)|}} \mid v_{j_k} \in \{v_1, \ldots, v_{i-1}\},$$

$$< v_{j_k}, v_i >\in E(d'), k = 1, \ldots, |A_1(d_i)|\}$$

and

$$A_2(d_i) = \{w \in A(d') \mid, < w, v_i >\in E(d')\}.$$

Note that in the above definition, the absent vertices $A(d')$ for the node d_i are adjacent to the node vertex v_i. The following proposition provides a method identifying the non-maximal clique path in a sequentially ordered backtracking tree.

B.4.1   PROPOSITION B.2

Given a graph $G = (V, E)$, let $p = \{d_0, d_1, \ldots, d_{|p|}\}$ be a path in the sequentially ordered backtracking tree of G. A sufficient and necessary condition for p mapping to a non-maximal clique is that there exists a node $d_i \in p$ an absent vertex $v \in A(d_i)$, such that $V(d_i) \in Ext(v \mid G)$, where $G(d_i) = (V(d_i), E(d_i))$ is the node graph for d_i, $A(d_i)$ is the set of absent vertex for d_i.

B.4.1.1   Proof

The necessity follows directly from Proposition 8.1. We now prove the sufficiency. We prove that the absent vertex v is adjacent to each node vertex along each path passing the node d_i, which means that each path passing the node d_i is not a maximal clique. Because $V(d_i) \in Ext(v \mid G)$ implies that v is adjacent to each node vertex descending from d_i, we only need to prove that v is adjacent to each node vertex v_j for the node $d_j, j = 1,\ldots,i$. Assume that v is inherited from father nodes because $d_{i-k}, i-1 \geq k \geq 0$. By the definition, the absent vertex v is adjacent to each node vertex $v_j, j = i-k,\ldots,i$. Because v is incurred as an absent node in the node d_{i-k}, v is a vertex of the node graph for the node d_{i-k}. Hence v is also a vertex of the node graphs for the nodes $d_1,\ldots,d_{i-k-1}$. Thus v is adjacent to the node vertex $v_j, j = 1,\ldots,i-k-1$. Putting these together, we conclude that the absent vertex $v \in A(d_i)$ is adjacent to each node vertex v_j of the node $d_j, j = 1,\ldots,i$.

B.5   OPTIMAL BRANCH CHOPPING

By now we have a tree whose paths are distinct and whose paths mapping to non-maximal cliques can be identified. We optimize this tree by further chopping the branches. For a node d with node graph $G(d) = (V(d), E(d))$, only subsets of $v(d)$ defined as *chief vertices* are used to create new branches. A vertex in a node graph $G(d) = (V(d), E(d))$ is a chief vertex if the following two conditions are met: there exists no vertex $u \in V(d)$ such that $Ext(v \mid G(d)) \subset Ext(u \mid G(d))$, and if $Ext(v \mid G(d)) = Ext(u \mid G(d))$, then u is greater than v in order. The following proposition shows that vertices other than chief vertices produce no distinct subpaths and thus can be left out when creating son branches.

B.5.1   PROPOSITION B.3

Given a graph $G = (V, E)$ and two vertices u and v of G, if $Ext(v \mid G) \subseteq Ext(u \mid G)$, then the set of maximal cliques over v is contained in the set of maximal cliques over u, that is, $MCS(v \mid G) \subseteq MCS(u \mid G)$.

B.5.1.1   Proof

Let $c = \{v_1,\ldots,v_m\}$ be a maximal clique over v. Then $v_i \in Ext(v \mid G), i = 1,\ldots,m$, because v_i is adjacent to v. As $MCS(v \mid G) \subseteq MCS(u \mid G)$, we have $v_i \in Ext(u \mid G), i = 1,\ldots,m$, which means v_i is also adjacent to u. Thus c is also a maximal clique over u.

B.6   THE MCE ALGORITHMS

We present the MCE algorithm in Figure B.2, which also shows the tree constructed using MCE over the graph in Figure B.1. It is clear that the tree paths are distinct, and the paths that are not mapping to maximal cliques are identified.

Algorithm   *MCE*(VertexinPath **p**, AbsentVertexofNode **A**
                         VertexSetofNodeGraph **V**, EdgeSetofNodeGraph **E**)
01   **CV** = subset of **V** that are Chief Vertices   //refer to the definition of ChiefVertices
02   Loop in sequential order on each vertex **v** in **CV**
10   **VertexSet(v)** = vertex of **V** adjacent to **v** and ordered after **v**
11       $A_1(v)$ = subset of **A** adjacent to **v**   //inherited absent vertices for **v**
12   If ($|A_1(v)| = 0$)   // if **v** has no inherited absent vertices
                 NullVertex(v) = false   // **v** will have branches
             Else   // otherwise, check if there exist absent vertex in $A_1(v)$
                                                     // that is adjacent to all vertices in **VertexSet(v)**
                 Loop on each vertex **x** in $A_1(v)$
                     If (**x** is adjacent to each vertex in **VertexSet(v)**)
                         NullVertex(v) = true   //vertex **v** will have no branches
                     Else
                         NullVertex(v) = false   //vertex **v** will have branches
13   If **NullVertex(v)** = false   // create branches for **v**
21   If |**VertexSet(v)**| = 1   // leaf node
                 output **p** + {**v**} as a maximal clique
22   Else   // apply *MCE* to create branches for **v**
                 $A_2(v)$ = subset of **CV** ordered before **v**   //incurred absent vertices
                 EdgeSet(VertexSet(v)) = edge in **E** having both vertices in **VertexSet(v)**
                 Call *MCE*(**p**+{**v**}, $A_1(v)+A_2(v)$, **VertexSet(v)**, **EdgeSet(Ext(v))**)

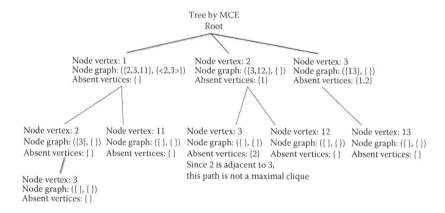

FIGURE B.2 Maximal cliques enumeration (MCE) algorithm and the illustration on the tree produced using MCE.

Str. Lev. Thre.	Data=WebView1					Data=WebView2					Data=BMS-POS				
	#V	#E	#bundles	MCE Time(ms)	MIS Time(ms)	#V	#E	#bundles	MCE Time(ms)	MIS Time(ms)	#V	#E	#bundles	MIS Time(ms)	MCE Time(ms)
0.00	483	9284	1186	3675		3324	60371	50228	34520		780	3364	1041	671	
0.05	465	3997	594	461		3269	13702	3997	4116		380	755	269	60	274574
0.10	415	2063	291	180		3027	6774	2222	2303		233	296	143	30	24626
0.15	356	1231	260	110	326049	2618	4031	1606	1583		157	140	81	20	6139
0.20	292	793	177	181	101185	2142	2572	1199	1001		112	84	58	21	1682
0.25	214	467	115	50	27689	1638	1687	866	661		84	57	41	10	691
0.30	147	268	77	60	5168	1261	1113	671	381		65	44	30	10	361
0.35	107	166	60	50	1943	884	695	463	210		53	38	24	10	180
0.40	86	105	49	30	881	594	433	309	110		49	36	22	10	201
0.45	63	63	33	50	290	387	271	195	50	250580	47	35	21	10	110
0.50	32	27	14	40	81	223	151	113	50	21762	29	26	12	50	50
0.55	27	22	12	50	30	131	84	69	20	3194	27	25	11	10	50
0.60	19	15	9	81	20	65	39	33	51	291	27	25	11	10	20
0.65	14	9	7	10	10	47	27	23	10	170	27	25	11	10	50
0.70	14	9	7	10	50	23	13	11	10	60	27	25	11	50	80
0.75	13	8	6	10	50	15	9	7	10	40	27	25	11	10	40
0.80	9	6	4	10	10	11	7	5	10	10	27	25	11	10	70
0.85	9	6	4	40	30	11	7	5	10	40	27	25	11	20	50
0.90	9	6	4	40	40	11	7	5	30	50	27	25	11	10	90
0.95	9	6	4	190	30	11	7	5	10	10	27	25	11	20	30
1.00	9	6	4	60	30	11	7	5	30	121	27	25	11	90	120

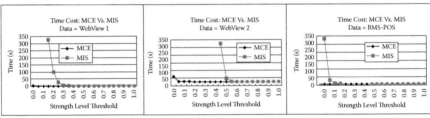

FIGURE B.3 Experiment: maximal cliques enumeration versus depth-first dynamic algorithm on three real-world data sets.

Index

Printed and bound by CPI Group (UK) Ltd, Croydon, CR0 4YY

18/10/2024

01776257-0009